Whitley Stokes

Irish glosses. A mediaeval tract on Latin declension, with examples explained in Irish.

To which are added the Lorica of Gildas, with the gloss thereon

Whitley Stokes

Irish glosses. A mediaeval tract on Latin declension, with examples explained in Irish.
To which are added the Lorica of Gildas, with the gloss thereon

ISBN/EAN: 9783337731298

Printed in Europe, USA, Canada, Australia, Japan

Cover: Foto ©ninafisch / pixelio.de

More available books at **www.hansebooks.com**

IRISH GLOSSES.

A MEDIÆVAL TRACT
ON
LATIN DECLENSION,
WITH
EXAMPLES EXPLAINED IN IRISH.

TO WHICH ARE ADDED
THE LORICA OF GILDAS, WITH THE GLOSS THEREON,
AND A SELECTION OF GLOSSES FROM THE BOOK OF ARMAGH.

EDITED BY
WHITLEY STOKES, A. B.

DUBLIN:
Printed at the University Press,
FOR THE IRISH ARCHÆOLOGICAL AND CELTIC SOCIETY.
1860.

THE

IRISH ARCHÆOLOGICAL AND CELTIC SOCIETY.

MDCCCLX.

Patron:

HIS ROYAL HIGHNESS THE PRINCE CONSORT.

President:

HIS GRACE THE DUKE OF LEINSTER.

Vice-Presidents:

THE MOST NOBLE THE MARQUIS OF KILDARE, M.R.I.A.
THE RIGHT HON. THE EARL OF DUNRAVEN, M.R.I.A.
THE RIGHT HON. LORD TALBOT DE MALAHIDE, M.R.I.A.
VERY REV. CHARLES RUSSELL, D.D., President of Maynooth College.

Council:

EUGENE CURRY, ESQ., M.R.I.A.	PATRICK V. FITZPATRICK, ESQ.
REV. THOMAS FARRELLY.	JOHN C. O'CALLAGHAN, ESQ.
REV. CHARLES GRAVES, D.D., F.T.C.D., M.R.I.A.	JOHN O'DONOVAN, ESQ., LL.D., M.R.I.A.
	GEO. PETRIE, ESQ., LL.D., M.R.I.A.
REV. JAMES GRAVES, A.B.	REV. WILLIAM REEVES, D.D., M.R.I.A.
THOMAS A. LARCOM, Major-General R.E., M.R.I.A.	WM. R. WILDE, ESQ., F.R.C.S.I., M.R.I.A.

Secretaries:

REV. J. H. TODD, D.D., Pres. R.I.A.	J. T. GILBERT, ESQ., M.R.I.A.

A MEDIÆVAL TRACT

ON

LATIN DECLENSION,

WITH

EXAMPLES EXPLAINED IN IRISH.

HE following tract on Latin declension is taken from a volume of parchment MSS. marked H. 2. 13, and preserved in the Library of Trinity College, Dublin. The volume is unpaged, but the tract commences at the back of the 35th, and ends at the back of the 38th folio from the beginning.

Dr. O'Donovan thinks the tract in question was written about the year 1500. Mr. Curry considers it somewhat older. I do not venture to decide on its age. It is clear, however, that the scribe was a copyist, not a composer; and that his original was produced at a period considerably before the transcription.

The chief, indeed the only, value of the tract lies in the large number of Irish words (about 1100) which are placed as glosses to the Latin vocables exemplifying the different declensions. Many of these words are unregistered in our dictionaries; of others, the meaning

meaning has hitherto been guessed at rather than known. Still, some persons may ask, why should the Irish Archæological Society expend its funds in publishing a document which merely illustrates the Irish language? Let such persons try to understand that every contribution to a more accurate knowledge of this Irish language is ultimately a contribution to Irish history. For this can never be written until trustworthy versions are produced of all the surviving chronicles, laws, romances, and poetry of ancient Celtic Ireland. Moreover, immediate results of high historical importance may be obtained by comparison of the words and forms of the Irish with those of the other Indo-European languages. Chronicles may, and often do, lie; laws may have been the work of a despot, and fail to correspond with the ethical ideas of the people for whom they were made; romances may misrepresent the manners and morals of their readers and hearers; and poetry may not be the genuine outcome of the popular imaginative faculty. But the evidence given by words and forms is conclusive—evidence of the habitat, the intellectual attainments, the social condition of the Aryan family before the Celtic sisters journeyed to the West—evidence of the period at which this pilgrimage took place as compared with the dates of the respective migrations of their kindred—evidence of the connexions existing between the Celts and other Indo-Europeans after the separation of languages. I trust that the subjoined commentary will be found to have done somewhat towards the attainment of the objects here indicated; and have now only to acknowledge the helpful kindness of my friends, the Rev. Dr. Todd, Mr. Eugene Curry, Dr. O'Donovan, Dr. Siegfried, and the Rev. R. F. Littledale.

W. S.

CARAIG BREACC, HOWTH,
August 16, 1858.

[IT

[It was at first my intention to have printed the following tract exactly as it stands in the codex. But so corrupt did this appear on closer investigation, that it seemed preferable to correct the text wherever it was likely to embarrass the reader, always, however, giving in a foot-note the lection of the MS. This I have done. Proper names have been spelled with initial capitals. Marks of punctuation have been introduced. The letters Q. and R. have been inserted before the Questions and Answers respectively. The examples have been numbered. All other interpolations have been enclosed in brackets.]

Q. Prima declinacio quot literas terminales[1] habet? R. Tres. Q. Quas? R. a, s, m. Q. Quot terminaciones habet? R. Quatuor. Q. Quas? R. a, as, és, am. Q. Da exempla. R. a ut poeta, as ut Eneas, és ut Anchises[2], am ut Adam.

Q. Quot genera habet hec terminacio .á. in prima declinacione?

R. Quinque, que sunt masculinum, ut hic poeta, femininum ut hec regina, neutrum, ut hoc pascha[3], commune, ut hic et hec avena, epicenum ut hic et hec aquila.

Q. Quot genera habet hec terminacio ás in prima declinacione?
R. Unum genus, ut hic Eneas.
Q. Quot genera habet terminacio es in prima declinacione?
R. Unum genus, ut hic Anchises[4].
Q. Quot genera habet hec terminacio am in prima declinacione?
R. Unum genus ut hic Adám. Unde regula[5]—

Rectius as, es, a, dat declinacio prima,
Atque per am proprie quedam ponuntur Ebrea, ut supra.

Q. Que est agnicio prime declinacionis nominum?
R. Hec est: cujus genitiuus[6] et datiuus singulares, nominatiuus et

---

[1] MS. tirmínales. [2] ansises. [3] pasca. [4] ancísses. [5] r̃. [6] genetiuus.

et vocatiuus plurales in æ diphthongo[1] desinunt, accusatiuus singularis in am productum desinit[2], accusatiuus pluralis in ás productum desinit, exceptis nominibus prime declinacionis que non declinant[ur], sic :—

1. hic poeta .i. ꝼιliŏ.
   hic propheta .i. ꝼáιτ[3].
   hic psalmista .i. ꞅaιlmcéτlaιꝺ[4].
   hic scriba .i. ꞅaí.
5. hic citharista[5] .i. cꞃuιτιꞃe.
   hic timpanista .i. τιmpanaċ.
   hic organista .i. oꞃꝹanaιŏ.
   hic sophista .i. ꞅophιꞃτιŏe[6].
   hic partista .i. ꞃannaιꞃe[7].
10. hic lanista .i. luċτaιꞃe.
    hic legista .i. leꞃaιꞃe.
    hic decretista .i. ꝺecꞃeꝺeċ.
    hic patriarcha .i. uaꞃalaċaιꞃ.
    hic scurra .i. cꞃoꞃan.
15. hic questionista[8] .[quaestionarius] .i. ceꞃτunaċ.
    hic archimandrita[9] .i. aꞃꝺeaꞃꞃoc.
    hic auriga .i. Ꝺιlla cιnn eιċ.
    hic birria .i. bιꞃꞃaċ.
    hic geta .i. Ꝺeιŏ.

Feminina haec sunt :—

20. haec regina .i. ꞃíꝹan[10].
    haec duxista. banτóιꞃeċ[11].
    haec abatissa .i. banab.
    haec priorissa. banꞃꞃιoꞃ.
    haec sacerdotista. banꞃaꝹaꞃτ.
25. haec ancilla. ιnnιlτ.
    haec galea. aτ cluιc.
    haec alea. τaιꞃlιꞃ.
    haec mitra[12]. baιꞃín.
    haec tunica[13]. ιnaꞃ.
30. haec manica. muιncιlle.
    haec allea [allium]. ꝹaιꞃleoꝹ.
    haec lacerna. ꞃleꞃτan.
    haec cirra [cirrus]. cιaŏ.
    haec chirotheca. lámann[14].
35. haec spica. ꝺιaꞃ.
    haec lasciuia. bꞃaιꞃe[15].
    haec falinga. ꞃallaιnꝹ.
                                    haec

[1] diptongo. [2] desinunt. [3] faidh. [4] sailmcetlaid. [5] sitarista. [6] sophistighi. [7] ri
[8] qonista. [9] arcimantrica. [10] righan. [11] bantaisech. [12] mittra. [13] toníca. [14] cirathcea.
amann. [15] h. lassiua braisi.

haec camisia¹. léine.
haec gena. gruaiḃ.
40 haec lingúa². tengaḋ.
haec pera. tiaċ.
haec trolla. loran.
haec decima. ḋechmaḋ.
haec candela. coinnill.
45 haec gelima. punnann.
haec fistula. feḋán.
haec barba. feróg³.
haec nouerca. lermátair⁴.
haec carruca. rerraċ.
50 haec phoca. rón⁵.
haec caphia .i. cennḃarr⁶.
haec claua long.
haec penna penn⁷.
haec pocna⁸ pian.
55 haec iolla [jula?]. maroc.
haec olla. crocan.
haec vesica. riaṫaire⁹.
haec creta cailc.
haec caustoria [καυστήριον?].
aḋarc.
60 haec plumba [plumbum].
luaiḋe¹⁰.
haec norina. riaġail.

haec tabella taḃaill.
haec cantilena cantairecṫ¹¹.
haec mitreta tuireog.
65 haec parra meḋan.
haec parricula gocan.
haec tabula clár.
haec ancora ancoire.
haec lympha .i. uirce imill¹².
70 haec aptempna [ἐπιδεμνια?]
rer no capp.
[haec] trabecula taeḃán tellaiġ no comlaḋ¹³.
haec caliga .i. arran.
haec ligula. lainḋer.
haec corrigia. traiġle.
75 haec corona. coroin.
haec clerica. coroin.
haec coma¹⁴. folt.
haec glabella. ḋeirgeċ in ḟuilt¹⁵.
haec palpebra. faḃra.
80 haec pupilla mac imperan.
haec theologia¹⁶. ḋiaḋact.
haec grammatica. gramma-
taċ¹⁷.

¹ haec camisa. ² linga. ³ fesog. ⁴ lesmathair. ⁵ foca. ron. ⁶ cenbar. ⁷ pond. ⁸ pena. ⁹ fessica. siadaire. ¹⁰ luaidhi. ¹¹ candaléna canntairecht. ¹² h. limpausci .i. imill. ¹³ naucula tuman callaigh l. comla. ¹⁴ cómma. ¹⁵ fuilt. ¹⁶ tethologia. ¹⁷ gramaticn. gramatach.

hacc dialectica[1]. oilectac.
haec ystoria. roaip.
85 haec mechanica. éolar oóip[2].
hacc patena. oigen.
hacc rhetorica[3]. oligi.
haec pantera nacaip[4].
haec maxilla. leca in ouini[5].
90 haec mala. letail[6].
haec bucca. áil.
haec gula. cpáep.
haec mataxa. ulbu.
haec palina. bapp.
95 haec alapa. bapog.
haec plannta. bono.
hacc mentula peam .i. ppiu.
haec cinenda .i. cáin.
haec vena. curle.
100 haec mamma. cich.
haec mainmilla. cichín[7].
hacc mammula[8]. uch.
hacc stella. pecla.
haec ethera [aether]. aoíp.
105 hacc aere. aiep.
haec cratera. pcala.
haec cretella gneioell.

hacc terra. calam[9].
haec tribula [tribulum].
ruipc no rgiuppe[10].
110 hacc villa. baile.
haec villula .i. apcán[11].
hacc via. rlige[12].
haec vita. becu[13].
hacc herba. lub[14].
115 hacc silua. coill.
haec virga[15]. plac.
haec virgula. rlaicín[16].
haec grunna. moin.
haec gleba[17]. poo.
120 hacc casa[18]. bochan.
haec cassula. cocall.
[haec casula]. cro[19].
haec camera. campa no re-
oinpa.
hacc porta. oopup.
125 hacc valua. comla.
haec creta [crates] chach.
haec digma[20]. mapcac na
comlao.
haec flamma[21]. lapaip.
hacc cloaca. campao.
hacc

[1] dilcta (with a hook over the *l*) [2] h. mecanica. cal. doc. (undulating line over the last *e*). [3] rethorica. [4] nathari. [5] duine. [6] leth ail. [7] cichin. [8] mamula. [9] talum. [10] sust l. sgiursi. [11] villola .i. urtan. [12] slighi. [13] beta. [14] luibh. [15] virgo. [16] virgola slaitin. [17] glebo. [18] cassa. [19] h. cassula cochall no cro. [20] or perh. drigma. [21] flama.

130 hacc auia. ꞃenmáċaıꞃ[1].
haec denia. ꞃeċꞁán[2].
hacc scama [σκάμμα]. lanꝺ.
hacc gemına. léᵹ lóᵹmaꞁ[3].
hacc fenistra. ꝼuınneoᵹ[4].
135 hacc furca. ᵹaḃal.
hacc sportula. pellec.
haec treuga[5]. oꞁꞁaꝺ.
hacc urna. mılan.
haec guerra[6] coᵹaꝺ.
140 haec alauda. ꝼuıꞃeoᵹ.
hacc garga[7] baıꞁᵹen.
hacc quarta .ı. ceċꞁamaꝺ.
hacc merenda. ꞃꞁuḃan.
hacc buccella ꞃꞁubán maꞁa[8] no ᵹꞁeım.
145 haec susurra [susurrus]. coᵹaꞁ.
hacc tibia[9]. colꞁa.
hacc festucula[10]. ꞇaıꞃ.
hacc honplata [ὠμοπλάτη?]. monᵹ ınꞇ ṗlınꝺéın[11].
hacc junctura[12]. cenᵹal.
150 haec gingiua. ꝼeoılnaꞁıacal.
hacc uvula[13] ꞃıne ꞃeaın.

hacc biturría vel biturrea buꞇun.
haec tectúra[14]. ꝺıꝺean.
haec lorica. luıꞁeċ.
155 haec antiquula. aıċleıne[15].
haec mica. míꞁ[16].
haec vaghina. ꝼaıᵹın.
haec famula. caıle ꝺaḃca.
hacc vacca[17]. bó.
160 hacc aqua. uıꞃce[18].
haec idiogina. aꝺḃ[aꞁ].
haec bínna. calꞁꞇaċ.
hacc benna. ᵹamaın aꞁaın.
haec juvenca[19]. calꞁaċ.
165 haec mulctrella[20]. cuınꝺeoᵹ.
haec mulcra. eꝺꞁaċ.
hacc opa[21]. coꞁꞁoᵹ.
hacc tunica sclerotica[22]. ᵹealan na ꞃúl[23].
hacc taberna. ꞇaıbeꞁꞁne.
170 hacc rectoria. peꞁꞁonaċꞇ[24].
haec vicaria. bıcaıꞁecꞇ.
haec capillanía. caḃıllanaċꞇ.
haec abbatia[25]. abꝺaıne.
hacc vaccaria[26]. buaıle.

haec

[1] aua. senmathair. [2] sechran. [3] gema. legh loghmar. [4] fuindeog. [5] treoga. [6] gerru. [7] leg. quadra? [8] buccalla. [9] tipia. [10] pestucula. [11] ın ꞇꞁlınꝺóın. [12] iuntura. [13] ugula. [14] dectura. [15] anticula aithleini. [16] mir. [17] vaca. [18] uisci. [19] iuvenccu. [20] múcledla. [21] oba. [22] h. tonica scilarotica. [23] sul. [24] persunacht. [25] abacia. [26] uacaria.

175 haec prouincia. pṗóuinṗe.
haec metrop[o]litica ca-
ṫhaiṗ aiṗoeaṗbuiʒ.
haec basilica. eaʒlaiṗ¹.
haec mellifolia [millefolium].
aṫaiṗṫalman².
haec testa. blaeṗc.
180 haec sabribarra bṗoṫṗaṫan.
haec uolua [valva?]. cen-
baṗan.
haec artemisia³. buaṫḃallan
liaṫ.
haec ferina. luṗ na ƒiaḃ.
haec brecia [brassica?]. biṗoṗ.
185 haec genista. ƒeclu ʒ.
haec ca. ʒaṗboʒ.
haec ganea. meṗoṗeṫ.
haec concha⁴. ƒaeṫoʒ.
haec gletcalla [clitellae?].
maṗclaṫ.
190 haec solea⁵. bonn.
haec urla [orlus] .i. bile.
haec impedica. uaṫṫaṗ.
haec medulla. ṗmiṗ.
haec coquilla⁶. ƒaecoʒ beʒ.
195 haec grangia. ʒṗainṗeṫ.

haec gallina. ceṗc.
haec aquila. iluṗ.
haec arca⁷ aṗʒ.
haec cista ciṗṫe⁸.
200 haec merula. ciaṗṗeṫ.
haec monedula⁹ caoʒ.
haec philomena¹⁰. ṗpioeoʒ.
haec columba. colum.
haec lucifugia .i. cṗeḃaṗ.
205 haec capreola. ƒeṗboʒ.
haec rostigola¹¹. coṗcaṫ ma-
ṗa¹².
haec aurigola. oṗeolan.
haec urtica. nennṫóʒ¹³.
haec arista .i. connlaṫ.
210 haec stipula coinnlin.
haec fistula¹⁴. ṗeimin.
haec moneta monaoan.
haec glaneta. ʒlacaṗba.
haec pharetra¹⁵. ʒlacṗaiʒeo¹⁶.
215 haec sagitta¹⁷. ṗaiʒeo¹⁶.
haec hasta. ʒa.
haec flabella. ƒeioeo ʒáiṫe
no bulʒa¹⁸.
haec fabrica. ceṗoṫa¹⁹.
219 haec massa. meṗʒan.
haec

¹ bacilica caglas. ² athair talman. ³ artimesia. ⁴ conea. ⁵ solia. ⁶ coquima.
⁷ archa. ⁸ sista cisti. ⁹ monetola. ¹⁰ pilomena. ¹¹ leg. rusticula? ¹² márn. ¹³ nenn-
tog. ¹⁴ festula. ¹⁵ faretra. ¹⁶ soiged. ¹⁷ sagita. ¹⁸ seideth gáibulga. ¹⁹ cordea.

220 haec baudaca [balducta ?]. bláṫaċ¹.
haec ceruisia². líno.
haec urina. ꝼual.
haec fabula. ꞃʓél³.
haec purpura. coꞃcaıꞃ.
225 haec cera. céıꞃ⁴.
haec serra⁵. ʓlaꞃꞃ.
haec rota. ꞃoṫh.
haec fauilla.
haec cauicula [cavernula] .i. ꞃoċlaıȯ⁶.
230 haec litera. lıṫeꞃ.
haec syllaba. ꞃıllaıȯı [?].
haec pagina⁷. leṫenaċ.
haec chiragra⁸. cꞃupán na lám⁹.
haec luna. eꞃʓa.
235 haec panca [pantex] meȯal.
haec aruina¹⁰. blonac.
haec moniꞃıcına [?]¹¹. monaȯ.
haec comprisura. ꝼaꞃcan.
haec troclia canṫaıꞃ.
240 haec cripica [rastrum]. clıaṫ ꝼuıꞃꞃıȯ[e].

haec situla¹². ꞃıṫeal.
haec pista. ṫaeꞃ.
haec glassia [γαλαξία] mulcan.
haec prissura. ıʓa.
245 haec pensa [pensum] cocan.
haec lapifulta. léċċ ın áꝓaın¹³.
haec presena. bancoıʓ.
haec rula. luċ ꝼꞃancaċ.
haec talpa. luċ ȯall.
250 haec lactura. lachṫ.
haec amusca. amaıꞃc.
haec ascia¹⁴. ṫál.
haec scindula¹⁵. caꞃnoıȯı.
haec scupa [scopae]. eꞃcaꞃṫ.
255 haec pustula. ʓuıꝓín¹⁶.
haec onesta. nuꞃ.
haec grimaga baıneachlaċ.
haec picuta. meall.
haec mustella. eáꞃ.
260 haec muscipula. ꞃıȯċaṫ¹⁷.
haec decipula .ı. concꞃo¹⁸.
haec sagena. ꞃꞃaṫaꞃ.
haec biga. caꞃꞃ.
haec antela [antilena]. uċṫaċ.

haec

¹ blathach. ² seruisia. ³ sgel. ⁴ ccir. ⁵ sera. ⁶ h. fauilla. fochluidh .i. cauicula. ⁷ pagena. ⁸ sirogra. ⁹ crupan na lam. ¹⁰ asugia. ¹¹ monifína (a hook rising out of the f). ¹² citola. ¹³ lec in arain. ¹⁴ assia. ¹⁵ sindola. ¹⁶ guirin. ¹⁷ musipula. fidhcat. ¹⁸ decipola .i. con cro.

265 haec postella [postilena]. ciapaċ.
    haec crapula¹. laichipt.
    haec uva. cáep pínemnaċ².
    haec lepra. lubpa.
    haec fragella. cnáimpiaċ³ no coppan.
270 haec parma. cocun.
    haec pyromantia⁴. nellavopacht.
    haec chiromantia⁵. vopnavopaċt.
    haec scunna [?] clap guail.
    haec catapulta. pblínaċ⁶.
275 haec edibulta. cpoicinn mapa allaiv.
    haec offa. coinmíp⁷.
    haec cavea⁸. vabaċ.
    haec calopoda. puipce⁹.
    haec trica. ió upċumail¹⁰.
280 haec parvispendia. cepaċt.
    haec ophthalmia. galap púla¹¹.
    haec pupina. cailleaċ ligeoc.
    haec coquina. coċtaip.
    haec babana. cappach.
285 haec creatura coippeagav.

Ista sunt propria nomina uirginum:—

haec Maria.
haec Catarina.
haec Margareta.
haec Anna.
haec Lucia.
haec Brigada.

haec Elina.
haec Petronilla.
haec Alathia.
haec Osanna.
haec Melén.
haec Tegea.

haec placenta. apan geal.
his dominabus. baincigepna¹².

his animabus. anim¹³.
his deabus. baihvea in copaiv.

his

¹ capula. ² vua. caer finemach. ³ cnaimfiach. ⁴ piromanxia. ⁵ ciromancia. ⁶ cadibulta. ⁷ coinmir. ⁸ caba. ⁹ callidiba. suisti. ¹⁰ urcumail. ¹¹ obtolmia. galar sula. ¹² báinntigerna. ¹³ ainím.

290 his filiabus. ingen¹.
his natabus. ingen.
his libertabus. banṙóeṗ².
his amicabus. banċaṗa³.
his equabus. láiṗ⁴.
295 his mulabus. múl⁵.
his asinabus. aṡṡal.

his lupabus. foġ allaiṫ.
Hoc pascha⁶. caiṗc.
hoc manna⁷. mainn.
300 hoc mammona. boṡluaiġeṫ⁸.
hoc all. a [alacrimonia?]. ṡu-
baċúṗ.

Communia⁹ sunt haec:—

hic et haec idiota. amaṫán¹⁰.
hic et haec áduena. ṫeoṗaṫ.
hic et haec indigena. uṗṗaiṫ.
305 hic et haec Hibernigena. eiṗ-
innaċ¹¹.
hic et haec Scotigena¹². alba-
naċ.
hic et haec Angeligina. ġall-
ṫaċ¹³.
hic et haec Normanigina.
noṗmanaċ.
hic et haec Francigena.
ḟṗanġcaċ.
310 hic et haec Romanigena. ṗo-
manaċ.
hic et haec romipeta¹⁴. oilit́-
ṗeċ.

hic et haec Almanigina al-
manach¹⁵.
hic et haec cristigina. cṗiṗcin.
hic et haec alienigena¹⁶ co-
maiġteċ.
315 hic et haec hermita [ere-
mita]. ṫit́ṗebaċ.
hic et haec homicida. ṫun-
maṗbtaċ.
hic et haec parricida. aṫaṗ-
maṗbtaċ.
hic et haec matricida. máth-
aṗmaṗbtaċ¹⁷.
hic et haec fratricida bṗáth-
aṗmaṗbtaċ¹⁸.
320 hic et haec sororicida ṡiuṗ-
maṗbtaċ.

hic

---

¹ ingin. ² banshaer. ³ bancara. ⁴ lair. ⁵ mul. ⁶ pasca. ⁷ mann. ⁸ h. mamona. bo sluaiged. ⁹ commonía. ¹⁰ amadan. ¹¹ ibernígina. eirindach. ¹² Scatigena. ¹³ galldacht. ¹⁴ romipida. ¹⁵ almaneach. ¹⁶ alinigena. ¹⁷ mathar. m. ¹⁸ brathar. m.

hic et haec uxoricida. bean-
mapbcaċ.
hic et haec genericida. cli-
amuinmapbcaċ.
hic et haec uerbigina. cpir-
caiġe¹.
hee bracce² cpibup.
325 hee insidie³. cealġ.
hee nuptie⁴. bainoe cíċ.
hee nundíne mópmapġaυ⁵.
hee rixe pepġa⁶.
hee tabe inaυa.
330 hee atene [Athenae?]. aċ-
píana.
hee tenebre. υopcaυup.
hee latebre. υopcaυup.
hee diuicie. inmupa.
hee diuine υiaυaċc.
335 hee none. noíne⁷.
hee calende⁸. caillné.
hee nebule. néll⁹.
hee schole¹⁰. pcola.
hee mine.˙baġaip.
340 hic Andreas. anopiap.
hic Thomas. comap.

hic Eneas. αenġup.
hic Barnubas. apostoli.
hic Lucas.
345 hic Nemías. ġilla na naom.
hic Malacias maolpech-
lainn¹¹.
hic Ysayas. çpac.
hic Tobias.
hic Elyas. elç.
350 hic Jermías. páiċ¹².
hic Annanias. páiċ¹².
hic Sacarias. páiċ¹².
hic Boreas¹³. an ġaeċ acú-
aiυ.
hic Ancises. ppimaiυeċc.
355 hic Nestorides¹⁴. en.
hic Peliades. en.
hic Fetomsiades. en.
hic˙Latoniades. en.
hic Tebaydes. en.
360 hic Eneades. en.
hic Adam. e.
hic Joram. e.
hic Abraham. e.
hic Cayn. e.

Q. Secunda declinacio quot¹⁵ literas terminales habet? R. Tres.
Q. Quas?

¹ cristaighi. ² bracc. ³ incidie. ⁴ nubtic. buindi. cich. ⁵ mormargad. ⁶ fergach.
⁷ nonne ndíne. ⁸ callende. ⁹ nell. ¹⁰ scole. ¹¹ maolechl. ¹² faith. ¹³ borius.
¹⁴ Nastorrades. ¹⁵ quat.

Q. Quas? R. r, s, m.

Q. Quot terminaciones habet? R. uí.

Q. Quas? R. er, ír, ur, us, ús, um. Q. Da exempla. R. er, ut magister, ir, ut uír, ur ut satur, ús ut dominus eus, [ut] Tatheus, um, ut templum. Q. Quot genera habet secunda declinacio? R. uí. Q. Quas? R. ut supra.

Q. Quot genera habet hec terminacio er in secunda declinacione? R. unum ut hic magister.

Q. Quot genera habet terminacio ír in secunda declinacione? Q. Unum ut hic uir.

Q. Quot genera habet hec terminacio us in secunda declinacione? R. quatuor.

Q. Que sunt? R. masculinum, ut hic dominus; femininum [ut] hec domina vel hec malus; neutrum, ut hoc vulgus; promisc[u]um siue epicoenum[1] ut hic [et haec] milgus.

Q. Quot genera habet terminacio éus in secunda declinacione? R. unum, ut hic Tatheus.

Q. Quot genera habet terminacio um in secunda declinacione? R. duo.

Q. Que sunt? R. femininum, ut hec dorcium, philorsium, glicerium; neutrum, ut hoc templum, simitherium.

Q. Que est agnicio nominum secunde declinacionis? R. hec est: cujus genitiuus singularís, nominatiuus et uocatiuus plurales in í productum desinunt, datiuus et ablatiuus[2] singulares in ó productum desinit, [et genitiuus pluralis in orum] nisi sincupacio [i. e. syncope] fiat, ut duum pro duorum, datiuus et ablatiuus[2] plurales in is productum desinunt; accusatiuus pluralis in os productum desinit, exceptis alis nominibus secunde declinacionis que non sic faciuntur.

hic

[1] episcenum.   [2] oblativus.

365 hic magister. maġirdeṗ.
    hic arbiter. bṗeiṫeam.
    hic presbyter¹. ṗaʒaṗc.
    hic minister cimċiṗiġ.
    hic faber. ʒabann².
370 hic puer. macam.
    hic liber. leabaṗ.
    hic caper. ʒabaṗ.
    hic aper. copc.
    hic cancer. paṗcán³.
375 hic fiber. dobṗan.
    hic linter. labaṗ no ṗlinncṗi-
        aḃ.
    hic gener. cliamuin.
    hic socer⁴ companaċ.
    hic liber .a. um. neaċ ṗaeṗ.
380 hic pulcher⁵.a. um. ṗochṗuiḃe.
    hic niger .a. um. duḃ.
    hic piger .a. um. leṗc.
    hic macer .a. um. cṗuaġ.
    hic acer .a. um. ʒṗuamda.
385 hic acer .a. um. aʒaṗb.
    hic dexter .a.um. deaṗ.
    hic sinister⁶. cle.
    hic anser. ʒeiḃ.
    hic onager⁷. aḃ allaiḃ.

390 hic ager. ṗeṗand.
    hic suber. ṗnámaċ⁸.
    hic in[s]cimagister maʒiṗ-
        deṗ aimpeṗaċ.
    hic eger a. um. cṗlán.
    hic tener .a. um. maeċ.
395 hic uir. ṗeṗ.
    hic semiuir. leċṗeṗ⁹.
    hic leuir. ṗeṗ clí.
    hic duum. uir cıʒeṗne¹⁰
        deiṗe¹¹.
    trium vir. cıʒeṗne cṗíṗ.
400 hic quadrum uir. caiṗeċ ceċ-
        ṗaiṗ¹².
    hic quinctum uir. caiṗeċ
        cúiʒiṗ.
    hic satur. ṗaċaċ.
    hic semisatur. leċṗaċaċ¹³.
    hic dominus. cıʒeṗne¹⁴.
405 hic deus. dıa.
    hic animus. anum.
    hic filius. mac.
    hic natus. mac.
    hic libertus. ṗaeṗ.
410 hic famulus¹⁵. baċlaċ.
    hic molossus. mílcú¹⁶.

                                      hic

¹ prespiter. ² gaban. ³ partan. ⁴ soces. ⁵ puplican (*sic!*). ⁶ senester. ⁷ on
aġ (*sic*). ⁸ snamach. ⁹ semuir. lethfer. ¹⁰ tigerna. ¹¹ deisi. ¹² cetráir. ¹³ leth hea-
thach. ¹⁴ tigerna. ¹⁵ famalus. ¹⁶ malosus. milcú.

hic bufulus. bacl[ać] bꞃe-
all[án].
hic amícus. caꞃa.
hic equus[1]. eać.
415 hic mulus. múl[2].
hic asinus[3]. aꞃꞃal.
hic lupus cu allaıꝺ.
hic ursus. maṫꝢamaın.
hic auus[4]. ꞃenaṫaıꞃ.
420 hic proauus[5] a aṫaıꞃ ꞃın.
hic atauus[6]. a aṫaıꞃ ꞃın.
hic clericus. cleıꞃeać.
hic laicus[7] ṫuaṫa.
hic vitulus. lóeꝢ[8].
425 hic oculus. ꞃúıl[9].
hic monoculus. leṫ[h]caeć.
hic cecus. ꝺall.
hic cetus. mıl móꞃ no ꞃuaın-
mech ꝺubaıꞃ[10].
hic orbus. mac ꝺıleċta.
430 hic luscus. mınṫꞃuıleć[11].
hic lippus maeṫꞃuıleć[12].
hic aduocatus. aꞃcoıꝺe[13].
hic juridicus[14]. ꝺlıꝢṫıneć.
hic causidicus. ꞃeꞃ cúıꞃı ꝺo
ċonꝢbaıl[15].

435 hic monachus[16]. manać.
hic homunculus[17] ꝺuıne beꝢ.
hic canonicus. cananać.
hic discipulus ꝺıꞃcıbul.
hic legitimus. ꝺlıꞃṫınać.
440 hic cnipulus. ꞃꝢıan.
hic cutellus. ꞃꝢıan.
hic ungulus [ungula]. cꞃuꞃ[18]
eıć.
hic clauus [clavis]. ṫaıꞃınꝢe[19].
hic camus bꞃaıꝢꝺeć.
445 hic baietus. ꞃaıꞃṫı bꞃóꝢ[20].
hic tegulus. ꞃcolꞃ ṫıꝢe[21].
hic archiepiscopus. aıꞃꝺeaꞃ-
boꝢ.
hic episcopus. eaꞃboꝢ.
hic archidiaconus. aıꞃċın-
neċ[22].
450 hic legatus. ṫeaċṫaıꞃe.
hic decanus. ꝺeꝢanach.
hic prelatus. ꞃꞃelaıṫ.
hic prepositus. ṫıꝢeꞃꞃe[23].
hic diaconus. ꝺeċáın.
455 hic subdiaconus. ꞃubꝺeċáın.
hic acolytus. aclaıꝺe[24].
hic chorus[25]. ıncoꞃaıꝺ.

hic

[1] cqus. [2] mul. [3] assinus. [4] aus. [5] proaus. [6] ataus. [7] lacius. [8] laegh. [9] suil. [10] ruaimnech dubain. [11] mintsuilech. [12] lipus mœthsuilech. [13] abhcoidí. [14] iuriticus. [15] condmail. [16] monacus. [17] honumculus. [18] cru. [19] tairrngi. [20] brog. [21] tigi. [22] airchindech. [23] tigerna. [24] acolitus. aclaidhi. [25] corus.

hic populus. ιn pupul.
hic agnus. uan.
460 hic angelus. aιngel¹.
hic gladius. cloιυeam.
hic arcangelus. apcaιngel.
hic pilus. ρuaιnυe no ϝoιl-
τín².
hic capillus. ϝoιlτnín³.
465 hic digitus. méρláιme.
hic articulus. méρ coιρe⁴.
hic psalmus. ρalm.
hic uirsiculus. ϝeρρán⁵.
hic sonus ϝoξuρ.
470 hic tonus. τoιn⁶.
hic semitonus⁷ [semitŏnium]
leττoιn.
hic ditonu[s]. υιτoιn.
hic pumnatus [prognatus ?]
macam ξenτe⁸.
hic punctus. punc.
475 hic circulus. ceρcall.
hic murus. múρ⁹.
hic cibus. bιaυ.
hic discus. ιn ξaιllmιaρ¹⁰.
hic cupus. copán¹¹.

480 hic cepus [cippus ?]. ceρ.
hic lectus. lebaιυ.
hic fimus. oτρać.
hic porcus. τoρc.
hic uannus ρξaιξneρ.
485 hic tignus [tignum] cleaτ.
hic collactaneus¹² comalτa.
hic decius.
hic phaselus¹³. cuρać.
hic forulus. ρacc.
490 hic mantellus¹⁴. maτal.
hic flosculus. blaτmaρ.
hic agnellus. uaιnín¹⁵.
hic porcellus. oιρcnín¹⁶.
hic pullus. ϝeρρać no ξeρ-
cać¹⁷.
495 hic palus. cuaιlle¹⁸.
hic talus. υιρle.
hic callus.
hic catulus. cuιlen.
hic murilegus¹⁹. caτ.
500 hic dolus. cealξ.
hic pediculus. míl éυaιξ²⁰.
hic manipulus. υoρnán²¹
buana.

hic

---

¹ angilus. aingil. ² ruaindi l. fuiltin. ³ foiltnin. ⁴ merlaime-mer coisi. ⁵ fersa.
⁶ tóin. ⁷ semitonus. ⁸ gennti. ⁹ mur. ¹⁰ ingaill. mias. ¹¹ cipus copan. ¹² collacanius. ¹³ facellus. ¹⁴ mancellus. ¹⁵ uainin. ¹⁶ oircnin. ¹⁷ serrac l. gerrcach. ¹⁸ cuailli.
¹⁹ morelius. ²⁰ peticulus. mil edaigh. ²¹ dornan.

A Mediæval Tract on Latin Declension.

hic curellus. cnáimḟiaċ¹.
hic columbus. colum.
505 hic curcolus [curlegius?]. corcaċ mara.
hic gallus. coileaċ.
hic milgus [milvus]. ppeċán².
hic figulus. cerv.
hic cygnus³. ın ela.
510 hic corus. coileċ gaiṫe⁴.
hic focus. ceallaċ.
hic sotus. oınmıv.
hic mimus geocaċ.
hic loculus. rborar.
515 hic pellicarius rgıngívoır.
hic locus. ınav.
hic diuersarius. aıbırreoır.
hic iocus. cluıṫe⁵.
hic Tartarus⁶. ırreann.
520 hic infernus. ırrenn.
hic catholicus. caṫolıca⁷.
hic locanus. loċan.
hic xpianus. gılla crırt.
hic Persianus. perren⁸.
525 hic Donatus. Donncav.
hic Martinus. gılla Marcaın.
hic Malcus vıabul.

hic Petrus. Pecar no Péċiur.
hic Robertus. Roıberv.
530 hic Valterus. Uacer.
hic Uillialmus. Uıll[ıam].
hic Gillialmus gıllıam.
hic Uirgilius. Fergal.
hic Gillibertus. gıllıberv.
535 hic Ruaricus. Ruaıorı.
hic Ouídius. voccor.
hic Patricius. gılla Pácrıcc.
hic Laurencius. Laurınc.
hic Clemencius. Clemenc.
540 hic Diarmicius. Oıarmaıv.
hic Lodauicus. Loċlann.
hic Mauricius. Murchav.
hic Eugenius⁹. Eogan.
hic Grigorius. grıgoır.
545 hic Cornelius. Concubar.
hic Thitheus. mac na hoıvċe¹⁰.
hic Orp[h]eus Uaıṫne.
hic Thateus. Cavg.
hic Matheus. maċa.
550 Hec diphthongus¹¹. veóır.
hec synodus¹². renav naom.
hec cristallus. [crystallum]. cloċ crırvaıl.
hec

¹ cnaimfiach, and leg. corvellus?. ² prechan. ³ cignus. ⁴ coilec gaithi. ⁵ cluithi.
⁶ tarturus. ⁷ cathholica. ⁸ presen. ⁹ augenius. ¹⁰ mach na hoidhchi. ¹¹ diptungus.
¹² sinatos.

A Mediæval Tract on Latin Declension.

hec paradisus. paiptur.
hec quercus. ɔaip.
555 hec malús. aball.
hec corylus¹. coll.
hec fraxinus. ꝼuinɔreog.
hec alnus². ꝼeptnog.
hec prunus³. ɔpoigin.
560 hec buxus. beiṫe⁴.
hec taxus. ibap.
hec ficus. piċaball⁵.
hec pinus⁶. cpanɔ ġiur.
hec laurus. cpanɔ lauíp.
565 hec brucus. ꝼpáeċ⁷.
hec cornus. cpanɔ mucop.
hec colus. cuigel.
hec fusus. ꝼeppaiɔ⁸.
hec domus. ṫeach.
570 hec socrus. bean ɔobpaṫap
 [*recte* máṫhaip ɔo mná].

hec nurus⁹. bean ʋomeic.
hec penus. cuġan.
hec jacinthus. léġ¹⁰ loġmap.
hec carbassus. long luaṫ.
575 hec abyssus¹¹. in ꝼaipġe¹².
hec aulus. bpu na hoiġe¹³.
hec byssus. rpoll¹⁴.
hec humus. in uip.
hec papyrus¹⁵. paipep.
580 hec porticus. ɔopur lir.
hec Egiptus. Eiġipt.
hec acirus. ꝼeopur.
Hic bubulcus. buaċaill bó¹⁶.
hic subulcus. buaċaill mucc¹⁷.
585 hic rubus. múine.
hic remulus. aipġeaċ.
hic dumus¹⁸. ɔpir.

Hec sunt nomina adiectiua que non comparantur:—

hic primus .a. um céɔ neach.
hic secundus .a. um inɔapa neaċ.
590 hic tercius .a. um. an tper neaċ.
hic quartus .a. um. in ceṫhpuma neaċ.

                                                                     hic

¹ corrolus. ² anlús. ³ brunus. ⁴ bruxus. beithi. ⁵ fichus. fidhabhall. ⁶ pinnus. ⁷ fracch. ⁸ forsad. ⁹ murus. ¹⁰ iacingtus. leg. ¹¹ abisus. ¹² infhairghi. ¹³ hoighi. ¹⁴ bissus. ¹⁵ papirus. ¹⁶ bo. ¹⁷ muc. ¹⁸ tomús.

hic quinctus .a. um. ın cuı-
ʒeḋ neać.
hic sextus ın ꞅeıꞃeḋ neać.
hic captus .ı. ʒabáılꞇeć.
595 hic cuculatus .a. um. cuꝑꝑa-
cać.
hic capuciatus .a. tum. aꞇa-
nach.
hic tunicatus¹ .a. tum. ına-
ꞃać.
hic ınanicatus. muıncılleć.
hic falingatus .a. tum. ꝼal-
laınʒeć.
600 hic bracatus² .a. tum. ꞇꞃı-
buꞃać.
hic coronatus coꞃonꞇa.
hic inuidus³ .a. dum. ꝼoıꞃm-
ꞇeć.
hic blaesus⁴ .a. um. ʒoḋ.
hic surdus . a. um. boḋaꞃ⁵.
605 hic claudus .a. um. baccać.
hic auratus .a. um. óꞃḋaıʒe⁶.
hic argenteus⁷ .a. um. aıꞃʒe-
ḋać.
hic ferreus .a. um. ıaꞃnaıʒe⁸.
hic plumbeus⁹ luaıḋeaṁaıl¹⁰.

610 hic stanneus¹¹ .a. um. ꞅꞇana-
ṁaıl.
hic aereus¹² .a. um. uṁaṁaıl.
hic fundatus ꝼunḋamınꞇeḋ.
hic féssus .a. um. ꞃcıꞇeć ón
ṗlıʒı¹³.
hic lassus .a. um. ꞃcıꞇeć ó
obaıꞃ¹⁴.
615 hic festinosus .a. um. [festinus]
cınnıꞃneć no cınnıꞃnać.
hic libidinosus .a. um. ꞃalać.
hic infestinosus neṁcınḋıꞃ-
neć.
hic procus .a. um. ꞃuıꞃʒeć.
hic fornicarius .a. um. aḋall-
ꞇꞃać.
620 hic famelicus .a. um. ʒoꞃꞇać.
hic strabonus .a. um, ꝼıaꞃ-
ṗuıleć h¹⁵.
hic orbatus .a. um. ḋallṗuı-
leć¹⁶.
hic cecus .a. um. ḋall.
hic monoculosus .a. um. leć-
ćaeć¹⁷.
625 hic linguosus¹⁸ .a. um. ꞇenʒ-
ꞇać.

hic

¹ tonicatus. ² braxatus. ³ inuidus. ⁴ blesus. ⁵ boghar. ⁶ ordhaighe.
⁷ argeteos. ⁸ iarn. i. ⁹ plumpeus. ¹⁰ luaigheam. ¹¹ staneus. ¹² aureús.
¹³ on shl. i. ¹⁴ o obair. ¹⁵ strubosus .a. um. siadshuilech. ¹⁶ dall shuilech.
¹⁷ léthcaech. ¹⁸ lingosus.

hic bilinguosus[1] .a. um. [bi-
linguis] ᴅótengtaċ.
hic caritatosus .a. um. ᴅép-
caċ[2].
hic uerbosus .a. um. bριaċ-
ρaċ.
hic aglossus [ἄγλωσσος] .a.
um. ρbezaċ.
630 hic rediculosus .a. um. ρona-
maιᴅeaċ.
hic egenus .a. um. ρaιlzeaċ.
hic crispus .a. um. caρτa.

hic sanus .a. um. ρlán.
hic insanus .a. um. eρlán[3].
635 hic zelotypus .a. um. éᴅ-
muρ[4].
hic densus .a. um. ᴅluιτh.
hic acidus[5] .a. um. zoιρτ.
hic urbiculatus .a. um. bal-
laċ.
hic lubricus .a. um. ρlemaιn.
640 hic amplus .a. um. ρaιρριnz.
hic neruosus[6] .a. um. luaċ-
zaιρeċ.

Nunc de nominibus significantibus plenitudinem :—

hic formosus .a. um. ᴅealḃḋa.
hic strumossus [ventosus]
.a. um. uċταρᴅ.
hic gulosus[7] .a. um. cρaeρ-
ραċ.
645 hic barbosus .a. um. ᶂéρó-
zaċ[8].
hic uentossus [ventosus] .a.
um. zaeċmaρ.
hic uentriosus .a. um. bρonn-
maρ[9].

hic pediculosus .a. um. mí-
leċ[10].
hic lendosus[11] .a. um. ρneċaċ.
650 hic peditentosus[12] .a. um. coι-
ρíneċ.
hic phlegmosus .a. um. cρo-
ιnᴅτιlleċ[13].
hic rugosus[14] .a. um. zeρbaċ.
hic maculosus .a. um. bocoι-
ᴅeċ.
hic animosus .a. um. anmaċ.
hic

[1] bilingosus. [2] caritatinus .a. um. d. cach. [3] slan. eslan. [4] celopidus .a. um. edmur. [5] accidus. [6] neurosus. [7] gulossus. [8] barbossus a. um. fesogach. [9] uentri-ossus .a. um. brondm. [10] milech. [11] lentossus. [12] pedidendus. [13] flegmosus .a. um. croindtilli. [14] rugossus.

655 hic famosus .a. um. clú-
map¹.
hic difamosus .a. um. míclú-
map².

hic spadosus .a. um. bpeal-
lać.
hic retrocosus .a. um. ppe-
bać.

Nomina adjectiua que comparantur :—

hic albus .a. um. ɓeal.
660 hic doctus³ .a. um. cegaipɼe.
hic bonus .a. um. maié.
hic malus .a. um. olc.
hic magnus .a. um. móp⁴.
hic paruuus .a. um. beɼ.
665 hic clarus .a. um. polup.
hic candidus .a. um. caiéne-
mać.
hic auarus .a. um. panncać.
hic dignus⁵ .a. um. oinɼbala.
hic indignus .a. um. míoinɼ-
bala⁶.
670 hic multus .a. um. imòa.
hic purus .a. um. ɼlan.
hic rarus⁷ .a. um. ceipc.
hic paucus .a. um. beɼ.
hic durus .a. um. oainɼen⁸
no cpuaiò.
675 hic madidus .a. um. pliuć.

hic ignauus .a. um. ooćené-
lać⁹.
hic longus .a. um. paoa.
hic curtus .a. um. cumaip.
hic firmus .a. um. oainɼen⁸.
680 hic infirmus .a. um. éoain-
ɼen¹⁰.
hic iustus .a. um. pípénać.
hic iniustus .a. um. ainpípé-
nać¹¹.
hic fetidus¹² .a. um. bpén.
hic sordidus .a. um. palać.
685 hic gnarus .a. um.
hic ignarus .a. um.
hic gnauus .a. um.
Hoc templum. cempoll.
hoc tabernaculum. caib-
epne¹³.
690 hoc pennaculum.

hoc

¹ clumar. ² míclomar. ³ doctus .a. um. tegaisgí. ⁴ mor. ⁵ dingnus.
⁶ midingbala. ⁷ rarrus. ⁸ daingin. ⁹ ignaus .a. um. docinclach. ¹⁰ cdaingen.
¹¹ firenach, ainfirenach. ¹² fetitus. ¹³ taiberni.

hoc simithcrium [κοιμητή-
ριον]. peilic.
hoc feritrum [elicpum hod.
O'D.].
hoc sepulcrum. aölucaö.
hoc lucrum. eoail.
695 hoc miraculum. mipbail.
hoc monaculum. baclog.
hoc cúnábulum. cliban.
hoc sinabulum.
hoc jentaculum¹. oinep.
700 hoc cribrum. cpiacap.
hoc molendinum². muilino.
hoc atrium. zappga.
hoc torritorium³. cipaö.
hoc uestibulum⁴. oplap.
705 hoc stirpidivortium. rcoc-
ponna⁵.
hoc lumbarium. cpip cpi-
buip.
hoc epiglotum. rzop-
nac[an].
hoc gernonum. cpombeol⁶.
hoc chartaceum⁷. rzeoca.
710 hoc sacritegium. rzeoca.
hoc pistrinum⁸. muilleano.

hoc cla[u]strum. cliacac.
hoc prostibulum. cech na
mepopeac.
hoc redimiculum in bpaic-
cin.
715 hoc silintrum.
hoc uentilogium. bile.
hoc stragulum⁹. in ceip.
hoc lolium oicen.
hoc plectrum cpano. zlepca.
720 hoc igniferrium. ceiní
[ceine] cpeapa.
hoc scrupůlum. oubpuoan.
hoc teretorium. cuaipgin.
hoc herbagium. cluain ga-
bála¹⁰.
hoc caldarium. coipe¹¹.
725 hoc castrum. longpopc¹².
hoc monasterium. mainip-
cep.
hoc suffragium. popcacc¹³.
hoc refectorium. ppoinocec.
hoc dormitorium. covalcec.
730 hoc coopertorium. rpeilp.
hoc dolium¹⁴. cunna.
hoc corium. peice¹⁵.
hoc

¹ gentaculum.   ² mulindinum.   ³ tritorium.   ⁴ uescibulum.   ⁵ stipifortifartium. stoc ronna.   ⁶ gernoodum. cromccol.   ⁷ cartesium.   ⁸ prostrinum.
⁹ straulium.   ¹⁰ .gabála.   ¹¹ colldarium. cóiri.   ¹² longport.   ¹³ sufragium. furtacht.   ¹⁴ dolcum.   ¹⁵ corcum. scichí.

A Mediæval Tract on Latin Declension.

hoc cotium.
hoc ingénium ıntlecṫ¹.
735 hoc seníum. ſenáıſ².
hoc ymagium.
hoc incendium. loſcaḋ.
hoc martyrium³. maſtſa.
hoc salarium. taıle⁴.
740 hoc solarium. ſoılen.
hoc sellarium. ſeallaḋ.
hoc equitium. ʒſoıʒ⁵.
hoc palatium
hoc collum. muınél⁶.
745 hoc dorsum. ḋſuım.
hoc gyrgyrium⁷. ceılebſaḋ eoın. no cſanḋ toċaſ-taıʒ⁸.
hoc cerebrum. ıncınn⁹.
hoc scamnum¹⁰. ſtol.
hoc firmamentum. ſıſma-mınt.
750 hoc rubigorium. mıſ pluc.
hoc inuentorium. luaċ ſaıſ-néıſı.
hoc exilium. ınnaſbaḋ.
hoc alimentum. oıl[emaın].
hoc armentum. aıſʒe¹¹.

755 hoc crementum. toſmaċ.
hoc incrementum [decre-mentum]. mıtoſṁaċ¹².
hoc indumentum. éḋaċ.
hoc iumentum. óʒḋaṁ.
hoc monumentum. aḋlacaḋ.
760 hoc testamentum. tımna.
hoc instrumentum. ınſtſu-mınt.
hoc tegmentum. ḋıoın.
hoc augmentum. méḋuʒuḋ¹³.
hoc fragmentum. ſſuıſeċ.
765 hoc folium. ḋuıllen.
hoc psalterium. ſaltaıſ.
hoc pulmentum. lıté.
hoc dipodium¹⁴. uaıténe.
hoc pavementum. bıóʒaḋ¹⁵.
770 hoc lamentum. caſ.
hoc sementum.
hoc centum. céḋ.
hoc ducendum [ducenti]. ḋá-céḋ¹⁶.
hoc tricendum [tercentum]. tſí céḋ¹⁷.
775 hoc quatricentum [quadrin-genti]. ceıtſſe¹⁸ .c.

hoc

---

¹ inntlecht. ² seonoir. ³ martirium. ⁴ tailſ. ⁵ groidh. ⁶ múinel. ⁷ g̅giuin ⁸ .dochartaigh. ⁹ cerebrum. incind. ¹⁰ scanum. ¹¹ airgi. ¹² mitormach. ¹³ me-dug. ¹⁴ ffodium. vaithne. ¹⁵ pavímentum. ¹⁶ da .c. ¹⁷ tri .c. ¹⁸ ceithri.

hoc quincentum [quingenti] cúig .c.
hoc sexcentum [sescenti] ré¹ .c.
hoc frumentum. cruitnect.
hoc hordeum². eorna.
780 hoc [a]mersiamentum. méir-ri.
hoc stagnum. loċ.
hoc mulsum. lemnact.
hoc serum. meög.
hoc butyrum. im [imm].
785 hoc unguentum. uinnimint³.
hoc aurum. ór.
hoc argentum. airged.
hoc plumbum. luaide⁴.
hoc stannum. roan.
790 hoc ferrum. iarunn⁵.
hoc metallum⁶. mitall.
hoc praesumpticium⁷ luaċ lera.

hoc alministrum. bealaċ.
hoc nuchum. rreban⁸.
795 hoc gladiolum. roilercar.
hoc propheticum⁹. rgar-taċ.
hoc falcastrum. fióba.
hoc bonum. mait.
hoc malum. olc.
800 hoc candidus. (*sic*) taitnea-mnaċ.
hoc album. geal.
hoc nigrum. dub.
hoc flauum. buide¹⁰.
hoc fuscum. riabaċ.
805 hoc multum. imda.
hoc paruum. beg.
hoc modicum. merurda. ·
hoc minimum. robeg.
hoc magnum. mór.
810 hoc porrum. lur.

Nunc dicendum de nominibus heteroclitis:¹¹—

——— ínleman.
hoc coelum et plur. hí coeli¹² nem.
hoc castrum. longrort¹³.

hoc rastrum. rartail.
815 hoc epulum ⁊ plur. hee epule. roigi.
hoc delicium héc. cie.

hoc

¹ sc. ² ordium. ³ vinnimint. ⁴ luaighi. ⁵ iarund. ⁶ mithallum. ⁷ proseumcti-cum. ⁸ arcbhand. ⁹ profeticum. ¹⁰ buidhi. ¹¹ creocledus. ¹² h. celum ⁊ plur híi celí. ¹³ longport.

hoc filum uel fila ꞅnáıꞇe¹.
hoc claustrum .ri. ra. clauꞅ-
ꞇꞃa.
hoc frenum .ni. na. ꞅꞃıaɴ.
820 hoc capistrum .ri. ra. aḃaꞅ-
ꞇaꞃ.
hoc scarletum.
hoc balneum .e. uel.a. ꝓꞇ-
ꞃaʒaḋ.
hoc nasturtium². bıꞃuꞃ.
hoc admidulum.

825 Hic Tartarus haec .ra. ıꝕ-
ꝼeꞃɴ³.
hic sibilus est hominis⁴, sibela
feminae prius ın ꝼéṿ ꝼoꞃċ
hic infernus. na. ıꝼeaꞃɴaḃa
hic menalus .a.
hic dindimus .a.
830 hic avernus .a.
hic pelleus [pileus] aꞇ pıll
hic intimus .a. ıbꞃaċ

Q. Tercia declinacio quot literas terminales habet? R. xi.
Q. Quae sunt? R. a, e, o, c, l, n, d, r, s, t, x.
Q. Da exempla. R. a, ut poema: e, ut sedile: o, ut uirgo: c, ut lac: l, ut mel: n, ut nomen: d, ut Dauid: r, ut pater: s, ut ciuitas: t, ut caput: x, ut felix.
Q. Quot genera habet hec terminacio a in tercia declinacione? R. unum genus, scilicet neutrum, ut hoc poema.
Q. Quot genera habet hec terminacio e in tercia declinacione? R. unum, scilicet neutrum, ut hoc sedile.
Q. Quot genera habet hec terminacio o in tercia declinacione? R. sex. Q. Quae? R. masculinum, ut hic ordo, femininum, ut hec dulcedo, commune, ut hic et hec homo, omne [i. e. omnigenum], ut centripondio⁵, promiscuum siue epicoenum⁶, ut uespertilio, dubium, ut hic vel⁷ hec margo.

Q. Quot

¹ snaithi. ² nastorsium. ³ ifern. ⁴ ecbelus .c̄. hois. ⁵ oc. ut cento p̄sto. ⁶ episenum. ⁷ et.

Q. Quot genera habet hec terminacio c in tercia declinacione?
R. unum, scilicet neutrum, ut hoc lac.
Q. Quot genera habet hec terminacio l in tercia declinacione?
R. quatuor. Q. Quae? R. masculinum, ut hic sol: femininum, ut hec Micol: neutrum, ut hoc mel: commune, ut hic et hec uigil.
Q. Quot genera habet hec terminacio n in tercia declinacione?
R. tria. Q. Quae? R. masc. ut hic Titan: fem. ut hec siren[1]: neut. ut hoc nomen.
Q. Quot genera habet hec terminacio d in tercia declinacione?
R. Unum, scilicet masc. ut hic Dauid.
Q. Quot genera habet hec terminacio r in tercia declinacione?
R. Sex. Q. Quae? R. Masc. ut hic pater: fem. ut hec mater: neutr. ut hoc cadauer: commune, ut uber: omne, ut par: prom[i]scuum siue epicoenum[2], ut turtur.
Q. Quot genera habet hec terminacio s in tercia declinacione?
R. Septem. Q. Quae? R. masc. ut hic abbas: fem. ut hec caritas: neutr. ut hoc uas: commune, ut hic et hec sacerdos: omne genus, ut sapiens: prom[i]scuum siue epicoenum[2], ut phoenix[3], ut cortex[4].

Q. Que est agnicio tercie declinacionis nominum? R. hec: cuius genitiuus singularis in is correptum[5] desinit, datiuus in i productum desinit, accusatiuus sing. in em uel in im correptum desinit[6]: uocatiuus similis suo nominatiuo: ablatiuus desinit in e correptum [uel i] productum desinit excepto[7] fame et nocte: nom. et acc. et uoc. plur. in es productum desinunt[8], genitiuus pluralis in um uel in ium correptum[5] desinit: datiuus [et] ablatiuus plurales in bus correptum[9] desinunt[10].

Nunc

[1] siren. [2] episcnum. [3] fenix. [4] corcortex. [5] coruptum. [6] coruptum desinit in i. [7] acepto. [8] desiniunt. [9] correbtum. [10] desinit.

Nunc de nominibus tercie declinacionis, ut sequitur:—

Hoc poema. ꝑɩlɩḃecꞇ.
hoc dindyma[1]. ʒeman.
835 hoc prolemma[2]. aḃbaṗⱱacꞇ.
hoc cataplasma. céɩꝑín[3].
hoc dogma. ꝼoɩꝑceⱱal.
hoc doma. mullac ꞇɩʒe[4].
hoc énighma. ꝼoꝑꝛʒaꞇ no ɩnʒaꝑ.
840 hoc chrisma[5]. cꝑɩꝑmal.
hoc nomisma[6]. monaḃ.
hoc sophissma. ꝼoɩꝼɩꝑꞇ.
hoc apostema[7]. neꝑcoɩⱱ.
hoc phlegma[8]. cꝑoɩnⱱꞇɩlle.
845 hoc anathema. coɩnⱱealbꞇaⱱ.
hoc fantassma. ꞇaḃbaɩꝑ.
hoc sperma. coɩmꝑeꝑꞇ.
hoc ídíoma. aḃbaꝑⱱacꞇ.
hoc thema[9]. aḃbaꝑ.
850 hoc sedile. ꝼuɩḃeocan.
hoc ouíle. cꝑo caeꝑac[10].
hoc mónile vel munile. ꝑꝑoɩꝑꞇé.
hoc missale. leḃaꝑ aɩꞇꝼꝼꝑɩnⱱ.

hoc gredale. ʒꝑeḃáɩl.
855 hoc trobiale. ꞇꝑoɩbel.
hoc lectóric. ꝼꞇuɩⱱɩꝑ.
hoc manuale. lámꞇuaʒ.
hoc cubile. leabaɩⱱ ɩn ⱱaɩm all[ꞇa].
hoc corporale. coꝑꝑoꝑaꝑ.
860 hoc mare. muɩꝑ.
hoc praesepe[11]. maɩnⱱꝑéꝑ.
hoc cepe[12]. uɩnneamaɩn.
hoc rete. lín[13] uɩꝑcí.
hoc gausape. ꝼcaꝑaɩⱱ.
865 hoc cete. míl móꝑ[14].
hoc tempe. macaɩꝑe.
Hec locucio. uꝑlabꝑaⱱ.
hec lectio. aɩcecꞇ.
hec accio. acꝑa.
870 hec oracio. ʒuɩⱱe[15].
hec constrùctio[16]. cumꞇac.
hec preposicio. ꝑemꞇeccaꝑ[17].
hec coniunctio. comꝑocul[18].
hec ínterjectio[19]. ɩnꞇeꝑɩacꞇ.
875 hec comparatio. comparáɩⱱ[20].

hec

[1] dindíma. [2] prolema. [3] ceirín. [4] tighi. [5] crisma. [6] momíssma. [7] apastema. [8] fethma. [9] téma. [10] caeirach. [11] p. cepe. [12] sepe. [13] lin. [14] mil. mor. [15] guidhi. [16] construccio. [17] remtoṡc. [18] comfoccul. [19] ínterdeccio. [20] comparaíd.

hec intencio. ınnꞇınꝺeaċ.
hec opinio. baꞃamaıl.
hec electio. ꞇoẋa.
hec racio. olıẋeꝺ.
880 hec consecratio. coıꞃꞃeẋꞃaꝺ.
hec ornacio. cumꝺaċ.
hec famulacio. muẋꞃaıne.
hec fornicacio. aꝺallꞇꞃaꞃ.
hec consolacio. comꞃólaꞃ[1] no
comaıꞃle.
885 hec nominacio. aınmneaċaꝺ.
hec dominacio. ꞇıẋeꞃnaꞃ.
hec generacio. ẋeınemaın.
hec correctio. ceꞃꞇaċaꝺ.
hec operacio. oıbꞃıuẋuꝺ.
890 hec planacio. ꞃeıꝺe[2].
hec castigacio. ceꞃꞇuẋuꝺ.
hec associacio[3]. comꞃanꞇuꞃ.
hec supplicacio. ẋuıꝺe[4].
hec monstracio[5]. ꞇaıꞃbenaꝺ.
895 hec annunciacio. ꝼoıll[ꞃıu-
ẋuꝺ].
hec collacio. comꞃaꞃáıꝺ.
hec communicacio[6]. comaın-
eachaꝺ.
hec ministracio. ꞇımeıꞃeċꞇ.
hec procuracio. ꝺénam[7].

900 hec fictio[8] ꝺoılbꞇıuẋuꝺ.
hec pericio [peritia]. eolaꞃ[9].
hec adulacio. molaꝺ.
hec coequatio. comꞇꞃomu-
ẋuꝺ.
hec simulacio. coꞃmaıluꞃ.
905 hec disimulacio. eẋcuꞃmaı-
luꞃ.
hec sequestracio. uꞃlamaꞃ.
hec prolongacio. ꞃaıoıuẋuꝺ.
hec satisfaccio. lóꞃẋním[10].
hec remuneracio aċcumı-
leꝺ.
910 hec deduccio[11]. ꝺıꞃluẋuꝺ.
hec compilacio. ceꞃẋal.
hec reuolucio. eıꞇellaꝺ.
hec computacio. comaıꞃem.
hec benediccio[12]. bennachꞇ.
915 hec malediccio. mallaċꞇ.
hec remigacio [reptatio ?].
lamaccan.
hec mitigacio. aılẋıneċ[ꞇ].
hec talliacio. comma.
hec caro. coluno.
920 hec fortitudo. laıoıꞃe[13].
hec multitudo. ımaꝺ.
hec magnitudo. méıꝺ.
hec

---

[1] comsholas. [2] reidhi. [3] asociacio. [4] suplicacio guidhi. [5] mostracio. [6] comuní-
cacio. [7] forcuracio denamh. [8] fixio. [9] colus. [10] lorgnim. [11] dedicacio. [12] benndic-
cacio. [13] laidiri.

hec paruitudo. loiǵev.
hec raritudo. ceipce.
925 hec latitudo. leicne.
hec celsitudo. aipve.
hec pulchritudo. maippe.
hec egritudo. eplane.
hec longitudo. paive¹.
930 hec triplicacio. cpipulca.
hec quadruplicacio. ceċapvublav.
hec limpitudo. uipṡemlacc.
hec arundo. cupċuplaċ² no ṡilcaċ.
hic hirundo³. painleoc.
935 hec hirudo⁴. náic. epcuinṡ upċoiveċ⁵.

Propria nomina:—

hic. Odo ɑov.
hic Catto. caiv.
950 hic Plato. plaic.
hic Uato. [Pluto?] ploic.
hic Apollo. ṡpian.
hic et hec homo vuine.
hic et hec uirgo. óṡh⁹.
955 hic et hec nemo. nemvuine.

hec ymago. vealv.
hec indago. lopṡapecc.
hec uorago. páevċoipe⁶.
hec rubedo⁷. vepṡe.
940 hec sangis suga [sanguisuga]. ṡeppṡuin.
hec fuligo. puithe.
hec calido [calor]. cep.
Hic ordo. opv.
hic cardo. meplaċ na coinla.
945 hic carbo. pmepóiv⁸.
hic mango. ṡilla naneaċ.
hic uel hec margo bpuaċ.

hic et hec latro placaive¹⁰.
hic et hec Brito bpecnaċ.
hic et hec pseudo. páiċ bpéṡaċ¹¹.
hic et hec praesto. piavnaipe¹².
960 hic et hec par. comcpom.

hic

¹ In the MS. teirci, leithní, airdí, maissí, eslaní, faidi. ² curcuslach. ³ crundo. ⁴ ¨írundo.¦ ⁵ urcoidech. ⁶ urago. saebhcoire. ⁷ rubido. dergi. ⁸ smeroid. ⁹ ogh. ¹⁰ slataidhi. ¹¹ ceudo [over which is the gloss ".i. longa fullsa"] faith bregach. ¹² psto. fiadhnaisi.

hic et hec impar. ⁊com-
ṫrom.

hic et hec dispar. ⁊com-
ṫrom.

Ista sunt nomina :—

hic Issac.
hic Melchisedech.
965 hic [hec] ambago¹.
hoc lac. bainne².
hoc allec. rgaḋan.
hic Daniel.
hic Michael.
970 hic Raphael.
hic Uriel.
hic Samúel. mascula sunt.
hic sol .ı. grian.

hoc mel. mil.
975 hoc fel. ḋomblar áe.
hoc animal. ainmiḋe³.
hoc sál et dicitur hic sal .ı.
  ralann.
hic tribunal.
hoc ccruical⁴. cércaill.
980 hic Aníbal. ainm ḋuini⁵.
hic et hec consul comairr-
  leaċ.

Propria [communia?] sunt nomina :—

hic et hec praesul. earpog.
hic et hec exul. ınnarbṫaċ.
hic et hec uigil. furaċair.

985 hic et hec [im]provigil.
  nemfuirećáir.
hic et hec pugil. glecaire.

Nomina indeclinabilia :—

hoc nil neımṫní.
hoc nul. neımṫní.

hoc Pean. grian.
990 hoc Titan. grian.

Hoc

¹ ambaca. ² bainde. ³ ainm .i. ⁴ scruical. ⁵ ainmidhi duine.

Hoc nomen. αınm.
hoc praenomen¹. ꝑemαınm.
hoc cognomen. comαınm.
hoc stramen. τuıɼ̃e².
995 hoc tegimen. ꝺıꝺın.
hoc pronomen. αꝑꝛon αn-
ma.
hoc flamen. ꝛıꝺαn. ɼαcıτc.
hoc lumen. ꝛoıllꝛe³.
hoc flumen. ꝛꝛuτ.
1000 hoc limen. ταıꝑꝛec⁴.
hoc polímen. ꝛlıꝛeoɼ.
hoc carmen ꝑılıꝺecτ.
hoc agmen. ꝛluαɼ.
hoc fragmen. ꝛbꝛuıleαc.
1005 hoc trolliamen. mαꝛóɼ.
hoc odomen. [abdomen]
blonαcc.
hoc culmen. mullαc.
hoc cacumen. ꝑınꝺ.

hoc semen. ꝛíl⁵.
1010 hoc geminen⁶. emnαꝺ.
Hic rén. áꝛα.
hic splen. ꝛeαlɼ no ꝺꝑeαꝛ-
ꝛαn.
hic lién. ınτınne ıαchτα-
ꝛαc⁷.
hic pecten ꝛlınꝺ.
1015 hic lyricen⁸. cꝛuıτıꝛe.
hic tubicen⁹. ꝛꝺocαıꝑe.
hic fidicen. τéꝺαıꝑe¹⁰.
hic cornicen. ɼılla αɓαıꝑce.
hic lamen [flamen?]. ꝛeı-
ꝺeαɓ¹¹.
1020 hic siren. muıꝛꝺuchu¹².
hic Caton.
hic Simon.
hic Samson.
hic Phaethon.
1025 hic Lycaon¹³.

Propria nomina villarum :—

Hᴇᴄ Calidon.
hec Babilon .ı. confusio.
hec Elicón.

hic delphin¹⁴. mucc mαꝛα.
1030 hic Cayn colach.
hic iubár. ꝺeαllꝛαꝺ.
hic

¹ áinm h. pronomen. ² tuighi. ³ soillsi. ⁴ tairrsech. ⁵ sil. ⁶ genímen.
⁷ .iasachtarach. ⁸ liricen. ⁹ tibicen. ¹⁰ tedaire. ¹¹ séideagh. ¹² cirén. muruchu.
¹³ foton hic licaon. ¹⁴ delipin. muc.

hic hepar[1]. áe.
hic sutolar. bɼócc.
hic lar. ιϲϲaɼ na comlaȯ.
1035 hic Cesar. pí.
hic Lastar. pí.
hic Nár. ɼɼuϲ.
hoc fár. ιϲ ιn aɼba.
hic naris (pars corporis)
ɼɼón (ιɼ fluuii Náris).
1040 hic sequester [sequax] len-
munaϲ[2] (extat hic se-
questris).

hoc calcar. ɼboɼ an eιϲ.
hoc pluuinar. ɼɼuϲ.
hoc torcular. cláɼ[3]. caɼϲa.
hoc bostar. buaιle ȯam.
1045 hoc nectar .c. ʒɼιnoí ɼoιlcí.
Hic pater. aϲhaιɼ.
hic frater. bɼáϲhaιɼ[4].
hic imber. bɼaen aιmɼιɼe.
hic cucumer. culaɼan.
1050 hic September[5]. mí.
hic October. mí.

Feminina[6] hec sunt :—

hec mater. máϲhaιɼ[7].
hec mulier bean.

hec linter. ɼlιnn cɼιaȯ.

Communia sunt :—

1055 Hic et hec puber caeϲaɼ-
[aϲ].
hic et hec uber. uϲh.
hic et hec degener. ȯocιné-
lach[8].
hic et hec et hoc pauper.
boϲϲ.

hoc uber ɼιne oϲϲa[9].
1060 hic campester ⎫
hec campestris ⎬ maϲaιɼe.
hoc campestre ⎭
hic siluester ⎫
hec siluestris ⎬ caιllϲea-
hoc siluestre ⎭ maιl.

hic

[1] opar. [2] "hoc naris sron .is. flui. náris Hic sequester lenmunach. párs corporis extat. hic sequestris hoc calcar sbor an eich hoc sequestro." [3] torculcar. clar. [4] brathair. [5] septimb. [6] feminea. [7] mathair. [8] docinelach. [9] apparently *senextus*.

A Mediæval Tract on Latin Declension.

hic pedester
hec pedéstris   } uaċtlanaıḋe.
hoc pedestre
hic celeber
hec celebris   } uaċtlanaıḋe.
hoc celebre
hic saluber
hec salubris   } uaċtlan.
hoc salubre
Video larem (.ı. familiam) per larem (.ı. per familiam) circa larem (.ı. ignem) in lare (.ı. in domo).

1065 Hic acer
hec acris   } ꞅnuamḋa.
hoc acre
hic volucer[1]
hec volucris   } eteċaıl.
hoc volucre
hic paluster
hec palustres   } ꞅóıtamaıl[2].
hoc palustre
hic alacer
hec alacris   } eıtıḋeamaıl.
hoc alacre[3]

Hoc polyandrium. uaıḋ[4].
1070 hoc uer. eappaċ.
hoc cadauer. copp leꞅap.
hoc piper. pıpup.
hoc iter. ꞅét ꞅlıgeḋ.
hoc spinter. ḋealꞅ.
1075 hoc ruter. cac. ꞅaḃap.
hoc iuger. la oıppti.
hoc uesper. nóın[5].
hic nutritor. aıḋe[6].
hic honor. onoıp[7].
1080 hic lector. leꞅtoıp[8].
hic amor. ꞅpaḋ.
hic doctor. ḋoctuıp.
hic decor. maıꞅe.
hic dedecor. mímaıꞅe[9].
1085 hic labor. ꞅaechap.
hic calor. tép.
hic color[10]. ḋaṫ.
hic odor. bolcanaḋ[11].
hic fetor. bréntup[12].
1090 hic factor. ḋénmupaċ[13].
hic fictor. ḋoılḃteoıp.
hic emptor. cennaıḋe[14].
hic protector. ḋıḋnıꞅteoıp.

hic

---

[1] hoc acris cithidemail Hic volucer. etechail hec uolacris, hoc volacre.   [2] gœtham.
[3] alice eathideam. h. alieris h. alierc.   [4] políandrium.   [5] noín.   [6] oidí.   [7] onar. anoir.
[8] leg. légtóir?   [9] maisi. dedicor. mímaisi.   [10] colar.   [11] bolltanadh.   [12] brentus.
[13] denmusach.   [14] cend.i.

F

hic tenor [tener]. boc.
1095 hic textor. ꝼıɉıꝺóıꞃ¹.
hic nitor. cꞃıallacóıꞃ.
hic liquor². ꝼlıuċıꝺeċc.
hic conditor³. cumꝺaıɉcóıꞃ.
hic rector⁴. maıɉıꞃceꞃ.
1100 hic senior. ꞃenóıꞃ.

hic auditor. eıꞃcıꝺóıꞃ.
Hoc cor. cꞃoıꝺe⁵.
hoc equor. ꝼaıꞃɉe⁶.
hoc marmor. maꞃmuꞃ.
1105 hoc castor. aınmıꝺe⁷.
hoc ador aꝺ⁸.

Nomina communia⁹ :—

hic et hec autor. uɉꝺuꞃ.
hic et hec decór. maıꞃı.
hic et hec dédicor. mímaı-
ꞃı.

1110 hic et hec memor. cuım-
neaċ.
hic et hec immemor. mıcu-
ımneaċ.

Nunc de nominibus comparatiuis tercie declinacionis :—

hic et hec doctior¹⁰ et hoc
.ius. nı́ꞃcecoıꞃce.
hic et hec fortior et hoc
.ius. nı́aꞃlaıꝺıꞃı¹¹.
hic et hec maior¹² et hoc
.ius. nı́ꞃmó¹³.
1115 hic et hec minor et hoc.us¹⁴.
nı́aꞃluɉa.
hic et hec melior et hoc
.ius. nı́ꞃꝼeꞃꞃ.

hic et hec peior et hoc .ius.
nı́ꞃméꞃa.
hic et hec durior et hoc .ius.
nı́ꞃ¹⁵cꞃuaıꝺı.
hic et hec mollior et hoc .ius.
nı́ꞃ¹⁵ buıɉı.
1120 hic et hec auarior et hoc.ius.
nı́ꞃꞃanncaıɉı.
hic et hec carior et hoc .ius.
nı́¹⁶aꝺıLé.

hic

---

¹ figidoir. ² licór. ³ cumdaightoir. ⁴ retor. ⁵ croidhi. ⁶ fairef. ⁷ ainmidhi.
⁸ adorad. ⁹ indecl.e. ¹⁰ doctor. ¹¹ nisalaid. ¹² magior. ¹³ mo. ¹⁴ .ius. ¹⁵ nis. ¹⁶ ni.

hic et hec clarior et hoc .ius. nírroillri.
hic et hec debelior et hoc .ius. nís'armeaca.
hic et hec albior et hoc .ius. nirgile.
1125 hic et hec amabilior et hoc .ius. nírrocapéanaig[1].
hic et hec legibilior et hoc .ius. nísarrolegca.
hic et hec laudabilior et hoc .ius. nírromolca.
hic et hec felicior[2] et hoc .ius nísarconaichi.
hic et hec sapientior[3] et hoc .ius. niargluca.
1130 hic et hec benignior et hoc .ius nírcainruaraigi[4].

hic et hec audacior[5] et hoc .ius. nírvana.
hic et hec amarior et hoc .ius. nírreipbe.
hic et hec loquacior[6] et hoc .ius. nírlabarcaige.
hic turibulus .i. raicec na cuire[7].
1135 hoc orologium .i. urralairci.
hoc collistrigium[8] .i. piloir.
hoc equicium .i. compar no paing ancrair.
hoc equilibrium .i. compar.
hoc manubrium .i. maive rgine.

[1] nisamcata. [2] felitorum. [3] crudelior. [4] cœnshuaraighi. [5] audatorum. [6] locatorum. [7] saithee na tuisi. [8] colosdrigium. [I have placed a mark of length over the *ni* in Nos. 1124, 1128, 1129.]

F 2

COMMENTARY.

[In the following Commentary I have made use of certain abbreviations, which, if not explained, might cause obscurity. Thus, "A. S." for Anglo-Saxon; "Beitr." for the *Beiträge zur vergleichenden sprachforschung auf dem gebiete der arischen, keltischen und slavischen sprachen*, herausgegeben von A. Kuhn und A. Schleicher, vol. i. Berlin, 1858; "Corm." for Cormac's Glossary; "gl." for "the gloss on;" "Glück" for C. W. Glück's *Keltische Namen* (München, 1857); "Lib. Hymn." for the Liber Hymnorum; "l. w." for "a living word;" "O. H. G." for Old High German; "O. Ir." for Old Irish; "O'R." for O'Reilly's Irish Dictionary (Dublin, 1817); "O. W." for Old Welsh; "r." for root; "Skr." for Sanskrit; "W." for Modern Welsh; "Z." for Zeuss, or Zeuss's *Grammatica Celtica* (Lipsiæ, 1853); "Zeits." for the *Zeitschrift für vergleichende sprachforschung* u. s. w. Berlin, now edited solely by Dr. Kuhn. Finally, I trust that Dr. O'Donovan and Mr. Curry will not be offended at finding their honoured names reduced to "O'D." and "C." respectively.]

1-5.—1. *Fílidh* (gl. poeta), in O. Ir. fili gen. filed, a masc. d-stem, may perhaps be connected with the W. r. gwel, "to see;" cf. Velleda? Fili is declined in O. Ir. as follows:—

Masc. *d*-Stem.
Stem, filid.

	Sing.	Dual.	Plur.
N.	fili	dá ḟili	filid
G.	filed	dá filed	filed (ṅ)
D.	filid	dib filedaib	filedaib
Ac.	filid (ṅ)	dá ḟili	fileda
V.	a ḟili	a dá ḟili	a fileda

Hence *filidecht* (gl. poema, gl. carmen), Nos. 853 and 1002, *infra*. The .i. which so frequently occurs is for idón, "to wit," "namely." 2. *Fáith* (= vâtis) gen. fátha (= vâtayas?) cognate with Lat. vâtes, a masc. i-stem, declined in O. Ir. thus:—

Masc. *i*-Stem.
Stem, fáthi.

	Sing.	Dual.	Plur.
N.	fáith	dá ḟáith	fúithi
G.	fátha	dá ḟáithe	fáithe (ṅ)
D.	fáith	dib fáithib	fáithib
Ac.	fáith (ṅ)	dá ḟáith	fáithi
V.	a ḟáith	a dá ḟáith	a ḟúithi

3. *Sailmchétlaid*,

3. *Sailmchétlaid*, from salm = psalmus, is also an i-stem, as is cétlaid, which is not found in O'R., but must mean "singer," cf. crochairchétlaid gl. tibicen Z. 198 (crochuir, acrachair gl. crus Z. 744). 4. *Sai*, leg. súi? a masc. t-stem? of obscure origin,—unless we assume that a *p* has dropped out. It occurs, spelt *sui*, in Lib. Hymn. 3ᵃ (p. 72, ed. Todd), "roleg [read rolég] iarsein i Corcaig corbo *sui*" (he afterwards studied in Cork till he became a *sui*, a learned man, sage) acc. pl. seems to occur in the same MS. in the pref. to S. Cuchuimne's hymn, fo. 6ᵃ: rolég *suthe* codruimne¹. 5. *Cruitire* (leg. cruittire, gl. citharista, gl. lyricen, *infra*), a masc. ia-stem = crottárias, formed from crott = crottá, W. crwth, a fem. â-stem. cf. chrotta Britanna, Venant. Fortun. 7, 8, cited by Z. 77, crottichther gl. charizatur Z. 77. Note in cruitire the vowel-change (umlaut) of the *o* of the root into *ui*, effected by the *i* of the penultima; note also the non-aspiration of the *t*, though flanked by vowels, in consequence of its original duplication. Engl. crowd-er (fiddler) is from W. crwth, where *tt* has, according to rule, become *th*. cfr. O. H. G. hrotta, Ang. Sax. rót (fem.).

6–10.—6. *Timpanach*. 7. *Organaidh*. 8. *Sophistidhe*. All formed by adding Irish terminations to foreign roots. 9. *Rannaire* (gl. partista), a personal noun (masc. ia-stem) from rann (a part) a fem. â-stem = W. rhan: cf. O. W. rannam (gl. partior) Z. 1078. In O. Ir. rannaire was thus declined:—

MASC. *ia*-STEM.
Stem, ranndria.

	Sing.	Dual.	Plur.
N.	rannaire	dá rannaire	rannairi
G.	rannairi	dá rannaire	rannaire (ṅ)
D.	rannairiu	dib rannairib	rannairib
Ac.	rannaire (ṅ)	dá rannaire	rannairiu
V.	a rannairi	a dá rannaire	a rannairiu

And

¹ Suthe may here be a derived abstract subst. which occurs, spelt súithe, in the Amra Choluim Chille (*Leb. na huidre*, 10 *a, a*): Bái sab *súithe* ceedind (gl. *no uas, no in .i. ba* [*sab*] *suithe in cach dindsenchas*) .i. *roba sab daingen nosoad cech niummus. No robosuiabb. No sabb cech denna .i. cecha aircchta cosaricced Colum cille. No basoabb isuthemlacht cechberlai coclethi. No robonertmar isint*[*s*]*uithe coriacht coclethi*. "He was a chief of science in every hill (gl. or above, or in, i. e. he was [a chief] of science in every hill-science), i. e. he was a firm chief who used to return every wealth [of knowledge]. Or he was a sage-abbot. Or a chief of every hill, i. e. of every assembly to which Columcille came. Or he was a good abbot in the knowledge of every tongue to perfection. Or he was mighty in the science to perfection" (coclethe, lit. according to C. "to the ridge or the top of anything"). In H. 2. 16 (T. C. D.) col. 691, the passage and

And rann was thus declined:—

FEM. á-STEM.
Stem, rannā.

	Sing.	Dual.	Plur.
N.	rann	dí rainn	ranna
G.	rainne	dá rann	rann (ṅ)
D.	rainn	dib rannaib	rannaib
Ac.	rainn (ṅ)	dí rainn	ranna
V.	a rann	a dí rainn	a ranna

luchtaire (gl. lanista) not in O'R., who, however, has luchdaire, "whirlpool," as to which meaning, quære. Perhaps we may compare the name of Luctorius, chief of the Cadurci, also spelt LVXTIIPIOS.

11–15.—11. *Lexaire* (gl. legista), a hybrid from lex, as 12, *decredech* from Lat. decretum, medializing the tenuis *t*. In O. Ir. we should probably have had erchoilidech. 13. *Uasalathair* (patriarch), a masc. stem, declined in O. Ir. like cathir (which, according to Ebel, is a stem in *r* taking the determinative suffix *e*—cf. Goth. brothrahans—but should, perhaps, like Ainmire, ruire, Fiachra, Fiacha, Lugaid, Echaid, cáera, nathir, &c., be rather considered a stem in *e*); cathir was thus declined:—

	Sing.	Dual.	Plur.
N.	cathir	dí chathir	cathraig
G.	cathrach	dá cathrach	cathrach (ṅ)
D.	cathraig	dib cathrachaib	cathrachaib
Ac.	cathraig (ṅ)	dí chathir	cathracha
V.	a chathir	a dí chathir	a chathracha

If uasalathair be a stem in r, it is compounded of uasal = óxala (óxalla?) high (cf. Uxellodunum) and athair = Skr. pitar, Gr. πατήρ, Lat. pater, Eng. father, with loss of the initial *p* as is common in Irish and Welsh: cf. lán (full) = W. llawn, Lat. plénus, Skr. root par; lear (many) with plêrus, πλήρης; iasc = W. pŷsg = piscis = fish; lia = πλείων; lethan (broad) with πλατύς, Skr. pṛthu; the O. Ir. intensive particle and verbal prefix ra-, ro- = Skr. pra, Lat. pro; the prefix il- = πολύ, Skr. puru, Goth. filu; ire (ulterior) = περαῖος, ath (ford) = πάτος, and other instances brought forward by Ebel, Beitr. i. 307. Athir was thus declined in O. Ir.:—

gloss above quoted stand thus: Bai sapb saithi cach dind .i. *robai corbasai* ꝛ *corbo hap saitheamlachta dindseanchas* .i. *iter ecna* ꝛ *fílidecht* ꝛ *faistine* (wisdom as well as philosophy and prophecy).

MASC. r-STEM (NOUN OF RELATIONSHIP).
Stem, athar.

	Sing.	Dual.	Plur.
N.	athir	dá athir	athir
G.	athar	dá athar	athre (ṅ)
D.	athir	dib ṅathraib	athraib
Ac.	athir (ṅ)	dá athir	athra
V.	athir	a dá athir	a athra

14. *Crosan* (gl. scurra), W. croesan (buffoon), primarily a cross-bearer in religious processions, "who also," says Dr. Todd (Irish Nennius, p. 182), "combined with that occupation the profession, if we may so call it, of singing satirical poems against those who had incurred Church censure, or were for any other cause obnoxious." The exercise of this profession was sometimes not unattended with risk—Muirchertach mac Erca having been expelled from Ireland ar na *crossana* do marbad (after having killed the Crossans, Ir. Nenn., *ubi supra*). In the Cornish vocabulary, printed by Z., *scurra* is glossed by barth, i. e. bard. 15. *Cestunach*, apparently formed from the base of the Lat. questio.

16–20.—16. *Ardeaspoc* (archbishop), O. Ir. ardepscop, where the first element ard (high) = Lat. arduus, Gr. ὀρθός for ὀρθFός, Skr. ûrdhva: epscop is of course from episcopus. 17. *Gilla cinn eich* (gl. auriga), "a servant (*gillie*) at a horse's head;" *gilla* = O. W. name Gildas, apparently a stem in *s* (Dauid in *gilla dana*, Colmán's hymn, "D. the bold youth"); *cinn* the locative of cenn (head), W. penn. a masc. a-stem, and thus declined in O. Ir.:—

MASC. a-STEM.
Stem, *cinna*.

	Sing.	Dual.	Plur.
N.	cenn	dá chenn	cinn
G.	cinn	dá cenn	cenn (ṅ)
D.	ciunn	dib cennaib	cennaib
Ac.	cenn (ṅ)	dá chenn	ciunnu
V.	a chinn	a dá chenn	a chiunnu
Loc.	cinn		

eich = eci = akvai, gen. of ech, a masc. a-stem = ecas = akvas, cf. Skr. açvas, Gr. ἵππος, Lat. equus, O. H. G. ehu, &c. v. *infra*. 18. *Birrach*, says C., is "a heifer between the ages of one and two years;" the Lat. birria is obscure to me. Festus (sub v. burrum, ed. Mueller) has "burra," a heifer with a red muzzle. O'R. has "biorrach," a boat, a cot, a currach (which word I have never met in a MS.). This reminds one of baris, a flat Egyptian rowboat, in Propertius, 3, 11, 44, βᾶρις in Herodotus. 19. *Geidh* (gl. geta), leg. *géidh*, is afterwards the gloss on anser (goose). 20. *Righan* (queen), a fem. â-stem. Cf. Skr. rājn͏ī, Lat. rēgīna. Skr. root, rāj, reg-ere.

21–25. In *bantóisech* (duchess), *banab* (abbess), *banprioir* (prioress) (leg. banphrioir), *bansagart* (priestess), the first element is ban (woman, female), W. bun (Myvyr. Arch. i. 575) = gvanâ, Gr. γυνή, Bœotian βάνα (see Ebel, Beitr., i. 160), tóisech (princeps Z. 61), a derivative from tús (initium), out of which a *v* has certainly fallen (cf. O. W. touyssogion principes Z. 6) as in dia (God) = Skr. dêvas, núe (new) = navius; cf. the Gaulish base novio in Noviodunum and Noviomagus, Vêdic navya, nói (a ship) = Lat. navis, Boind, the Boyne = Bovindâ (Βοουυίνεα, Ptol.) &c.; *sagart* is of course from sacerd-os, with the provection of the medial frequent in derived words (cf. apgitir [alphabet] = abecedarium). 25. *Innilt* (gl. ancilla), "a handmaid."—O'R.

26–30. *At cluic* (gl. galea), "hat of (the) skull," cf. clogad, "helmet," O'R. We should, I suspect, read atchluic; cf. *atanach*, gl. caputiatus, *infra*. 27. *Taiplis* (alea), perhaps nothing but the English "tables" (backgammon, or some such game with dice), with the provection of the medial above alluded to. 28. *Bairín* (gl. mitra) leg. bairrín? and cf. barr gl. cassis, gl. frons, frondis Z. 51. 29. *Inar* (gl. tunica) *inarach* (gl. tunicatus) *infra*, loc. sing.: Senoir broit buide (leg. buidi?) *inair* glais go glanmét (leg. glanméit), "an old man in a yellow cloak, in a blue tunic of full size." Harleian 1802, fol. 5ᵇ (tunica is glossed by fúan in Z., W. gwn, Eng. gown). 30. *Muincille* (gl. manica), afterwards *muincilleeh* (gl. manicatus), "a sleeve, cuff," O'R.

31–35. *Gairleog*, from Eng. garlick, A. S. garleac, garlec. 32. *Slestan* (gl. lacerna) not in O'R., is apparently a deriv. from sliassit (gl. poples Z. 22), of which the dat. pl. sliastaib is glossed by femoribus in the Leabhar Breacc copy of Gildas' Lorica: slestan, therefore, is probably a cloak, covering the thighs and hams. With the connected O. Ir. sliss, cf. W. ystlys (side, flank). 33. *Ciabh*, "a lock of hair," O'R., l. w. Cirrhus is glossed by mong in Z. 34. *Lámann* (a glove); cf. W. llawes, deriv. from lám (hand) = lûmâ, lâbâ? and this, perhaps, from the root LAB (Skr. labh), cf. λαμβάνω—the root-vowel being lengthened (vriddhied?). 35. *Dias* (gl. spica, "an ear of corn," O'R., probably W. twyson, although W. *t* = Ir. *d* is irregular), occurs in Z. 577 : nin (leg. nín) *dias* biis archiunn fochcirt (non ἡ spica est antequam seminas). Oengus célé dé (Félire, Nov. 24) calls Cianan of Daimliac "cain-*dias* diar tuirind" (a fine ear to our wheat).

36–40. *Braise*,

36-40. *Braise*, "hastiness, rapidity, intrepidity, boldness," O'R., which does not agree very well with lascivia (playfulness, licentiousness). The dat. sing. of the word occurs in the Leabhar Breacc copy of the Félire of Oengus (June 19):—

Luid afuil foroenu (.i. *foroenchaire*)
fiadsluagaib comBRASSI : (.i. *coslatra no cosolam*)
donrig batar uissi (.i. *batar uiss no umla no innraice no comadais*)
Geruassi Protassi (.i. *duos* [duo] *fratres erant, et in Elcidie sunt reliquia suo qui* [reliquiae suae quae] *per somnium Ambrossio ostensa* [ostensae] *sunt*).

Their blood flowed at the same time (i. e. at the one accusation)
Before hosts, with boldness (i. e. strongly or quickly):
Just unto the King [of heaven] were (i. e. they were obedient, or humble, or fit, or suitable).
Gervassi [and] Protassi.

Cf. W. brysiaw, "to hasten, hurry." 37. *Fallaing*, l. w. (mantle) a fem. i-stem, *fallaingech* (gl. falingatus), *infra*, occurs in Giraldus Cambrensis, Topogr. Hib., 3, 10, "gens ista, hibernica, vice palliorum *phalingis* laneis (al. falangis nigris) utitur," cited Z. 95; fallaing is perhaps connected with pallium. Cf. the W. adage, *mal y Gwyddyl am y ffaling*, "like the Irishman for the cloak." 38. *Léine* (gl. camisia¹ = chemise), gen. leined, Corm. v. Lendan, a shirt, probably connected with lín (flax), W. llin, lin-seed, lin-um, λίν-ον. 39. *Gruaidh* (a cheek), occurs in Cormacan éeces' Circuit of Ireland, ed. O'D., v. 23. (I have restored the ancient spelling):—

rob imde dér dar *gruaid* ngrinn
oc bantracht Ailig foiltfind.

(There was many a tear over a comely cheek among the fair-haired women of Ailech), cf. O. Ir. gruad, gl. mala, Z. 28, Corn. grud. 40. *Tengad* (tongue), whence *infra tengtach, dotengtach*. In O. Ir. this was tenge gen. tengad, a d- (or t- ?) stem, but identical in root with the Lat. lingua = dingua, O. H. G. zunga, Engl. tongue, Skr. jihvâ. Very remarkable is the irregular representation of a Latin medial (*d*) by the Irish tenuis (*t*); cf., however, ithim = admi, edo. The W. form tafod (Corn. tavot, tongue) is to me altogether obscure; it seems to occur in the corrupt Gaulish plant-name ταρβηλοδάθιον, which Z. reads ταρβοταβάτιον (ox-tongue).

41-44. *Tiach* (gl. pera), "a bag, pouch, wallet," O'R. The word seems to occur in an obscure

[1] "Volo pro legentis facilitate abuti sermone vulgato: solent militantes habere *lineas* quas *camisias* vocant."—Jerome, cited by Diez, Etymolog. Wörterbuch, 82.

obscure passage in the St. Gall Priscian (Z. præf. xv.), "Tiach didiv mad ferr lat. i. d. o. o." 42. *Losad*, leg. losaid? Corn. losait, a "kneading-trough," gen. loisde, O'D. Gram. 90. If losad be the modern form of losait, it was a fem. i-stem, the declension of which is in the oldest Irish identical with that of the masc. i-stem. 43. *Dechmadh*, a tithe, tenth, identical with the ordinal (dechma-d = da(n)kama-tha, formed by adding the superl. suffix *tha* to the ordinal?). 44. *Coinnill*, Corn. cantuil = candela, and probably borrowed from the Lat., a fem. â-stem, gen. coinnle, O'D. 90, for cainnle, caindle; cf. caindlóir, gl. acoluthum, i. e. candelarium, Z. 1060.

45–50. *Punnann*, punán in O'R., gelima is a "corn-sheaf;" and O'D. informs me that in his boyhood the word was used in this sense in the county of Kilkenny; the primary meaning, however, is "load," and the word seems borrowed from the Lat. pondus—like W. pwn, pyniaw. 46. *Fedán* (gl. fistula), perhaps derived from fid (arbor) = vidu (wood), gen. feda, W. and Corn. guiden, Breton, gwezen. Cf. O. Sax. widu, Ang. Sax. wudu, O. H. G. witu, the Gaulish Viducasses, and the name of the Irish river Ουίδουα (vidvâ) in Ptolemy (see Glück, 116). 47. *Fésóg* (a beard), fésóc, Corn. v. Crontsaile, apparently a diminutive. 48. *Lesmáthair* (stepmother), cf. W. llysfam, Bret. lesvamm; so Ir. lessmac (stepson) = Bret. lesvab: lessathair (stepfather), Corn. W. llysdad, Bret. lestad: lesainm (nickname), W. llysenw. I am not sure that Z. is right (p. 1104) in identifying this *les* with the Cornish *els*(privignus). 49. *Sesrach* (gl. carruca, a plough, Fr. charrue), fem. â-stem, absurdly derived by O'R. (who spells the word seisreach) from seiscar each. 50. *Rón* (gl. phoca) Corn. W. moel-ron (sea-calf, seal).

51–55. *Cennbarr* (gl. caphia), by which the scribe probably meant some kind of covering for the head. 52. *Lorg* (a club, cudgel), Corn. lorch, gl. baculus, Breton, lorchen (temo). 53. *Penn*, obviously from penna, as is—54. *Pian* (= pêna) from poena. In— 55. *Maroc* (leg. maróc), gl. iolla, the Irish and Latin are equally obscure; maroc once seemed to me connected with W. myr (emmets), Engl. pismire, Zend, baêvarĕ maoirinām, decem millia formicarum (Spiegel), &c. (see Kuhn, Zeitschr., iii. 66; Försteman, *ib.* 80; Pictet, *ib.* v. 349). And if so, iolla might well be considered a blunder for iulus, ἴουλος (centipede). But Dr. Todd has pointed out in Du Cange the word jula, "piscis genus," which comes nearer to iolla; the gen. sing. maróci for maróce occurs in a passage from Mac Conglinni's Dream cited by Dr. Petrie (Round Towers), but the context affords no assistance in determining the meaning of the word. Is maróc identical with maróg (gl. trolliamen) *infra*?

56–60. *Crocan*, gl. olla (leg. croccan, W. crochan, boiler, pot), now crogan, "a pitcher" —O'R., seems a different word from crocann, gen. crocainn, which occurs in a gloss on fel. Z. 740; ainm in *chrocainn* im bí bilis, i. e. name of the membrane [the gall-bladder]

bladder] wherein is the bile, and of which crocenn gl. tergus (Z. 80) seems a by-form = W. crocn (a skin, hide); crocann is certainly not olla, but tergus, in the poem of Cormacan éces above quoted:—

<blockquote>
rob iat ar taigi cen rainn
ar cochaill chorra (?) <i>crocainn</i>.
</blockquote>

And on the whole we may safely say that Z. erred in comparing (p. 740) Ir. crocann with W. crochan. 57. *Siataire* (gl. vesica, if I am right in so reading "fessica, siadaire") seems connected with siataim, O'R., "I puff, swell up," cf. W. chwythu, "to blow, to breathe." 58. *Cailc* (gl. creta), "chalk, lime," O'R., W. calch, perhaps a deriv. from calx, calcis. 59. *Adharc* (gen. adhairce, *infra*) is "a horn, trumpet," O'R., the adj. adarcdc, gl. corneta is in Z. 780. Here adharc probably means "a drinking-horn." With caustoria compare "Costarium, Costerium, ut Costrellus, Poculum vinarium," Du Cange. What is the *adharc leaga* (cornu medici) of Irish medical MSS.? A substitute for a cupping-glass? 60. *Luaidhe* = Engl. lead.

61-65. *Riaghail*, gl. norma, cf. regula, whence, of course, it is derived, but apparently with a change of declension, regula being a fem. â-stem, whereas the umlaut in riaghail points to a stem in *i* (in Z. 22, riagul, riagol, are exactly = rêgula). A similar remark applies to—62. *Tabhaill*. 63. *Cantairecht*, apparently a hybrid from the Lat. cantor, but possibly a pure Irish word from the root CAN, Skr. çans; though the first *t* is hard to account for. 64. *Tuireog*, gl. mitreta: here both Irish and Latin are obscure to me. 65. *Medar* (gl. parra): parra is said to be a wheat-ear; I have not met medar elsewhere.

66-70. *Gocan* (gl. parricula): gogan is "cackling, prating," according to O'R., but I suspect gocan to be the name of some small bird, cf. *gocan* na cubhaig, "avicula quæ cuculum comitatur" (Highland Society's Dict., i. 500). 67. *Clár* (gl. tabula) in Z. claar (W. claur, clawr, O.W. o cloriou, tabellis, Z. 170), abl.: hi *claar* cridi (in tabulâ cordis), Z. 1082. 68. *Ancoire* = ancora is from the Latin; ingor is the pure O. Ir. form, see Z. 1107, W. angor, Corn. ancar, Bret. cor. 69. *Uisce imill* (lympha), "water at the edge" (uisceán, gl. aquula, Z. 281; lán di *uisciu*, "full of water," Z. 595); uisce is perhaps an example of the rare derivative suffix -scia; cf. the man's name Muirsce = moriscias; but may possibly be connected through the Vedic form utsa, "a well," with the root und (vand), to which belong ὔδωρ, ûdus, water, &c.; *imill*, nom. imell, in O'R. imeal, W. ymyl. 70. *Sess no carr* (seat or car). Sess from the root sad, Lat. sed-eo, ἕζομαι, &c.; cf. fiss and fid, &c.; sess ethar in Corm. is the thwart of a boat (ethar, gl. stlata, Z.); perhaps the abl. may be in that obscure passage in Patrick's hymn, Crist illius, Crist *issius*, Crist inerus; *carr*, which subsequently glosses biga,

biga, is the well-known Gaulish carrus. The four-wheeler of Cæsar and Livy is now represented by the Irish carracutium. What *aptempna* can be, is to me exceedingly problematical.

71–76. *Taebhán*, which I have written for tæman (aspirated *m* for aspirated *b* is not uncommon in O. Ir.), C. explains to be the cross-beam between each pair of rafters; *teallaigh* is gen. sing. of teallach, which glosses focus, *infra*; taebhán teallaigh may therefore mean the little beam (trabecula) over a fire, from which pots are hung; taebhan *comladh* would mean the bar of a door (comla, gl. valva, *infra*). 72. *Assan* (caliga), in O'R., asán s. f. "a stocking or hose," W. hosan. 73. *Lainder* (a shoe-strap, shoe-string); O'D. suggests that this may be connected with the Engl. lanyard. It seems identical in meaning with—74. *Traighle;* neither word is in O'R. Can traighle be connected with O. Ir. traig (foot), acc. pl. traigid, a neuter t-stem = Corn. truit, O. W. traet (plur.), and cf. τρέχω, Goth. thragja, Skr. tṛksh, and the Scythian name Ταργι-ταος mentioned by Herodotus (Ebel, Zeits. vi. 400)? The Celtic root TRAG occurs (as Z. 6, has shown) with the intensive particle ver in the Gaulish vertragi: αἱ δὲ ποδώκεις κύνες αἱ κελτικαὶ καλοῦνται μὲν οὐέρτραγοι κύνες φωνῇ τῇ κελτικῇ, Arrian. de Venat. c. 3. 75, 76. *Coroin*, gl. corona, gl. clerica (leg. coróin?), from corona, apparently with change into the fem. i-declension; but probably an instance in the sing. of that usurpation by the acc. of the place of the nom. which is common in the plur. The acc. plur. occurs in the Book of Armagh, 180, *a*. 2—coirnea, gl. coronas—which shows that the word belonged to the â-declension. Corn. curun.

77–80. *Folt* (gl. coma), falt, Z. 251, abl. o folt, Z. 65, = W. gwallt, Corn. gols, gl. caesaries, Z. 1101, occurs in a quatrain concerning the Norsemen, quoted by Z. 928, from the St. Gall Priscian [Z.'s reading of the last line is dondlaechraidlainn oaloth lind]:—

    Is acher in gáith innocht,   Bitter is the wind to-night:
    Fufuasna fairgge find-*folt:*   The white-haired sea is enraged:
    Ni ágor[1] reimm mora minn   The passage of a clear sea is not undertaken
    Dond laechraid lainn oa Lochlind.   By the fierce heroes from Lochland.

The gen. sing. in—78. *Deirgech in fuill*, stripping (?) of the hair, i. e. baldness (for deirgech I suspect we should read deirgechht); *in* O. Ir. ind. gen. sing. masc. of the article, which was thus declined:—

STEM,

---

[1] A'gor (for agthar = agitur? cf. *agat* clesamnaig "agant joculatores," Seirgl. Conc.) is probably the O. Ir. form of *aghar*, which is thus explained in O'Davoren's Glossary (Mus. Brit. Egerton, 88): "Aghar .i. gaibther no innsaighther, *ut est* Athgabáil *agar* a fai[th]che neme[d] is cóir dia dítiu." *Aghar*, i. e. is taken or is advanced, *ut est*, a distress that is taken from a privileged person's green ought to be protected. Ní agor might be rendered non timeo. Cf. agathar, Gr. ἄχεται, Z. 45.

STEM, SAN(D)A.

	Masc.	Fem.	Neut.
Sing. N.	int, in :	ind''	an, a (= sanad ?)
G.	ind', in'	inna :, na :	ind', in'
D.	(s) ind', (s) in'	(s) ind', (s) in'	(s) ind', (s) in'
Ac.	(s) in (ṅ),	(s) in (ṅ)	(s) an, (s) a (= sanad ?)
Plur. N.	ind', in'	inna :, na :	inna :, na :
G.	inna (ṅ), nan		
D.	(s) naib, (s) nab	in the three genders.	
Ac.	inna :, (s) na :		

In the dual *in* appears in every case, and for all genders.

79. *Fabra*, according to O'R., is not only "eyelids" and "eyelashes"—both which meanings may be attributed to palpebra—but also "eyebrows;" cf. O. H. G. *prawa*, ὀφρύς, Skr. bhrû. 80. *Mac imresan* (pupil of the eye), mac = O. W. map = maqvas (gen. maqi, in two of Dr. Graves' Ogham inscriptions), originally son, is here obviously in a transferred sense like pupilla, primarily an orphan girl. In Early Middle Irish mac imresan was mac *imlesen* (leg. immlesen), lit. "son of exceeding light"? Is hé tene na súla in *mac imlesen*, "the fire of the eye is the pupil;" Seirglige Conculainn, edited from Lebar na huidre, by Mr. Curry, Atlantis II. 383.[2]

81-85. *Diadhacht* (gl. theologia), a fem. â-stem, from dia (God), gl. deus, *infra*, a masc. a-stem = dêvas, which was thus declined in O. Ir. :—

	Sing.	Dual. (Not yet observed.)	Plur.
N.	dia : = dêvas		dé' = dêvi
G.	déi', dé' = dêvi		déa (ṅ) = dêvân
D.	dia' = dêvu (dêvâi ?)		déib : = dêvâbis
Ac.	dia (ṅ) = dêvan		déo : (for déu) = dêvûs (dêvâns)[3]
V.	a dé' = dêve		a déo :

Grammatach,

[1] The turned comma (') indicates that aspiration (of the initial letter of the word following) is caused by the forms to which it is added, and which therefore must have ended in a vowel. The mark (:), which has been suggested by the Skr. *visarga*, represents a lost final *s*. The forms to which *visarga* is added do not aspirate. N. B.—The *s* in brackets is found after the non-aspirating prepositions, and certainly belongs to the article. Dr. Siegfried was the first to make this important observation. This article in O. W. was *ir*, in Corn. and Bret. *an*.

[2] "In the Hebrew Bible," writes Dr. Todd, "the pupil, or 'apple of the eye,' is literally 'Daughter of the eye.'—Ps. xvii. 8."

[3] Compare Goth. vulfans, Gr. ἵππους (Ahrens, Diall. ii. § 14, 1), O. Prtss. daivans and Skr. forms like kumârâṅç-cha (puerosque) Nalas, 8, where the dental s of âns (= -a + ans) has regularly become ç

Grammatach, dilechtach, sdair, are obviously *fremdwörter* (grammatica, dialectica, historia). 85. *Éolas dóir*—if I read aright—("an ignoble art"); éolas occurs in Z. 42, spelt houlas: the nom. pl. masc. of the related adjective óolach (gnarus) in Z. 252; ammi néulig (where the so-called prosthetic *n* is nothing but the old termination of the 1st pers. plur. of the verb subst. ammi (ṅ) = ἐσμεν, W. ym, asmasmi); dóir is the opposite of sóir (free, noble), which words are produced by prefixing the inseparable particles of quality *do* (= Skr. dus, Gr. δυς?) and *so* (= Skr. su, Gr. ευ), to a root which remains obscure to me[1]. Perhaps we should read caladan doenna, "scientia humana."

86–90. *Oighen* (a pan) seems to stand alone; O'R. spells it oigheann. 87. *Dlighi* (gl. rhetorica): here there is either an omission (? labradha, i. e. of speaking) or a blunder: for dlighi must stand for O. Ir. dliged, lex, regula (cf. W. dleet, Z. 166, pl. dilehedion, Z. 293, O. Sloven. dlŭgŭ, debitum), passing into the consonantal declension, like the Mod. Ir. pearsa, gen. pearsan = O. Ir. persan, gen. persine (a person). 88. *Nathair*, gl. panthera, is surely a blunder, nathair (O. Ir. gen. nathrach), declined like cathir, *suprà* = W. nadr, being "a snake, adder, viper, serpent"—O'R., perhaps originally a water-snake, &c. = Lat. natrix. 89. *Leca in duini* (maxilla), leaca in O'R. (gen. leacan), is, however, not jaw-bone (maxilla, the mobile os), but "cheek;" duini, gen. s. of duine (homo), n. plur. in O. Ir. dóini, a masc. ia-stem, originally, perhaps, as Dr. Siegfried conjectures, related to Zend daêna faith, and the root ΔΗΥΛΙ (think, meditate), as Skr. manu (homo), Engl. man, is from the root man (think). 90. *Lethail* (gl. mala), apparently one of the class of compounds noticed by O'D. (Grammar, p. 338), who, after quoting in his text leathcluas (one ear), leathchos (one foot), leathlámh (one hand), leathsúil (one eye), gives the following note:—"When leath, which literally means half, is thus prefixed, it signifies 'one of two,' such as one ear, one eye, one leg, one hand, one foot, one shoe, one cheek. It is never applied except where nature or art has placed two together; but in this case it is considered more elegant than aon, one." We shall find lethchaech (gl. monoculus), *infra;* leth retains its original meaning in the following words: lethchil (half-biassed), Corm. v. Cil; lethfer (gl. semivir), *infra;* lethgute (a semivowel, Z. 968); lethmacthail (half a cheese), Corm. Prull; ledmarb (half-dead), Z. 825, lethóm (half raw, Adamnán's Vision, óm = Skr. âmá, Gr. ὠμός); lethsathach (gl. semisatur), *infra;* mala is glossed by gruad in Z. 28.

91–95. *Aïl* before the palatal ch. The hypothetical dat. devâbis is to be compared with a Japetic instrumental dalvâbhis, for which we should find in the Veda dialect devêbhis, and in classical Skr. devâis.

[1] My reason for hesitating to identify *do* with *dus* and δυς is, that *do* aspirates (cf. dochrud gl. indecor dochruidigther gl. turpatur, Z. 833); and should therefore have originally ended in a vowel. The *s* may, however, have dropt off at so early a period that its former presence was unrecognised when the practice of aspiration was introduced.

91-95. *Aíl* (gl. bucca) is probably connected with the root al, nourish, Lat. ăl-o (cf. lúm from r. lab, Skr. labh); ail gl. esca occurs in Z. 996, and cf. iráil (nom. irál?) in the following gloss: hi precept sos[celi] ocus in *iráil* hirisse, "in preaching the Gospel, and in nurturing (?) faith", Z. 996. 92. *Cráes*, gl. gula; *craessach*, gl. gulosus, *infra*, also means "gluttony," as in the following passage cited from the Leabhar Breacc by Dr. Todd (Ir. Nennius, pp. 170, 171): isé focuinn malarta dona tuathaib ⁊ dona cellaib icambít na ríg ⁊ na aircindig atta (?) dilsi do *craes* ⁊ do raebaidecht int sacgail; and in Z. 41, where the word is spelt crois; cf. W. crocsaw, to welcome? 93. *Ulbu* (gl. mataxa), I have never found elsewhere; mataxa (μάταξα) means in Martial "raw silk;" it also meant "a cord or line." W. ulw (cinders) is the only Celtic word I know resembling ulbu. 94. *Bass* (gl. palma), acc. pl. bassa, gl. palmas, Leabhar Breacc copy of Gildas' Lorica. 95. *Basog* (gl. alapa) is obviously a derivation from bass.

96-101. *Bonn* (gl. planta), bonn gl. solea, *infra*, = W. bon (base, sole), found in most Indo-European tongues: Skr. budhna, Gr. πυθμήν, Lat. fundus for bundhus, O. H. G. bodam, Engl. bottom, O. Norse botn (Kuhn, Zeitschr., ii. 320), Huzváresh and Parsi buñda, "ground, root" (Spiegel, Zeitschr., v. 320). 97. *Feam* (gl. mentula), "a tail," O'R., who also has feamach, "dirty," which adjective Pictet (Zeitschr., v. 348) compares with the Skr. root vam, vomere, ἐμέω, &c. As to *priv*, I doubt if I read the contraction (p̃u) rightly, and cannot explain it, unless perhaps as a derivative from the Lat. privus. 98. *Cáin* (gl. emenda, i. e. " damni reparatio," "satisfactio de jure laeso vel de illata injuria," Du Cange) a fem. i-stem; "rent, tribute, a fine, amercement," O'R., cáin seems to occur in Z. 592: Is tacáir dúnn, achdin fochell asarchorp. 99. *Cusle* (gl. vena), with the *u* infected, cuisle, O'R. The voc. sing. is frequently heard in the conversation of the Irish peasantry: achushla (i. e. a chuisle) mochridi, "O vein [or pulse] of my heart!" Cuisle is a fem. stem in *n*, and perhaps derived (by the frequent change of *p* into *c*) from Lat. pulsus. The W. word for vein, gwyth, must on no account be compared with O. Ir. féith, gl. rien, gl. fibra, which, as Dr. Siegfried remarks, is the W. gwden, Eng. withe, Lat. vitis, vieo, ἰτέα, O. H. G. wida, Skr. vițiká, a tie, fastening (Kuhn, Zeits., ii. 133). 100. *Cích* (gl. mamma), dat. pl. cichib (gl. mamillis), Leab. Breacc. Gild. Lor. 101. *Cichín* (gl. mammilla) should probably be written cích, cíchín, as the present Irish is cioch, "a woman's breast," O'R.

102-105. *Uth* (gl. mammula), leg. úth? = (W. uwd pap, i. e. pulmentum?), if connected with Skr. ûdhas, Gr. οὖθαρ, uber, udder, M. H. G. euter, is an instance of an Ir. tenuis irregularly representing a Skr. aspirate medial. 103. *Retla* (gl. stella), gen. retlan (Vis. Adamn.), in O'R.; "readhlann, s. m. a star." 104. *Aoir* (aether) is W. awyr

awyr = Lat. aer = O. Ir. aér, Z. 114: dat. sing. *responsit mulier*, lus atcondaire hisind *aeur* ⁊ ni accai hi talmain a leitheid ⁊ athélsa no abéla ingein fil imbroind no abélam diblínaib mani thomliur inlussin. "The woman answered, 'the herb thou perceivest in the air, and on earth thou seest not its like, and I shall perish, or the child in my womb will perish, or we shall both perish, unless I eat that herb."—Trip. Life of Patrick, iii. 36. Cf. r. var, to surround. Whether in—105. *Aier* (gl. aera), the aera is for aer, or whether *aier* is era, is to me obscure.

106-110. *Scala* (gl. cratera), "a great bowl," O'R.; Corn. scala (gl. patera), Z. 1122, Goth. skalja, Eng. shell, O. H. G. scala (O. French jale, jalon, galon, Eng. gallon?). If Z. is right (G. C. 1122) in thinking scala a German word, when and how could it have come into Irish? 107. *Greidell*, "a gridiron," O. W. gratell (gl. graticula, Z. 1094), Ital. gradella, Fr. greille, Engl. grill, from craticula (Mart. 14, 21), Med. Lat. graticula, a dimin. of crates (see Diez, E. W. 180). 108. *Talam* (gl. terra), gen. talman (= talmanas), a fem. n-stem, perhaps identical with W. talm, the m of which, by the phonetic laws of Welsh, must stand for mn, mm, or mb. Talam has nothing to do with Skr. dhanvan, which Kuhn (Beitr., i. 368, 369) has identified with the Lat. tellus for telvûs; talam was thus declined in O. Ir.:—

FEM. *n*-STEM.
Stem, talaman.

	Sing.	Dual.	Plur.
N.	talam	dí thalam	talmain
G.	talman	dá talman	talman (ṅ)
D.	talmain	dib talmanaib	talmanaib
Ac.	talmain (ṅ)	dí thalam	talmana
V.	a thalam	a dí thalam	a thalmana

109. *Suiste no sgiurse* (tribulum), "a flail or a scourge," suist = fustis, W. ffust as srian = frênum, W. ffrwynn, seib = faba (Skr. r. bhaksh, Gr. φαγ), W. plur. ffa, srogell = flagellum, W. ffrowyll, &c. *Sgiurse* seems taken from the Engl. scourge. The etymology of—110. *Baile* (gl. villa), the Bally so common in Irish topography, is obscure to me. If, notwithstanding the singleness of its *l*, we connect it with the Med. Latin ballium, we are only led from one difficulty to another—for who shall explain ballium? The earliest instance I have met of the occurrence of bailo is in the Trip. Life of Patrick, iii. 12: tanic victor do ingabail (leg. imgabáil?) patrice asin port corraboi immuiniu draigin boi i toeb in *baile*. "To avoid Patrick, Victor went from the house till he was in the brake of thorns at the side of the *baile*."

111-115. *Artán,*

111–115. *Artán*, as I venture to read the urtan of the MS. (gl. villula), I have not met elsewhere. It is a dimin. of art, "a house, tent, tabernacle," O'R. 112. *Slighe* (gl. via), a base in *t*, if sligthib, gl. naribus, in Gildas' Lorica be correctly spelt. Says Cormac: *Slige*, din, do scuchad charpat sech araile, dorónta fri himcomarc dá carpat .i. carpat ríg ocus carpat epscoip, con dechaid each áe díb sech araile. "*Slige*, then, for the passage of chariots by each other: made for the passage of two chariots, to wit, a king's chariot and a bishop's chariot, so that each of them may pass by the other." 113. *Bethu* (gl. vita), a masc. t-stem = O. W. bywyt, Bret. buez, O. Ir. gen. sing. bethad acc. bethid (ṅ) = bivataten (or -tin ?). The root is biv (the adj. biu = bivas); cf. Skr. jiva for giva, Goth. qvius, Eng. quick, Gr. βίος, Lat. vivus. 114. *Lubh* (gl. herba), gen. lubae, lube, Z. 18, 777; abl. dind luib (gl. de rosa), Z. 232, = Eng. leaf, Goth. laufs: lub-gartóir (gl. olitor), Z. 45; lub-gort (a garden), in the so-called Annotations of Tirechan preserved in the Book of Armagh; cf. the Corn. luworch guit gl. virgultum, Z. 817. 115. *Coill* (silva), a fem. i-stem, W. cell, pl. celli, Corn. kelli, gen. coille in Cormac v. Ana:—Ba bind gair *choille* loinche Um ráith Fiachach maic Moinche, i. e. "Sweet is the voice of the wood of blackbirds [ad v. vox silvae merulo-sae] round the ráth of Fiacha son of M." Coill in Z. is always spelt caill, and only occurs in compounds: mirtchaill, gl. myrtetum, escalchaill, gl. osculotum, olachaill, gl. olivetum, gen. pl. innan olachaille, gl. olearum, Z. 821. May we identify this word with Lat. collis?

116–120. *Slat* (gl. virga), a fem. â-stem = slattâ, is, with its diminutive *slaitin*, to be compared with the W. llath, yslath. Compare—118. *Móin* (gl. grunna, a bog), apparently a fem. i-stem, with W. mawn (turves). In W. migu (masc.), migen, mignen (fem. a bog, quagmire), the *g* must have been a *c*, which could hardly have fallen out in Irish. 119. *Fod* (gl. globa), leg. fód, "a clod of earth, sod, soil, land."—O'R. 120. *Bothan* (gl. casa); perhaps we should read bothán ("a little tent," according to O'R.), from both (house), W. bod, cf. Eng. booth; *both* seems to occur in composition in Cormac: tic íarum Find don fuar-*boith* deóg lai, con faca in colainn cen cenn: "colann sund cen cenn," ol Find; [afterwards Find came to the hut in the evening, and he saw the body without the head: "a body is here without a head!" said Find].

121–126. *Cocall* (gl. cassula). Cf. "The cuculla, sometimes called casula and capa, consisted of the body and the hood, the latter of which was sometimes specially termed the casula." In a note, Dr. Reeves, from whose noble edition of the Vita Columbæ I have made this quotation, spells the word cassula. Cocall is one of those Celtic words which,

which, by the influence of the Church, has become universal. Diefenbach (Celtica, i. 122) quotes Martial:—

> Gallia Santonico vestet te bardocuculло;
> Circopithecorum penula nuper erat.

And compares Bret. kougoul, Corn. cugol, Engl. cowl. 122. *Cro* (leg. cró?), before which I have ventured to put casula, the dimin. of casa, occurs *infra* (cro cáerach, gl. ovile), and is explained "a hut, hovel, pen, cottage, fortress" (?) by O'R. 123. *Camra no seomra* (gl. camera); the former is from the Latin, the latter from the Anglo-Norman. 124. *Dorus* (gl. porta), W. drws, Corn. darat [*sic* in Z., but daraz in Lhwyd] (ostium), Lithuanian durrys, Skr. dvâra, Gr. θύρα, Lat. fores, Goth. daur, Slav. dver, Engl. door, dat. plur. dinaib *doirsib* (gl. de portis), Z. 749. 125. *Comla* (gl. valva), gen. comladh, *infra*, occurs in the Leabhar Breacc, cited by Petrie, R. T., 400: *comla gered friss ┐ gerreend maróci* (leg. maróce?) furri (a gate of suet to it, and the short head of a *maróc* upon it). 126. *Cliath* (= crates, *hurdle*), Med. Lat. cleta, O. W. and Corn. cluit = clêtâ, mod. W. clwyd, occurs in the Irish name of Dublin, Baile an atha cliath (the town of the ford of hurdles), also in Z. 21, 114. Fr. claie, Provençal cleda.

127-131. *Marcach na comladh* (gl. digma) is altogether obscure to me; marcach is literally horseman—W.; "marchauc (equestris) ortum e Gallico vetusto marca (μάρκα, τριμαρκισία, ap. Pausan.)," Z. 47. 128. *Lasair* (gl. flamma), gen. lassrach, marg. gloss on Patrick's hymn in Lib. Hymn. The 3rd pers. sing. pret. act. of the verb lasaim occurs in Fíac's hymn:—

> Dofaith fades co Victor, ba hé aridrálastar:
> Lassais in muine im bai, asin ten adgládastar.

> He went southwards to Victor, be it was that spoke to him:
> The bramble-bush wherein he [Victor] was flamed—from the fire he called.

The word is probably connected with loscad, Z. 143, W. llosg, Corn. leski. 129. *Camradh* (gl. cloaca). O'R. cites from Shaw, camrath, "a gutter, sewer, jakes;" I have not met the word elsewhere. 130. *Senmáthair*, "a grandmother" (O. W. henmam), from sen (old) = sinas, W. hen; cf. Zendhana (Spiegel), Gaulish senomagus, Lat. sen-ex, Sen-e-ca (compar. siniu, Z. 283, and sinithir [Lib. Hymn. gloss on the Altus Prositor]), O. W. superl. hinham, leg. hinam, Z. 305, and máthair = μήτηρ, mater, mother, Skr. mâtṛ (mâtar), from the root mâ (to create?), was declined in O. Ir. like athir (v. *suprd*), except in the gen. plur., which was máthar(ṅ). 131. *Sechrán* (gl. devia, i. e. deviatio), O'R. seachrán, "an error, straying," has been taken into the Anglo-Irish dialect in the phrase, "going on the shaughraun."

132-136. *Land* (gl. scama), if we take scama to be for scamma, an arena = σκάμμα,
"a place

"a place dug out and sanded"¹, land is the W. llan, "area, yard, church." It occurs as the last element of a compound in Z. 168: isind ith-*laind*, gl. in area (i. e. in the threshing-floor). If, however, as is more likely, scama is for squama, we may quote O'R.: "lann, s. m. a scale of a fish." 133. *Lég lógmar* (a precious stone), lég (stone), O. Ir. liacc, W. llech; cf. the river-name Licca in Venant. Fortun. Z. 174, and the O. Sax. leia, i. e. leja for lêa = lêha lapis, Glück, 19. In O. Ir. liacc is a cc-stem, and either masc. or neut., I have not ascertained which. *Lógmar* is an adjective, formed by adding the common suffix -mar to lóg (merces, pretium): gen. sing. "*stipendium* ainm ind *lóge* doberr do míledaib ar mílte" (stipendium is the name of the price that is given to soldiers for military service), Z. 577; hill*uag* mo saethir ("in reward of my labour"), Book of Dimma macc Nathi; lóg, W. llog, is perhaps connected with Lat. lŏcare, loc-arium. May we also venture to adduce Goth. laun, Engl. loan? 134. *Fuindeog*, "fuinneog, s. f. a window," O'R., reminds one of the O. Norse vindauga (wind-eye), Engl. window; Ir. scinistir, W. ffenestyr, Corn. fenester, Bret. fenestr, are directly from the Latin. 135. *Gabhal*, gl. furca, (W. gafl, hardly gebel, a pickaxe), in Z. 731 is gabul (gl. furca, gl. patibulum), which spelling is strange, as the Med. Lat. is gabalus, gabala, gabalum, O. H. G. gabala, Engl. gavelock. 136. *Pellec* (gl. sportula, a small basket) is "a basket made of untanned hide," as O'D. considers. It occurs in Cormac's Glossary, and comes, of course, from pelliceus (made of skins), and this from pellis = Eng. fell, &c.

137-141. *Ossadh* (gl. treuga = truce). 138. *Milan* (gl. urna), not in O'R., is one of a long series of names of different-sized water-vessels, of which we shall hear more when C. publishes his invaluable glossaries. 139. *Cogad* (war), gen. cogaid, n. plur. cogtha, O'D. Gr. 87, like some other nouns of his first declension (a-stems) is, I strongly suspect, a neuter. How else can we account for the vowel-ending in the nom. plur. of aonach, ualach, mullach, eádach (O. Ir. étach, a neut. a-stem), bealach, órlach, sgéal (O. Ir. scél, a neut. a-stem), &c.? Neuter a-stems were thus declined in O. Ir.:—

A NEUTER *a*-STEM.
Stem, forcitala.

	Sing.	Dual.	Plur.
N.	forcetal (n)	dá forcetal	forcetla
G.	forcitil	dá forcetal	forcetal (n)
D.	forcitul	dib forcitlib	forcitlib
Ac.	forcetal (n)	dá forcetal	forcetla
V.	a forcitil	a dá forcetal	a forcetla

With

¹ See an interesting note by Dr. Todd, Lib. Hymn., 75.

With cog-ad Glück compares the Gaulish name Cog-i-dumnus, *sed qu.* as the *g* is unaspirated in Mod. Irish. Cf. Marti *cocidio?* hardly the Lat. pugna. 140. *Fuiseog* (gl. alauda), "s. f. a lark"—O'R.; cf. W. guichell, "a bird," Pughe. The Welsh name for a lark is uchedydd, Corn. evidit, Bret. echouedez. 141. *Bairgen* (gl. garga) = W., Corn., and Bret. bara (panis), Z. 1122¹; in O'R. *báirghean*, "a cake;" gen. sing. for dénma *bairgine*, gl. pistor, i. e. vir faciendi panis, Z. 462. The word often occurs in the conversation of Anglo-Irish children, barnbrack (O. Ir. bairgen brecc, speckled cake) being one of their favourite comestibles. Garga I have been unable to find in any Lat. dictionary.

142–146. *Cethramadh* (fourth, O. W. petguared, now pedwyryd, m. petguared, now pedwared fem.). The -ma- here seems inorganic, and introduced from the false analogy of sechtm-ad, ochtm-ad, nóim-ed, dechm-ad. A similar remark applies to óenmad = W. unvet, Z. 330. 143. *Sruban* (gl. merenda, a luncheon) I have not met with elsewhere. O'R. has srúbóg, "a mouthful of any liquid;" and srubhóg, "a cake baked before the fire." With the latter our sruban is probably connected. 145. *Srubán mara* (buccalla, i. e. buccinula?), is apparently a "cockle" (srubán, O'R.). *Greim* (gl. buccella, a morsel), stem in n; cf. O. Sax. gruomon (mica). 145. *Cogar*, "s. m. a whisper," O'R. 146. *Colpa* (gl. tibia, the shinbone) does not agree very well with O'R.'s "calpa, s. m. the calf of the leg." The word occurs in Corm. v. Ferend.

147–151. *Tarr* (gl. festucula, a little stalk or straw), now means "the lower part of the belly," and is still found in a phrase used in reference to a childless man, viz., nír' fas dadam assa tharr. 148. *Mong intálindein* (gl. honplata), "hair of the shoulder," i. e. mane, which meaning does not agree well with that of ὠμοπλάτη (shoulder-blade), for which word I am indebted to one of my friend Littledale's ingenious conjectures. Observe the form of the gen. sing. masc. of the article before aspirated *s*. In O. Ir. *d* before an *s*, or *sr*, or *sl*, which has been flanked by vowels, regularly becomes *t*. The proof of this proposition, which would occupy overmuch room here, may be found in Part IV., vol. I., of the "Beiträge" before referred to. It is enough here to say that int élindein may be proved to have been sandislindeui; and that the Mod. Ir. ant ech, "the horse" (phonetically written an t-ech) was of old san(d)as akvas. 149. *Cengal* (gl. junctura), W. cengl, both probably from Lat. cingulum. 150. *Feoil na fiacal*, "flesh of the teeth," i. e. gums; feoil, a fem. i-stem in Z. 23, ind *féuil*, "the flesh;" fiacal, gen. pl. of fiacail, a fem. i-stem², which occurs in one of the St. Gall incantations

---

¹ Bara and gouin (wine) compose the Fr. word baragouin (gibberish).

² In the gen. pl. Mod. Ir. has lost all declensional distinction between fem. stems in *d* and *i*; in the old language the gen. pl. of fiacail would have ended in *e*. Thus nime, dúle, caille, are respectively the genitives plur. of nem or nim (heaven), dúil (a thing), caill (a wood).

incantations, Z. 926: ind ala *fiacail* airthir a chinn (one of the two teeth in the front of his head), the adj. *fiaclaich* gl. dentatam, acc. sing. fem. of fiaclach, is in Z. 22. 151. *Sine seain*, the uvula, lit. John's teat; sinsean in O'R.

152–156. *Butun* (biturría); *butun*, according to O'D. and C., is now used for a blacksmith's paring-knife. The Lat. biturría is obscure; perhaps it may be for biturrius, bitorius, Fr. butor (bittern); if so, we should probably read the Irish word *butur*, which word, however, is not known. Batura (patena in Diefenbach's valuable collection of Med. Lat. Germ. glosses) is the only other Med. Lat. word I know like biturría. 153. *Didean*, "protection, defence," O'R., which corresponds well enough with tectura, occurs *infra* in the form *didin* (gl. tegmentum, gl. tegimen). In O. Ir. the word is *dítiu* (gl. teges, gl. velare, Z. 79), gen. *díten*, dat. *dítin*. 154. *Luirech*, W. lluryg, from Lat. lorica (a corslet of thongs), which alone furnishes the etymon, viz., lorum. The earliest instance of the occurrence of this word is in Fíac's hymn, v. 26:—

Ymmon doroega it' biu bid *lúrech* díten do cách:
Immut il laithiu in messa régat fir hérenn do bráth.

The hymn thou hast chosen in thy lifetime shall be a corslet of protection to every one:
Around thee on the Day of Doom the men of Ireland shall come for judgment.

(Here *luirech* is used in its secondary signification of a religious composition supposed to protect the soul in the same way that a corslet guards the body.) In the poem commencing "Cris finnáin," Z. 933, we find the word with its primitive meaning: *lurech dé dum'* indegail ota [leg. ótá] m' ind gom' bend, "God's corslet to protect me from my crown to my sole." 155. *Aithléine* (gl. antiquula, if I read the Latin rightly) means, according to C., "a shirt cast-off" (on account of its age); cf. *aithle*, "an old cloak" —Corm. "*Aith*, or *ath*," says O'D. (Gram. 272), "has a negative power in a few words, as *aithrioghadh*, 'to dethrone;' *aththaoiseach*, 'a deposed chieftain;' *aithchléireach*, 'a superannuated or denounced clergyman;' *athlaoch*, 'a superannuated warrior, a veteran soldier past his labour.'" I have not met examples of this power of *aith-* in Z., where *aith-* (= Skr. ati, beyond) generally has the force of the Latin *re-*. 156. *Mir* (mica, offula) occurs in Z. 25 (with the neut. article), as the last element of a compound: *a conmir* (gl. medicatis frugibus offam), "the dog's-bit."

157–161. *Faighin*, W. *gwain*, Corn. *guein*, Bret. *gouin* = vagina; whence Ital. guaína, Fr. gaîne. 158. *Caile dabhca* (gl. famula), "girl of (the) tub;" *caile*, a fem. iâ-stem, occurs in Corm., and is compared by Bopp with Skr. kanyâ, Z. kainê (maiden), as aile (another) = anya. Hence the diminutive *cailín*, so often heard in the conversation of the Irish peasantry. *Caile* was thus declined in O. Ir.:—

A Fem.

A FEM. *iá*-STEM.

Stem, *caliá*.

	Sing.	Dual.	Plur.
N.	caile	dí chaili	caili
G.	caile	dá caile	caile (ṅ)
D.	caili	dib cailib	cailib
Ac.	caili (ṅ)	dí chaili	caili
V.	a chaile	a dí chaili	a chaili

Dabhca, gen. of *dabhach*, which subsequently glosses caba; cf. Eng. tub? 159. *Bó* (a cow), O. W. *bou* (in *boutig*, gl. stabulum, i. e. domus vaccarum, Z. 1079) = βοῦς, Lat. bos, bov-is, Skr. gâus, gen. sing. "monasterium quod Latine Campulus Bovis dicitur, Scotice vero *Achcd-bou*," *Vita Columbæ*, ed. Reeves, p. 121, where two other readings of the Irish are given, viz., *achetbbou*, *achadh bó*: gen. dual. macc dá *bó*, Corm. sub v. *Deal*. 160. *Uisce*, "water" (whence "whiskey," i. e. *uisce beathadh*, aqua vitæ), has been considered *supra*. 161. *Adhbar*, gl. idiogina (ideogina?), afterwards glosses thema, and is, according to O'R., "a cause or motive; a subject or matter to be converted into some other form." Terdelbac[h] a mac, *adbur* ardríg crend: "Terdelbach his son, *materies* of a monarch of Ireland" (i. e. crown-prince), Annals of Boyle, cited and translated by O'D., Gram. 445. Adbar occurs in Z. 337: rotbia *adbar* fáilte "erit tibi causa lætitiæ."

162–166. *Calptach* (gl. bínna); Ir. and Lat. here equally obscure to me. O'D. thinks *calptach* an unfledged bird, sed qu.; binna is explained præsepe in the Med. Lat. Dictionaries. 163. *Gamain arain* (gl. benna) is also obscure to me; O'D. says that *gamain* is a yearling calf; but what is *arain*, and what is benna? 164. *Calpach*, gl. juvenca (spelt colpach by O'R.) is, according to C., a heifer from her second to her third year. 165. *Cuindeog*, O'R., *cunneog*, "s. f. a churn, a pail" = W. *cunnawg*, milk-pail. 166. *Edrath* gl. mulcra, or, perhaps, mulca), is, according to O'D., "milking-time; but we may also read the Ir. word *edradh*, and compare O. Ir. étrad (libido), the dat. and acc. sing. of which are found in Z. 433, 452.

167–172. *Corrog* (gl. oba, for which I have put opa, is obscure, opa, i. e. a hole) seems connected with O'R.'s *corr*, "a pit of water." 168. *Gealán na súl*, "the white of the eyes;" *gealán*, from *gel*, white; O. Ir. comp. gilither, O'D., Gr. 120. Christ is called by Oengus céle dé, "the white sun that illuminates heaven with much of holiness" (*gel*-grian forosna riched cu méit nóibe); *súl* gen. pl. of *súil*, of which more

infra.

infra. 169. *Taiberne*, from Lat. taberna, as—170. *Personacht* from persona, *Bicairecht*, from vicarius, and—171 and 172. *Cabillanacht*, from Med. Lat. capellanus.

173-176. *Abdaine*, better *abbdaine* (abbey), a fem. iâ-stem; gen. sing. occurs in Leab. Breacc, cited by Dr. Petrie (Tara, 76), isin nomad (leg. noi maid?) bliadain déc *abbdaine* Cormaic (in the nineteenth year of the abbotship of Cormac), whence it appears that abbdaine is applicable to the office as well as the place. 174. *Buaile* (gl. vaccaria, a cow-house), spelt *buaili, buailidh*, in O'R., occurs *infra* in *buaile dam*, gl. bostar. It is from the Lat. bovile, with loss of the *v* between vowels, according to rule in Irish. 175. *Proúinse* (province) is proibhinnse in Keating, who calls the Pale *proibhinnse Gallda;* it is, of course, from the Lat. provincia. 176. *Cathair airdeasbuig* (oppidum archiepiscopi): *cathair* has been considered *supra*, No. 13. Note in airdeasbuig the transposition (p) s-b-g for p-s-e-p; and compare eengeedais with πεντηκοστή, coisreachad (*infra*) with consecratio, cisdeacht = O. Ir. étsecht, and beurla = O. Ir. bélre.

177-181. *Eaglais*, O. Ir. *eclais*, gen. *ecaillse, ecolso*, a fem. i-stem, from ecclesia, with change of declension. 178. *Athairtalmhan*, yarrow, milfoil; literally *pater telluris;* wrongly spelt by O'R. atairtalmhuin. *Athair* and *talmhan*—gen. sing. of talam —have already been noticed. Observe the non-aspiration of the *t* in talman, in consequence of athair being a consonantal base. 179. *Blaesc* (gl. testa) is *blaosc*, a shell in O'R. 180. *Brothrachan* (gl. sabribarra). *Brothrach*, according to O'D., is a royal garment. 181. *Cenbaran* (gl. uolua); here again the Ir. and Lat. are equally obscure to me.

182-186. *Buathbhallan liath* (gl. artemisia, wormwood, mugwort) is, according to C., "the great thistle;" according to O'D., "the gray ragweed;" *liath* (gray) = O. Welsh *luit* (fuscus), now *llwyd*. 183. *Lus na fiadh* (herb of the deer); *lus*, W. *llysieuyn*, pl. *llysiau; fiadh* gen. pl. of *fiadh* (s. m. gen. *fiaidh*); W. *hydd?* though certainly Irish *f* can never be = W. *h*. 184. *Biror*, afterwards spelt *birur* (gl. nasturtium), W. *berwr*, Corn. beler, is now *biolar* (cresses), with change of *r* to *l*. Biror is fancifully derived by Cormac from *bir*, edge, and *or*, hair, the cresses being, as it were, the hair on the edges of wells and rivers. 185. *Feclug* (gl. genista, broom), not in O'R. 186. *Garbog* (gl. ea) is "the coarse brassica," according to C.

187-191. *Merdrech* = meretrix, from which it is derived. 188. *Faechog*, a shell, cockle? occurs *infra* (194). 189. *Marclach*, "a horse-load," according to C. (marclach cruithnechta occurs in the Trip. Life of P.), from *marc* (horse)—W. and Corn. *march*, which we have met above in *marcach*. 190. *Bonn* (gl. solea) = *bond*, v. *supra*. 191. *Bile*, masc. ia-stem, correctly explained "a border" by O'R.; W. byl, masc. "brim, edge." The word occurs in a beautiful old poem attributed to Columbcille, and quoted in full by Dr. Reeves. (Vita Columbæ, 285, 288.) Unfortunately the spelling has been modernized. I will try to restore the pure orthography, and adopt Mr. Curry's translation :—

Diambad lim Alba uile	Were all Alba mine,
O' thú brú co á bile,	From its centre to its border,
Rop ferr limsa ait taige	I would prefer to have the site of a house
Occam ar lár caem-Daire.	In the middle of fair Derry.
Is aire caraim Daire	The reason I love Derry is
Ar á reide, ar á glaine	For its quietness, for its purity,
'Sar imad á aingel find	And for the multitude of its white angels
On chiunn co roich araile.	From the one end to the other.

192-196. *Uachtar* (gl. impedica); uachtar is the upper part, O'R.'s *uachdar*; but impedica is altogether obscure to me. *Uachtar* also means "cream;" and uachtar go tóin, "cream to the bottom," is, according to C., "a plant supposed to possess the property of turning all the milk into cream when the milk-pail is scoured with it." 193. *Smir* (marrow); W. *mer*, cf. O. Norse smior (butter), Eng. smear, occurs in the exceedingly old tale of the "Fled duin nan géd," ed. O'Don. p. 70 :—Ní roan sum din co tardad cnáim for móis dó . . . ocus toimlid á *smir*, ocus á feoil asáaithli; "he stopped not till a bone was brought on a dish to him, . . . and afterwards ate [eats] its marrow and flesh." 194. *Faechog beg*, a periwinkle, lit. "a little shell." 195. *Grainsech* (gl. grangia), *grainseach*; O'R. "a grange, a farm." 196. *Cerc*, O'R. *cearc*, a hen; cf. *cercdae*, gl. gallinaceus, Z. 765; the resemblance to the Gr. κίρκος seems accidental.

197-201. *Ilur* (eagle); W. *eryr*; Corn. gl. *er;* Bret. *erer, er;* Goth. ara, gen. arins; O. H. G. aro. 198. *Arg* (from arca), "a chest, coffer,"O'R.; so 199—*Ciste* is from cista. 200. *Ciarsech*, a hen blackbird, perhaps connected with ciar (fuscus), whence the name Ciarán, which occurs in an old obituary notice (Z. praef. xxxii.), bás Muirchatho maic Mailedúin hi Cluain maccunois á imda-*Chiarain* (death of Muirchad, son of Mailedúin, in Clonmacnois, from Ciarán's bed). With ciar = cêra, we might, perhaps, compare κελαινός, Skr. kâla, Lat. cal-igo. 201. *Caog* (gl. monedula, a jackdaw); cf. W. *coeg*-fran = coeg + bran. Engl. chough.

202-206. *Spideog* (gl. philomena), "a nightingale," O'R.; generally applied to the robin redbreast. 203. *Colum*, for columb = columba; cf. Lat. palumba; *ciadcholuim*, gl. palumbes, Z. 752; cf. Corn. *colom;* gl. columba, *cudon;* gl. palumba, Z. 1113; W. *colomen;* Bret. *koulm, klom*. The final b is still retained in *Colomb* cille (Book of Armagh, 15 b, 2), gen. sing. "eductio martirum, i. e. ossuum *Coluimb cille*" (ib. 16 a, 1), "*Columb* crag" (Vita Col., ed. Reeves, 19, 20); and in the tenth century inscription on the case of the Book of Durrow (see Vita Col. ed. Reeves, 327), which Rod. O'Flaherty has copied on a fly-leaf at the beginning of that MS. :—✠ Oroit acvs

acvs bendacht *cholvimb* chille do flavnd macc mailsechnaill dorig herenn lasandernad acumddachso ([the] prayer and blessing of Columb of [the] Church for Fland, son of Mailsechnall, for [the] King of Ireland, by whom this case was made). 204. *Crebhar* (gl. lucifugia); *creabhar* is a woodcock, according to O'R.; cf. W. creyr, a heron. 205. *Ferbog* (gl. capreola, a roebuck), in O'R. *fearboc, earb, earboc*; Gael. *earb, earbag*, Corn. yorch, gl. caprea, Z. 1115; W. iwrch, Bret. iourc'h. The unaspirated *b* in ferbog is a medialized *p*; cf. heirp (gl. dama, gl. capra), Z. 78. May we also compare Lat. hirpus, hircus, Sabine fircus, with which Weber (Zeits. vi. 320) connects Tacitus' alces, A. S. elch (Eng. elk)? 206. *Corcach mara* (gl. rostigola, *infra* gl. curiolus), some kind of sea-bird, perhaps the curlew. The nearest thing I know to rostigola is rusticula, but this is a heath-cock.

207–211. *Dreolan* (leg. dreólan?); W. drywyn, a wren, = Ir. drean, "the king of all birds;" the "avis regulus," for which aurigola seems to stand. 208. *Nenntóg* (gl. urtica, a nettle), spelt with two n's—O'D. Gr. 19; O'R. *neantóg, neanta;* nenuid (nettles) occurs in Cormac, but I omitted to note where. 209. *Connlach* (gl. arista), a collective, "stubble," "straw"—O'R.; applied in Clare, according to C., to *stalks* of rape; arista, however, is the beard of an ear of grain. 210. *Coinnlin* (gl. stipula, a corn-stalk), applied, according to C., to a *single* stalk of rape; cf. connall, gl. stipulam, colligendo, Z. 731; W. *cynnull* yd, "ingathering of corn." 211. *Seimin* (gl. fistula, reed), "a bulrush"—O'D.; "blackheaded bog-rush," O'R.; probably a deriv. from séim (gl. macer; gl. tenuis, Z. 23, 261).

212–216. *Monadan* (gl. moneta), bogberry, leg. mónadán, l. w., perhaps connected with móin, a bog. 213. *Glacarba* (a handful of corn); *glac* (hand, palm); *arba* (for *arban?*) O'R.'s "*arbha*, s. f. corn" he is wrong as to the gender, for ith *in* arba, gl. far, occurs *infra*); cf. W. erfin. 214. *Glac saiged* (gl. pharetra); here *glac* must mean a quiver-like receptacle; soiged, better saiged, = sagittân; gen. pl. of *saiged*, anciently saiget; W. *saeth*, from Lat. sagitta; for if the word were Celtic, the initial *s* would have become *h* in Welsh. Thus, in Colmán's hymn (Lib. Hymn. fol. 5 *b*):—

    Cech martir, cech dithrubach, cech nóeb robai in genmnai,
    Rop sciath dunn diarn imdegail, rop *saiget* uan fri demnai.

    Let every martyr, every hermit, every saint who lived in purity,
    Be a shield to us, to defend us; be an arrow from us against demons!

216. *Ga* (gl. hasta) = gaisas; gaide (gl. pilatus, Z. 64) = gaisatias, the *s* being lost between vowels, as in siur (sister); íaran (isarn = iron); giall (a hostage) = O. H. G. kisal; iach = esox, esucius, W. cawg (salmon), Corn. chog, &c. Cf. with gaisatias, n. pl. masc. gaisatii, gaisati, the Gaulish tribe-name Γαισάτοι, Polyb., which, however, seems

seems a stem in *a*, not in *ia*. See Z. 64, note; W. gwaew, pl. gwewyr, Z. 119, Corn. gew, Z. 152, seem the O. Ir. faebur (edge), Corm. v. *Dimess*.

217–221. *Seidedh gáithe no bulga*, gl. flabella (a blast of wind—cf. flabra—or a bellows; cf. flabellum); *seideadh*, O'R.; W. chwythiad, Ir. siataim = Bret. c'houézaf Corn. huethaf; *gáithe*, gen. s. of *gáith*, a fem. i-stem, which we have already found in the quatrain quoted from the St. Gall Priscian; *bulga* (bellows?) must be connected with *bolg* (bag); O. Ir. bolc, gl. uter; bulgas Galli sacculos scorteos vocant, Festus, Z. 17; Goth. balgs, and Aeol. βολγος (= μολγός, hide). 218. *Cerdcha* (gl. fabrica), a smithy, forge, occurs twice in Cormac (sub vv. *Ca* and *Nescóit*). In Z. 70 it is spelt cerddchae, and glosses officina; *cerd* (formator, faber), gen. *cerda* (cerdcha, .i. teg cerda, Corm.); acc. *ceird* (Brogan's hymn, 79) is a masc. i-stem, from the root CAR, Skr. kṛ, to make, whence also *cerd* (art), a *fem.* i-stem; gen. dual; mic dá *cerda*, pseudo-Oengus, cited by Dr. Todd, Lib. Hymn, p. 85. *Cae, ca* (W. cae, caiou, gl. munimenta, Z. 291), has probably lost a *g*; cf. O. H. G. hag (stadt), N. H. G. gehege, Fr. haie, Eng. hedge. 219. *Mesgan* (gl. massa), leg. mesgán, now, I believe, applied to a lump of butter, shaped like a sod of turf. 220. *Bláthach* (gl. baudaca) is buttermilk; gen. *bláthaigh*. 221. *Lind*, leg. *linn?* (gl. cervisia), ale; O'R., linn, lionn, s. f. Gael. *leann*, W. llyn.

222–226. *Fual* (gl. urina), stem, *vòla*; cf. Skr. vâr, vâri (water); οὖρον, harn?; gen. *fuail*, occurs in one of the St. Gall incantations (Z. 926). "Ar galar *fudil*" (against disease of the urine, strangury?). "Domesuresa diangalar [mo] *fudil*-se" (I save myself from great disease of my urine). "Focertar inso dogrés i maigin hi tabair *thúal*" [thúal = do fúal]. (Let this be placed continually in [the] place wherein thou makest thy water). 223. *Sgél* (gl. fabula), O. Ir. scél (narratio, nuntius), nom. and acc. plural scéla; a neuter a-stem[1]; gen. plur. scél (ṅ), which before *b* becomes scél (ṁ),

---

[1] The mod. Irish nom. and acc. pl. is *sgéalta* (*sgéal-t-a*), as in *seol-t-a* (sails); *ceol-t-a* (melodies); *néal-t-a* (clouds), where the *t* is what Bopp would term an inorganic addition to the base, but what Curtius would call a determinant. Another inexplicable *t* is found in some dialectical verbal forms: thus, *biomuis-t* (let us be), in S. Leinster and E. Munster (O'D. Gram. 169); glanamuis-t (let us cleanse), in Kilkenny (ib. 180); *glanfamuis-t, glanfabhuis-t* (we would, you would, cleanse), Kilkenny (ib. 182). All through Ireland this *t* occurs (sometimes medialized) in the 1st and 2nd pers. plur. pres. act., and 1st pers. sing. fut. act., as *glanamai-d* (we cleanse); *glan-t-aidh* (ye cleanse); *glanfa-d* (I will cleanse). Cf. ar sein *bera-t-sa* einech do agena [ib.], "on him I will take revenge (?) of daggers" (Rumann, Petrie, R. T.); compare also tánais-t-e (second), O'D., Gram., 123, for Z.'s tanise. The so-called determinant is not used in the O. Ir. declension, but a *t* occurs in two or three conjugational forms. Thus, *guidmi-t*, Z. 143 (we pray); *logmai-t* (we forgive); *proimfimi-t* (we shall prove); in perfects like *asrubur-t* (I said), *asrobar-t* (he said), and in the third pers. plur. of the secondary present, e. g., *domel-t-is* (they were

(ṁ), as in a verse in a poem on the characteristic virtues of the saints of Ireland (Rev. Dr. Kelly's "Calendar of Irish Saints"):—

> Caras Scuithin na *secl* ṁbinn (bendacht ar chách doroinne!)
> Aindre áilne uchtgela, etarru dogní oige.
>
> Scuithin of the sweet legends loved (a blessing on every one who hath done so!)
> Maidens beautiful, white-bosomed, [and] among them preserved his chastity.

The long ê seems to indicate the loss of a consonant. 224. *Corcair* (log. *corcuir?* gl. purpura), from which it seems formed by changing the *p*'s into *c*'s (as in case, from pascha; cengcodais from pentecoste; cf. necht = neptis (W. nith, Skr. naptrî, N. H. G. niftel); secht (ṅ) = saptan; fescor = vespera = a Skr. divas-para, Bopp), and altering the declension. Perhaps, however, corcuir is not a foreign word. Z. 744, has dub-chorcur, gl. ferrugo, and compares the name of the Dalmatian island, Κόρκουρα, Corcyra. The Welsh is *porphor*. 215. *Céir* (wax); W. *cwyr* = cêra; but the Irish *céir* seems an i-stem. The Cornish and Bret. are *coir*, *koar*. 226. *Glass* (gl. serra), a lock, manacle, occurs in the poem of Cormacán éces (ed. O'D.), v. 57:—

> Ocus ní thardad air *glas*   And there was not put upon him a manacle,
> Na geimel alainn amnas.   Nor polished tight fetter.

The dimin. glasán (gl. serrula) occurs in Z. 281.

227-231. *Roth* = Lat. rŏta (a wheel); Z. 82, the *t* being aspirated between the *o*, and the *a* which originally ended the word. Under such circumstances in Welsh *t* always becomes *d*. We find, accordingly, that the Welsh for wheel is *rhod*; cf. Lith. ratas, O. H. G. rad. We may also compare Skr. ratha (waggon), Zend, ratbaêstâ. 229. *Fochlaidh*, "a cave" in Cormac, occurs in the Irish Nennius, p. 116: int ochtmad ingnad, *foelaid* fil i tír Guent ocus gaeth tribith ass (the eighth wonder, a cave which is in the land of G., and wind for ever [blowing] out of it). Cf. O. W. claud (fossa), Z. 622, W. goglawdd, Ir. cláidim (I dig), W. cloddiaw. 230. *Liter* (a letter) = Lat. littera. Double *t* becomes *th* in Welsh; we find, accordingly, *llythyr-en*. 231. *Sillaidhi* (if I read the word rightly) seems a curious hybrid, consisting, as it does, of the first syllable of syllaba, *plus* an Irish termination. Cf. *siolla*, O'R.; W. *sill*. In Z. 968, eating); *asber-t-is* (they were saying). The declensional *t* occurs frequently in the plurals of O. Welsh nouns, cf. *ætin-et* [now *edned*], *bronnbreith-et* (volucres ventre variegatæ), *merch-et* (filiae, now *merched*). I do not find a *t* in the British conjugation, except in perfects act., like *a gant* (cecinit), *ae gwant* (feriit). In this *t* (= *dd* ?), and in that of the corresponding Irish perfects, I am inclined to recognise the redaplicating root dhâ.

968, the word is, as might be expected, sillab, fem.; sillaid occurs in Leab. Breacc in the nom. pl. of sillad, Gael. *siolladh*.

232-236. *Lethenach* (gl. pagina, a page of a book); the gen. *lethinig* (leg. lethenig?) occurs in Harl. 1802, 13 *a*; line moite [O. Ir. m' aite] hí tus ind *lethinig* sea. Rob connnis dia for anmain maclissu, "a line of my tutor's [written by him] is at the beginning of this page. God be gentle to Maclissu's soul!" Is *lethenach* weakened from lethanach? 233. *Crupán na lám* (gl. sirogra, i. e. chiragra, χειράγρα, gout in the hand); crupán I have not met elsewhere. O'R. has *crúpadh* (contraction, Gael. *crupadh*); *crúpaim* (I contract); *crupog* (a wrinkle), to which it seems allied. 234. *Esga* (gl. luna); in O. Ir. aescae, Z. 247; gen. ésci, Z. 1074, s. n. The adj. esca, which occurs in the Félire of Oengus, is glossed by cain no alaind no *lucida* in the Leabhar Breacc copy of that (philologically) valuable composition. Note neph-éscide, unmoonlit (gl. σκοτομήνη), isin nep[h]-œscaidiu (gl. in σκοτομήνη), Z. 830. 235. *Medhal* (gl. panca = paunch?) though the unaspirated *d* in O'R.'s maodal, "a belly, a paunch," is certainly correct. Gael. *meadhail* is "mirth," "joy." 236. *Blonac* (lard); cf. W. *bloneg* (lard, grease). Corn. *bloneg*; gl. adeps.

237-241. *Monadh* (subsequently glossing momissma, i. e. νόμισμα, coin), seems here to mean a mint. In Gaelic *monadh* means a mountain; cf. W. mynydd, di-minid sursum, lit. ad montem, Z. 571, and also a heath. 238. *Farcan* (gl. comprisura), (leg. *farcán?*), is "a knot in wood," according to C.; O'R. has "*farcán*, s. m., a corn or welt on hands or feet." 239. *Cantair* (gl. troclia), "cantaoir, a press"—O'R.; "into which wood is put to be straightened," adds Mr. Curry. In Gaelic *farchan* is "a little mallet." 240. *Cliath fuirsidh* (gl. eripica, a harrow); as to *cliath*, v. *supra*; *fuirsidh* seems the gen. sing. of *fuirse*, harrowing, O'R. 241. *Sitheal* (gl. situla, bucket) is "a bowl, a cup," according to O'R.; W. hidl, a cullender?

242-246. *Taes* (= dough, Goth. daigs, N. H. G. teig?), W. *toes*. 243. *Mulcan* (gl. glassia, i. e., γαλαξια? a kind of milk-frumety) is O'R.'s *mulachán*; s. m., "a kind of soft cheese; cheese curds pressed, but not in a vat." Cf. Goth. miluks, Eng. milk, O. H. G. miluh, mulgere, mulcere, ἀμέλγω. 244. *Igha* (gl. prisura), perhaps O'R.'s *iodha*, "the cramp, rheumatism, any kind of pain;" "a stitch in the side," according to C. 245. *Cocan* (gl. pensa, a day's ration) is *cucan* (gl. penus, store of food, provisions) in Z. 80. This is a different word from *cucann*, gl. pistrinum, gl. coquina, gl. culina, Z. 740, though they come from the same root, viz., CAK, or PAK. Cf. O. W. coc, gl. pistor; Cornish *cog*, gl. coquus; whence *keghin*, (gl. coquina), Z. 1095, 1122; cf. Skr. pacâmi; Lat. coquo, coqu-in-o, and popina; Lithuanian kēpu; Gr. ἀρτοπόπος, ἀρτοκόπο-ς (bread-baker), which last word Messrs. Liddell and Scott derive from ἄρτον and

and κόπτω. See Curtius, Zeitschr. iii. 403[1]. 246. *Lécc in árain* (calculus in the kidney); as to léce v. *supra*; *árain*, abl. of aru; gl. rien, Z. 20; Welsh *aren*, perhaps connected with Lat. rên; *sed qu.* Lapifulta is, perhaps, a blunder for lapillula.

247–251. *Bancoig*, gl. preseua. Both words obscure, and probably corrupt. Shall we read *banchoigle* and proseda, a prostitute? *Banchoigle* occurs in O'R., with the meanings, "a female companion, a cup gossip." *Banchoigreach* in Gaelic is "mulier aliena." 248. *Luch francach* (lit. French mouse) is certainly a rat (cf. Welsh *llygod ffrengig*, rats), but what is rula? With *luch* (O'R. s. f. a mouse), cf. W. *logod*, Z. 82, *llyg* (a field-mouse). 249. *Luch dall* (gl. talpa, a mole), lit. blind mouse; *dall* (blind), which glosses caecus, *infra*, and occurs in composition with *súilech*, in *dallsúilech* (gl. orbatus), *infra*, is the Welsh *dall*, pl. *deillion*, Z. 296. 250. *Lacht* (gl. lactura), in in O'R. *laed*, "milk;" Corn. lait (leg. laith); W. *llaeth* = Lat. lact (lac, lactis) is, perhaps, as Bopp has suggested, an old passive participle formed by the Skr. suffix ta[2]. On this word, and on the interesting identification of Ir. bliocht, W. blith, with γάλακτ (γλακτοφάγος, γλάγος), where the Celtic *b* and the γα are the last remnant of the word for cow (Skr. gav, Ir. bó), see Grimm, Gesch. d. d. Sprache, II., p. 1000. 251. *Amaisc* (gl. amusca) I cannot explain.

252–256. *Túl* (gl. ascia, adze), cf. Lat. tâlea (a cutting for planting); inter-taliare, and the crowd of words connected therewith; Ital. taglia; Span. tajo; Fr. taille, tailleur; Engl. tailor, and fee *tail* (feudum talliatum); and M. H. G. teller (a plate), Diez, E. W. 339. 253. *Casnoidhi* (gl. scindula, shingle), leg. casnaidhi? is "chips, or shavings of wood," according to O'D. and C. The nom. sing. *casnaidh* is in O'R. 254. *Escart* (gl. scupa, i. e. scopae, a besom?), probably from *es* (= Lat. ex), and the root SCAR, whence etarscar-tha (separationis), Z. 254–5. But scupa is probably a blunder for stupa, and we may compare the Gaelic *eascard*, or *ascart*, s. m. "tow," "coarse lint." 255. *Guirtn* (gl. pustula), Gael. *guirean*, W. goryn, from gur (pus); Corn. v. Nescoit; W. gor; cf. French gour-me, and perhaps O. Norse gor (dung), gor-m-r (slime). 256. *Nus* (gl. onesta, i. e. colostra?) is, says O'D., the beestings or new milk of a cow after calving: "*nus* quasi novus," says Cormac; and though it is

of

---

[1] Dr. Smith, in his Latin Dictionary (sub v. coquo), is wrong in including the English *bake* in this class of words. *Bake*, as Curtius points out, is the Greek φώγειν.

[2] This suffix (Lat. -tus, Gr. τός) is found (without addition) in Irish, not, as might be expected, in the part. perf. pass., but in the pret. pass. in -d, plur. -tha (Ebel. Beitr. i. 162). Ebel here speaks of *vocalic* verb-stems. The tenuis is preserved in the sing. of the pret. pass. of *consonantal* verb-stems: e. g. rocet (was sung) = pra-can-ta, tairchet (was prophesied), ad-ra-nac-t (was buried), &c. The termination of the part. perf. pass. O. Ir. -the, te, mod. Ir. *-tha, -ta*, really stands for ta + ya (see Ebel, Beitr. i. 162).

of course absurd to identify *nus* with novus, the word may really come from the root nov, which in Irish would lose the *v*. Gael. *nùs*, *nôs*, gen. sing. *nùis*.

257-261. *Baineachlach* (gl. grimaga), a female servant, a she-post-boy! if O'R. be right in his explanation of *eachlach*. 258. *Meall* (gl. picuta, i. e. picota), a mound, hillock, a masc. a-stem, with which Glück, 138, has connected Mellodunum and Mellosectum. W. *moel* (a conical hill) is represented by the Mod. Ir. *maol*. 259. *Eás* (gl. mustella, weasel), a dimin. form in O'R., viz., casóg; another mod. word for this animal is *nas*, which is nes in Z. 60. 260. *Fidhchat* (gl. muscipula), literally wood-cat, a humorous word for a mouse-trap. 261. *Concro* (gl. decipula, a snare, a trap), " a wolf-trap," conjectures C., from *con*, base of *cu* (dog, a wolf is called *cu allaidh*), and *cro*, gl. casula (*supra*).

262-265. *Srathar* (gl. sagena, a fishing-net or seine), Gael. *srathair* (clitellae). I suspect the scribe has blundered here, for srathar is certainly "a straddle," as O'R. explains the word; W. ystrodyr, f. from Med. Lat. stratura. It occurs (with its *s* aspirated by the nom. sing. of the fem. article) in the St. Gall Priscian, Z. 929:—

Galb do chuil isin charcair:	Take thy corner in the dungeon:
Ni róis chluim na colcaid:	Thou gettest neither down nor flockbed:
Truag insin, amail bacbal,	That wretched one! like a slave,
Rot giuil ind *srathar* dodcaid.	The miserable *srathar* sticks to thee.

This, however, does not enlighten us much as to its meaning. 263. *Carr* (gl. biga, a two-horsed chariot) has been noticed *supra*. 264. *Uchtach* (gl. antela), a poitrel, or breast ornament for horses, from *ucht*, breast (also the brow of a hill, as in conrici *hucht* noinomne, "to nine-oaks' hill," Book of Armagh, 17 *a*, 1), mod. gen. ochta, a masc. u-stem. The following is a paradigm of these stems:—

MASC. *u*-STEM.
Stem, bithu.

	Sing.	Dual.	Plur.
N.	bith	dá bith	betha
G.	betha	dá betha	betha (ṅ)
D.	biuth	dib bethaib	bethaib (*for* bithuib)
Ac.	bith (ṅ)	dá bith	bithu
V.	a bith	a dá bith	a bithu

In—265. *Tiarach* (gl. postella, i. e. postilena = W. *pystylicyn*), a crupper, may, I suspect, be found the *tiar* conjectured by Z. 567, as a designation for the western regio mundi. In Ireland the west is the back; the east, the front (airthir a chinn, in the front

front (east) of his head); the south is the right hand (des) (cf. Dekkhan, from the Skr. dakshiṇa) the north, the left (tuath). In Kerry I have heard an English-speaking peasant talk of a tooth in the *wesht* side of his jaw, meaning the back part.

266-270. *Laithirt* (gl. capula, i. e. crapula, drunkenness, debauch, also the headach resulting therefrom) is pleasantly derived by Cormac from *laith* (ale), and *ort* (killed) thus: *Laithoirt* .1. laith ron *ort* .1. ol cormac, "laithoirt, that is, *laith*, which killed us, i. e. a drink of ale (*corm* dat. s. *cormaim* = W. *cwrw*, κοῦρμι, Dioscor., see Dief. Celt., i. 123). 267. *Cáer fínemnach* (gl. uva), literally bacca vitea: cáer, gl. bacca, Z. 37; W. cair: *fínemnach*, an adj. formed from *fínemain*, a vine, which is found in the Leabhar Breacc Sermon on S. Brigit, cited by Dr. Todd (Lib. Hymn. 65): Is aire sin isé á samail etir dúlib, colum eter énaib, *fínemain* eter fedaib, grian uas rennaib. ("Hence it is that her type among created things is the Dove among birds, the Vine among trees, the Sun above the stars.") 268. *Lubra* (gl. lepra, leprosy), cf. W. llyfrith, "eruptive, pimpled." 269. *Cnaimfiach no torpan* (gl. fragella, cornix *frugilega*?): *cnaimfiach* (which glosses curellus, *infra*, No. 503) means, according to C., "the great eagle," and is also applied to a raven (*sic* O'R.); to a rook in Scotland. It is hard to say what the first element of the compound can be: if we read *cnáimfiach*, we might compare *cnám*, bone, a masc. i-stem, o chnáim gl. ex osse, Z. 1002, n. pl. in chnamai, Z. 237, acc. pl. cnámi, Z. 609, cf. κνήμη, and *fiach*, gl. corvus, Z. 1030; cf. N. H. G. weihe, O. H. G. wiho, wigo (milvum), uuiio (milvus). *Torpan* is a crab (cancer), according to C., Gael. *tarpan*. 270. *Cotun* (gl. parma, a small round shield) I have not met elsewhere.

271-275. *Nelladoracht* (gl. piromanxia, pyromantia?) is, according to C., "astrology," Gael. *neuladaireachd*, from *neuladair* (astrologer). The first element of the word seems *néll*, a cloud. I know not if the Irish practised νεφελομαντία. 272. *Dornadoracht* (gl. ciromancia, leg. chiromachia, pugilism?), Gael. *dórnadaireachd*, from *dornadóir* (a boxer): cf. *dorn*, W. *dwrn* (fist, hand): whence *dornán*, *infra*: nom. *durni* (gL ut me colaphizet), Z. 336. 273. *Clas guail* (gl. sturna?), "the place on which charcoal was made," C.; *clas* here seems = the W. *clas* (a space, region). Its usual meaning is "furrow," "trench." *Guail*, gen. sing. of *gual* = Eng. coal, W. glo. 274. *Sblinach*, gl. catapulta (if I read this rightly), seems connected with *splín*, "a sharp dart of the eye;" *splincin*, "one who gives a sharp glance out of the corner of his eye;" and *spline*, "a point of rock," "an overhanging cliff," O'D. 275. *Croicinn madra allaid* is "hide of a wolf," lit. "of a wild dog." What *edibulta* can be, or be put for, I cannot conjecture.

276-280. *Coinmir* (gl. offa), conmír in Z., *v. supra*, No. 156. 277. *Dabach* (gl. caba, i. e. cavea), gen. *dabhca*, *supra*, No. 158. 278. *Suiste* (flail), a lengthened form of of *suist* = fustis. *Calopeda* (if this be what the scribe's callidiba meant) seems a barbarous hybrid formed from καλον (wood), and pes (foot). 279. *Idh urchumail* (gl. trica, i. e. tricæ, hindrances) is a spancelling-chain: *idh*, a collar, chain; urchumail for érchumail, and this = *cumail* (holding), with the intensive particle *ér* = Gaulish ver, Lat. per, Gr. περι, prefixed. 280. *Cessacht* (gl. parvispendia, penuriousness). The adj. *cessachtach* occurs in S. Brogan's poem on Brigit:—

> Ní pu for seotn santach; ernais cen neim, cen mathim:
> Nír' bu chalad,[1] *cessachtach*: ni car in domuin cathim.

281-285. *Galar súla* (gl. obtolmia, i. e. ophthalmia), "disease of the eye;" *galar*, gen. galair in O. Ir., a neut. a-stem = W. *galar* (mourning, grief), *súla*, gen. sing. of *súil*, No. 425, *infra*. 282. *Cailleach ligeoch* (gl. pupina) is nearly unintelligible to me; *cailleach*, anciently *caillech*, has the meanings of "old woman" and "nun:" in Gaelic, *ligeach* is "sly," ligheach, "flooded." 283. *Cochtair* (gl. coquina = cuisine), *vide supra*, No. 245. 284. *Tarrach* (gl. babana); of these two words I can make nothing as they stand. May we read torrach (pregnant), and babúna, an Hiberno-Latin fem. subst. formed from babán (baby), and meaning a pregnant woman? In Gaelic *tarrach* is "the belly-thong of a pack-saddle, a girth." 285. *Coisreagad* (gl. creatura, i. e. the consecrated wafer?); for coisegrad = consecrata: the *n* being lost before *s* as in *mis* = mensis, *cis* = census, *mias* = mensa, &c.

286-298. *Aran* [leg. arún] *geal* (gl. placenta, a cake), "white bread." 287. *Baintigerna* (gl. dominabus). Here, and in the following twelve articles, the Latin words are in the dat. or abl. pl., the Irish being in the nom. sing. In baintigerna (lit. female-lord), note first the non-aspiration of the *t*, though originally between vowels, the Irish phonetic laws not admitting the combination *nth* (cf. banterismid, gl. obstetrix, Z. 820; o chaintaidliuch, gl. satisfactione, Z. 826, and verbs in the 3rd sing. pres. pass., such as frisduntar, gl. obstruitur, Z. 464); secondly, the change of the O. Ir. final *e* (= ia) to *a*; thirdly, the change of the *a* of *ban* to *ai*, which is owing to the influence of the vowel in the following syllable, viz., *i*, which has the power of changing a preceding *a* into *ai*; so *e* changes a preceding *a* to *i* (ai); but *o* causes no vowel-change. See Ebel, Beitr. 288. *Ainim*, in Z. anim (Corn. enef; Armor. éné) = anima, and declined like a fem. â-stem[2], but also declined as a stem in *n*[3] (= a Latin animo, -onis, if there were such a word), which curious fact Ebel (Zeits. vi. 213) was the first to notice. 289. *Baindea in toraid* (goddess of the fruit, Pomona? or growth, Ceres?); baindea, bandea

---

[1] = Goth. hardus, Eng. hard.
[2] Gen. anme, dat. anim; cf. *anam*-chairtea, gl. doctores, lit. soul-friends, Z. 10 (= anamacarant-i-ans).
[3] Dat. sing. anmin, acc. anmin(n), pl. anmin, anman(n), anmanaib.

bandea, Z. 279 (not bandia); where the ban seems superfluous, as dea = dêvâ = Lat. dea; *toraid*, gen. s. of torad; dat. torud (fructui), Z. 231; n. pl. *toirthe*, O'D. 88, for tortha, whence it would seem to be a neut. a-stem. Ebel (Beitr. 428) would connect this word with the root RAD; but consider the *t* in *toirthe* and in the adj. toirtheeh (fruitful), which occurs in Z. 778. 290, 291. *Ingen* (filia, nata), a daughter, girl; now *inghean*, Gael. *nighen*, which Bopp and Pictet, I venture to think, erroneously, have compared with the Skr. anganâ, is literally, I suspect, "one who does not bring forth," from the neg. particle *in* (Z. 829), and the root GAN[1] (Skr. jan), to produce. Cf. the word *ingenas* in the following gloss (Z. 492), ma eterrosera fri a fer, ni teit co fer naile, act bed *ingenas*, which I render literally thus, "if she have separated from her husband, let her not go to another husband, but let there be not-bringing forth"—impartitudo, impartura, if I may coin a Latin word. Z. translates *bed ingenas* by sit innupta, obviously taking *ingenas* for an adj., or a concrete subst.; but the termination -*as* is only, so far as I know, used to form abstract substantives; see Z. 759 (eurchas, gl. arundo, has yet to be explained). Ingen may, however, be for andegena (adgnata), cf. Cintugena.

292-295. *Banchara*, a female friend; *cara* = W. *carant*, pl. *ceraint* (O. Ir. gen. carat = carantas, as Skr. bharatas = φέροντος[2]), is a stem in *ant*, like náma (hater, enemy), gen. námat (= na + amantas); fiadu (God); dínu (ewe-lamb); bráge, throat (= Welsh *breuant*, windpipe); lóche (lightning); Nuada (a man's name); Brega (?) plur. Βρίγαντες (= in the Irish of Z.'s glosses, Bregait, Skr. brhantas), an Irish clan mentioned by Ptolemy. This class of nouns represents the Gr. participles in ων, οντος. Cara was thus declined in O. Ir.:—

MASC. *ant*-STEM.

Stem, carat from *carant*.

	Sing.	Dual.	Plur.
N.	cara	(Not yet observed)	carait
G.	carat		carat (n)
D.	carait		cairtib
A.	carait (n)		cairtea
V.	a chara		a chairtea

294. · *Láir*

---

[1] The root GAN, when it means to be born, reduplicates in Irish (cf. no gigned, gl. nascebatur, Z. 417), as well as when it means to produce (nis gignetar tola, Oingus, Félire).

[2] The loss of the *n* before *t* in Irish is, however, purely the result of a phonetic law; the same loss in the Skr. gen. bharatas, and in the other weak cases, is the consequence of what may be called the *dynamics* of the language.

294. *Láir* (a mare); gen. lárach (declined like cathir, *supra*, No. 13). 295. *Múl* (afterwards glossing mûlus, W. mul, N. H. G. maul); cognate with Lat. mûla, a she-mule. The adj. múldae, gl. mulionicus, is in Z. 30, where also are quoted the O. British name Epomulus = equomulus, and múlu, the O. Ir. acc. pl. of mûl = mulus.

296–301. *Assal*, glossing, *infra*, asinus (W. asyn, he-ass; asen, a she-ass), I cannot believe to be a Celtic word. The vowel-flanked *s* would have been lost in Irish. Assal (O'R. asal) I believe to stand for asan, and to have been taken from the Lat. asinus: cf. Gaul. Ep-*asn*-actus, Gr. ὄνος for ὄσνος, Goth. asilus, O. H. G. esil, Lith. asilas. 297. *Sogh allaid*, she-wolf, lit. a wild bitch; as *cu allaid*, lit. wild dog, is lupus (v. *infra*); *sogh*, also *sagh*, *saidh*, *saith*, O'lt., Gael. *saigh*. Hence *saighln*, "a little bitch," O'R.; saigir, "a bitch's heat," O'D. 298. *Caisc* = pascha, from which it is taken. Note, however, that it has become a fem. i-stem. In the O. Ir. the nom. is casc, which is declined like a c-stem; gen. casc = cascas; dat. caisc = casci; acc. caisc (ṅ) = cascin (or -en?). So—299. *Mainn* (manna) is mann in Z. 593; ni pu imdu do (leg. dó) in *mann* cid trén oc tecmallad; "non fuit abundantius ei manna quamvis sollerti in collectione;" whence it appears that the word was either masc. or fem., which is curious, as the O. Ir. foreign-words generally follow the gender of the original vocables. 300. *Bosluaiged* (gl. mammona, riches), leg. bósluaiged, a deriv. from bósluag, "cow-host;" cf. Goth. faihuthraihns (μαμμωνᾶς), originally "cattle-throng," "*fee*-throng," v. *infra*, No. 1003. 301. *Subachus* (gl. all. a, leg. alacrimonia?), glossed by lætitia, Corm., and ilaritas (*sic*) in Egerton, 88, fo. 70: from subach (cheerful), opposed to dubach (v. *supra*, No. 85).

302–304. *Amadán* (gl. idiota, here a fool, idiot, *omadhaun*), which Pictet (Zeits. v. 325) rightly connects with Skr. a-mati, stupidity—mati is understanding—and Lat. amens. The root is MAN (think), whence Skr. manu, Eng. MAN, quasi thinker. 303. *Deorad* (gl. advena, a stranger, alien = the Scottish name Dewar, Gael. *deóradh*) also means a pilgrim, an exile, a stranger settling in an Irish chieftain's territory. See a valuable note by Dr. Reeves (Vita Col., 366), and one by O'D. (Battle of Magh Rath, p. 163), in which page the nom. pl. deoraid occurs. 304. *Urraidh* (gl. indigena), a native, also meant "a solvent yeoman," C.

305–310. *Eirinnach* (gl. Hibernigena), from the old name of this island, which is declined in the Book of Leinster and Lib. Hymn. nom. hérinn (Maolmura Othna's poem) dat. dond crinn, gen. and acc. hérenn (see Flacc's Hymn, vv. 7, 8, 10, and the *orthain* at the end, and the quatrain from Marianus Scotus, Z. 944). The origin of this name, notwithstanding the labours of Z. (G. C. 67) and Pictet (Beitr. 87), still remains obscure. One of Z.'s ideas is, that it is compounded of the intensive ér and rind (a star), (a star), which he thinks may also have signified an island, "quasi signum maris." Another conjecture of his is, that érrend is for iar-rend ("insula occidentis"). There are three objections to these theories: 1°, as Pictet observes, we never find the *r* doubled; 2°, the gen. of rind is renda, but the gen. of hérinn is hérenn; 3°, rind never means an island, though it certainly has the meanings of "star," "headland," and "point." Pictet, citing the Teutonic names for the Irish—Norse Irar (Irishmen), Anglo-Sax. ira, ire (Irishman), asserts that Eirinn is derived "ohne zweifel aus dem ältesten volksnamen der Iren, der etwa Er oder Eir gelautet haben muss." The following theory has been suggested to me: Hérinn, which certainly is a stem in nn, iver-inn being the base in the nom. gen. and dat., iver-ann in the acc., represents a petrified AVARASMA (cf. Skr. avara, posterior, western, declined with the pronominal -sma, Ir. iar, after, aniar "in the west," Pictet, Beitr. i. 89). By weakening the vowels¹, dropping the final *a*, and changing *m* into *n* (cf. sni, "we," ex ASMI) we obtain ivarisn. From ivarisn hérinn may have arisen, by the assimilation of the *s* (cf. immunn = Skr. abhyasmân = N. H. G. um uns) the passage of *v* into a spiritus asper, the shifting of this breathing, and the drawing together of the i-a thus produced (cf. orthuaiscertach (gl. euroaquilo, Book of Armagh, 188, *b.* 2) = iarthuaiscerddach (gl. ctesiarum, Z. 777); nauairchinniuch = naui-airchinniuch):—

    Nom. Sing. hérinn = hiarinn = iharinn = ivarinn,

        G. hérenn = hiarinn-as = ivarinn-as

        D. and Loc. hérinn = hiarinn-i = ivarinn-i

        A. hérenn = hiarann-en (-in?) = ivarannen (-in?)².

311–314. The only words here calling for remark are—311. *Oilithrech* (gl. romipeta, i. e. Rome-seeker), "a pilgrim" in O. Ir., alither, ailither, and—314. *Comaightech* (gl. alienigena, foreigner), now written *coimhtheach*, Gael. *coimheach*.

315–325. *Dithrebach*

[1] Cf. Ptolemy's Iver-n-ioi, Iver-n-is, Iver-n-ia ('Ιουερνια), and the W. Ewyrdonic (hibernicus, "westmanish"), Z. 814. But for these forms with *e*, Hérinn might be connected with Skr. apara.

[2] The most unfortunate circumstance in the investigations respecting the etymology of "Hérinn" is, that Prof. Pictet, to whom Celtic philology is much indebted, should have been deluded by our wretched O'Reilly, who actually has the following:—"Ibh, s. a country, a tribe of people."

Will it be believed that this Ibh is nothing but the mutilated dat. plural of the Mod. Ir. *ó* or *ua* (grandson, descendant, in O. Ir. haue, Z. 1029, boa, Fiacc, v. 2, nom. pl. háui, Z. 39, dat. pl. auib, *ibid.*)? See O'D. Gr. 108. Irish districts were often called after the tribe that possessed them: thus, Ia aum censelich, in the Book of Armagh (literally apud nepotes Censalaci), is correctly translated by O'D. (Gr. 436) "In Hy-Kinsellagh;" auu (leg. háuu) is here the accus. pl. Dat. pl.: mac ind [r]irdana do *ib* Birnn, i. e.

315-325. *Dithrebach* (hermit), *supra*, dithrubach ; cf. W. didryfwr from dithrab, "a desert," = di-trab : cf. A(d)trebates (possessores), from trab = W. treb (vicus), Lat. tribus, Goth. thaurp, Eng. thorp, N. H. G. dorf (Ebel, Zeits., vi. 422). *Marbtach* (slayer), in the following compounds, is from marb, "dead," = martva = Lat. mortuus? root MAR, Skr. mr̥. 320. *Siurmarbtach* (gl. sororicida), "sister-slayer :" siur = W. chwaer, chwïawr = svasâr, N. H. G. schwester, occurs in Z. in the dimin. siurnat, gl. sororcula, p. 282, acc. sing. : conuargaib foectoir in *siair*, "he straightway lifted up the sister" (Trip. Life of Patrick). A second form, sethair (?), occurs in sethar-oirenid (gl. sororicida), Z. 767 : a third form, pethair (?)—the Gaelic *piuthair*—in the Táin bó Cuailgne (Leb. na huidre); mac dechtere do *phethar*-su ; and a fourth form, fiar, fiur (Lib. Hymn. ed. Todd, p. 72), acc. sing. in the Trip. Life of Patrick : roboi bara do patricc fri *fiair* (lit. fuit ira Patricio contra sororem). 322. *Cliamhuin*, gen. *clémhna*, "son-in-law," in the plur. commonly signifies, in the Highlands, "any near relations by marriage." 324. *Tribus* (gl. braccæ), = W. trws, trows-ers.

326-330. *Cealg* (gl. insidiæ, *infra*, gl. dolus); cf. W. cele (trick). 326. Nubtie. *baindi. cich*, is very obscure ; bainne cích would be "breast-milk" (bainne, a drop); but this hardly agrees with nubtie, which can scarcely be for anything but nuptiæ. Dare we read *banais caich* nuptiæ cujusvis—*banais*, a deriv. from *ban*, as to which *vide supra*, and *caich*, the gen. sing. m. of each ? 327. *Mórmargad* (gl. nundinæ, market-day), great-market, margad, Corn. marhaz, is perhaps not derived from Engl. market (mercatus). 328. *Fergach*, leg. fergacht (gl. rixæ, quarrels), Gael. *feargachd*. Fergach is "angry," in Z., fereach for forgaeh, from ferg, anger, s. f., which Z. 71, compares with O. W. guerg, gl. efficax, and Gaulish Vergobretus, and Glück and Ebel (Beitr., i. 160) with Gr. Ϝέργον, Ϝοργή. Hence fairge, foirge, "the sea," Οὐεργίουιον (Vergivios) ὠκεανὸς, Ptol., and perhaps W. gweilgi (torrent, ocean). 329. *Inada* (gl. tabe), and—330. *Athfiana* (gl. atene), are obscure to me. Perhaps we should read
Athenæ

("Son of the poet of Hy B." as Gilla mac Liace is called in Harl. 1802, last page), literally "of the descendants of B." And yet the Professor compares with this fragment of the termination of a fragment (ib = háuib = ἀγαυᾶβο ? Cf. Vedic âyu proles, Dr. Siegfried), the non-existing Skr. root ibh, ibha (elephant) ἶφι, ἶφιος, and placing it before an imaginary "crna," soberly sets down "ibberna das land der Ernen oder Iran, oder vielleicht ibh-erin, mit hinzugesetzter griechisch-lateinischer endung," Beitr. i., 89). I cannot believe that the h which occurs in our MSS. so constantly at the beginning of Hérinn, háue (grandson), huile (all), huáir (hour), huasal (high, ὑψηλός), &c., is merely a freak of the scribe's. In Hérinn I am inclined, as above suggested, to attribute its presence to a shifting of the spiritus asper into which v has passed. Cf. in Greek ἴππος for Ἴκϝος, Skr. açvas. A similar displacement has been remarked by Dr. Siegfried in biaira ("of iron"), *infra*, where the h has arisen from a vowel-flanked s. So, as Kuhn remarks, ἱερός = Ved. ishirû.

Athenæ for atene; if so, the glossarist absurdly meant to derive the city-name from áth fiana, "champion's ford."

331-364. *Dorchadus* (gl. tenebræ, gl. latebræ): dorchæ, obscurus (Z. præf. xv., 84); na dorche (tenebræ), Z. 237; cf. sorcha, "bright" (so-r'ch-a), Skr. r. ruch, and *v. supra*, No. 85. 333. *Inmasa* (gl. divitiæ), pl. of inmas, O'R.'s *ionmas, ionmus*, "treasure, riches." 337. *Néll* (for nebl = neblas?), "a cloud," hod. *néul*, W. nifwl, niwl, N. H. G. nebel, Lat. nobula, νεφέλη. 338. *Scola*, "schools," from schŏla: gen. sing. in Colmán's Hymn, v. 40 (Lib. Hymn., 5 *b*):—

Robet maccáin¹ flatha dé itimchuairt naaculese!
May the little children of God's kingdom be around this school!

339. *Bagair* (gl. minæ), n. sing. *bagar*, "threat," O'R.; dare we compare W. bwgwth, bygyliaeth (minatio), O. W. bicoled, vecordia, Z. 802 ? 342. *Aengus* (Oingus, Book of Armagh, 13, *b*. 1, 19, *a*. 1, 19, *a*. 2), gen. Oingusso, *ib.* 18 *b*. 2, oingoš, leg. Oingosso, *ibid.*, a masc. u-stem, like Doilgus, gen. Doilgusso, Z. 18; Fergus, gen. Fergusso, Book of Armagh, 15, *a*. 2, fergosso, *ib.* 16 *b*. 2 (= W. Gwrwst?), Muirgus, Congus, Uarghus, and other nouns in -gus, = gustù? as Dr. Siegfried suggests to me². 345. *Gilla na naom*, "servant of the saints:" *naom* in O. Ir. is nóib, an adjectival *a*-stem. 353. *An gaeth atúaidh* (gl. Boreas), "the wind from the north," Gael. *gaoth á tuath*; *an gaeth*, O. Ir. in gáith (Z. 929), *a* (from) O. Ir. á; *túaidh*, cf. antúaid, "in the north;" anfartúaid, "in the north-west;" anairtúaid, "in the north-east;" fa dess no fa thuaith, "to the right or the left," Z. 566. 354. *Primaidhecht* (gl. anchises), inexplicable by me: primaidecht would be "prime-tutorship," *vide* oide, oite, *supra*.

365-389. *Magisder*, W. meistyr, Corn. maister, all, of course, from the Lat. magister: O. Ir. acc. pl. magistru, Z. 615. 366. *Breitheam* (gl. arbiter), Z.'s brithem judex, a masc. n-stem, gen. brithemon, in a mutilated gloss preserved in the Book of Armagh, 187 *b*, 1, viz., suide bri[th]emon, gl. tribunal: dat. s. brithemain, Z. 269; cf. breth judicium, and the Gaulish Vergobretus (judicium exequens). A sister-form is found in

---

[1] MS. maccan.
[2] Dr. Reeves has favoured me with a list of names in -gus, which he has collected from the Annals, Calendars, and Pedigrees. From this I select the following, in hopes that some may be identified with Gaulish or Cymmric names: Alldghus, Artgus, Baothghus, Cuangus, Doedhghus, Donnghus or Dongus, Fachtgus, Faelgus, Fiangus, Fianngus, Flathgus, Lergus, Miodhgus, Nialgus, Saergus, Suedgus. If Dr. Siegfried's conjecture be established, we have here the Celtic representative of the Skr. r. jush, γεύω, Lat. gustus, Eng. choose, Goth. kiusan. Cf. láimtech a des, diglach a *gus*, Seirgl. Conc. *Atlantis* ii. p. 382.

in O. Ir. bráth, O. W. braut, an u-stem, and is contained in the Gaulish *Bratu*spantium. Cf. A. S. braðcan (sententiam dicere). 367. *Sagart* (gl. presbyter), from sacerd-os. 368. *Timthirigh* (gl. minister), leg. *timthiridh?* and cf. timthir-thid, servus, Z. 256; timthir-echt servitium, Z. 237; gl. ministratio, *infra.* 369. *Gabann* (gl. faber); cf. the Gaulish man's-name Gobannitius, Bret. Corn., and W. gof, all perhaps etymologically connected with fab-er; O. Ir. nom. goba, gen. gobann. Patrick invokes divers virtues fri brichta ban ocus *gobann* [MS. goband] ocus druad (against the incantations of women, and smiths, and druids). 370. *Macam* (gl. puer), a deriv. from mac, as to which *vide supra.* 371. *Leabar* (gl. liber, "a book"), W. llyfyr, Corn. liuer, is here apparently spelt according to "leathan re leathan," but the vowel-change in the penult is either owing to *umlaut* or assimilation; in O. Ir. either lebar or libur, a masc. a-stem. A Mid. Ir. gen. sing. occurs in a gloss on *a folaire* (leg. a phólaire), H. 3, 18, p. 523, viz., ainm do teig *liubair*, "a name for a book-satchel," where, by the way, note *téig,* dat. sing. of *tiach* (gl. pera, *supra,* No. 41), a fem. â-stem, obviously from thêca, θήκη. A dimin. of lebar occurs in a quatrain which the scribe of the St. Gall Priscian seems to have extemporized while producing his invaluable MS. (see Z. 929):—

Dom'farcai fidbaide¹ fál,	The grove makes a festival for me,
Fom'chain lóid luin lúath, nad cél—	A blackbird's swift lay sings to me—I will not hide it—
Uas mo *lebrán* indlinech	Over my many-lined booklet
Fom'chain trirech inna én.	A trilling (?) of the birds sings to me.

372. *Gabhar*, gabor, gl. caper, Z. 744, W. gafr (pl. geifr), a masc. a-stem, irregularly = Lat. caper. (I say irregularly, because the Lat. and Gr. tenues (c, t, κ, τ) are, as a rule, represented by the same letters in Irish: so the Lat. and Greek medials (d, g, b, δ, γ, β) by Irish medials, which last (as in Gothic, Slavonic, and Lithuanian) regularly represent the aspirates: b = φ, Lat. f, d = θ, g = χ, Lat. h.) But by Benary's important law, the Lat. cap-er might be regarded as arising from a r. GABH, and thereby the Celtic form with two medials would become intelligible; cf. Gaulish Gabromagus (goat-field), O. Brit. Gabrosentum (goat's-path), Glück, 43. 373. *Torc* (gl. aper), acc. sing. torcc, Book of Armagh, 18 b, 1, hence torcde, gl. aprinus, Z. 85. *Torc* = W. twrch, Bret. tourc'h, "a hog," Corn. torch, gl. magalis. 374. *Partan* (gl. cancer, "a crab"), etymologically inexplicable by me. The W. is cranc = cancer? 375. *Dobhran* (gl. fiber), masc. a-stem, is now an "otter" (ἔνυδρις), not a "beaver,"

---

¹ Cf. Lenb. Breacc, 121 *aa*, cited O'D., Gr. 370: is liriu feoir no folt *fidbuide* illratha in marbnuda noibsea; literally, 'Tis more numerous than grass or a grove's hair, the many-blessings of this holy elegy (marbnud = W. marwnad).

ver," from dobur (water), which Pictet compares with dabhra, said to be Skr. for "ocean." The W. for "otter" is dufrgi, i. e. dufr + ci, "water-dog;" cf. W. rivername, Camdubr, and the Gaulish Verno-dubrum, Dubra, Dubris. 376. *Labar no slinncriadh* (gl. linter), " an ewer (?) or a clay-tile." 378. *Companach* (gl. soccs, i. e. socer, socius?), formed from Lat. compaganus, the *g* being lost between vowels, as *always* in W., and sometimes in O. Ir. (*vide infra*, 550). 380. *Socruidhe* (pulcher), i. e. εὔμορφος: cruidhe from cruth (forma), an u-stem: gunated gen. sing. in O. Ir. crothu = crutavas, non-gunated, crutto = crutvas. 381. *Dubh* (gl. niger) dub in Z., is in W. and Bret. du, Corn. gl. duv; cf. the river-name Dubis; and perhaps Lat. fuscus (blackish), for fubiscus? Engl. dusk? Dub also meant ink: is tana an *dub*, "thin is the ink" (Z. praef. xv.): cf. Danish blæk. 382. *Lesc* (gl. piger), n. pl. m. neb-*leisce*, gl. non pigri, Z. 830; *vide* leisg, O'R., W. llesg, Lat. laxus? 383. *Truagh* (gl. macer), = tróg, "miser," Z. 28; trogán (gl. misellus), better spelt in the Book of Armagh, 38, *a.* 1, trógán, a marg. gloss on "Judas scariothis," W. truan. 384. *Gruamda* (gl. acer) cf. W. grwm?, "surly, sour," O'R. 385. *Agarb* = acerbus, as *sagart*, O. Ir. sacart = sacerdos, which shows that the Lat. *c* before *e* was pronounced like *k* by the Irish. 386. *Deas* (gl. dexter), O. Ir. des, = W. deheu, Corn. dyghow, dex-ter, δεξιός, Skr. dakshina; cf. the Gaul. goddess-name, Dexsiva, Dexivia. 387. *Cle* (gl. sinister), leg. *clé*, is obviously a mutilation of a *cledh*, W. cledd, Bret. kleiz, which Diefenbach and J. Grimm have compared with Goth. hlei-duma (-duma = -timu, in Lat. dextimus). A sister-form clí occurs in the dat. sing. for laim *chlí* (gl. a sinistris), Z. 67; duc*hli* (gl. ad sinistram), Book of Armagh, 184, *b*. This comes close to Goth. hlei, and also to Skr. çrî, which Bopp equates with hlei ("Vergl. Gramm." ii. 30, 2te aufl.). "Wenn ich recht habe," says the Master, "den goth. primitivstamm *hlei* auf das Skr. çrî = krî, glück zurückzuführen, mit der äusserst gewöhnlichen vertauschung des *r* mit *l*, so sehen wir in der gothischen benennung des linken einen euphemismus, gleich dem worauf die griechischen ausdrücke ὀριστερός und εὐώνυμος sich stützen." 389. *Adh allaidh* (gl. onager), leg. *agh* allaidh: *agh*, "a beast of the cow-kind," O'R., gen. *aighe*, masc. and fem.: in Gael. "a hind," "a heifer," "often applied to cattle two years old, without regard to gender." If *gh* here stands for *ch*, we may compare *agh* with Skr. paçu, pecus, Goth. faihu.

390-394. *Ferand* (gl. ager), glosses iathmaige in the *orthain* after Fiacc's Hymn; ferann, which Dr. Reeves (Vit. Col., 449) explains as "jurisdiction of a monastic order," is perhaps the same word: induxit niuem supra totum agrum pertinguentem *ferenn*, Book of Armagh, 5 *a*. 2; cf. W. grwn, pl. gryniau, " a ridge, a lay, or land in a field." 391. *Snámach* (gl. suber, "the cork-tree"), something, apparently, that swims

swims or floats; cf. Skr. snâ, W. nawf. Odran is called abb sáer *snámach*, "a noble, swimming abbot," by Oingus, Fél., Oct. 27. 392. *Magister aimfesach*, "an ignorant master;" aimfesach from the neg. prefix am (Skr. sâmi, ἠμι, semi?), and the root fis, the connexion of which with fid, Skr. vid, Fιδ, wit, seems to rest on a desiderative formation. Only a gunated base VIVAITS would explain O. Ir. forms like fésur, fiasur (scio), fiastar(scit), fésid (scitis), fiasmais(sciebamus), fiastais(sciebant); and perhaps we should read aimfésach. 393. *Eslán* (leg. esslán), from es = Gaul. ex, W. eh and slán, with which W. llawen may be identified, if we assume the existence of an original slavana. 394. *Maeth* (gl. tener, i. e. tener), irregularly = W. mwyth; compar. moithiu, gl. molliorem, Z. 283.

395–409. *Fer* (= vira-s, a masc. a-stem) = Lat. vir, Goth. vair, Lith. wyras, Skr. vara. 397. *Fer cli* seems to mean not levir (husband's brother), but a left-handed man (*supra*, No. 387), as if levir (for dêvir = ἐaϜήρ, Skr. dêvara) were a compound of lœvus and vir. 398–401. *Deise*, *trír*, *cethrair*, *cúigir*, respectively the genitives sing. of dias (fem.), triur, cethrar (dunaib chethrairib, gl. quaternionibus, Book of Armagh, 178 *b*. 2), cuigur, O. Ir. cóicur (which respectively mean a combination of 2, of 3, of 4, of 5 persons); four of those numeral substantives which form so remarkable a feature in Irish. O'D. and Z. suggest that the numeral substantives in -r are compounded with fer. If so, the original *a* is preserved unweakened in nonbar (a combination of 9 persons), Corm. v. Nós = Skr. navanvara-m, hod. *nonbhar*, and in deichenbar, a combination of 10 persons, (gen. sing. deichenboir occurs in one of the inscriptions copied by my revered friend Dr. Petrie) now *deichneabhar*. Others, I may observe, compare fer, &c., with Skr. víra (hero), *sed qu.* on account of the long *í*. 402. *Sathach* (gl. satur). 403. *Lethsathach* (gl. semisatur); cf. Lat. sat-is. 404. *Tigerne*, *dia* (O. W. duw, Corn. duy), *anum* (anam) *mac* (O. W. map, Corn. mab), *saer* (sóir), have been already considered. *Libertus* is glossed by sóirmug, i. e. free servant, in Z. 825.

410–418. *Bachlach* (gl. famulus, a slave) is "a herdsman, a rustic," according to O'R. 411. *Milchú* (gl. malosus, i. e. molossus, i. e. κύων Μολοττικός, a wolf-dog, guitter in the Cornish Vocab.) is explained "greyhound" by O'R., who spells the word *miolchu*; plur. mílchoin occurs in Lebar na Cert, 252, W. milgi, pl. milgwn. 412. *Bachlach breallán* (gl. bufulus) is obviously a term of great reproach; but what breallán is exactly, I know not; "a lubberly fellow with a hanging under-lip," says C.; perhaps it is connected in meaning with spado; cf. *breallach*, gl. spadosus, *infra*, *breall*, "foreskin," l. w. 418. *Mathghamain* (a bear), of uncertain derivation.

419–423. *Senathair* (gl. avus, grandfather), literally "old-father," *v. suprà*, No. 13. 420. *A athair sin* (gl. proavus, great-grandfather), "*his* father," i. e. the father of the

avus;

avus; so the same words at No. 421 mean the father of the *proavus*. *A*, O. Ir. *á* (the gen. sing. of the masc., and neut. pronoun of the 3rd pers. sing.) aspirates, must, therefore, have ended in a vowel, and has long since been identified by Bopp with Skr. asya. As to *sin* (for O. Ir. som, sem, Mid. Ir. sium, now *sean, san*), it is here placed as an emphasizing particle. The O. Ir. som has been compared by Bopp and Pictet with Skr. svayam; and their view is confirmed by the fact that the *s* in som is unaspirable (cf. dossom, ci, Z. 334), and must, therefore, represent a combination of consonants. *Tuata* (gl. laicus); cf. τοντιους in what, up to the recent appearance of M. de Belloguet's work, was presumed to be the oldest monument of the Celtic language, the Gaulish inscription, found at Vaison (Département Drôme):—CEΓOMAPOC OYIΛ-ΛONEOC TOOYTIOYC NAMAYCATIC EIωPOY BIIΛIICAMI COCIN NEMHTON, which Dr. Siegfried has thus translated:—"Segomaros Villoneos, a citizen of Nemausus (Nîmes), dedicated (?) this temple to Belesama"[1]. Cf. also Toutio-rix (a Gaulish name for Apollo) from tuath (people), O. Brit. tût, Z. 39, now tud, a widely scattered word. Oscan tovto, Umbrian tuta, tota (urbs), Goth. thiuda, O. H. G. diota, Lith. Tauta (Germany), all from the root tu (to grow, to be strong), as Aufrecht and Kirchhoff, Grimm and Kuhn have shown. 424. *Lóegh* (gl. vitulus, calf) = W. llo, pl. lloi, Corn. loch, Bret. lue; cf. uenierunt ad fontem *loig*les in scotica nobiscum vitulus ciuitatum, Book of Armagh, 10 *b*, 1, and perhaps the man's-name, Loiguire, *ib.*, 7 *a*, 1 (but see Z. 126). The nom. and gen. sing. occur in Brogan's poem on Brigit, l. 52:—

> In *loeg* lla clam l carput, la bó indlaid ind *lóig*.
> The calf with her leper in the chariot, the cow behind the calf.

425-428. *Súil* (gl. oculus), "eye," frequent in Z. It is also found in the Book of Armagh, 219, *b*, 1, where a grotesque profile occurs, opposite to which is written: [f]éccid in[s]róin *súil* bél, "behold ye the nose, eye, mouth." Súil is a fem. i-stem: its etymology is obscure to me. 426. *Lethcaech* (leg. lethchaech, gl. monoculus, "blind of an eye"); here, if caech be not a foreign-word (Corn. cuic, gl. luscus), we have a trace in Irish of aksha, oculus, auge, eye, &c., for caoch is = Lat. caecu-s = câ-icu-s, Skr. kâ-aksha (Pott, E. F. i. 126, Benfey, Zeits. ii. 222). But I suspect caech is taken from the Lat., as Skr. ksh would have become *s* in Ir., as in Gr. cf. akshi with ὄσσε, ὄσσομαι. 427. *Dall* (gl. caecus), v. *supra*, No. 249, and cf. the adj. dallbrónach (blind, sad),

---

[1] Is not *Villoneos* the gen. sing. of Villoneus, governed by a *mapos* (filius), understood? Compare Correus, Abareus. Ειωρου in the other Gaulish inscriptions seems always ιενην (ieuru). See De Belloguet, Ethnogénie gauloise, p. 197, ss.

sad), of which the gen. sing. m. occurs in the Book of Armagh, 11 *a*. 1, as a man's name: super fossam *dall*bronig. 428. *Míl* (log. míl) *mór*, *Ruaimnech dubair*, gl. cetus (if I read the two last Irish words aright) are names for a whale, míl mór, "great beast," ruainmech dubair, i. e. r. of the water; ru-ainmech, great-animal? ru being an intensive prefix (= Skr. pra), and ainmech being probably, like ainmidhi, gl. animal, *infra;* anim, Lat. animal, &c., a deriv. from the root AN, to breathe. I have only once found ainmech, viz., in a poem attributed to Rumann (Bibl. Bodl. Laud, 610, fo. 10):—

| Rola curu¹ in gaeth ganmech | The sandful wind sent circles |
| Im iuber na da *ainmech*. | Round the estuary of the two *ainmechs*. |

Perhaps, indeed, the reading of the MS., *ruaimnech dubain,* "the hair-line of a fish-hook," may be correct. *Ruaim* is "the long hair of a horse's or cow's tail," O'D.; "cetus," would, accordingly, stand for seta.

429-439. *Mac dilechta* (gl. orbus, orphan, properly "bereaved"), "son of milkless-ness," according to C., *sed qu.* Gael. *dilleachdan.* 430. *Mintšuilech* (gl. luscus, here "purblind"), leg. mintšuilech, is O'R.'s mionšuilech, "weak-eyed" (the *t* in min-t has yet to be explained). *Min* = W. mwyn, main, Bret. moan, Gr. μᾰνός, Glück, K. N. 99. 431. *Macthšuilech* (gl. lippus, blear-eyed, which is fliuchdere in Z.), macth, gl. tener, *infra,* W. mwyd. 432. *Abhcoide,* taken from advocatus. Note the bh = dv, as in aibbersóir, *v. infra,* = adversarius, and cf. the Lat. bellum, bis = dvellum, dvis. 433. *Dlightinech* (gl. juridicus), the guttural assibilated in the sister form *dlistinach* (gl. legitimus), *infra,* from the root DLIG (dligim, debeo, Z. 431, Goth. dulg, *v. supra,* No. 87). 434. *Fer cúisi do chongbail* (gl. causidicus), "a man to maintain causes;" cúisi acc. pl. of cúis, from causa, with change of decl., acc. sing. cois, Z. 443. With congbail = con-gab-áil, cf. O'R.'s cungbhailim, O. Ir. congaibther, Z. 842; congbhalas, "stay, help, support," O'R. 435. *Manach* (Corn. manach)—437. *Cananach,* and—438. *Discibul* (W. dysgybl, Corn. discibel), respectively from monachus, canonicus, discipulus. 439. *Duine beg* (gl. homunculus, ad v. homo parvus), *beg,* in Z. bccc, bcc; gl. paulum, Z. 281, be[c]ca, gl. modicus, Book of Armagh, 183, *a,* 2, is the W. bach, cc always becoming ch in Welsh.

440-444. *Sgian* (gl. cnipulus, gl. cutellus), a knife, dagger, gen. sgine, *infra;* O. Ir. scian, gen. scine; W. ysgïen fem. ("a slicer, cymetar"), a fem. â-stem ; cf. W. ysgïaw, Bret. skéja, to cut. Note, that *ia* here does not stand for an original *é* (if it did,

---

¹ Curu (gl. gyros, Z. 1072) = Lat. curvûs.

did, the Welsh would have been ysgwyn, and the Irish gen. sing. scéine). Perhaps the original base was skidyanâ, from which first *d* and then *y* may have fallen. If so, we might compare scindo, scidi, $\sigma\chi i\zeta\omega$, Skr. chhid, &c. 442. *Crubh eich* (gl. ungulus), "a horse's hoof;" eich, gen. of ech. 443. *Tairnge*, "a nail, pin, peg," O'R. 444. *Braigdech* (gl. camus, horse-collar, *hame*); O. Ir. brúigtech, from bráge, gen. brágat, neck, throat, = W. brouant, an ant-stem, *supra*, No. 292.

445-456. *Paisti bróg* (gl. haietus), a patch on a shoe; paisti (leg. paiste?) is, perhaps, taken from Eng. patch; bróg, fem. according to O'R., O. Ir. bróce; cf. the Gaulish bracca. 446. *Scolb tige* (gl. tegulus); scolb is a wattle ("scollop"), pointed at both ends, used to bind down straw-thatch. *Tige*, gen. of teg (house), a neut. i-stem = tagi; cf. tegere, *et v. infra*, No. 446. 449. *Airchinnech* (gl. archidiaconus), princeps in Z., has been before noticed: dat. sing. naucirchinniuch (gl. nauiclero), Book of Armagh, 188, *b.* 2. 450. *Teachtaire* (gl. legatus), messenger, envoy, O. Ir. techtaire, tectaire, a personal noun, from techt, tect (venire), cf. Zend. tac (ire), Lith. tekù (curro), W. taith (journey), the Gaulish tribe-name, Tectosages, O. Ir. man's name, Techtmar. Techtaire is wrongly explained dispensator, gubernator in Z. 743, 888, though one would have thought the gloss in Z. 888 was decisive as to the word's not meaning gubernator: is hé in tecttaire maith conduig indocbáil dia thigerni, "he is the good *tectaire* (ambassador), who obtains glory for his lord." At p. 78 Z. probably mis-read tecttaire, gl. dispensator, for recttaire, which word is better spelt rectaire (ónd rectairiu, gl. a villico, Z. 743), and rectire (gl. praepositus, Z. 245). 451. *Deganach*—452. *Prelait*—454. *Decháin*—455. *Subdecháin*—456. *Aclaidhe*— 458. *Pupul*—460. *Aingel*—462. *Arcaingel*, all from the Latin. Note, however, in pupul (Corn. pepel) the assimilation of the *o* of populus to the succeeding *u*, and note also that the stem of aingel, a masc. a-stem (Corn. ail) seems in O. Ir. to be extended in the acc. pl., which is always aingl-i-u, not angelu, anglu. Cf. Lagn-i-u (Leinstermen), Z. 944: coirn-e-a (coronas), a fem. â-stem: Boind-e-o, gen. sing. of Boind (Bovinda, Boyne), Book of Armagh, 16 *a*, 2, 16 *b*, 1: ins-e-o, gen. sing. of inis (island), *ibid*. 18 *a*, 1: ailichth-i-u, gl. alternationes, Z. 256, an u-stem: cairt-e-a, friends, and náimt-e-a, haters, enemies, both ant-stems in the acc. pl.

457-464. *Coraidh*, a choir, is, like W. cor, from chor-us, or $\chi o\rho$-ós, but with an Ir. termination. 459. *Uan* (lamb), W. oen, Corn. oin, Bret. oan, a masc. a-stem, whence uainín, *infra*, has certainly lost a *g*, *v. supra*. 461. *Cloideam* (sword), W. cloddyf, in O. Ir. claideb, Z. 442. 469. *Ruainde* (leg. ruainne?), a single hair; *foiltín*, a dimin., and—464. *Foiltnín*, a double dimin. of folt, hair, as to which *v. supra*, No. 77.

465-479. *Mérláime*, a finger (lit. digitus manus, as toe is—466. *Mér choise*, digitus pedis), mér (digitus), acc. dual; imber in dá mér (infer duos digitos), Z. 926; abl. pl. in o meraib (in digitis ejus), Z. 347. Mér seems to have lost a letter (*t* ?) before *r*; cf. W. motrwy, a finger-ring; *coise*, gen. sing. of cos, a fem. â-stem = Lat. coxa. 467. *Salm*—468. *Fersán*—470. *Toin*—471. *Lethtoin*—472. *Ditoin*—474. *Punc*—475. *Cercall*, all taken from the corresponding Lat. words: *fersán*, with the addition of the Ir. dimin. suffix án. 469. *Foghur*, gen. foguir (sonus, pronuntiatio), frequently in Z., see pp. 964, 965; root ᴏᴀɴ, whence gair (vox), gairim (voco), &c., Skr. gir (vox). 473. *Macam gente*, a child begotten; gente, part. perf. pass. of gcinim, root ɢᴀɴ, as to which *v. supra*, No. 291. 476. *Múr*, W. mur = mûrus, is probably taken from the Lat. "Mur," says C. (Cath Maighe Léna, 78, note ᶜ), "means simply a circular¹ wall, bank, or mound of earth; but it does not imply a dwelling, except for the dead." It sometimes meant a mound only, as in the passage to which the note is appended. 477. *Biadh* (gl. cibus); biad = bivata, βίϝοτο-ς, in O. Ir. is neuter, like the Skr. jivita (Lat. vita = vivita is fem.); cf. arbiathim, gl. lacto, gl. nutrio, Z. 431, gen. sing. in O. Ir. biith (Z. 250) = bivati, in Mod. Ir. *bídh* = W. bwyt, Corn. buit. 478. *Gaillmias* (gl. discus), i. e. *gall* + *mias*; *gall*, foreigner (v. Galldach, *supra*), *mias* = mensa, O. W. muis, Z. 137. 479. *Copán* (gl. cupus), a deriv. from Eng. cup?

480-493. *Cep* (gl. cepus) I can hardly explain, unless as = Lat. cippus: *ceap* occurs in O'R., with many meanings, of none of which, save two, do I feel certain (ceap is a shoemaker's last, and isna ceapaibh is certainly "in the stocks"). Cf. icip, gl. in ligno (Book of Armagh, 181, *b*. 2; Acts, xvi. 24). 481. *Lebaid* (gl. lectus, a bed), O. Ir. lepaid: the abl. sing. occurs in the Leabhar Breacc (pref. to Secundinus' Hymn, Lib. Hymn, ed. Todd, p. 28): batar i oen *lepaid*, "they were in the same bed," and the gen. sing. at the beginning of the *Táin bó cuailgne*: Fect nóen do ailell ⁊ do meidb iarn dergud a *rígleptha* dóib i cruachan rúith chonrach arrecaim comrad chindchércaille eturru, "once upon a time, after Ailill and Medv had spread their royal couch in C. R. C., a pillow-conversation took place between them." 482. *Otrach* (gl. fimus, dung), O'R., also a dunghill, Gael. *òtrach*. 483. *Torc* (gl. porcus), *v. supra*. 484. *Sgaignen* (gl. vannus, a winnowing-van), also a cullender, according to O'D.; in O'R. *sgaighnean*. 485. *Cleath* (tignum, a log, beam) is explained "a rib, rod, stake," by O'R. 486. *Comalta* (gl. collactaneus—ὁμο-γάλακτ-ος—a foster-brother), com-al-ta, involves the root ᴀʟ nourish (Lat. al-o), -ta, perhaps for -tava. Comalta occurs in the Scirglige Conculainn: fobith ba haite dó Fergus ocus ba *comalta* Conall Cernach,

"because

---

¹ Cf. Skr. r. mur, circumdare, vestire; Bopp.

"because F. was his foster-father, and C. C. was his foster-brother," Atlantis, ii. 372. 488. *Curach* (gl. phaselus, "a kidney-bean-shaped vessel, made (sometimes) of wickerwork," which answers tolerably well to the Irish curragh, W. cwrwg-l, whence Eng. corac-le. 489. *Sacc* (gl. forulus), W. sach = Lat. saccus, Gr. σάκκος, Goth. sakkus, Eng. sack (saco is incorrectly spelt sac in O'R.). 490. *Matal* = Lat. mantêlum? whence it is probably derived, the *n* being lost before *t*, as in sét, a road, W. hint, Goth. sinths, Eng. send, etar (between), Lat. inter, Skr. antar, and in the termination of the third pers. plur. pres. and fut. active of verbs (-at [= Lat. ant], -et, -it: -fet, -fit = Lat. -bunt). W. mantell (pl. mentyll, Z. 787) = Lat. mantellum. 491. *Blathmar* is "flowery" (W. blodeuog), not "floweret" (flosculus), from bláth, flower = W. blawd, Corn. blez, Lat. flos, N. H. G. blüte. 492. *Uainin* (gl. agnellus), dimin. of uan = agnus. 493. *Oirenin* (gl. porcellus), double dimin. of orc = porcus, W. porch, with loss of initial *p*.

494-514. *Serrach no gereach* (gl. pullus, "a foal or a chicken"); gereach, "an unfledged bird," "a squalling child," C. 495. *Cuaille* (gl. palus, W. pawl), a pole, stake. 496. *Disle* (gl. talus), a die, W. dis. 498. *Cuilen* (gl. catulus, whelp), leg. cuilenn? (cuilenn*bocc*, gl. cynyps, Z. 740), W. colwyn, Corn. gl. coloin, Bret. kolen, compare Eng. whelp. 499. *Cat* (murilegus, cat, lit. mouse-catcher), for catt, W. cath, Corn. kat, Bret. kaz, a masc. a-stem; cf. Med. Lat. cattus, catta. 500. *Cealg, v. supra*, No. 326. 501. *Mil edaigh* (gl. pediculus, louse), lit. beast of the clothes; édaigh = O. Ir. étaig (ætig, Z. 857), gen. of étach, a neut. a-stem. 502. *Dornán buana* (gl. manipulus, small handful of hay), dorn, W. dwrn, a fist: buain, gen. buana, "s. f. cutting, reaping, shearing," O'R. 506. *Coileach* (gl. gallus) = W. ceiliawg, Corn. cheliec. 508. *Prechán* (gl. milgus, i. e. milvus), a kite; cf. Gr. κίρκος? note in the Lat. *g* for *v*, as in ugula (*supra*) for uvula. 508. *Cerd* (gl. figulus), v. *supra*. (In the MS. the letters *cg* are just visible before cerd, but the scribe has evidently tried to efface them.) 509. *Ela* (swan), O'R. eala: W. alarch, pl. eleirch, Lat. olor. But who can account for ela? Can it have lost a *g* before the liquid? cf. Ἄγλυ, ὁ κύκνος ὑπὸ Σκυθῶν, Hesych. 510. *Coilech gaithe* (W. ceiliog gwynt), i. e. gallus venti, weathercock? 511. *Teallach* (gl. focus, fire-place, hearth), perhaps for tenlach, tened-lach. 512. *Oinmid* (gl. sotus), an oaf, W. ynfyd. The -*mid* = O. Ir. mit = manti, and probably involves the root man. 513. *Geocach* (gl. mimus), apparently from jocu-s (*sed* cf. N. H. G. geck), now "a strolling player." 514. *Sboran*, "a purse," O'R. sporán, W. ysbur.

515-533. *Sgingidoir* (leg. sgingidóir? gl. pellicarius, "a furrier"), is, according to C., a "packsaddle maker;" cf. W. ysgin (fur) = Eng. skin, scing, O'R., "part of the trappings of a horse." 516. *Inadh*, a place, O. Ir. inad, frequent in Lib. Hymn.

517. *Oibhirseoir*

517. *Oibhirseoir* = adversarius. 518. *Cluithe* (gl. jocus), also cluiche, game, sport, an iu-stem. The dat. sing. occurs in the Trip. Life of Patrick: Fecht aili do patricc ic *cluithiu* iter a comaistiu (.i. *a comaltud*), "at another time P. was playing amongst his coevals" (i. e. *his foster-brothers-and-sisters*). With cluiche cf. cluichech (gl. ludibundus), Z. 778. 519, 520. *Iffearn*, iffern = infernum, W. uffern, Corn. iffarn, gen. sing. of iffern, viz. iffirnn in Z. 51. 522. Locanus (Lucanus), here identified with the Irish man's-name, Lochan; see O'D., Four Masters, A. D. 606. 533. *Fergal* is connected with ferg (anger), fairge (sea), Ούεργιόνιος (ὠκεανός) Ptol. "The proper meaning of the word [ferg] is," says Glück (K. N. 131), "motio, agitatio (compare Gr. ἔργον for Ϝέργον, ὀργή for Ϝοργή, from the root varg, Germ. werk)." Cf. Zend verez (agere). If Fergal be the W. Gwral-deg and = a Gaulish Virogalos, the elements are for "man" (Skr. vara), and the root GAL, as to which see Z., 993 n.

534–548. Of the rest of the proper names note *doctor*, glossing Ovidius. Hence there would seem to have been some Irish word resembling this name, and corresponding with W. ofydd, with which, however, Z. 3, would connect the Irish ogham. 540. *Diarmaid* seems = Derbomantis. 541. *Lochlann* is curiously like the old name for Scandinavia, Lochland, of which the dat. sing. occurs in one of the S. Gall quatrains above quoted. 542. *Murchad*, leg. muirchad, gen. muirchatho, Z. xxxii. = moricatus, a masc. u-stem. 543. *Eogan* is from εὐγενής. 545. *Concubar*, leg. Conchubar, the Anglo-Irish Connor; cf. Conchuburnensium (Book of Armagh, 9 *a*, 2), Conchobor, Z. 1133, Glück, 66, where note the aspiration of *c*. Does Con- stand for Cono- (cf. Cono-maglus, Cunobelinus), or is *c* aspirated in the combination *nc*, as in sancht (Brogan's Hymn, l. 23) = sancta; conchoimnucuir (efficit), Z. 853; conchechrat (amabunt), Z. 495; and perhaps tenchor (gl. forceps), Z. 84? 546. *Mac na hoidhche* means "son of the night;" *oidche*, O. Ir. aidche, a fem. iâ-stem, Z. 257; aidchide, "nocturnal," Leab. Breacc, cited Lib. Hymn. ed. Todd, 27. In the *h* prefixed to *oidche* here, and to *oighe*, *infra*, No. 576, Bopp would see a relic of the *s* which terminated the fem. article in the gen. sing. 547. *Uaithne* is placed opposite orpeus, i. e. Orpheus, because Uaithne is said to have been the inventor of music, under the singular circumstances described in a legend, which C. tells me is preserved in the Book of Leinster. 548. *Tadhg* (the "Teague" of English writers) is said to mean "poet."

550–554. *Deóir* (gl. diphthongus), in Z. deoger = defoger (gair, sonus), the *g* being dropt between vowels, as is the rule in Welsh, and as sometimes occurs in Irish. 551. *Senadh naom* ("holy synod"), cf. W. senedd, Corn. sened, from synodus. 552. *Cloch crisdail*, "stone of crystal." 553. *Parrtus*, leg. partus from paradisus, W. paradwys, the medial *d* being provected, as sometimes happens in foreign words: cf. aipgitir

gitir = abecedarium. Perhaps, however, the *t* may be owing to the practice pursuant to which *b, d, g* are written respectively *p, t, c*, when preceded by either *l* or *r :* see Z. 70, 71. 554. *Dair* (gl. quercus, oak-tree), gen. darach = daracas, a c-stem; cf. daur, gl. quercus, Z. 8; dairde, daurde, gl. quernus, Z. 764; daurauch, gl. quercetum, Z. 779, deruce, gl. glans: W. derw-en. Cf. δρῦν, δόρυ, Goth. triu, A. S. treóv, trýv, Eng. tree, Skr. dâru (timber), Δαρούερνον (Britanniæ oppidum), Z. 8.

555–566. *Aball*, O. W. aball-en, Corn. auall-en = apple, apfel, Aballum, &c. Ubull *quasi* abull; aball, imorro, o burgg Etale dianid ainm Abellum .i. is ass tucad sfl nan aball *prius* (Cormac's Glossary, Book of Leinster), "*Aball*, now, from a town of Italy called Abellum, i. e. it is thence that the seed of the apples was brought formerly." 556. *Coll* (W. coll-en, Corn. col-viden, Bret. kel-vézen) = coslas = hasel, corylus, whence κόρυλος. Z. 1118 compares the name Coslum, hod. Kusel, and the Slav. sheol, virga, baculus, "primitus colurnus?" whence, he says, the names of places Scheslа and Scheslitz. The adj. collde, gl. coluruus, in Z. 81. 557. *Fuindscog* (gl. fraxinus, ash-tree), leg. fuinnscog ? and cf. O. Ir. huinnius (gl. fraxinus, Z. 751), uinsenn (Irish Nennius, 116); and, perhaps, Lat. ornus for osnus: Corn. onnen, Bret. ounn-en. 558. *Fernog* (gl. alnus, alder), W. and Bret. gwernen, f., Corn. guernen, "gall. vet. vern [vernâ] in nomine fluvii Vernodubrum ;" cf. Vernosole (Glück, 35, 125). 559. *Droighin* (gl. prunus, blackthorn, sloe-tree), leg. *draighen ;* draigen is used to gloss pirus in Z. 738 ; cf. W. draen, pl. drain, *sed vide* Z. 139 *n*. 560. *Beithe* (gl. buxus, box-tree), bethe, gl. buxus, Z. 728, apparently = W. bedw, birch, Lat. betula. The word occurs in a note on Christ's cross (Lib. Hymn. 7 *b*. in marg.): cedir a cos ⁊ cupris a tenga ⁊ gius in geind deratad trethe ⁊ *bethe* in clar in roseribad in titul, i. e. "Cedar its shaft, and cypress its tongue [the upper segment], and deal the piece (?) that was put across it, and box the board whereon was written the title." 561. *Ibhar* (yew), ibar in Corm. Another Irish word for yew, *eo*, is the W. yw, Corn. hiuin, Bret. ivinen, O. H. G. iwa, N. H. G. eiben-baum, Fr. if, Sp. and Port. iva. 562. *Fichabhall* (as I read for the senseless fidhabhall, wood-apple), a fig-tree, from ficus and aball (malus), No. 555 ; cf. Corn. fichren, gl. ficus, Z. 1118. 563. *Crand gius* (pine-tree). 564. *Crand lauir*, laurel-tree (leg. erandgiús, crandlauir), with giús, perhaps cf. bí, gl. pix, Z. 25, 764. 565. *Fraech* (gl. brucus, heather), O'R.'s *fraoch*, nom. pl. neut. inna dærcæ *fróich*, gl. vaccinia, i. e. rubræ ericæ, Z. 890, which Z. calls a solitary example of the occurrence of flexion in an adjective *preceding* a substantive. Cf. however, doadhadar sunt atá *níli* dána in spirto *et* as nóindæ in spirut (Z. 360), "here is shown that there are many gifts of the Spirit, and that the Spirit is single." With fraech cf. W. grûg. 566. *Crand mucor* (gl. cornus, cornel-cherry, dogwood-tree), "dogbriar," C.

567–568. *Cuigel*

567-568. *Cuigel* (gl. colus, distaff) = W. cognil, Corn. kigel, Bret. kigel, kegel = O. H. G. cuncla, N. H. G. kunkel, all, like Fr. quenouille, It. conocchia, from Med. Lat. conucula, for colucula, from colus. 568. *Fersaid* (gl. fusus, spindle) cf. W. gwerthyd, Corn. gurhthit, Bret. gwerzid, and Lat. vert-o, verticillus, versatilis, Med. Lat. vertebrum, verteolus, "Et colus et fusi digitis occidere!"

569-575. *Teach*, tech in Z. 73, house (cf. coitchen communis = con-tech-en? Z. 73; tec-nate, gl. domesticus, Z. 769; cum-tach, ædificatio, Z. 843; daltech (gl. forum), Book of Armagh, 189 *b*. 2), apparently a sister form of teg, Z. 73 (gen. ind idultaigæ, gl. fani, Z. 822; dat. i *taig* ríg, gl. in prætorio, Z. 280), which last is W. ty, pl. tai, Corn. and Bret. ti, τέγος, *thatch* (Skr. r. sthag?). 570. *Bean do brathar*, "thy brother's wife;" *bean do meic*, gl. nurus, "thy son's wife;" as to *bean v. infra*, No. 1053. *Brathar*, leg. bráthar, gen. of bráthair, a stem in tar, declined like athair, *supra*, No. 13; and = Skr. bhrâtṛ, Goth. brôthar, Lat. frâter, Gr. φρητήρ, ἀδελφός, Hesych.; *do*—O. Ir. du, do—the possess. pron. of 2 pers. sing.; W. dy, Bret. da, = Skr. tava, the original *t* having been worn down to a medial in this frequently used word. The *d* of this pronoun, however, becomes *t* when the vowel is elided. Cf. tesérge, "thy resurrection," Book of Armagh, 18 *b*, 1; conicim tanacul, "I am able to save thee," *ibid.*, 186 *a*. Note that no word corresponding to Skr. snushâ, Gr. νυός, Lat. nurus, Goth. snur, has yet been found in Celtic. Skr. çvaçrû, Gr. ἑκυρά, Lat. socrus, Goth. svaihro (mother-in-law), are represented by the W. chwegr, but no such Irish word can be quoted. It would, however, be rash to draw conclusions from circumstances like this, till we make more progress in collecting our ancient words and names, of which, perhaps, scarce one-third is accessible to the philologer. 572. *Cugan*, gl. penus, Z. 80, cucan, gl. penus. 573. *Lég loghmar* (read lóghmar), a precious stone = O. Ir. liacc lógmar, liacc = W. llech, a *flag*, a flat stone. Liacc is a fem. â-stem: is[ed] béss didu *ind liacc:* berir ilbeim friss *et* intí dothuit fair conboing a chnámi; intí for a tuit som, imorro, atbail side: "It is this, now, that the stone is: many a blow is given to it, and he that falls on it breaks his bones; but he on whom it falls *he* perishes," Z. 609: gen. in accclesia magná aird*licce*, Book of Armagh, 9 *b*, 2: dat. for *leice* luim, Fiacc, 16, "on a bare stone." 574. *Long luath* (gl. carbassus), "a swift ship;" long, gen. luinge (W. llong, fem., whence llynghes, a fleet), a fem. â-stem: is *long* from the Lat. navis *longa*, or may we refer it to the Skr. root langh (salire, ire)? The acc. sing. loing glosses vas in the Book of Armagh, 177 *b*, 1; carbasus, "eyn schiff das keyn bodem hat."—Dief. Med. Lat. Dict. 575. *Fairge* (sea), *v. supra*, No. 328, a fem. iâ-stem, O. Ir. fairgge, Z. 928; fairggæ, foirggæ, Z. 1125.

576-579. *Bru na hoighe* (gl. aulus), "the virgin's womb," leg. *brú na hóighe* (gl. alvus).

alvus). 577. *Sroll* (gl. byssus, βύσσος) is spelt sról, and explained "silk, satin, gauze, crape," by O'R., but byssus is a yellowish linen. With—578. *Uir* (gl. humus, the ground), Pictet compares εὐρύς, Skr. uru (large), fem. urvî (earth); gen. úire, Corm. v. Gaire; Corm. v. Mur, glosses ur by talam: so also sub v. *Ur.* Ur. tréide fordingair, úr chetamus .i. talam, ⁊ úr cech nuæ amail asmberar imb úr; úr dana cech nolc, inde dicitur isna br. n. [brethib nemed] lán dosíntbach cach núr .i. cech nolc. "Ur: three things it means; úr, in the first place, i. e. the earth; and úr, everything new, as is said, *imb úr* [fresh butter]: úr, then, is everything bad. Hence is said in the *Bretha nemed*, "fully *dostathach*(?) is everything *úr*, i. e. everything bad.'" Adj. búrde, "ad humum portinens," Z. 764. 579. *Paiper*, of course from papyrus, πάπυρος.

580–587. *Dorus lis*, "door of a *less*," now spelt lios, an a-stem, cf. Lissus: "a Dun, pronounced Doon [dún, cf. Eng. town] is an elevated, circular, enclosing wall or bank, within which a dwelling-house was erected. A Dun required to be surrounded by a wet fosse or trench [a moat] to distinguish it from the Rath which had not a trench ... Lios was another name for the Dun, but that it often contained within it more than one dwelling-house." (C. *Cath Maighe Léna*, 78, 79.) Cf. W. llys, a court, hall. The dat. sing. of less occurs in the Book of Armagh, 17 b, 1: Dirrógel ... ochter nachid con a scilb it[ar] fid ⁊ mag ⁊ lenu con al*lius* ⁊ allubgort; also in Patrick's Hymn: Crist il *lius*, Crist iś sius, Crist in erus, "Christ in the court, Christ in the chariot-seat, Christ in the poop," i. e. Christ be with us while at home, or travelling by land or sea; the gen. pl. occurs in loig-*less*, before cited: in Gaelic, *lios*, gen. *lise*, is fem., and means "a garden." 582. *Feorus* (gl. acirus), *feoras* is explained "the spindle-tree, prick-wood," by O'R. (on whom, of course, no reliance can be placed), which reminds one of W. grwysen, gooseberry. Should we read acinus for acirus, or is it for acerus, galingale, sweet flag? 583. *Buachaill bó*, ad v. bubulcus bovum; buachaill (gen. muine *buachaille*, Book of Armagh, 17 b, 1) is bóchaill in Z. 28, 67; cf. W. bugail, Corn. bugel, gl. pastor. 584. *Buachaill muce* (swineherd) is lit. bubulcus porcorum; buachaill, like bubulcus and βουκόλος, merging its special meaning of cowherd in that of herdsman; cf. ἱπποβουκόλος, horseherd, and see Max Müller, *Oxford Essays*, 1856, p. 17. 585. *Múine* (gl. rubus, bramble-bush) occurs, as we have seen, in Fiacc, 24, and in the Book of Armagh. 586. *Airgeach* (gl. remulus, a small oar), but airgeach is a plunderer, O'R., also an owner of herds (nirbu airgech air slébe, Brog. 11; cf. *airge*, gl. armentum, *infra*, No. 754), and there is probably some mistake here. 587. *Dris* (gl. tomús, i. e. dumus, bush, bramble); cf. dris-tenach, gl. dumetum, Z. 777, driss, gl. vepres, Z. 139, Corn. dreis, gl. vepres, Z. 1118, W. dryssien (frutex), Z. 301.

588–593. As

588–593. As to these ordinals, *céd* (céd neach, "first anyone") is only found in Z.'s glosses in fochetoir, leg. fochétóir, statim, illico, lit. sub prima hora. The lengthened form cét-ne is used instead. But we find the adverbs cétu, ciatu, céta (primùm), and Corm. has cétamus (imprimis), cét-aidche (first night), Fíacc, 32; cétbliadain, first year, Z. xxviii. The *t* is unaspirated, owing to *n* having been lost before it; this *n* is found in W. kentaf, kyntaf, Z. 230; Gaulish *Cintu*-genus, "first-born," = O. Ir. Cetgen, Book of Armagh, 11 *b*, 2. *Indara neach* seems simply the old indala nech (the second anyone), the liquid *l* becoming *r*, as in imlesen, *supra*, &c.; ala = W. eil, alter, secundus; ala occurs in Z. 313, with the meaning of "second," in connexion with the numeral deac, 10: cethar brottae, 7 *ala* rann deac brotto (4 moments, and the 12th (2 + 10) part of a moment): with the meaning of "one of two:" indala fiacail, Z. 926. With ala we may, perhaps, connect the prep. al, gl. ultra, Z. 602, which occurs with a suffixed pronoun in Colmán's Hymn, 50: Benedacht for Columcille con nóebaib Alban *alla*, " blessing on Columcille, with the saints of Scotland besides him." *Tres*, third, O. Ir. triuss, tris, gen. tres, Z. 316, is not easily explained: can it have been a distributive = Zend thrishva? or an old superlative in -istha? But how is gen. tres to be accounted for? A passing over to the *s*-declension is possible, but unlikely. *Cethruma*, O. Ir. cethramad, v. *supra*, No. 142. The dat. sing. neut. occurs in the Book of Armagh, 177 *b*, 2: iár *cethramad* laithiu (gl. a nudus [nudius] quartana die). *Cuigedh*, O. Ir. cóiced = O. W. pimphet, Lat. quinctu-s: *Seis-ed* = O. W. chuech-et = svecs-a-ta, Lat. sextu-s.

594–604. *Gabáiltech* (gl. captus), from gabáil, W. cafael, cavail, Z. 160, capere. 595. *Curracach* (gl. cuculatus, i. e. cuckolded?), lit. crested. Horne Tooke was not so original as he supposed when he wrote, "In English we do not call them cuculi, but cuculati (if I may coin a word on this occasion)." 596. *Atanach* (gl. capuciatus), cf. Corn. hot, gl. caputium, W. hotan, hotyn (a cap). 597. *Inarach*—598. *Muincillech*—599. *Fallaingech*—600. *Tribhusach*, adjectives, and—601. *Coronta*, a participle, from bases considered *supra*. 602. *Foirmtech* (gl. invidus). The subst. format, O'R.'s *formad* (envy, ex man, like μῆνις): acc. s. appears in the pref. to Patrick's hymn, Lib. Hymn., cited in Petrie's Tara, 32: bid ditin do ar cech neim ⁊ *format*, "it will be a protection to him against every poison and envy;" cf. W. gorfynt. 603. *God* (gl. blaesus, lisping, speaking indistinctly), "stammering," according to C., who tells me that the Danes were called by the Irish na Gaill *guit;* cf. W. gyth (a murmur). 604. *Bodhar*, deaf, W. byddar, Corn. bothar, Bret. bouzar, Skr. badhira. (Hence Eng. bother?)

605–614. *Bacach* (gl. claudus, limping, halting, lame, W. bachawg, "crooked") occurs

occurs in the acc. pl. masc., spelt bacachu, as a gloss on the word luscu, in the second line of the 17th couplet of Fíacc's hymn :—

> Iccaid luscu la truscu, mairb doeflnscad do bethu.

> He used to heal the halt, with the lepers; the dead he used to raise them to life.

606. *Ordaighe* (gl. auratus), *ór*, gl. *aurum*, *infra*, gen. óir, from the Lat. aurum for ausum (Skr. root ush, urere). If the word were Celtic, the *s* would have been lost between the vowels. 607. *Airgedach* (gl. argenteus), from *airged*, gl. argentum, *infra*, in O. Ir. argat (gen. arggait, argit, Book of Armagh, 17 b, 1) = W. ariant, Bret. arc'hant, Corn. arhanz, Old Keltic Argento-ratum, Argento-magus, &c., Zend erezata, Lat. argentum, Osc. aragoto, Skr. rajata. 608. *Iarnaighe* (leg. íarnaidhe?), gl. ferreus, from íarn, for ísarn (iron), W. haearn, Corn. hoern, Z. 120; cf. the Gaul. Isarnodurum (iron door?), *iarunn*, gl. ferrum, *infra*; the gen. sing. seems to occur in Z. 926, ar fuilib híairn for fhairn = ísarni, the aspirate being displaced as in the W. and Corn. forms); cf. Skr. ayas, Eng. ore, Goth. eisarn (ferreus), from which the Celtic stem ísarno can hardly be taken, the deriv. suffix -arn being common in Celtic, but rare in Gothic. 609. *Luaidheamhail* (gl. plumbeus), from luaidhe, gl. plumbum, *infra* (cf. Eng. lead, load?), and *samhail* = samalis = W. hafal, Lat. similis, Gr. ὁμαλός, &c. 610. *Stanamhail* (gl. stanneus), from stan (sdan, gl. stannum, *infra*). 611. *Umamhail* (gl. aereus), from umae (*humae* fogrigedar, "aes quod dat vocem, sonat, Z. 445), O. W. emed, Mod. W. efydd. 612. *Fundamintech* (gl. fundatus), from fundamentum. 613. *Scithech ón éligi* (gl. fessus, "wearied from the way," i. e. journey). 614. *Scithech ó obair* (gl. lassus, "wearied from work"), leg. scithech, and compare scíth, Z. 26, sciith, Z. 669: ni confil bas *sciith* lim act rop ar Christ, "death is not a burden to me if only it be for Christ."

615–621. *Tinnisnech* (O'R. tinneasnach), "speedy, hasty." 617. *Nemhtindisnech*, "unspeedy, unhasty." 616. *Salach* (salacious, lustful), perhaps borrowed from salax, root sal (sal-io, ἅλλομαι, for σάλjομαι). Salach subsequently glosses sordidus, dirty = W. halawg, cf. halou, gl. stercora, Z. 1095 (the man's name Connsalach, gen. sing. Coinnselich, Book of Armagh, 18 a, 1, comes from cennsal, imperium), and hence would seem connected with O. H. G. salo, not clear, troubled, Fr. sale. 618. *Suirgech*, gl. procus, wooer (in O'R. suireach), perhaps connected with στοργή, στέργω; cf. serce, amor, W. serch, with the *s* preserved (*st* at the beginning of a word in Welsh, as a rule, loses the *t*, not the *s*). 620. *Gortach* (gl. famelicus, famished, starved), O. Ir. gorte (famine), a fem. iâ-stem, Z. 1006 = gardh-ti-â, Skr. r. grdh (avidum esse). 621. *Fiarsúilech* (if I read the word aright), gl. strabonus, squint-eyed; fiar, crooked = W.

gŵyr.

gŵyr. Bopp may be right in comparing fiar with Lat. vârus, Skr. vakra curvus, flexuosus. So Gaulish mûros seems Gr. μακρός.

625–629. *Tengtach* (gl. linguosus), dótengtach (leg. dothengtach?), gl. bilinguosus, hypocritical, double-tongued, from tenge (tongue), gen. tengad, *v. supra*, which, from these adjectives, would seem to have been a t-stem. 626. *Dércach* (leg. déircach?), charitable, from déire, alms, deserce (amor), Z. 78. 628. *Briathrach* (gl. verbosus), from briathar (word), a fem. â-stem. 629. *Sbegach* (ἄγλωσσος, clinguis, not glib of tongue), not in O'R.

630–634. *Fonamaideach* (gl. ridiculosus, facetious, droll), O'R. has fanamhad, ridicule, and fonamadach, which he translates by "contemptuous;" "making game," is, O'D. tells me, the meaning now attributed to the word; cf. Eng. *fun?* 631. *Failgeach* (gl. egenus, needy, indigent). 632. *Casta* (gl. crispus, curled, crisped), from *casaim*. 633, 634. *Slán* (gl. sanus) *eslán* (gl. insanus), have been connected, *supra*, with W. llawen.

635–639. *Edmur* (gl. zelotypus), O. Ir. étmar [= Gaulish Iantumarus, Glück, 78], from ét zelus, Z. 22, æct, Z. 343 (fern *ét* fri saibapstalu darmchensa, "vestra æmulatio pro me contra pseudoapostolos," Z. 607, Skr. r. yam(niti)? 636. *Dluith* (gl. densus), an adjectival i-stem; glosses dense in Gild. Lorica. Z. seems to have mistaken for the adj. dlúith the subst. dlúthe, wrongly rendered "apertus" in Z. 30, notwithstanding his glosses contain tri beulu *dlutai*, gl. fixis labris, Z. 1015, *dluthe* in tinf[id] denaib conso[naib], Z. 1021; literally, connexion (coherence) of the aspiration to [i. e. with] the consonants (in χ, θ, φ). Dlúithe also means a chink: huand *dlúithi* scim, gl. tenui rima, Z. 261; and cf. dlúth, gl. stamen (the warp in a loom), Z. 30; tre chomdluthad, gl. per synæresin, Z. 985, rundlúth, gl. densaverat, Z. 435. 637. *Goirt* (gl. acidus), perhaps connected with the verb in "ma *gorith* loch cith in e chuis nu in e laim," which Z. renders (p. 1006) "si dolet locus vel in ejus pede vel in ejus manu." 638. *Ballach* (gl. urbiculatus) is now not "rounded, circular," but "freckled," from ball (spot). Cf. W. ball, "eruption, plague." In Z. ball, a masc. a-stem, always means membrum, and agrees in form, declension, and gender with φαλλός. 639. *Slemain* (gl. lubricus, slippery, smooth), an adj. i-stem: a sister-form, of the a-declension, is slemon, which occurs in a marginal gloss on the Lib. Hymn. copy of the Altus Prositer; nom. pl. neut.: is airi asbertar étrumma ꝛ *slemna* huare nád techtat tinfed, Z. 1022 (i. e. therefore are they called light and smooth, because they have not aspiration); slemna, gl. levia, Z. 737, slemon = W. *llyfn*, fem. *llefn*. Cf. N. H. G. schleifen, Eng. slip.

640–649. *Fairsing* (gl. amplus, spacious, roomy), farsinge, the subst. from this, occurs in Lib. Hymn., 5 *b*, Colman's Hymn, line 43, as a gloss on lethu:—

Robbem

Robbem cen es illethu la ainglin imbithbethu.

May we be without age, in space¹, with angels in eternal life!

641. *Luathgairech* (gl. nervosus), generally means "rejoicing," "exulting," from luath (swift), and gáire (joy), W. gware (play). Here it seems equivalent to energetic, vigorous in expression (quis Aristotele *nervosior?* Cic.). 642. *Dealbhdha* (gl. formosus), O. Ir. delbde, from delb (forma, figura, imago, paradigma), fem. W. delw, Z. 99, and cf. doilbthid figulus, Z. 987, indoilbthid, gl. figurate, Z. 984, dolbud (figmentum), Z. 768, leads one to think the root DAL which is, perhaps, etymologically connected with Lat. forma, Skr. r. dhṛ. 643. *Uchtard* (gl. strumosus, wenny) rather seems "high-breasted," from ucht and ard. 644. *Craessach*—645. *Fésógach*—646. *Gaethmar*—648. *Milech*, all from nouns noticed, *supra*. 647. *Bronnmar*, from brú, gen. s. bronn, W. bru (womb): a dimin. from brú occurs in the dat. sing.: his *bronnait* (gl. infra ventriculum), Z. 593. 649. *Snethach*, leg. snedhach (nitty), W. neddog, is interesting, furnishing, as it does, a hint as to what must have been running in the heads of the European Aryans at an early period, for sned, Z. 1126 (W. nedd-en, Bret. niz) is Slav. gnida, Gr. κόνις, κόνιδ-ος, N. H. G. nisse, Lith. gli(n)da, Lat. le(n)s, le(n)dis.

650–653. *Coisinech* (if I read the word rightly) means, I presume, taking short steps, going pedetentim, step by step, slowly. 651. *Croindtilli* is probably a blunder for crointsilech, an adj. formed from croutsaile, phlegm, spittle, derived by Corm. from grant (grey), and saile = saliva. 652. *Gerbach* (gl. rugosus, wrinkled, shrivelled) is now "scabby." 653. *Bocoidech* (gl. maculosus, spotted), leg. bocóidech? from bocóid, a spot, O'R.

654–659. *Anmach*, from anim, *v. supra*. 655. *Clúmar*—656. *Michlúmar*, from clú (gl. rumor, Z. 68, also fama), W. clyw; cf. Slav. slovo (verbum, sermo), slava (gloria), Gr. κλέϝος, Skr. çravas, rumor. The W. for famosus is clodfawr = clotomâros (the O. H. G. Hlodomâr, Glück, 81); cf. with clod, Ir. cloth (fame, praise) = cluta-s, Gr. κλυτός, Lat. in-clytus, Eng. 'loud; Ir. cluas (ear) = W. clust (cf. Eng. *'list*). The root reduplicates in Celtic. Thus in Irish: rot-cho-chlad-ar (hears thee), Z. 496; ecchluista .i. nocluinfitbea (auditum erit, Brehon Law gloss). And in Welsh: ciglif (audivi), Z. 420 = Skr. çuçrâva. 657. *Breallach* (gl. spadosus) I cannot explain with any certainty; spadosus is, perhaps, a med. Lat. adj., from spado (σπάδων), an impotent person. 658. *Prebach*, kicking (preabaim, I kick, O'R.). Is retrocosus for calcitrosus?

¹ Perhaps we should rather translate "in greatness," "in grandeur;" lethe and fairsinge, like amplitudo, may well have attained to this secondary signification.

citrosus? or a barbarous hybrid from retro and the Irish cos (= coxa), leg from knee down, foot? 659. *Geal* (white), O. Ir. gol, *v. supra*.

660–669. *Tegaisge* (gl. doctus), *tecoisce*, gl. doctior, *infrd*: cf. sochoise, gl. docibilem, Z. 832; cose (institutio) Z. 53; cossce, *ib.* 61; cosce, *ib.* 78: *coscitir* ind fir et doairbertar foréir dé, "the men are taught and brought under the will of God," Z. 618. I know not if O. Ir. écosc (habitus, forma), Z. 832, 235, or W. *dangaws*, demonstration; *arddangos*, to demonstrate, be connected with this word. 661. *Maith*, good, O. Ir. nom. pl. maithi, Z. 883 (an i-stem), W. mad; cf. the Gaulish name Teutomatus. 662. *Olc* (bad), n. pl. masc. uilc, uilec, Z. 252; acc. pl. masc. ulcu, Z. 457. In the nom. and acc. pl. neut., when followed by *sa*, this adjective drops its proper termination: inna *olc*-sa, Z. 354, 676. 663. *Mór*, O. Ir. már, mór (W. mawr), great = μακρός? (the guttural was lost even in Gaulish; cf. Virdomarus, Brogi marus [W. *bro*, country], Segomaros [Skr. sahas, strength], Iantumarus [Ir. étmar], Nertomarus [Ir. nertmar¹]); cf. μέγας, mag-nus, Skr. mah-at, for maghânt, Goth. mik-ils, μεγάλου. 664. *Beg* (small), O. Ir. becc, W. bach, cf. Gaul. "*Becco* Mocconis fil.," Z. 77. 665. *Solus, v. supra.* 666. *Taithnemhach* (gl. candidus), from do + aith + nemh; cf. W. ednyf, ednyw (purity, vigour), with which we may, perhaps, connect Adnamatius, Namatius (Glück, 39), *namhain*, and Namnetes (Glück, 140). 667. *Sanntach* (greedy, avaricious, covetous) occurs in Z. 78, from sant, with which Z. wrongly compares the Gaulish tribe-name Santones, for W. and Bret. chwant (invidia, desiderium) points to an Old Celtic svanataka. Cf. Suanetes, Consuanetes (Glück, 28, 64). 668. *Dingbala* —669. *M'idingbala* (worthy, unworthy), I can in nowise explain, unless, indeed, dingbala be from do-ind-gabál (acceptabilis).

670–674. *Imdha* (gl multus), in Z. 75, imde (multus, abundans) = ambitias, imda, gl. opulentus, *ib.* = ambitvas? cf. Ambitui, a Gaulish tribe-name; imbed (gl. ops copia, Z. 75), all from the prep. imm, W. amm, Gaulish ambi (circa) = Lat. amb, Gr. ἀμφί, Skr. abhi, Eng. um (in umstroke = circumference, Fuller), which has often an intensive meaning. 671. *Glan* (purus, mundus, clarus), mod. W. glân, with inorganic lengthening of the vowel (Glück, 187, justly compares the Keltic river-name Glana), act ranglana, gl. siquis emundaverit se, Z. 454, glantar as (cliditur, Z. 985), hói ní roglante and, Z. 1060; cf. Eng. clean, N. H. G. klein? 672. *Teirc* (gl. rarus), whence

---

[1] Curiously enough, we find many O. German names formed with this adj. and identical with Celtic appellations, e. g., Hadumar (= a Gaulish Catumâros), W. catmor, Illodomar (= a Gaulish Clotomâros), W. clodfawr, &c., Glück, 78, 81. So Hincmar = Ex-cincomarus, Sigumar, Segimerus, bod. Siegmar = Segomaros.

whence teircc, *infra* (gl. raritudo), thin, scanty. 673. *Beg, v. supra.* 674. *Daingen no cruaidh* (gl. durus), daingen glosses firmus, *infra, édaingen* (infirmus), O'R.'s daingean, "strong, secure, close;" isin dun *daingen*, Z. 30, "in the strong fort;" daingnigim (gl. moenio), Z. *ib.* Apparently donjon, Eng. dungeon, are Celtic words, perhaps cognate with O. H. G. dwingan, Eng. twinge, tongs, tack (Zwecke) : *cruaidh*, "hard, callous, severe," O'R.

675–694. *Fliuch*, moist, wet = W. gwlyp (= vlievas ?) ; cf. *fliuchidhecht* (gl. liquor), *infra*, fliuchaide (humidus, Z. 272 ; fliuchaidatu humiditas, Z. 66 ; fliuchaigim, gl. lippio, Z. 65 ; fliuchdere, gl. lippus, Z. 65 ; cf. Corn. glibor (moisture) = W. gwlybwr [= Lat. liquor], and O. W. rogulipias, gl. olivavit, Z. 420. If fliuch, gwlyp, be, as conjectured, from vlievas, we may be correct in comparing the word with Lat. lippus for vlippus (where *pp* may have sprung from *kv*, as in ἵππος, from *akva*, Skr. açva), O. Slov. vlŭgŭkŭ, humidus. 676. *Dochenélach*, low-born, ignoble ; cenél genus, gen. ceneiuil = O. W. cenitol, Z. 172. The dat. sing. of cenél occurs in the following passage in the Book of Armagh, 17 *a*, 2, now for the first time correctly printed : Conggab patricc iarnaid puirt indruimm daro .i. druim lias, Fácab patricc adaltæ .n. and benignus aainm ⁊ fuitinse xuii. annís. Gabais caille lapatricc lassar ingen anfolmitho di*cheniul* caicháin. Baiade and tarési .m. benigni trifichtea bliadne, "Patrick afterwards abode at a place [or house—observe the locative of *port*] in Druimm Daro, i. e. Druimm Lias. Patrick left his pupil there. Benignus was his name, and he was therein for 17 years. Lassar, a daughter of Anfolmid (?), of the race of Caichán, took the veil from Patrick [lit. cepit velum apud Patricium]. Three scores of years was she there after Benignus." 677. *Fada* (long), O. Ir. fota, Z. 942 ; fote, Z. 966, n. pl. bithfotai, semper longi, Z. 824. The subst. is fot, Z. 230, gen. fuit, Z. 66. 678. *Cumair* (short, brief), O. Ir. cumbair, whence cumbro (brevitas) ar *chumbri*, Z. 1074 ; cf. W. byr, Lat. brevis. 681. *Firénach*—682. *Ainfirénach* (just, unjust) ; cf. fírián (verax, justus), Z. 115, &c. ; gen. pl. hignimaib fer *firean* (Patrick's hymn), firianugud (justice, justification), Z. 53, 346 ; firianigedar (justifies), Z. 445. Cf. W. gwirion, from gwir-iawn : *iawn* is "equity," "just," "meet ;" cf. O. Ir. án ("wealth," nom. pl. and gen. pl. ane, dat. pl. ánib, acc. pl. anu, Z. 934, a masc. u-stem), with which Dr. Siegfried is inclined to connect the Zend yâna (see Haug, *Die Gáthá's*, p. 42). 683. *Brén* (gl. fetidus), brénaim (puteo), bréntu (foetor), Z. 1085 ; cf. W. braen (rotten), braenu (to moulder) ; perhaps connected with braigim pedo, Z. 431, the *g* being lost before *n*, as in the instances quoted *supra*. 684. *Salach* (gl. sordidus), *v.* No. 616. 688. *Tempoll*, from templum, as—689. *Taiberne*, from taberna, and—691. *Reilic* (gl. simitherium, a cemetery), from reliquiæ (observe the hard

$c = qv$,

c = *qv*, as in mac), gen. sing. timchell na *relgi*, "round the cemetery" (Leab. Breacc. cited Lib. Hymn. ed. Todd, 31). 693. *Adhlucadh* (gl. sepulchrum), *Adhlaead* (gl. monumentum), *infra*, No. 759, are etymologically obscure to me. Can they be a corruption of adnacul (sepulcrum), Z. 731 (i slebti *adranact* cremthann, "C. was buried in Sletty," Book of Armagh, 17 *b*)? with which, perhaps, νέκυς, Zend. naçu, Skr. r. naç, "to die," Lat. nex, nox, Ir. nocht, may be connected. 694. *Edail* (gl. lucrum), O'R. cadail, leg. éadail, W. *ennill* (masc.) = antalli ? (gain, profit, acquired wealth). Gael. *eudail*, "treasure," cattle, feudail, "cattle," "herds," (with inorganic prefixing of *f*?).

695–699. *Mirbail* (gl. miraculum, wonder), an i-stem, acc. pl. dogni in noemog-sa na *mirbuli* mora (this holy virgin performed the great miracles), Leabhar Breacc, cited by Dr. Todd, Lib. Hymn. 65. This word is taken from mirabile. 696. *Bachlog* (gl. monaculum, i. e. monaculus?); should we read bachlóg, and is this a playful dimin. from bachal = baculus, crozier? Or is this word connected in meaning with bachlach (famulus), *supra*? and is monaculum a contemptuous word for servant, slave, a meaning often attributed to manach (monachus) in Irish, as will be seen from a note on S. Hilary's hymn in Dr. Todd's ed. of Lib. Hymn. 699. *Diner* (gl. jentaculum), from the English *dinner*.

700–708. *Criathar* (gl. cribrum, sieve) = crétara, Corn. croider, Bret. krouczer: glosses cerebrum in Z. 22 (the scribe having obviously mistaken cerebrum for cribrum): Skr. root kṛi, to pour out. Cf. κρησέρα, Benfey, G. W. ii. 171. 701. *Muilind* (gl. molendinum), *Muileand* (gl. pistrinum), *infra*, No. 711, mulenn (gl. pistrinum), Z. 740, is probably, like W. Corn. and Bret. melin, from the Latin mŏlendīnum (mŏlo); cf. muilneoir, a miller, O'D., Gr. xxxiv. Though the word for mill may be a foreign word, the root is certainly in Celtic: cf. Ir. meilim (I grind), W. malu (to grind); and cf. μύλη, O. H. G. muli, Lith. malunas, Eng. mill. 702. *Garrga* (gl. atrium, hall), said to be "court-yard," "enclosure" (but read garga, and cf. Skr. gṛha, house?). 703. *Tiradh* (gl. territorium, if this be what our careless copyist had before him), leg. tíradh (kiln-drying), for tirsadh? tirme (ariditas), tírim (aridus), both in Z. 1070, gl. 15, ho tirmai .i. co na bí tirim (from dryness, i. e. that it be not dry), tír (terra), all from Skr. r. tṛsh (tars), to thirst, "ursprünglich offenbar trocknen, vgl. gr. τέρσ-ομαι. Das goth. thaursja ich trockne, euphonisch für thursja (und dieses für tharsja) stützt sich wie das lat. torreo (aus torsco) auf die skr. causalform tarsháyâmi" (Bopp, vergl. gramm. 2te ausg. i. 105). One would have expected the *r* doubled as in *carr* (*supra*), Skr. karsha, "dragging." 704. *Orlar*, leg. orlár? (gl. vestibulum, a forecourt), lár, W. llawr is solum. Can the *or* be = παρά? cf. Ar-morica, παραλία, or is *or* for

for *aur*, and this for *air*, Gaul. *are*, as in do*aur*chanim (gl. sagio), Z. 10. 705. *Stocronna* (stirpidivortium, separation of a stock), from stoc (stirps)—cf. Corn. stoc, gl. stirps—and ranna (leg. rannadh?), a division, parting. Note the assimilation of the first *a* in ranna to the *o* of stoc, and cf. ocond, ocon, oco, Z. 594. 706. *Cris tribhuis* (gl. lumbarium), "belt of the trowsers" (tribhus, *v. supra*). 707. *Sgornachan* (gl. epiglotum, the epiglottis): sgornachán, says C., is now "a long-necked fellow," cf. Gael. *sgòrnach*, "throat, neck." 708. *Crombéol*, gl. gernonum (if I read the words rightly), a moustache (cf. with gernonum O. Fr. grignon, grenon, guernon, "bart sowohl der oberlippe wie des kinnes," Diez, E. W. 182, and O. H. G. grani (plur.), M. H. D. gran, O. N. grön, there cited. I know not if there ever was such a word as granni, "long hair," O'R., but it is possible there was, as grannaidh (hair) occurs in Gaelic. I have never met crombéol, except in the Anglicised form crommeal:—

"They tell me the stranger has given command
That *crommeal* and coolun shall cease in this land."

S. FERGUSON.

709–719. *Sgeota* (gl. cartesium), spelt—710. *Sgéotha* (gl. sacritegium) seems to be a bag or wallet for carrying ecclesiastical books or utensils. C. quotes: *Sceóta* nan aidbheadh ar muin chléirig riachois, Book of Fermoy, 88 *b, b*. 711. *Muilleand*, leg. muileann (gl. pistrinum, a pounding-mill), *v. supra*, No. 701. 712. *Cliathach* (gl. clastrum) seems to be an enclosure made of hurdles, from cliath, as to which *v. supra*. In Gaelic this word means "the frame of the ribs," "the chest." 713. *Tech na merdreach* (gl. prostibulum), "the harlots' house." 714. *Braicein* (gl. redimiculum, a band, girdle), is, perhaps, a garter (from brace-a?). 716. *Bile* (gl. ventilogium, a weathercock, Dief.) seems a blunder; *bile*, so far as I know, has in Ireland only the two meanings: "border," and "old tree" (such, e. g., as grows by a holy well or in a fort). In Scotland it also means "leaflet," "blossom." 717. *Ceis* (gl. stragulum, covering, rug, horse-cloth) is the Corn. peis, gl. tunica, powe (tunica), Z. 123, *peus* gruee, gl. toral, Z. 124, W. pais, pl. peisiau, Z. 1121. Cf. eass-ock? 718. *Dithen* (gl. lolium, darnel), O'R.'s dithoin, W. llys *dyn*. 719. *Crand glesta*, leg. *glésta* (gl. plectrum, the stick for striking the chords of a harp or other stringed instrument); *crand* (W. pren), O. Ir. crann, has occurred frequently, *suprd: glésta*, gen. sing. of glésadh; cf. Gael. gleusadh, "a tuning," "act of tuning," &c. O'R. has gleusaim, "I prepare, tune, arrange;" gléus, "key or gamut in music." Cf. W. glwys, "pure, pleasant."

720–724. *Teine creasa* (gl. igniferrium), fire of [the] girdle, i. e. flint-steel-and-tinder; as to *teine* (MS. teini), *v. supra*, and compare Zend tafnu (hot) ex TAPNU, as Ir. suan (sleep), W. hun is from SVAPNA; *creasa*, gen. of cris, which occurs *supra* in *cris* tribhuis, gl. lumbarium. 721. *Dubhradan* (gl. scrupulum), leg. dubhradán? I have never met elsewhere; perhaps it is a dimin. of dubhradh, "shade, eclipse," O'R., and may mean "trouble," "anxiety," figurative meanings of scrupulus, properly a pointed pebble. 722. *Tuairgin* (gl. teretorium, i. e. tritura). The O. Ir. verb and subst. occur in Z. 853: dofuairec (triturat): ar is bés leosom in daim do *thúareuin* ("for it is a custom with them for the oxen to thresh"); and pistor is glossed by fer dénma bairgine *tuarcain*, dofuaircitis inna grán la arsidi, "a man who makes bread [lit. a man of making of bread] by pounding: among the ancients they used to pound the grains;" and tuarcun glosses tribulatio, comthúarcon, contritio, Z. 738. 723. *Cluain gabála* (gl. herbagium): *cluain*, of which the dat. occurs in Z. xxxii. hi *cluain* maccunois, is a meadow, a lawn, in Scotch Gaelic also "a bower," = clôni, W. clyn, "brake," "thicket:" cf. Cluniûcum, hod. Clugny; *gabála*, gen. of gabáil (capere, captio), and cluain gabála is, according to C., an Irish legal term for "an appropriated field, a field not held in common." 724. *Caire* (gl. caldarium, "a vessel containing warm water for bathing"), W. pair (caldron), Corn. pêr, Fr. pair-ol, generally means caldron (as in *Coire* Breccáin, Corm., now Corryvreckan). It also means "a hollow or cul de sac in the mountains," Reeves, Vit. Col. 88, where Coirc Salchain occurs, and in this sense has been adopted into the English language as "corry;" coire = ΚΑΕΡΙΑ or ΡΑΕΡΙΑ, Γ. ΚΑΚ, ΡΑΚ (No. 240, *suprà*), as dér = δάκρυ, Goth, tagr; fiar, W. gŵyr = vakra, vârus; sár = Skr. çakra, Lat. sacer; mắr = μακρός.

725–729. *Longport* (gl. castrum), leg. longphort = W. llongborth (ship-harbour); *longport* glosses *sosad* in H. 3, 18, p. 523. It is not easy to see how its elements—*long* ship (v. *supra*) and *port* (a house, place, harbour)—can when combined express the idea of castrum. *Port*, gen. and loc. sing. puirt, dat. sing. purt (Lib. Hymn. ed. Todd, 13) is, perhaps, connected with Zend peretu, Eng. ford. Dief. G. W. ii. 365. 726. *Mainister*, gen. manestrech, Z. xxviii., from monasterium, but with a remarkable change to the *c*-declension. 727. *Fortacht* (gl. suffragium), here "a favourable decision;" cf. fortachtid, gl. fautor, Z. 766, 845; acc. s. fortachtain, Z. 270, a fem. n-stem, generally "assistance." The verb occurs in Leab. Breacc (cited by Todd, L. H. 65), is hí *fortaigess* da [leg. dona, dna?] cech oen bis cumca ocus in guasacht (she it is, then, that helps every one who is in anguish and in danger); fortacht, Z. 195: co fordumthésidse, "that ye may help me," Z. 335: fortiag (gl. conniveo), Z. 438. 728. *Proindtech* (gl. refectorium), and—729. *Codaltech* (gl. dormitorium), are, respectively, compounds of *tech*, house, with *proind*, W. prain, from Lat. prandium, and *codal*, whence *codlaim*, I sleep, O'R. The O. Ir. contul (?) dormio (ma *conatil* si dormis, Z. 1053, *contuil* cach úadib forsét, Fíacc, 31) appears connected with this.

Proindtech

Proiudtech (spelt praintech) occurs in the Book of Armagh, 18 *b*, 1 : airm ifuirsitis in torcc arimbad and furruimtis *apraintech.*

730–739. *Speilp* (gl. coopertorium, i. e. cooperimentum ? cooperculum ?) is explained "a belt, armour," by O'R., but by C. "a girdle or swathe of linen." 731. *Tunna* (gl. dolium, a large jar), exactly O. Norse tunna, is "a cask" in O'R.; hardly a Celtic word; cf. W. tynell, Corn. tonnel, Bret. tonel, French tonneau, M. H. G. tonne, Eng. tun, &c. 732. *Seiche* (gl. corium), "a hide, or skin," O'R., Gael. *seiche, seich, seic.* 734. *Intlecht* (gl. ingenium), in O. Ir. intliucht, intšliucht (= andeslictus ?), intellectus, sensus, Z. 42, 849, 230, gen. intliuchta, Z. 63 : sliucht, Z. 970, a masc. u-stem, compounded with the prep. ind (= Gaulish ande) which aspirates, and the *d* of which becomes *t* before aspirated *s.* 735. *Sendis*, old age, from sen (old) = sena-s (Gaulish Seno-magus, Zend. hana), and áis (age), a masc. i-stem, which Ebel would connect with Skr. âyus, but this would be a solitary instance of the preservation of an original final *s.* Áis, perhaps, stands for âissi-s ex âivs-i-s: cf. O. W. *in ois oisoudh,* the mod. W. yn oes oesoedd, Z. 298 : Corn. huis. 737. *Loscad* (gl. incendium, burning); dat. sing. do *loscud,* Z. 768, loisedib (gl. essis), *ib.* forloiscthe (gl. igne exanimatus), Z. 845 ; cf. Corn. losc (arsura, ustulatio), W. llosg, Bret. losk. 738. *Martra* (gl. martyrium), like martir, a martyr, Colm. 19, W. *merthyr*) is a foreign word. O. Ir. martre : filus trechenclœ *martre* dancu adrimiter ar cruich du duiniu[1] mad esgro bann martre ocus glas martre ocus derc martre, "now there are three kinds of martyrdom which are considered as man's cross, that is to say [lit. if thou sayest], white martyrdom, and green martyrdom, and red martyrdom," Z. 1007; dul *martre* tarfarcennsi, Z. 618, "to suffer martyrdom for your sake;" hence martre appears to be a fem. iâ-stem. 739. *Taile* (gl. salarium, wages), cf. W. tal, pl. talion (payment), τέλος, τελέω.

740–744. *Soiler* (gl. solarium, sun-dial ? house-top ? Germ. söller), Corn. soler (Z. iii.); solarium is glossed by solam in Z. 733, which looks a genuine Irish word, and gives a favourable idea of the material civilization of the Irish ecclesiastics in the eighth and ninth centuries, especially when we consider their native words for napkin (lambrat bís tar glúne, gl. mappa, gl. mantile, i. e. a napkin that is over the knees, Z. 613 ; lámbrat (gl. gausape), Z. 820), for canal, or, perhaps, water-pipe (lóthur, gl. canalis, lothor, gl. alveal, Z. 744, for bath : fothareud, Z. 893, *infra* fothragad); but, above all, for usury (fogbaidetu for fogaibthetu, Z. 844). 741. *Seallad* (MS. seall.), (gl. sellarium) a pantry, *séalladh,* "a cell, O'R. 742. *Groigh* (gl. equitium), a stud of horses, Gael. *greigh,* s. f., an i-stem = gragi-s, cf. Lat. greg (grex), W. *gre* (herd, stud).

[1] Lit. are counted for a cross to a human being : glas = glasta : cf. glastum, woad.

stud). 744. *Muinél* (gl. collum, neck), Gael. *muineal*, gen. *-eil* = W. mwnwgl; cf. muinde, gl. collarium, muinntore, gl. torques, Z. 764, where is also muinœ, which I suspect is a misreading or misprint for muinee (necklace); cf. mong, W. mwng, mane.

745-749. *Druim* (back, ridge): gen. sing. drommo, dat. druimm, occur in the Book of Armagh, 17 *a*, 1 : Issí inso coibse fétho fio ┐ acdocht dibliadin rembas daú dumanchuib *drommo* liás ┐ dumaithib callrigi it[er] crochaingel ┐ altóir *drommo* liás nadconfil finechas for*druimm* leas act conél fétho fio ma beith nech besmaith diib bescráibdech beschuibsech dinchlaind manipé duécastar dús inétar dimuintir *drommo* liás l. diamanchib Manićtar dubber décrud dimuintir pátrice into ... ["This is the communication of Féth Fio and his bequest, two years before his death, to the monks of Druim Liás and to the nobles of Callrige, as well the chancel as the altar (i. e. as well the laymen as the clerics) of Druim Liás : Let there not be *finechas* (inheritance of kindred, *fine?*) on Druim Liás (i. e. let it not devolve according to the law of *finechas*) but the race of Féth Fio, if any one of them be good—if any one of the clan be pious and decent. If there be not, let it be seen if there be one of the family of Druim Liás, or of its monks. Unless one be found, place a member of Patrick's family into it."] Druim occurs in Z. in composition with the numeral nóin (9): mochoe noin-*drommo*, "Mochoe of Nendrum" (Nine-ridge), now Mahee Island, in Strangford Lough (Todd, L. H., 100). 746. *Ceilebradh eoin* is "a bird's warbling," *ceilebradh*, from celebratio : the verb ceilebraim means "I bid farewell;" lase *celebirsimme* (gl. cum ualefecissemus), Book of Armagh, 184 *b.*; *ceileabhar*, "chirping like birds," O'R.; eoin gen. sing. of én (Z. 82: gen. inde*iúin*, Z. 24) = atina, W. edyn. Cf. O. W. *etn*-coilhaam (gl. auspicio), Z. 130; œtinet (volucres), Z. 169; Corn. idne (auceps), Z. 784. Has an initial *p* been lost by these words, and dare we compare (with Dr. Siegfried) πέτομαι, πετεηνά, Lat. penna (for petna—W. *adan*), Eng. feather (O. W. eterinn, avis, singularis, Z. 300: atar, aves: collect. *ib.*). *Grand tochartaigh* is "a reel;" cf. tocharaim, "I wind up, I reel," O'R., Gael. *tachras*, "winding, act of winding yarn;" gyrgyrium (if I read the word rightly—in Med. Lat. generally girgillus) seems formed by reduplication from gyrare. (See Pott as to this word, Zeits. i. 309.) 747. *Inchinn* (gl. cerebrum), the brain, Gael. *eanchainn*, W. emennyd, Corn. impinion, Bret. empenn: gen. inchinne : La sodain dolléci dia feraib fidchilli don techtaire com boi for lár a *inchinne* (Táin bó Cuailgne in the Lebar na Uidre), thus rendered by O'D., Lebar na Cert. lxiv.: "With that he cast [one] of his chessmen at the messenger, so that it pierced to the centre of his brain ;" inchinn is an i-stem, from *in* (= ande ?), and *cenn*, head. The word is formed like ἐγκέφαλον. 748. *Stol*, leg. *stól* (gl. scanum, i. e. scamnum),

scamnum), W. ystawl, fem.: both, no doubt, from Eng. stool, A. S. stól. 749. *Firmamint*, like Corn. firmament, W. *ffurfafen*, of course from firmamentum. 750–758. *Mir pluc*, gl. rubigorium, is altogether obscure to me. Possibly it may mean "the (top) red part of the cheeks." Cf. Gael. *mir*, "the top or summit:" *pluc, pluic, ploc*, "cheek," O'R. 751. *Luach faisnéisc*[1] (if I read the last word aright) is "reward of information,"; inventorium from invenio, in the sense of discover (" scis, Pamphilam meam *inventam* civem?"). 752. *Innarbad* (gl. exilium), for indarbad; cf. indarpe (ejectio), Z. 591, gen. -pi, dat. -pu, Z. 246; indarbad expulsus est, O'D. Gr. 291; isan *indarbe*, gl. in repulsam, Z. 247; aren *indarbe* analchi ood (that he banish vices from him), Z. 1003; tre *indarpae* .de. asin mascul (per ablationem syllabæ *de* a masculino), Z. 848; nachimr'indarpai-se quod non me repulit, Z. 848; nachitr'indarpither (ne sis exheredatus); *innarbar* hires dam trí drochgnimu, "Faith also is banished by evil deeds" (note the assimilation of the *d*); the *ind* (Gaulish ande, Skr. adhi) here signifying motion from something (Z. 848), which something is, in the present instances, arbe, orpe, heritage (gen. orpi), Z. 234, a neut. ia-stem, which = N. H. G. erbe, Ang. S. yrfe neut., as in Beowulf, 6093, ed. Thorpe. Cf. also na berat an *erpther* doib, " let them (slaves) not take away what is committed to them," Z. 458 : nom*érpimem* (me trado, confido), Z. 431 : nobirpaid (confiditis) ro *airp*tha (commissum est), Z. 7. 753. *Oilemain*, gl. alimentum, root al, as to which *v. supra.* 754. *Airge*, " a herd," O'R., *v. suprá.* 755. *Tormach* (increase). 756. *Mithormach* (decrease), *tormach*, leg. tórmach = do-for-mac-a, Z. 1051, gl. 26; tormachtaid (auctor), Z. 766; tormachtai (aucta), Z. 983; doförmgat (augent), Z. 854; doformagar, tórmagar(augetur), doformmagddar (augentur), Z. 854. Here again we find the Skr. root mah. 757. *Edach* (clothing), O. Ir. étach, Z. 442, éitach, Z. 1050, gen. átig, Z. 857, aítich, Z. 1051, a neut. a-stem, as in Z. 235, gaibid immib an*étach* macc cóimsa, " put around ye the raiment of sons of mercy." 758. *Oydhamh* (gl. jumentum, a beast of burthen), lit. young ox; cf. ógbho, leg. ogbhó, O'R.; óg = O. Ir. óc (óclachdi, gl. juvenilia, ocmil (= yavanca-milit), gl. tyro, Z. 60; ocmiledu, gl. athletas, Gildas). Oc = O. W. iouenc, W. *ieuanc* = Eng. young = juvencus, which shows that our Irish word has not only lost *v* and *n* in the middle of the word, but *j* (*y*) at the beginning. The original is YAVANKA, the *a* in the first syllable being found in the Skr. comparative and the superl. yavishṭha, and in Ἰάοϝες, which Lassen has equated with juvencs. The stem has been recognised by Dr. Siegfried in the O. Ir. comparative óa, "less" (= W. iau = Skr. yavīyāṅs), and superlative oam (gl. minimus, Z. 286) = W. icuaf. Z., p. 60,

---

[1] In the MS., fulni, with an oval mark over ai, and a mark like a long z between n and i.

60, points out another word in O. Ir. which has lost initial *j*, viz., aig (gl. cristallus, Z. 60), the corresponding W. word iâ (= yag), ice, and the Breton adj. yen (= yagin), icy, still retaining the semi-vowel. Cf. also uisse with Lat. justus, from which, however, I do not think it taken. Consider A. Weber's remark (Ind. Stud. iv. 398), "yôs for yâvas, from √yu, to join : cf. Lat. jus, Zend yaos, in the verb yaozhda." In other words, such as ísu (Jesus), íce (salus), W. iechyt, íth (gl. puls, Z. 60), W. iot, the *j* has blent with the following vowel, and produced i. *Damh* will be considered *infra*, No. 858.

760–769. *Timna* (gl. testamentum), O. Ir. timne : "is taschide *timne* déc do chomalnad," Z. 897 ("it is necessary to fulfil God's commandment"). This timne is a neut. ia-stem. 761. *Instrumint*, like—766. *Saltair* (gl. psalterium) is a foreign word. 762. *Didin* (gl. tegmentum), O. Ir. dítiu, gen. díten, *v. supra*. 763. *Médugud* (gl. augmentum), from *méid*, gl. magnitudo, *infra*. 764. *Spuirech* (gl. fragmentum), from the same root, probably, as W. ysbwrial, sweepings, ysborion, refuse, *Spruilleach*, gl. fragmen, *infra*. 765. *Duillen* (gl. folium), W. dalen, deilen, Corn. delen, Bret. delien, pl. deliou, Gaulish dula in πεμπέδουλα quinquefolium : πεντάφυλλον 'Ρωμαῖοι κινκεφόλιουμ, Γάλλοι πεμπέδουλα [alia lectio πομπαιδουλά] Δάκοι προπεδουλά. Dioscorides, 4, 42, cited Z. 324. Z. thinks that dula = folium, b-l-at. Celtic *d* may certainly sometimes be = Lat. *f*, because we know that at the beginning of a word the latter often represents DH. The double *l* in duillen seems due to an original semi-vowel. Cf. φύλλον = φυλjον, fol-i-um. But what is the -en ? A trace in Irish of the singulativo forms of her Celtic sisters ? 767. *Lité* (gl. pulmentum), Gael. *lit*, *lite*, is porridge. Cf. W. llith, "meal soaked in water." 768. *Uaithne* (gl. dipodium, if I rightly read this strangely contracted word, *ff* = *di f*, i. e. two *f*'s) is a kind of rhyme in Irish verse, discussed in O'D. Gr. 418. Our scribe does not seem to have been very deep in Greek, δίποδία being "two feet combined into one metre." 769. *Bidhgadh* (gl. pavementum), O'R.'s *biodgadh*, "stirring, rousing, startling;" Gael. *biodhgadh*, "a stirring up, sudden emotion."

770–777. *Caí* (gl. lamentum, "wailing, weeping") occurs in Corm., but I omitted to note where, also (spelt coí) in Lib. Hymn. (fol. 3, *a*, and p. 72, ed. Todd, where the mark of length is omitted). 772. *Céd* (gl. centum), O. Ir. cét, Skr. çata-m, Zend çatĕ-m, ἑ-κατό-ν, Lat. centu-m, Goth. and O. H. G. themes, hunda, hunta. Here the Welsh and Bret., as usual, surpass the Irish and Cornish in retaining intact the combination nt ; W. and Bret. cant, Corn. cans. In composition cét aspirates. Thus Conn cétchathach "100-battled Conn." 773. *Dá* (2), in O. Ir. inflected with dual-endings, nom. masc. and n. dáu for dvâv (originally dvâm ?), gen. dá

not

not aspirating = Skr. dvayôs? dat. dib(ṅ)¹ (= Skr. dvâbhyâm?), acc. dá for dvâv. The fem. was nom. dí = dvaí, Skr. dve, Lat. duae, gen. dá, dat. dib(ṅ), acc. dí. In composition this numeral was dé, which is curious, as the Skr. is dvī, and Gr. δῖ, Zend and Lat. bi-, A. S. tvi. In O. W. dou masc. dui fem. 774. *Trí*, masc. and neut. (3) does not aspirate, having ended in the nom. originally in *s*; the O. Ir. forms for the fem. of this numeral are teoir, teora, gen. teora (ṅ), dat. teoraib, acc. teora. Of these, teoir is obscure to me; teora, teora (ṅ), seem to be formed from an extended theme. In O. Welsh, tri masc. teir fem, which last is the mod. *tair*. 775. *Ceithre* (4), I have never met in O. Ir., though cethri occurs in the Lib. Hymn. (a MS., I should say, of the eleventh century). The O. Ir. forms are cethir, masc. and neut. (= W. petuar, Skr. nom. masc. chatvâras, neut. chatvâri, Goth. fidvór), and cetheora fem. Corn. (We may expect to find a cethcoir = W. peteir, Skr. chatasra².) 776. *Cúig* (5), O. Ir. cóic = Lat. quinque, Skr. pánchan, Zend. panchan, πέντε, Æol. πέμπε, Goth. fimf, Eng. five. The non-occurrence of what may be called a transported *n³* after cóic before vowels and medials (except of course in the gen.) might be regarded as confirming Bopp's assumption that the final nasal in the Indo-Zend pancha-n is a later addition, were it not that the Welsh *pump* nasalises an initial medial, and should therefore, according to Aufrecht, Beitr. i. 105, have ended in *n*. However, this phenomenon seems quite modern (cf. pump gwraged, 5 women, not pump ngwraged, Z. 325, quoting the Mabinogion, iii. 101), and is probably owing to the influence of the *m*. 777. *Sé* (6), W. chwech = svees, originally ᴋsᴠᴀᴋs, Zend. khsvas, the final *s* (= Lat. *x*, Gr. ξ, Skr. sh, Goth. hs) is retained in the ordinal *ses*-e-d, W.

[1] As in the following examples: for *deib ṅdillib* (according to two declensions), Z. 277; in *dib ṅuarib deac*, Z. 312 (in 12 [2 + 10] hours); in an *dib ṅairechtaib* dermaraib (in their two vast assemblies), Adamnán's Vision, and with the *n* changed to *m* before *b*: Doluid Oengus con *dib* mbuidnib aracheud dia marbud (O. went with two troops before him to slay him), Trip. Life of Patrick.

[2] A curious Celtic (Pictish?) form of this numeral is found in composition in the name *Cothír*-thiacus, given to S. Patrick, "because he served four houses (households?) of druids." It occurs in the following passage (Book of Armagh, 9, *a*, 2):—" Tirechán episcopus hec scripsit ex ore uel libro ultani episcopi cuius ipse alumpnus uel discipulus fuit. Inueni .iiii. nomina in libro scripta patricio apud ultanum episcopum conchuburnensium sanctus magonus qui est clarus [cf. "Apolloni Granno *Mogovno*"] succetus qui est [deus belli—see the gloss on the Lib. Hymn. copy of Fiacc's Hymn, v. 2, where this name is spelt *succat*] patricius cothirthiacus quod seruiuit .iiii. domibus magorum et empsit illum uons ex eis cui nomen erat milluc maccuboin magus." (See Lib. Hymn. ed. Todd, p. 27.)

[3] Z. calls this a prosthetic *n*, which conveys an erroneous idea. Irish grammarians call it an eclipsing *n*. I have, I believe, proved that this *n* has almost always originally belonged to the termination of the word immediately preceding that to which it seems prefixed.

W. chwechcd. A remarkable form of this numeral is involved in mór-fes-er, seven persons, literally great-six-persons. I incline to the opinion that here, as in the forms fiur, fiar (= Skr. svasṛ), above quoted, the ƒ was unaspirable, and stands for sv (cf. Ϝεξήκοντα, Ϝεξακάτιοι, Ϝέκτον, on the Tabulæ Heracl.)—that for this ƒ we sometimes find *ph* written (cf. mo *phethar*-su for mo *fehar*-su, urphaisiu, gl. cancer, for urfaisiu); but that there is no good ground for regarding a form like the Gaelic *piuthair* as ancient.

778-788. *Cruithnecht*, gl. frumentum; gen. sing. cruithnechta, Z. 193; cruithnechtide, gl. ceritus, Z. 765. 779. *Eorna* (gl. hordeum), barley: here, as in óc (= young), perhaps both *y* and *v* have been lost; and, if we assume the addition of the Celtic derivative syllable -arn-, we may compare Skr. and Zend yava, Gr. ζέα. 780. *Méirse* (gl. merciamentum), cf. Fr. merci, Lat. merces. 781. *Loch*, gl. stagnum = lacu-s, gen. sing.: ótha crích drommo .nit. euglais tamlachtæ dub*locho*, Book of Armagh, 17 *a*, 2, a stem in *u*, gen. dual: dún dá *lacha* (Fled dúin nan géd, 80) = lac(u)ás? Loch = Lat. lacus, Bret. and Corn. lagen. 782. *Lemnacht*, gl. mulsum, i. e. wine mixed with honey (lemnach, gl. mulsum, Z. 777), is O'R.'s leamnachd, "sweet milk," *et sic hodic*. 783. *Medhg* (gl. serum, whey), W. maidd, O. Fr. mègue, Germ. matten. 784. *Im*, leg. *imm* (gl. butyrum), in Corm. imb (O. W. emmeni, Z. 130, W. ymenin, Bret. amann). Imm occurs in the nom. sing. with the masc. article in a MS. of T. C. D. (H. 3, 18, p. 433), cited in Petrie's Tara, 190: ni ba leghtha int*im*, "the butter was not dissolved;" gruth ┐ *imm*, pref. to Secundinus' hymn (Todd, Lib. Hymn. p. 32), "cheese and butter" (gruth = Eng. curd). Gen. sing.: Fecht naile luid rechtaire ríg bretan do chuinchid chísa grotha ┐ *imme* comuime pátrice, "at another time the steward of the King of the Britons came to Patrick's nurse to demand tribute of cheese and butter."—Trip. Life of Patrick. Dr. Siegfried has acutely suggested that the *b* of imb may be for *g* (cf. bó = Skr. gâus, broon [gl. molac, Book of Armagh, 10, *a*, 2] = Goth. qvairnus, bíu = Skr. jíva), and that the word may, accordingly, be connected with the Skr. anji, ointment, *ungere*, &c. Cf. Germ. *anke*, butter, and see Grimm, Gesch. d. d. Spr. ii. p. 1003. 785. *Uinnimint* (gl. unguentum), seems derived from a Med. Lat. ungimentum, or perhaps from Eng. ointment. *Ór*, *Airged*, *Luaidhe*, *Sdan*, *Iaran*, have been noticed *supra* (606-610). 791. *Mitall*, from metallum. 792. *Luach lesa* is, says C., "the reward paid by a pupil to his tutor;" for lesa, he says, is "a guardian." Cf. *leasughadh*, "education," O'R.; Gael. *leasachadh*, improving: *luach* seems a sister-form of ló-g, lua-g, gen. lóge, Z. 432, dat. luag, *supra*. The root seems LAV, found in Lat. Lav-erna, lú-cru-m, Skr. lô-ta (booty, *loot*), λη-ΐ-ς, λά-τρι-ς (hired servant), Goth. lau-n, anda-launi, Curtius, G. E. i. 329. 793. *Bealach* (gl. alministrum)

alministrum) I cannot explain: alministrum is like almunicium (amice?), Dief. Lat.-Germ. Gloss.: bealach generally means "a road," or "a mountain-pass," "defile." *Beoladh* is "anointing." 794. *Srebhan* (gl. nuchum, a membrane): *srebhan na hinchinne*, "membrane inclosing the brain," C.; cf. sreibnaide, gl. membranaceus, Z. 765.

795–808. *Soilestar* (gl. gladiolum), sedge, flaggers, fleur de lis, O'R.'s *feleastar, feleastrom, seilistrom, sileastar, seilisdeir*, and *soileastar*! The last form comes nearest to the Lat. salicastrum, "bitter-sweet," and if this be the etymon, we should write *sailestar*: W. and Corn. elestren. 796. *Sgærtach* (gl. propheticum) is "roaring out," according to O'D., Gael. *sgairteach* (clamosus), from *sgairt* (exclamatio). 797. *Fidhba* (gl. falcastrum) is the W. gwyddif, "a hedging-bill," O. W. gudif, gudhyf scalprum, from fid = wood, and the root BEN, BE, Z. 44. With gudif I should be inclined to compare a word *uudimm*, which Z. gives as a gloss on lignismus (a woodman's axe, lignicisimus, Ducange). But in the facsimile, published by Vicomte H. de la Villemarqué, of the part of the MS. (Bibl. Bodl. 572, fo. 42) from which Z. purports to take this form, it stands distinctly *undimin*[1]. *Maith, Ole, Taithneamach, Geal, Dubh, Imdha, Beg, Mór*, have been noticed *supra* (from 659 to 673). 803. *Buidhe* (yellow), buide, gl. flavus, Z. 727, an adjectival ia-stem. Such stems were thus declined:—

		Masc.	Fem.	Neut.		Masc.	Fem.	Neut.
Sing.	N.	núe	núe	núe (ṅ)	Plur.	núi	núi	núi
	G.	núi	núe	núi		núe (ṅ)	núe (ṅ)	núe (ṅ)
	D.	núu	núi	núu		núib	núib	núib
	Ac.	núe (ṅ)	núi (ṅ)	núe (ṅ)		núu	núi	núi (núe)
	V.	núi	núe	núi		núu	núi	núi (núe)

And adjectival a-stems were thus declined:—

		Masc.	Fem.	Neut.		Masc.	Fem.	Neut.
Sing.	N.	mall	mall	mall (ṅ)	Plur.	maill	malla	malla
	G.	maill	maille	maill		mall (ṅ)	mall (ṅ)	mall (ṅ)
	D.	maull	maill	maull		mallaib	mallaib	mallaib
	A.	mall (ṅ)	maill (ṅ)	mall (ṅ)		maullu	malla	malla
	V.	maill	mall	maill		maullu	malla	malla

Adjectives agreeing with nouns in the dual are always put in the plural. 804. *Riabhach*

[1] In the "Archives des Missions Scientifiques et Littéraires," v^e vol., facsimile Nu. IV., Paris, 1856.

ach (gl. fuscum, swarthy): etymologically obscure to me. 807. *Mesurdha* (gl. modicum), from mensura, with the usual loss of *n* before *s*. Cf. mesraigthe (gl. modestus), Z. 743, O. W. doguomisur (gl. geo, i. e. mensuro), Z. 1076. 808. *Robeg* (gl. minimum), from beg, by prefixing the intensive particle *ró*, *ro* = Lat. pro, Skr. pra.

810-816. *Lus* (gl. porrum) = look, Corn. les, W. llysiau, "herbs." What (811) *inleman* can be, I know not. 812. *Nem* (heaven) also once *nim*, in Z. ní artu ní *nim* ní domnu ni muir ar noibbriathraib rolabrastar Crist assa chroich, "neither height nor heaven, nor depth nor sea surpasses[1] the holy words that Christ spoke from his cross," Z.; W. and Corn. nef, Bret. énv : cf. Slav. nebo, "heaven." Nem (gen. sing. nime, gen. pl. a choimdiu secht *nime!* "O Lord of seven heavens," Oingus)—is a fem. i-stem = nami, perhaps for nabi, originally a stem in *s*, like Skr. nabhas, Gr. νέφος—(*m* from *bh*, as in lám, from r. labh). Original stems in *s* have, with the exception of mí, month, gen. mís, invariably ceased to be inflected according to the consonantal declension. Thus, clú, "glory" = Skr. çravas, κλέϝος. The following have gone over to the vocalic declension: geine, Lat. genus, γένος: lige, "bed" = λέχος: suide, "seat," Skr. sadas, ἕδος: corp, Lat. corpus: ucht, Lat. pectus. With the suffix *arn*—híarn, iarann (Gaulish ísarno-), Skr. ayus, Lat. aes. What the *s* in áis, óis ("age," which Ebel compares with Skr. âyus) can be, is not easy to say, *v. infra*, No. 1071. 814. *Rastail* (gl. rastrum), rastal in Corm., O'R.'s rásdal (a rake), perhaps from the Lat. rastrum; cf. W. rhasgl, O. W. rhasel, gl. sartum, Z. 1093. 815. *Foighi* (gl. epulum), leg. foighdhe? and cf. Z. 1059: leisce na pronn .i. fri fognam gréssich *foigde*, ad v. "pigri τῶν prandiorum, scil. in servitio continuo epuli," acc. sing. inn áis déed caras *foigdi* cáich, Z. 457; dat. sing. nírbommar utmuill oc *foigdi*, Z. 481. In the last two quotations foigde seems to have the meaning of the Gaelic *faighe*, *faighdhe*, "begging, a public begging from house to house;" "an asking of aid, in corn, clothing, or other stuff, usual with young persons newly married, or about to stock a farm."

817-825. *Snáithe* (a thread), snáthe, gl. filum, Z. 20; dat. sing. snáthiu, Z. 232; Corn. snod-en, W. ysnoden (vitta), *snood*, W. and Corn. noden, filum, Bret. neud, neuden. Cf. also O. W. notuid, "needle," Bret. nadoz. O. Ir. verbal forms, apparently connected with these words, are: co atomsnassar (gl. uti ego inserar), Z. 472; insnastis (gl. consuerunt exserere), Z. 452; nach nastad [leg. *nascad:* cf. ronaisc, Ir. Nennius, lxxii., Mod. Ir. nasgaim] in cretmech ┐ na coméitged dó, "Let him not bind the believer, and let none accompany him," Z. 599.—1 Corinth. vii. 15. The connexion of these words with Skr. r. nah, Lat. nectere; νέ-ω, Lat. ne-o; νήθω, NADH-, no

---

[1] Lit. [is] over.

no doubt exists, but is not easily made out. 819. *Srian*, a bridle = frênum, W. ffrwyn, all perhaps connected with the Skr. root dhr̥ tenere (see Pott, Zeits. i. 120). But whether srian, ffrwyn, are taken from the Lat., we shall not be able to decide till the nature of initial Welsh *ff* is more thoroughly understood. 820. *Adhastar* (halter), O'R.'s adhastair, cf. W. oddestr, oddestl, oddestlawr, a steed. 822. *Fothragadh* (gl. balneum), gen. sing. a conclæ *fothairethe*sin, Z. 893, "this kind of bath," dat. pl. fothairethib, Z. 238, an u-stem. 823. *Birur* (cress), Mod. Ir. *biolar*, W. berwr, berw, berwy, Corn. and Bret. beler. 825. *Iffern* (gl. Tartarus), *v. supra*.

826–832. *Inféd fosë* I cannot explain, unless we read *in féd fosclaidh*, "the whistling (sibilus) of a chink;" *féd* = W. chwyth, blast, chwythell, whistling: cf. *sétfeth*chaib, flatibus, Z. 856. 827. *Ifearnadha* seems a neut. adj. plur., formed from iffern = infernum. 831. *At pill* (gl. pelleus, pileus, πῖλος, hat of felt? But indeed *pill* may be an hibernisation of the Latin pellis. *At* is of course from the English *hat* = Lat. stem *cas*-sid, from *cad*-tid (Lottner, Zeits. vii. 180), *v. supra*, *at* cluic. 832. *Ibrach*— if I read the word rightly—(gl. intimus) is obscure to me; the only word I know resembling it is *iubrach*, which C. and O'D. say is a wooden drinking-vessel, broad at bottom and narrow at top.

833–841. *Filidhecht*, *v. supra*, No. 1. 834. *Geman* (or perhaps gemon, gemin), gl. didyma, δίδυμα, apparently from Lat. gĕminus, as W. gefell from gemellus. 835. *Adhbardacht*, πρόληµµα (afterwards glossing idioma), πρόληµµα, literally "what is taken beforehand," here apparently equivalent to "advantage" (πρόληµµα ποιεῖν τινι, "to give one an advantage"), a formation from the prep. *ad* and the r. BAR, Skr. r. bhr̥ (bhar), φέρ-ω, fer-o. 836. *Céirin*, κατάπλασµα, a plaster, probably from céir, wax; cf. W. cwyren, a cake of wax. 837. *Foircedal*, gl. dogma, O. Ir. forcetal, forcital (doctrina), gen. -til, a neut. a-stem[1]. The verb forchun, forchanim, præcipio, frequent in O. Ir., occurs in Z. 195, 440, fut. part. pass. forcanti (leg. forcantí), Z. 84; forcitlid, preceptor, Z. 85; forcitlaidecht (magisterium), Z. 771. The root CAN (Skr. çans, Lat. can-ere, cens-ere, Goth. han-a, καν-άζω), also occurs in doarchet, doairchet, tairchet, "it was predicted," Z. 468; doaurchanim (gl. sagio), Z. 440; foacanim (gl. succino), Z. 440; dorencanas, perspexit, Z. 856; isdo fordoncain, Z. 1060, leg. iscd do fordoncain, "this is what it teaches us." The root in question reduplicates: forduboechna (-cc-ch'n-a), gl. qui vos commonefaciat), Z. 496: tairchechuin, gl. predixit, tairchechnatar predixerunt,

ibid.;

---

[1] *For* (the Gaulish ver-, as *foirge* is to be compared with *Vergivios*) has been compared with Skr. upari (Ebel, Beitr. l. 309). *Sed quære*, for Celtic *v* never (so far as I know) is = Skr. *p*. And as Gaulish exhibits no tendency to eject *p*, the theory that *ver* arose from *uari* [u(p)ari] is untenable.

ibid.; rochachain, cecinit, Lob. na Cert, 136; doairrcechnatar .i. rotairnngestar, Brehon Laws, O'D.[1] 838. *Mullach tighe* (gl. doma), mullach (gl. culmen, *infra*, gl. vertici, Gildas' Lorica), generally means top, summit, head. Here "roof," a meaning which doma has in Eccl. Latin. 839. *Forsgath no ingar* (gl. enigma). I can throw no light on these Ir. words (which I have never met elsewhere), unless we read the first forsgáth, and connect it with sgáth = shade, shadow, αἴνιγμα being a dark saying. Cf. furastar (= furasctar?), gl. fuscetur, Z. 472. The Gael. iongarach is "purulent." 840. *Crismal* (gl. chrisma, anointing, unction), a hybrid from Eccl. Lat. chrisma, or perhaps Gr. χρῖσμα. 841. *Monadh* (νόμισμα, a coin), from Lat. moneta, generally means "money," whence W. mwnai.

842-850. *Soiphist* (sophisma) is certainly a foreign word, and perhaps involves a blunder. 847. *Nescoid* (gl. ἀπόστημα = imposthume, abscess) is nescoit in Corm. Its etymology is obscure to me. 844. *Croindtille, v. supra*, No. 651. 845. *Coindealbthadh* (gl. anathema), cursing with bell, book, and *candle*. 846. *Tadhbais* (gl. phantasma) is O'R.'s tadhbhas, "a spectre." Taidbsiu, a stem in tiûn (= du-ati-*bhás*-tiûn?) occurs in Z. 581, 196, 233, 456, 1016, with the meanings of manifestation, proof.

[1] Other reduplicating roots in O. Ir. are BA (die), bebais, Félire, 23rd April: rembebe, Z. 496 (where several instances are collected): beba Fiacc, 12. DAN (bear, Skr. bhṛ) dubbert, "he gave," Book of Armagh, 18 *b*, 1: atrópert [*p* for *bb*] flaith ⁊ aithech inso huile itosuch iar tabuirt baithis dúaib, "prince and peasant granted all this immediately after the administration of baptism to them," *ibid.*, 17 *a*, 2. BU (BHAV), "be:" Is airi doroigu dia geinti hore nár'*bube* la Iudeiu creitem, "for this cause it is that God chose the Gentiles, because the Jews had not faith" (ad v. "quia non fuit apud Judæos fides," Z. 602): robba (fuit), Z. 481, is, according to Lottner, an imperfect, and is for ro-bv-u, not (as one would think at first) for a Skr. prababhûva. CANG, "go :" cechaing (.i. roching) Félire: dacheachaing, "he advanced," Fled d. n. géd 66. CAR, "love," conchechrat "they will love," Z. 495 (for conchecharfat). CLU, "hear," rotchechladar, "hears thee," Z. 496. CLUS, "hear :" cechluista .i. rochluinfithea, O'D. DÁ, "give," adcho-*dad*-ossa, Z. 852; adcotedae [ad-cont-*ded*-ae], "he granted," Book of Armagh, 18 *a*, 1: cf. Ιαρται .... λλανοιτακος δ ε δε ματρεβο ναμανσικαβο βρατουδε, in the Nismes inscription (*Rev. Archéol.* 1858, p. 44), translated by Professor Siegfried, "Iartai .... llanoitacus [Illanoitacis *filius*?] dedit Matribus Nemausicis ex imperio [ipsarum]." GÁ, "go :" bit hé magistir don*gegat* inhi (leg. indi) asindisset a tola feisne doib, Z. 1057, "these are the masters to whom they will go, those who preach their own wishes to them." GAN, *v. supra*, No. 290, note 1. GES, "beseech :" gigestesi dia linn ara fulsam ar fochidi, Z. 496, "Ye used to beseech God that we might endure our tribulations." GRANN, "follow :" adrolgegrannatar, "they were persecuted," Z. 496 (cf. in*gre*nted, persecutor, Z. 265 ; ingrimmim ingraimmaim [in-grann-man-bi] persecutioni, Z. 268 ; ingramman, ingremmen, persecutiones, Z. 266, 463). STA, "stand :" sesaimm = ἵστημι for σίστημι, Skr. tishṭhâmi (Zend hiçtâmi). r. sthû, Lat. si-st o, Bopp, Gloss. 387. Whence is siasair .i. rosaidestar, Brog. 1 ?

proof. The related verb is also of frequent occurrence: doadbat, tadbat, demonstrat, Z. 852, 360, for tadbad-d; doadbadar, taidbadar, demonstratur, *ibid.*; *taidbdid* forn doscire friss, Z. 458, "show your love to him;" *doaidbdetar* físi doib, "visions are revealed to them," Z. 521; an donaidbdem, "when we shall demonstrate," Z. 670; from these forms it would seem that the root was B-D. The D, however, may represent a later formation (cf. $\phi a\text{-}\epsilon\text{-}0\omega$, and $\phi\acute{a}\text{-}os$); perhaps the root DHÁ agglutinated. 847. *Coimpert* ($\sigma\pi\acute{\epsilon}\rho\mu a$, seed, semen genitale, offspring), obviously a compound of co-imb-bert (r. bar, Skr. bhr), the *bb* becoming *p*, as in idpart, oblatio, &c. The genitive singular of coimpert, in the sense of "conception," occurs in the following passage from the Wanderings of the Curach of Maelduin, cited and translated in Dr. Petrie's Round Towers, 378: gabais Ailell a laimh lais ⁊ dodatrascair, ⁊ dogni coibligi fria ⁊ asbert an cailleeh fris: "ni segda," ol si, "ar comrue, ar is aimsir *comperta* dam." 848. *Adhbardacht*, and—849. *Adhbar* have been already noticed. 850. *Suidheocan*, leg. suidhechan (a seat, bench), an extended form of suide (seat), Z. 60, 140.

851–855. *Cro caerach* (gl. ovile, sheepfold), as to *cro*, *v. supra*; *caerach*, leg. cáerach, gen. pl. of cáera, a c-stem = cáirax, *v. supra*, No. 13: cf. cáirchuide, ovinus, Z. 37, 235, and the Gaulish tribe-name, Cacracates, Caerosi. This curious word may, perhaps, be connected with $\kappa\rho\iota\acute{o}s$. 852. *Proisté* (gl. monile, vel munile, a necklace) is said by C. to mean "a goad, a spike," which agrees well with the Cornish gloss on monile: scil. dole, leg. delch = Ir. delg spina. Proiste is probably taken from the Fr. *broche*, and this, according to Diez (E. W. 71), from Lat. brocchus, broccus, a projecting tooth. 853. *Lebhar aithffrind*, a missal, lit. liber offerendæ: aithffrind, leg. aiffrind, gen. of aiffrend, now aifrin, from the Lat. offerenda, with change of declension and gender, as scríbent, scríbend, from scribenda, and legend, gen. -ind, from legenda, Z. 462. 854. *Gredhdil*, gl. gredale, i. e. gradale, Eng. grail, "that book which containeth all that was to be sung by the quire at high mass; the tracts, sequences, hallelujahs; the creed, offertory, trisagium; as also the office for sprinkling the holy water," Burn, Eccl. Law, ii. 303. 855. *Troibel*, gl. trobiale, i. e. troperium? "the book which containeth the sequences, which were devotions used in the church after reading the epistle," *ibid.* iii. 799.

856–860. *Stuidis* (gl. lectóric, leg. lectoriale), a deriv. from the base of Lat. studium, studeo, here, perhaps, having the meaning of the Eng. "lectureship." 857. *Lámtuagh* (gl. manuale), lit. hand-axe or hand-bow, *tuagh* (axe), O'R., tuag nime "arcus coeli," Z. 28. 858. *Leabaid in daim allta* (gl. cubile), lit. bed of the wild ox, *daim*, gen. sing. of dam, ox; dat. sing. daum, Z. 250; n. pl. ar is bés leosom in *daim* do thúareuin, "for with

with them there is a custom for the oxen to thresh," Z. 853. *Dam* would also appear to mean a deer: cf. the adj. damde, gl. cervinus, Z. 764; but perhaps this is from the Lat. dâma (fallow-deer), and we should read dámde. I know not if W. dafad, pl. defeid, sheep, dafates, a flock of sheep, can be connected with *dam*. 859. *Corporas*, gl. corporale, I cannot explain. 860. *Muir* = Gaulish mŏri, W. and Corn. mor, Lat. măro, which I cannot think Bopp is right in comparing with Skr. vâri, water (Ir. fual?). Rather hold with Curtius (Zeits. i. 33) in referring it to the Skr. root mr̥ (mar), "welche in der bedeutung sterben am geläufigsten, in μαραίνω und dem mit c weiter gebildeten marceo die allgemeinere bedeutung des welkens hat (vgl. Skr. mr̥iṇ). In Skr. maru, die wueste, so·wie in marut, wind, tritt noch bestimmter der begriff des verwuestens hervor; mare bezeichnete demnach das meer als das unfruchtbare, als den tod der vegetation, wie nach der gangbaren erklaerungsweise ἀτρύγετος." Curtius also compares Ἀμφί-μαρο-ς, Lith. mar-ios, Goth. mar-ei. Muir in Z. is a fem. (or neut. ?) i-stem (gen. s. mora, Z. 1000), as appears from the termination of the adj. agreeing with its nom. pl. in Mora són nítat lora [leg. lóra] sidi leu, which Z. (1000) correctly translates maria hic, non sunt sufficientia ipsa eis. But note here, if *muir* be fem., the anomaly of an i-stem passing over to the â-declension in the nom. pl.

861-865. *Maindsér* (gl. praesepe) is of course from the Eng. manger. 862. *Uinneamain* (gl. cepe, onion), Gael. *uinnean*, W. *wynwyn-in*. These forms remind one of the Lat. ûnio, whence Fr. oignon, &c., are said to be taken. Perhaps the name of the vegetable is originally Gaulish (einnio?), which the Romans may have assimilated to their ûnio, "a single large pearl." The word foltchep is, I may observe, glossed by barr *uindiuin* (leg. uinniuin) in H. 3, 18 (MS., T. C. D.), p. 526. 863. *Lin uisci* (gl. rete), fishing-net, water-net, lit. "net of [the] water:" lin, gl. retis, Z. 25 : ished insin al*linn* ingaib diabul peccatores (gl. laqueum diaboli), Z. 1052, "this is the net in which the devil takes sinners." 864. *Sgaraid* (gl. gausape), O'R.'s scóráid, scároid, table-cloth. 865. *Mil mór, v. supra*, No. 428.

866-870. *Machaire* (gl. tompe, i. e. feld, anger, awe [aue], Dief.), a field, plain :—

    Adaig dúnn uili mallei
    Im*machaire* (leg. machairiu?) hǔue Carpri.—Corm. Ecces, vv. 119, 120.

gen. sing. fo diamraib in *macairi* moir minscothaigsin; *Cogad Gaedil re Gallaib* (ed. Todd, 76), a masc. ia-stem: Gael. *machair*, gen. macharach, s. f. machaire bán, is still a living expression for a grass-field: W. magwyr, "wall, enclosure, field," Bret. môger, "wall" = Lat. mâcĕria, "wall, enclosure." 867. *Urlabradh* (gl. locutio), Corn. lauar, W. llafar. Another form of this word is erlabra, which occurs in Lib. Hymn. (pref. to the

the Magnificat): ocus is inti doratad *erlabra* do Zachar¹ ("and it was there that speech was given to Zacharias"), and, apparently with a transitive meaning, is an infin. in Patrick's noble hymn: cluas Dé dom' éstecht, briathar Dé dom' *erlabrai* lám Dé domm' immdegail "God's ear to hear me, God's word to plead for me (*erlabraidhe* advocate, O'R.), God's hand to protect me." 868. *Aicecht* (gl. lectio), I have never met elsewhere. It seems to occur in the "*Uraicecht* nan Eiges," O'D. Gram. p. lv., but this is, perhaps, a corruption of the Lat. præceptum. 869. *Acra* (gl. actio), is a lawsuit, pleading, perhaps from the prep. ad, aith, and GAR; cf. adgaur, gl. consentio, i. e. addico, Z. 987, adobragart, "he addressed you," Z. 838. 870. *Guidhe* (gl. oratio), in Z. guide is sometimes a fem. iâ-stem; tri *guidi* acc. sing. Z. 258: and sometimes masc. or neut.; oc du *guidiu*-siu a dæ, "in supplicating thee, O God," Z. 346. The verb guidim occurs at pp. 55, 993, *guidimse* Dia ṅerutsa² (I pray God for thee), guidimm vel adjuro (gl. testor), Z. 1050, gl. 21; nosṅguid som "he asks them," Z. 441. Can this be connected with gúid in the gloss con dartin do ar rogdid dom, Z. 450, "that I should give him what he asked of me," ro*gad* (rogavi): 1st pers. plur. pret. act. rogadammar, Z. 442, 443; 3rd plur. in Fiacc's Hymn, 9:—

> Gadatar co tissad in noeb, aran imthised lethu
> Aru tintarrad o chlóen tuatha herenn do bethu.
>
> They besought that the saint should come, that he should journey far and wide,
> That he should turn the tribes of Ireland from evil unto life;

for the latter forms seem referable to the Skr. r. gad, to speak, of which, however, Böhtlingk and Roth give no Vedic examples. The W. gweddi seems connected with the Skr. r. vad.

871–875. *Cumtach* (gl. constructio) is generally used in the spiritual sense of edificatio in Z. (*cumtach* necolso, Z. 229), sometimes in that of structure, and glosses fabrateria, Z. 777³. I agree with Z. in regarding the word as a compound, cum-tach; the *cum* being a frequent form of the prep. con, and tach (= taca), being radically connected

---

[1] In the Leabhar Breace this passage runs: ocus is indte thucad *hirrlabra* do Zach.

[2] Observe the so-called prosthetic *n* here: it is nothing but the *n* of the old accusative termination, dêvan.

[3] In the Book of Armagh: dubbert Pátricc *cumtach* du Fiacc idon clocc ┐ menstir ┐ bachall ┐ poolire, i. e. Patrick gave a *cumtach* to Fiacc [containing] to wit, a bell and a *menstir* and a crozier and a booksatchel. This cumtach, a neut. a-stem, seems a deriv. from the root of cum-main, box, or basket, Lib. Hymn. 3 a, culmin, "a little chest or box," O'R. O'D. Gram. 437, derives it "from the verb comhad or coimead [O. Ir. *coimet* arfuacht, "a defence against cold," Corm. cited O'D. 294] to keep or preserve."

nected with tech (house): cf. Foirtchernn (Book of Armagh, 16 a, 2) = Ver-*tig*-erna-s, Vortigern, cuimtgim (gl. architector, gl. construo), Z. 439, comrótgatar, Z. 843. Is this root ΤΑΚ, in the Vedic *tak*-ma-s, "child," with which Curtius connects τέκ-ος, τόκ-ος, τέχ-νη, τεῖχ-ος, τοῖχ-ος, τύκ-ος, and of which Skr. r. taksh, to fabricate (whence takshan = τέκτων¹), seems an intensive. But indeed there are three roots, T-O, T-GH, T-K, the relations of which I am unable to settle. 872. *Remthechtas* (gl. prepositio), see Z. 750; rem, a form of ren (before), and *techtas*, an abstract from techt, venire (cf. W. taith, Gaul. Tecto-sagi, "march-sustaining:" and Skr. and Zend r. tanch, ire). Remthechtas also meant anteposition: alaaili diib hí *remthechtas;* alaili dam it coitchena eter *remthechtas* et tiarmoracht, "some of them are in anteposition; others also are common between anteposition and postposition," Z. 985. As an infinitive, the word occurs in Patrick's Hymn: Intech dé dom remthechtas, "God's way to come before me." Cf. tairm-*thechtas* (transgressio), Z. 750. 873. *Comfocul* (gl. conjunctio), com + focul: focul dictio, Z. 968, taken from the Lat. vocabulum (focbhul, focvul), which would account for the non-aspiration of the *c*. Focul occurs in the nom. of the sing., dual, and plural in the following passage, from a fragment of Cormac's Glossary, preserved in the Book of Leinster: Trefocla .i. trifoccuil bíte ind .i. dáfoccul dimolud dobrith forculu indimderggtha dofarci antross (leg. in tress) foccul .i. foccul indimdorgtha ⁊ aire; "*Trefocla*, i. e. three words that are in it, i. e. two words of praise it gives behind the reproach, which makes the third word, i. e. a word of reproach and satire." From which curious definition it would seem that *trefocla* was a composition apparently satirical, but really laudatory. 874. *Interiacht*, and—875. *Compardid*, from the Latin. (The O. Ir. words for preposition, conjunction, interjection, and comparison, were remsuidigud, comaccomal, interiecht, and condelgg, Z. 982.)

876–880. *Inntindeach*, like—880. *Coissegradh*, a hybrid from the Latin. 877. *Baramail* (gl. opinio), baramhuil, O'R., Gael. *barail*, an opinion, conjecture, supposition, apparently a compound of samail, but what *bar* stands for I cannot conjecture. 878. *Togha* (gl. electio), O. Ir. togu, a stem in *d* (or *t?*) = du-VAGH-ad (or -at?): is dichéin immunr'ordad condan maicc togu, lit. it is long ago we were ordained that we should be sons of election, Z. 475: Gael. *tughadh*. 879. *Dlighedh* (gl. ratio), *v. supra*. 880. *Coissegradh* (gl. consecratio), like W. cysegriad, a hybrid from the Latin consecro (the *n* being lost before *s*, as usual), O. Ir. coisecrad: Asbert fiacc frisinaingel nandrigad

---

¹ Cf. the Gaulish con-*tex*-to-s (in the inscription of Autun), and perhaps O. Ir. Tassach (St. Patrick's artificer) = Tax-aca-s.

drigad contísed patricc dothoorund a luic leis ⁊ dia *choisecrad* ⁊ combed húad nuggabad [gg, γγ = ng, Z. 282] alocc Dulluid iarsuidiu patricc cufíacc ⁊ durind alocc les ⁊ cutsccar [leg. cu-t-śccar], "Fíacc said to the angel that he would not go till Patrick came to measure his place with him, and to consecrate it, and so that it might be from him he should receive his place. Patrick afterwards went to Fíacc, and measured his place with him, and consecrated it," Book of Armagh, 18 *b*. 1.

881–885. *Cumdach* (gl. ornatio)—so O'R. *cúmhdach*, "an ouch, an ornament;" in Z. 1046, *cumtach* bas uisse fri hiriss (gl. cum verecundia et sobrietate *ornantes* sc), "an adornment that is fitting to faith." 882. *Mughsaine* (gl. famulatio, service, servitude), from *mugh*, O. Ir. mug, gen. moga, a masc. u-stem (= Goth. magus), and *saine*, which termination, forming abstract substantives from other substantives, occurs twice in Z. 739, viz., in cocéilsine (gl. societas, céle, socius), and in faithsini (gl. prophetiæ, fáith, propheta). The termination is probably = -ss-an-ia, st-an-ia. 883. *Adhalltras* (gl. fornicacio), adhaltras, Z. 750, a hybrid from adulter. 884. *Comsólás no comairle* (gl. consolatio), "consolation or counsel:" comsúlás, sólás, from Lat. sôlâtium, which the Irish of old probably pronounced sôlâtsium[1]. (N. B.—I doubt if this be a different word from solás, happiness, the opposite of dolás, grief, which latter may either be derived from dolore, or have been produced on the erroneous hypothesis that the first syllable of sólas was the well-known particle of quality): *comairle*, in putting down which the glossarist evidently took consolatio for consultatio, occurs in Z. acc. sing. tre dag*comairli*, Z. 826, nom. pl. ni rubtar gáitha for *comairli*, Z. 481, "your counsels were not wise," whence the word appears to be a fem. iâ-stem. The acc. sing. of the airle in com-airle occurs in the following gloss (Z. 1060): arna érbarthar ochretsit nintá *airli* arnban, ad v. "ne dicatur ex quo crediderunt non-est-nobis animus nostrarum mulierum," and the nom. sing. (compounded with dag, "good") in "ban buidich, is sí ar dag*airle*," Z. 1051, where I suspect Z. should have read arndagairle. Comairlle (with two l's), occurs in Z. 51, and he explains it by voluntas. I have never found the word with this meaning: but if Z. be correct, we might, perhaps, regard it as = com-are-valiâ, and recognise therein (with Dr. Siegfried) the Skr. r. वृ (ex var), to choose, *wale*, *will*, velle, cf. W. ewyll (du-valya), to will, Bret. ioul, Ir. tol (du-valû). Cf. airlam (paratus, promtus), Z. 733 : irlithe (obediens), Z. 766 : irladigur (obedio), Z. 839. 885. *Ainmneachadh* (gl. nominatio), a deriv. from ainm, a name, declined *infra*, No. 991.

886–890.

[1] *C* before *i*, in Latin words, was probably also pronounced *ts* : cf. comirsire, Z. 233 = commerc-i-ari, kommerziren.

P

886-890. *Tighernas* (gl. dominatio), W. teyrnas, "kingdom," from tigerne, as to which *v. supra*. 887. *Geinemain* (gl. generatio), from r. ᴏᴀɴ, "to produce," as to which *v. supra*, Gael. *gineamhuinn;* cf. Vedic janiman, janman, "birth." 888. *Certachadh* (gl. correctio), Gael. *ceartachadh* (W. ceryddu, corrigere, seems for cerythu, and connected with correctus); cf. Lat. certus. The element cert enters into the composition of many words in O. Ir. Thus, cocert (mendatio), cocart, corrige, cocarti, emendandum, Z. xiv.; conaicertus (emendavi), foceirt deponit, &c. 889. *Oibriugudh* (gl. operatio), from *obair* (in Corm. opair, gen. *oibre*, a fem. i-stem = from Lat. opera (not opus, Skr. apas); cf. oipred, Z. 80, 476, gen. oipretho, Z. 766: dat. (sensu obsceno) oc ind oipred, Z. 593, acc. amal rongab comadnacul dúun ata comeisséirge act rocretem *oipred* dúé, Z. 1040, gl. 15, "as we have co-burial there is co-resurrection, if we believe in the working of God." 890. *Reidhe* (gl. planatio), leg. *réidhe*, levelling, smoothening, from *réidh,* "plain, level, smooth," which occurs in Z. 1067 (with the meaning of "easy"), is *reid* foglaim in besgnai, "easy is the learning of morality;" and in Colman's Hymn, v. 33 :—

> Amal foedes in aingel tarslace Petrum a slabreid
> Doroiter[1] dun diar fortacht, rop *reid* remunn cech namreid.
>
> As He sent the angel that delivered Peter from his chain,
> Let him be sent to us to help us, let everything unsmooth be smooth before us.

Cf. Bret. *reiz*, "aisé, facile."

891-896. *Cestugadh* (gl. castigatio), W. cystwyad, is, I suspect, a foreign word, as certainly is—892. *Compantus* (gl. associatio), from compagan-u-s; cf. however, O'R.'s *céasnugadh*, which suggests a connexion with césad (W. cystudd?), rocéss, pertulit, passus est, Z. 434. 893. *Guidhe* (gl. supplicatio), *v. supra*. 894. *Taisbenadh* (gl. monstratio), Gael. *taisbeanadh*, "act of revealing, showing, or disclosing," O. Ir. taispenad : ó ruscaith tra do Sechnall in moludsa do dénam, luid dia *taispenad* do patraic, i. e. "now when Sechnall had finished making this hymn [lit. this praise] he went to show it to Patrick" (Pref. to Secundinus' Hymn, cited from Leabar Breace, by Dr. Todd, Lib. Hymn. 31); gen. sing. ó dochotar imorro icenn *taispenta* ind immuin do griguir, "when, however, they had done showing [lit. come into the end of showing] the hymn to Gregory" (Lib. Hymn. pref. to Altus Prositor). Taispenad for taispenad (taid-bs-ten-ad) *v. supra*, No. 846. 895. *Foillsiugudh* (gl. annunciatio), rather manifestatio: this word occurs, spelt foilsigud, in Z. 16, the gen. sing. foilsichtho,

---

[1] Read dorfoiter, i. e. do-ro-foid-ther.

sichtho, Z. 85, foilsigthe, 255, and is derived from follus, Z. 664, folus, Z. 748, 751, "plain," "manifest." *Soillsiughadh* is, perhaps, a sister-form (soillse, light, Z. 51, 257).

896–900. *Comparaid* (gl. collatio, cf. comparit, Z. 973, W. cymharu, to compare), and—897. *Comaineachadh* (gl. communicatio), both appear foreign words; compare, however, with the latter comnactar: aní nad *comnactar* dóini trian cene, "that which human beings do not comprehend (or conceive of) by their understanding," Z. 447, 702 : comain occurs in Cormac, and also in Z. 1050, gl. 18, with the sense of "obligation," "debt." Comman occurs in Fíacc's Hymn, v. 27, with the meaning of "communion," "the Lord's Supper :"—

> Anais tassach di[a]áis, intan dobert *comman* dó :
> Asbert monicfed¹ pátrice : briathar tassaig nirbu gó².
>
> Tassach remained after him, when he had administered the communion to him :
> He said that Patrick would come : Tassach's word was not false.

The cognate W. words are cymyn, "bequest, testament," cymanfa, "congregation" (m = mm). Cf. Lat. communis from commoinis, Goth. gamains, O., M. and N. H. G. gemein. 898. *Timthirecht* (gl. ministratio), cf. *timthirigh*, *supra*, occurs in Z. 260: *timtherecht* cacha dúlo "servitus omnis creaturae," and also spelt timthirect, timthrecht, at pp. 771, 237, timdirecht (acc. sing.), p. 777 (do-imm-tir-echt). The root seems TAR, Skr. tṛ, to go; compare ἀμφίπολος and Skr. parichara, "servant," lit. "one who goes about." 899. *Dénamh* (gl. procuratio), O. Ir. dénom, dénum, gen. sing. dénmo, Z. 733, means "a doing," "to do" (cf. dénmusach, gl. factor, *infra*), a stem in u. Cf. denim (facio), Z. 430; dene (fac), Z. 457; dened (facite), Z. 458 (leg. dénim, déne, dénid); dénti (faciendum), Z. 473; denmid, gen. denmada (gl. factoris), Z. 766. 890. *Doilbtiugud* (gl. fictio), from delb, as to which *v. supra*.

901–906. *Eolas* (peritia), leg. *eólas?* et *v. supra*. 902. *Moladh* (gl. adulatio) laus, cf. molor (I praise), Z. 444; Bret. meulet laudatus, Z. 107, W. *mawl*. The etymon may be ΜΑΟΑΛΑ, cf. μεγάλου, and the Gaul. Magalus, Magalius, Glück, 50, as móidim, another verb for I praise, is to be compared with Gaulish Mogit-marus. Molad occurs in Z. 989: Is béos donaib dagforcitlidib *molad* in gni innantside ara carat an rochluinetar, "it is a custom of [lit. "to"] the good teachers to praise the intelligence of the hearers,

---
¹ Gloss: .L cosabull iterum, "that is to Sabull [Saul, in the county of Down, lit. "barn"] again."
Note the interesting form mo-n-icfed wherein mo, also spelt mu, is a verbal prefix, only occurring four times in Z. See Z. 419. Tassach was Patrick's artificer, and Bishop of Ráith-Cholptha, now Raholp.
² Gloss : quia uenit patricius iterum co sabull.

hearers, in order that they may like what they hear:" is huisse a *molath* (gl. laudandus), dat. sing. molud, *supra*, No. 873, Z. 459.   903. *Comtromugud* (gl. coaequatio), leg. comtrummugud, equalization, balancing, lit. "making-equally-heavy," from trumm, tromm, W. trwm (nipsa *tróm*—leg. trom̃—for nech, gl. nulli onerosus fui, Z. 585); *tromm* occurs subsequently in composition: tromchride (gl. jecur), Z. 825, i. e. heavy-heart; cf. étrumma, "non gravia," Z. 252; etrumme "dissimilis," Z. 843; cutrummus, similitudo, Z. 751; hi cutrumus, ad instar, Z. 451; cutrummi, similes, Z. 843; fortrumme, opportunitas, Z. 843.   904. *Cosmhailius* (gl. simulatio), cosmilius in Z. (cf. écsamlus, diversitas, Z. 751, 831), from the adj. cosmail (W. cyfal, cyhafal), i. e. co-samail con-samali-s, the *simplex* of which Bopp has justly compared with Lat. similis (an i-stem, as in Irish), to which we may add W. hafal, Gr. ὁμαλός (an o-stem); cf. also Skr. sama, Goth. sama, Eng. same, Slav. samŭ.   Observe in—905. *Egcosmailius* (gl. dissimulatio) an example of the mod. Ir. practice of writing the so-called eclipsing letter before the original tenuis.   It need hardly be said that all the phenomena of eclipsis (amongst which I by no means count the apparent change of *s* into *t*) are explicable by reference to the medializing influence of *n* on *c, p, t,* and *f*, and to the tendency of *b, d,* and *g*, respectively, to become assimilated to a preceding *m, n,* and *ng*.   *Egcosmailius*, however, seems merely an example of the ordinary sinking of the O. Ir. tenuis to the corresponding medial.

906-910. *Urlamas* (gl. sequestratio, properly "a depositing of money, &c., in dispute") is wildly guessed at by O'R. "possession, supreme power and authority; captivity," but is correctly explained by C. (who spells the word *urlámas*) "the placing anything in the custody of a person; as in the laws *urlámas coitcenn* means the placing of contested property in the hands of an indifferent custodian, until its true owner is defined by law." Cf. irlam (paratus), Z. 252; erlam, Z. 7; compar. erlamu, Z. 284. 907. *Faidiugud* (gl. prolongatio), from fot, length, *v. supra*. 908. *Lórgním* is exactly satis-factio. With lór, lour, laur, Z. 123, 309, 607, 889, 1000 (enough), cf. W. *llawer* multus, multitudo, Z. 123. Hence O. Ir. loure, sufficientia, and Z. 30, compares Lauro, Lauriacum, Laurentius. *Gním*, gen. gnímo, is of frequent occurrence in Z., and is connected with the root of do-gníu, facio (= du-genâiû?). 909. *Athcumiledh* (gl. remuneratio) seems from aith = ati (Gaulish *ate*), which stands for the Lat. re-, and *cumal* (a fem. â-stem), said to mean the value of 3 cows, which occurs twice in the following passage: digéni cummen cétaig ríthæ friéladach m[acc]maile odræ tigerne cremthinnæ arech[1] .n. donn ríthæ intechsin fricolmán. nam bretan ar*chumil* .n. arggit[2] Luid in
*chumal*sin

---

[1] Observe the transported *n* of the acc. sing. of ech, viz. ech (ṅ).

[2] Observe the transported *n* of the acc. sing. of cumal, viz. cumil (ṅ). The passage above quoted is

*chumal*sin duforlóg ochtir achid: "Cummen made a mantle, *which* was given to Éladach, son of Máel Odræ, lord of Cremthinne, for a brown horse. This horse was given to Colmán of the Britons for a *cumal* of silver. This *cumal* went in addition to the price of Ochter Achid" (Book of Armagh, 17 *b*). 910. *Disliugudh* (gl. deductio), if I read the word aright, seems literally "a leading away from the road, or path," di-slig-ud, *v.* sligo, *supra*, and cf. *disligeach*, "deviating," O'R., Gael. *dísleach*, "straggling."

911–916. *Cengal* (gl. compilatio), *v. supra*, No. 147. 912. *Eitelladh* (gl. revolutio, leg. evolatio?) I have never met elsewhere. O'R. has *eataladh*, a flight, *eiteallach*, "flying, bouncing," Gaelic, *itealaich*. 913. *Comairemh* (gl. computatio), Gael. co-máircamh, apparently a weakened form of comáram, W. cyfrif numeratio, from áram, numerus, W. cirif, rhif, A. Sax. rím, gerim (cf. rhyme?), see Z. 912. 914. *Bennacht* (gl. benedictio), O. Ir. benedact, bendacht, W. bendithio, "to bless." 915. *Mallacht* (gl. maledictio), O. Ir. maldacht, maldact, gen. maldachtan, acc. maldactin, Z. 584, from maledictio, Z. 270, W. melldith (*ct* always becoming *th* in Welsh, *cht* in Irish). 916 *Lamaccan*, leg. *lámagán*, which, according to O'R., means "groping," Gaelic, *lámhagán*, "handling."

917–921. *Ailginecht* (gl. mitigatio), connected with O'R.'s *ailghean*, soft, smooth, kindly; álgenaigim, algenigim (gl. lento, gl. tardo), Z. 431. 918. *Comma* (gl. talliatio); there is probably some blunder here (leg. *comain*, remuneratio?). I have never met "comma" elsewhere. 919. *Colund* (gl. caro), in Z. 740, colinn, gen. colno, colna, perhaps connected with kravya, κρέας, caro, O. H. G. hréo, gen. hrêwes, cadaver. Cf. the W. calaned, "carcasses;" perhaps, also, calon, "heart." 920. *Laidire* (gl. fortitudo), deriv. from *láidir* (fortis), of which the compar. occurs *infra*. 921. *Imad* (gl. multitudo), O'R.'s *iomad*, for immad, imbad, imbed, gl. ops, copia, Z. 75 (cf. Ambitui), a deriv. from imb = Gaulish ambi = Skr. abhi, Gr. ἀμφί, Lat. amb-, N. H. G. um, Eng. um-, in Fuller's umstroke, circumference.

922–926. *Méid* (gl. magnitudo), in Z. méit = W. maint, Corn. myns, a fem. i-stem = maganti? 923. *Loighedh* (gl. parvitudo), *laget*, Leab. Breacc, cited Lib. Hymn. ed. Todd, 30, W. lleiad (diminution); cf. laigiu minor, Z. 283, W. llai (= ἐλάσσων for ἐλαχιων, and levior, Skr. laghîyâṇs), superl. lugimem, Z. 1128, W. lleiaf. 924. *Teirce* (gl. raritudo), from teirc, gl. rarus, *supra* = duscirg; cf. scirg-lige, "bed of consumption,"

difficult. *Rithæ* seems the 3rd sing. imperf. pass. of an irregular verb, the 3rd plur. imperat. act. of which occurs in Z. 238: ni *riat* na dánu diadi aran indeb domunde (gl. non turpe lucrum sectantes, sint diaconi), "let them not give the divine gifts for worldly advantage," 3rd pl. pret. pass. ro-*ratha*, Fiacc, 25. Cf. the Cornish *ry*, *rey*, "to give" (Norris' *Cornish Drama*, ii. 282), W. rhoi.

tion," ar ni aill *seirge* oc cúrsagad, "for no loss (?) is weakness in reproaching," Z. 1056. 925. *Leithne* (gl. latitudo), W. llydanedd, from the adjectives lethan, llydan (Z.'s lethit, p. 770, acc. sing. is from *leth*). 926. *Airde* (gl. altitudo), derivatives from *lethan*, broad, and *ard*, high, as to which *v. supra*.

927–931. *Maisse* (gl. pulchritudo), O'R.'s *maise, maisi* (gl. decor), Mímaisi (gl. indecor), *infra*, 1083, 1084, 1108, 1109. Maisse occurs in Z. with the intensive er-prefixed: is fuasnad dut' menmainsiu tuisled ho *ermaissiu* firinne trimrechtrad na tintathach, Z. 1064, gl. 4, "It is a disturbance to thy mind to fall from the loveliness of truth, owing to the variance (trimrechtrad = tri in-brechtrad?) of the interpreters." Hence maisse in O. Ir. must have been either a masc. or a neut. ia-stem; cf. W. maws, "pleasant." 928. *Esláne* (gl. aegritudo). 929. *Faide* (gl. longitudo), from *slán* and *fot*, as to which *v. supra*. 930. *Tripulta* (gl. triplicacio), W. triphlygiad, a deriv. from tripul, triplex, threefold, not met elsewhere. *Diabul*, of which the dat. sing. occurs in Z. 968: a buith ar consain *diabuil* (gl. pro duplici consonante digamma positum, i. e. "its being for a double consonant"), has, perhaps, lost the guttural (but cf. ἁπλόος, διπλόος), which is preserved in the W. plygu, to double, root PLIK, Skr. preh, πλέκ-ω, plic-o, plec-t-o, O. H. G. flch-t-an. 931. *Cethardubhladh* (gl. quadruplicatio), W. pedwardyblyg (cf. Ir. dublaighim, I double), the Ir. and W. -dubladh, dyblyg, losing their primitive meaning of "two-folding" in the general idea of "folding." Cf. cóicdíabail, "five-folded," *infra*, note on No. 1053.

932–936. *Uisgemlacht* (gl. limpitudo), a deriv. from uisgemail (uisce-samail). 933. *Curchuslach no gilcach* (gl. arundo): for curchuslach perhaps leg. curchaslach, the middle syllable being represented by a contraction which may be read either *as* or *us* (curchas, gl. arundo, Z. 84.). The syllable -lach, perhaps originally a subst., occurs frequently in Z.: teglach, "family;" góithlach, "swamp;" mátharlach, "matrix;" mimasclach, "hinge;" óclach, "a body of youths;" aslach, "persuasion;" ellach, "union," &c. Here, perhaps, the scribe mistook arundo for arundinetum. Z.'s curchas seems derived from a stem identical with that of the Lat. cârex. 933. *Gilcach* (O'R.'s *giolcach*, "reed," "broom," also a place where reeds grow: Gael. *cuilcearnach*), occurs in Corm., and also in a passage from the Brehon Laws, cited by Dr. Petrie, R. T. 62. Iosa feada, raith, aitcand, dris, fraech, eidcand, *gilcach*, spin, which he thus translates: "The Losafeada [shrubs] are fern, furze, briar, heath, ivy, *broom*, thorn." 934. *Fainleoc* (gl. hirundo), leg. fainleóc, a dimin. of fannall (= W. gwennol, Corn. guennol, Bret. guénnéli), which glosses hirundo in Z. 731, Gael. *ainleag*. Cf. *vanellus* cristatus, the lapwing. Does the diminutival suffix eóc stand for yavanka? 935. *Náit. escuing urcoidech* (gl. hirude, horsclecch): *náit* (cf.
"naid,

"naid, sf. a lamprey," O'R.), seems = nânti. *Escuing erchoidech* is lit., according to O'D., "noxious eel." *Escuing* (= O'R.'s *eascu, easga easgan*, Gael. *easgann*) I have not seen elsewhere; *urchoidech* is Z.'s erchoitech, gl. nocens, Z. 199. 936. *Dealbh* (gl. imago), W. *delw*, a fem. â-stem = a Gaulish delva.

937-941. *Lorgarecht* (gl. indago, investigation, tracing from), lorg, m. track, W. llyr, which occurs in Corm., and also in Z., spelt lorc, gl. trames, whence also lorgairim, I track, investigate; lorgaire, tracker, investigator; lorgair, a dog (cf. Eng. lurcher); lorgad = W. llyriad. Compare also fin*lorg*, which word I have only met in Bishop Sanctáin's hymn, l. 2: dia dam *finlorg* [.i. darmesi] dia tuathum [.i. frim atuaith] dia dom thuus [.i. remum] dia dessam [.i. frim asocr], "God to follow me, God at my left hand, God to precede me, God at my right hand." In Corn. and Bret. we have *lergh, lerc'h*: see Norris, C. D. ii. 428, where the old Cornish trulerch (gl. semita) is ingeniously explained as = truit-*lerch*, "foot-trace." 938. *Sáebchoire* (gl. urago, i. e. vorago, whirlpool) is spelt in Z. 37, sáebchore, in Z. 827, sáibchore, and glosses syrtium. The first element of the word is obviously sácb, sóib, falsus; the last, coire, core, Z. supposes to mean "places" (cf. coór, gl. locus, Z. 29), but perhaps it is the *coire*, gl. caldarium, *supra*: cf. Corryvrecan, i. e. Coire Bhreccáin. 939. *Derge* (gl. rubedo), rust, lit. "redness," from *derg*, O. Ir. derc (cf. dere martre, *supra*), whence the diminutive adj. dercaide (gl. rubronus), Z. 1008¹. 940. *Gerrguin* (gl. sanguisuga, leech, "bloodsucker") is O'lt.'s gearrghuin, "a horseleech." The deriv. is obscure, but cf. Gael. geàrr, "cut," "bite," Irish gearradh, "cutting:" *guin* seems an i-stem from r. gonaim, vulnero, gonas, who wounds, Corm. náram*gonat* fir, "let not men wound me," Z. 933; *gerrguin* may therefore be lit. "that which wounds by biting. *Geal tholl*, a Gaelic word for leech, seems connected with W. gel, gelen, gelue, Corn. ghel, Bret. gwelaouen, gweleounen: Pictet compares Skr. jalukâ. 941. *Suithe* (gl. fuligo, soot) = W. swta, where the sibilant and tenuis are preserved, because swta is from the Eng. soot.

942-946. *Tes* (gl. calido, *infra*, gl. calor), "heat;" so in O. Ir.: gen. in *tesa*, gl. caloris, Z. 231, Corn. tes, gl. fervor, Z. 1112, W. tes, Bret. tez. Can tes be = tepsu? Skr. r. tap, Lat. tep-ere, the ultimate connexion of which with Skr. dah, Vedic dabh, ταφ, is not yet clearly understood. 943. *Ord* (gl. ordo), W. urdd, is órd, ordd in Z.: ní pu libsi int*órd*-so act ba la amiressehu (this order was not with you, but with the unbelievers), Z. 666, gen. uird, Z. 70. Hence it appears that the word is a masc. a-stem

---

¹ Other adjectives formed by this suffix are rotaide, "reddish," Vit. Adamn., and fliuchaide, "moist," "damp," from fliuch, "wet."

a-stem = árda, and cognate with, but not, like N. H. G. ordn-ung, taken from Lat. ordo, a stem in n.. Orddan, a deriv. from this word, occurs in Fiacc's Hymn, v. 25 :—

Asbert [t]*orddan* do mache : do crist atlaigthe¹ buide :
Dochum nime mosrega : roratha duit du guide.

He said, "Thy dignity *shall be* at Armagh : to Christ offer thanks :
To heaven thou shalt come : thy prayers have been granted to thee."

The dat. sing orddain occurs in Ultan's Hymn to Brigit. Cf. also with órd the Gaulish Ordo-vices. 944. *Merlach na comla* (gl. cardo, hinge), "the *merlach* of the door." I have never met *merlach* elsewhere ; shall we read mérlach, and connect it with mér, "finger"? 945. *Smeróid* (gl. carbo), O'R.'s "*smearóid*, s. f. a burning coal, an ember ;" cf. perhaps, W. marwydos and Germ. schmoren. 946. *Gilla naneach* (gl. mango), "servant of the horses :" in the MS. the article is written along with its subst. (*nancach*), and in Mod. Ir. nan each would be written phonetically na n-each, but this transportation of the termination of the gen. plur. of the article must be of very recent origin, as in Scottish Gaelic it is preserved at the present day with the na. In O. Ir. there can be no question that the final *n* of the longer form "innan" was transported to the following substantive beginning with a vowel or medial ; but I never find any indication that this was the case with the short form "nan."

947-951. *Bruach* (gl. margo), *sic* in Z. 28 ; a word still used by Lowland Scotch curlers ; cf. the Gaulish Ande-brocirix, Brocomagus, Eng. brink? 948. *Aodh*, in the Book of Armagh, Áed, a man's name, O. Ir. gen. Áedo, Áeda, Áido (connected with the Gaulish tribe-name Aedui, for áidvi). Aed, Z. xxxii. means "fire" (aed .i. tene, Corm. W. *aidd*), and is related to Gr. $\alpha i\theta\omega$, $\alpha i\theta o\varsigma$, $\alpha i\theta i o\psi$, $i\theta\alpha i\nu\epsilon\sigma\theta\alpha\iota$, Hesych., Lat. ædes, æstus, æstas (Curtius, Griech. Etymol. 215), Ved. édha, m. édhas, n. "fuel ;" vriddhi-form âidh, f. or âidha, m. O. H. G. eit, "fire," Ang.-Sax. âd, &c. The name Áed is either an i- or an u-stem, I cannot say which : it is formed by vriddhation from a root IDH = Skr. indh, to kindle. The name in question occurs in the following passage from the Book of Armagh, 18 *b*, 1 : Epscop *aed* bói isléibti luid duarddmacho

---

¹ Observe this interesting form of the 2nd pers. sing. imper. It also occurs in Z. 840, atlig-the buide, and in the Book of Armagh, 178 *b*, 2 : nutasigthe (nu-t-asigthe) du gallasu (gl. calcia te gallicas tuas), which gloss should have been cited *supra*, No. 72. Compare the Mid. Ir. forms notgebtha darahési ol pátraice, "put thyself in his place, said Patrick."—Pref. to Fiacc's Hymn. Gaibthi cloich isin tailm ; a Loig! "Put a stone into the sling, O Loeg !" Seirgl. Conc. Dr. Lottner regards these forms as taken from the 2nd pers. sing. of the secondary present, which in the indic. ended in -*the* (noscomalnithe, Z. 1054, gl. 29).

duarddmachæ birt edoct cusegéne duarddmachae dubbert segene oitherroch aidacht du*áid* ⁊ adopart *áed* aidacht ⁊ achenól ⁊ a celis dupátrice cubbráth Fáccab *ded* aidacht la conchad lnid conchad du art machæ contubart fland feblœ acheill dóo ⁊ gabsi cadossin abbaith. "Bishop Áed was in Sléibte (Sletty): he went to Armagh: he gave a bequest to Segéne of Armagh. Segéne gave another bequest to Áed, and Áed gave a bequest and his race and his church to Patrick for ever [lit. "to the Judgment"]. Áed left a bequest with Conchad. Conchad went to Armagh. Fland Feblae granted his church to him, and he himself (cadessin = fadessin) took the abbey." Coilboth mac oingusso maic eogin, brecán mac *aido, ibid.* 18 *b,* 2. 951. *Ploit* (gl. uato) seems for *Plait* (gl. Plato).

952-956. *Grian* (gl. Apollo, *infra*, gl. sol, gl. Pean, gl. Titan), sun = grêná, gen. sing. gréne, gréine, a fem. á-stem, and possibly connected with the name of the Gaulish Apollo, Grannos, which Dr. Siegfried compares with the Vedic ghraṇs, or ghraṇsá, m. "sun-glow, sunshine, light." This is referred by Böhtlingk and Roth to the root ghar, whereto also belong Skr. gharmá, "heat," ghṛṇi, "sun;" θερμός, fervere, Ir. garaim, and Eng. warm. The Gaulish Grannos appears in many Latin inscriptions along with Sirona (= Σελήνη? or perhaps, with Glück, goddess of long life, Ir. sír, W. hir); cf. also Apollini Granno Mogouno, with which Dr. Siegfried has compared Skr. maghavan, gen. maghônas, an epithet of Indra, &c. As to—953. *Duine* (gl. homo), W. dyn, Corn. den, and—954. *Nemduine* (gl. nemo), *v. suprá*. 955. *Ogh* (gl. virgo) = ôgâ, is apparently connected with óg integer, óge integritas, virginitas, Z. 28, and occurs in Ultán's Hymn in praise of Brigit, line 7:—

    Dorodba innunn ar colla[1] císu
    In chroeb com bláthaib, in máthair ísu:
    Ind fír-*óg* inmain, con orddain adbail (leg. aidbil?)
    Biam sóer cech inhaid lam' nóeb do laiguib.

    She has abolished within us our flesh's taxes,
    The branch with blossoms, the mother of Jesus:
    The beloved true-virgin, with vast glory—
    I should be safe at every time with my saint of Leinster.

The abl. plur. in Colmán's Hymn, line 48:

    Bendacht for órlam Brigit con *ógaib* hérenn impe,
    A blessing on Patron Brigit with Ireland's virgins around her!

Sometimes

[1] Note here an instance of the governed preceding the governing substantive.

Sometimes in the nom. sing. the ó is resolved, and we find *uag*, gen. *uaige*: foil már Muire *uaige* (the great festival of Mary the Virgin), *Félire Oingusso*, May 3. 956. *Slataidhe* (gl. latro), apparently from *slat* (gl. virga), *v. supra*. Gael. *sladaidh*.

957–966. *Bretnach*, from Bretan (Colman nam *bretan*, *supra*, No. 909), for Brettan = Britt-ana. Zeuss thinks that O. W. brith (gl. pictus) is connected with this name, W. *th* arising from *tt*. But W. *th* may also represent an original *ct*. Cf. O. W. ætinct hronn-*breithet*, "volucria pectore variegata," Z. 1087, and O. Ir. mrecht, varius, mrechtrad, varietas, ilmrechtrad, multa varietas, Z. 822. The following forms connected with a word so famous as *Briton* will probably interest: D. M. Phileti *Brittae* (Mommsen Röm. inschriften der Schweiz, 124). Com-bretonium (Glück, 66). Marti *Britouio* (Orelli, No. 1358). Matribus *Brittis* (from *Britte*burgum, in Bavaria, Orelli, 2094). The Greeks write Βρεττανία, Βρεττανοί = W. Brython. 958. *Fáith brégach*, lit. "lying prophet," O. Ir. brécach, from bréc, a lie, acc. s. bréic dolum, Z. 79, hreic, gl. mendacium, Z. 23; im brecairecht (gl. in astutia), Z. 580. 959. *Fiadhnaise*, in Z. fiadnisse, a neut. ia-stem, "witness, testimony," root ᚃᛁᛞ, gunated; cf. nuiadnisse (novum testamentum), Z. 823, 824, for nufiadnisse. Fiadh = W. gwydd. As to—960. *Comtrom* (gl. par), and—961, 962. *Egcomtrom* (gl. impar, gl. dispar), *v. supra*, No. 903. 966. *Bainne* (gl. lac), milk, occurs in Cormac v. Arg, and is probably connected with banna "drop" (ni contesbad *banna* ass, Brogan, l. 88), and the Corn. banne, gl. gutta vel stilla, Bret. bannec'h, Z. 1119, from bann, a jet?

967–976. *Sgadan* (gl. allec), in Corm. scatan, is a herring, W. ysgadan, cf. Eng. shad, N. H. G. schade; probably a foreign word. 968. *Mil* (gl. mel), honey, cf. Lat. mel, mellis, for melt-is, Gr. μέλι, μέλιτ-ος, Goth. milith : Mod. Ir. gen. *meala*, a fem. i-stem, W. Corn. and Bret. mel. Neither in Irish nor in Greek does the *l* stand for *d*; cf. *meadh* = W. medd = μέθυ, Skr. madhu, O. H. G. metu, Lit. med-u-s, "honey" (in the Mid. Ir. mesce, "drunkenness" (= med-scia), *d* has been lost). 995. *Domblas de* (gl. fel), lit. "bitterness of the liver;" *do-mblas*, opposite of so-mblas, gen. somblais, "sweetness, sweet," which occurs in the Ir. Nennius, 196, tipra uisce *somblais* i taeb in corainn, "a well of sweet water in the side of the Corann;" blas = W. blas, "taste:" the -m- perhaps for -imm. As to *de*, *v. infra*, No. 1032. 976. *Ainmide* (gl. animal), beast, brute; hence *ainmidheach*, brutal, brutish, O'R. 977. *Salann* (gl. sal), salt, *sic* in Z. 740, acc. sing. dinchloich derigne *saland* (leg. salann), "of the stone she made salt," Brogan's poem on Brigit, 40: sailti, "salted," Lib. Hymn. ed. Todd, 20; cf. ἅλς (masc.), sal, sâle, Goth. and Engl. sal-t, Lett. sahls, Slav. solŭ. "In Greek," says Lottner (Zeits. vii. 24), "ἅλς, as is well known, also means 'sea' [it is then feminine], and is radically connected with ἅλλομαι [from σάλjομαι], Lat. salio, which we find again

in

in Sanskrit in the forms sal, sar (sr̥), 'to go.' Thence salila, 'water,' sarit, 'river,' saras, 'lake' = ἕλος. Hence it clearly results that water is denoted by all these words as the 'bounding, leaping, billowing,' just as this meaning also lies in the Greek σάλος, Lat. salum, 'the (leaping) sea-flood.' The passage from this fundamental idea (*grund-anschauung*) to that of the 'salty,' could only take place on becoming acquainted with a great salt sea. And so there can be no doubt that the European peoples were still unsevered when they reached the sea, whilst the primeval abodes (*ursitze*) of the stem lay remote therefrom;" W. halen, Corn. haloin, halcin, Bret. hal, halen, holen; Z. compares the Gaulish name Salusa.

979-981. *Cérceaill* (gl. cervical), and no doubt taken from the Latin, which, of course, is from cervix, neck or nape. Note the lengthening of the *e*, produced by way of compensation for the loss of the *r*, and cf. futures like taiccéra, dogéna, asbéra, dobérat (Z. 1126), for taiccerfa, dogenfa, asberfa, doberfat. 980. *Aníbal* (Annibal), *Ainm duini*, "nomen hominis." 981. *Comairleach* (gl. consul), from comairle consilium, *v. supra*.

982-986. *Easpog* = O. Ir. epscop, from episcopus; cf. O. W. pl. escip, Z. 684, Corn. ispak. 983. *Innarbtach* (gl. exul) = indarbtach, *v. supra*. 984. *Furachair* (gl. vigil). 985. *Nemfuireachair*, "unwary." O'R. has *furachar*, "watching, watchful, wary;" Gael. *furachail*, careful, *furachras*, vigilance. Cf. W. gwarchad, "a guarding," gwarchadw, "to watch," gwarched, "to ward, to watch," &c. 986. *Glecaire* (gl. pugil), cf. O'R.'s gleic, "wrestling, jostling, combat, conflict, contest;" Gael. *gleachdair:* pugil is glossed by cuanene in Z. 27.

987-996. *Neimthní* (gl. nil, gl. nul), leg. *neimhní*; nem, nemh, is a mod. form of the O. Ir. neb, neph (pronounced nev?), and ní is a thing: cf. do nephní, gl. ad nihil, Z. 830. The acc. sing. *ní* occurs in Z. 584, 586; and the nom. (or perhaps the acc.) pl. in Z. 442; na ní ararogartsom (res quas mandavit). This is one of the stems in *i* (like Hí, "Iona," lit. "humilis") noticed in the Beitr. 462. 991. *Ainm* (gl. nomen), name, W. *enw*, has been noticed *supra*. It may here be further observed that ainm seems = âgnâmant = Gr. ὄ-νομαт, the -gnâmant, -νομαт being the Lat. gnomen in cognômen, agnomen (for ad-gnômen)[1]. If, however, ainm was originally an *ant*-stem, it is, so far as I know, the only one in which the *t* has been medialized, and then assimilated

---

[1] It is well known that the Gr. stems in μαт represent Skr. bases in *man*, Latin, in *men*. To identify these we must assume a common prototype *mant*. Curious, if a trace of this prototype be preserved in the second *n* of anmann.

assimilated to the preceding *n* (cf. clann, cland = W. plant). At all events, in the oldest Irish, ainm is a neuter *ann*-stem, and thus declined :—

	Sing.	Dual.	Plur.
N.	ainm (ṅ)	dá ṅainm	anmann
G.	anma, anmae	dá anma?	anmann (ṅ)
D.	anmaimm	dib ṅanmannaib	anmannaib
Acc.	ainm (ṅ)	dá ṅainm	anmann
Voc.	ainm (ṅ)	a dá ṅainm	a anmann

992. *Remainm* (gl. prænomen), W. rhagenw, and—993. *Comainm* (gl. cognomen), W. cyfenw, are compounds with *rem*, *com*. 994. *Tuighe* (gl. stramen, i. e. stratum), "straw-thatch," O'R.; cf. W. to, pl. toau, "layer, roof," toad, "roofing," Z. 163, 874; comtoou, gl. stemicamina, Z. 291; cf. the Gaulish names Togirix, Togidia, Togiacus, Τογοδουμνος (leg. Τογιοδουμνος?), Togius, Togitius, &c., and O. Ir. Toiguire, Book of Armagh, z *a*. 995. *Didin* (gl. tegimen), O. Ir. dítiu, g. diten, *v. supra*. 996. *Arson anma* (gl. pronomen), a pronoun, lit. "in lieu of a noun."

997–1001. *Sidhan gaeithe* (gl. flamen), "a blast of wind," leg. *sidan g.*, and cf. Gael. *séideag*. 998. *Soillse* (gl. lumen), *v. supra*. 999. *Sruth* (gl. flumen, gl. pluuinar, No. 1042), a river, gen. srotha, srotho, W. ffrwd, in O. Ir. a masc. u-stem. Pictet compares Skr. srotas, river, from sʀᴜ, fluere (from sbhrav?). Cf. the Gaulish rivername Φρουτις (Frutis), as Glück, 35, reads Ptolemy's Φροῦδις. Cf. also the Gr. r. ρυ in ῥέω ῥεύ-σω, ἐ-ῤῥύη-ν, ῥεῦ-μα, ῥυ-τός, &c. Lat. ru-o, riv-us, ru-mis (mamma), Lith. srov-e, srav-a. Curtius, G. E. i. 318, 319. The O. H. G. strou-m, Eng. *stream*, have a *t* which I do not understand. 1000. *Tairsech* (gl. limen), threshold; so in Cormac : *táirsech*, O'R., perhaps a deriv. from the prep. tars, Skr. root tar, to stride over or across, an old participle of which Bopp finds in the Lat. trans : cf. W. trothwy, and traws, tros; Bret. treûzou, from treûz. 1001. *Sliseog* (gl. polimen), Gael. *sliseag*, "a chip, shaving;" cf. the Eng. "slice." The glosser seems altogether to have mistaken the meaning of polimen.

1002–1006. *Filideeht* (gl. carmen), *v. supra*, No. 1. 1003. *Sluagh* (gl. agmen) = slôga, W. llu, Corn. luu : so in Z. 27, who justly compares the Gaulish (Belgic) Catuslôgi, "battle-hosts." He also compares λόχος, a troop, which seems a different word from λόχος, an ambush, childbed. Dare we compare O. H. G. slahan, Eng. slay, slaughter? 1004. *Sbruileach* (gl. fragmen), in O'R. *spruilleach*, "a small scrap, crumbs, fragments, offal," cf. W. ysbwrial. 1005. *Maróg* (gl. trolliamen). I now feel convinced that *maróg* (Gael. *marag*, "gut of an animal," "sausage," "pudding") is the modern
form

form of maróc, gl. iolla, i. e. hilla, *supra*, No. 55. Trolliamen is obscure to me.
1006. *Blonacc* (gl. odomen, i. e. abdomen), the same as *Blonac*, which glosses arvina, No. 236. So in A. S., we have the same word for lard and paunch. Blonaco : W. bloneg : : sebocc : hebawg. Perhaps the *ce* (W. *g*) stands for ancâ. Cf. the Gaulish derivatives in aneo, eneo, inco, unco, Z. 773, 774.

1007-1011. *Mullach* (gl. culmen), *v. supra*, No. 838. 1008. *Rind* (gl. cacumen), frequent in Z., nom. s. ar *rind*-siu, 254, generally a neut. i-stem, gen. s. renda, rendo, acc. frisa *rind*, Z. 236, nom. pl. n. rind, Z. 257 : na rind astoidet (gl. signa radiantia), but renda (masc.) in Adamnán's Vision (early middle Irish) : Isat lána *renda* nimo ocus redlanda ocus firmamint ocus ind uli dúl don uallguba dormair dognfat anmanna na peedach fo lámaib ocus glacaib inna námut nemmarbdasin, "Full are the constellations of heaven, and the stars, and the firmament, and the whole world of the mighty lamentation which the sinners' souls make under the arms and hands of those immortal enemies." The following is a paradigm of the O. Ir. declension of neuter i-stems :—

NEUT. *i*-STEM.

Stem, fissi.

	Sing.	Dual.	Plur.
Nom. and Acc.	fiss	dá fiss	foss
G.	fessa, fesso	dá fisse ?	fisse (ṅ) ?
D.	fiss	dib fissib	fissib
V.	a fiss	a dá fiss	a fess

Rind is always rendered signum coeleste, constellatio, by Z., and unquestionably this must be its meaning in "ainm renda, gl. pisces," Z. 255; but its primary meaning seems "point," "mark" (cote in *rinnd*, gl. ubi ... aculeus ? Z. 361, where note the *masc.* article, in dá *errend*, gl. stigmata, Z. 254, and in this sense it is connected with the verbs toruther, Z. 595 (leg. torndcr); dofoirnde, Z. 974; tóirndet (do-fo-rindet), dofóirndet, Z. 433, significant, tororansom, gl. signavit (do-fo-ro-rand-som), Z. 854 ; trimirothorndiussa (gl. transfiguravi), Z. 850 (where the *d* of the root is dropt or assimilated : in dofoirde, dofoirdet, Z. 56, the *n* of the root is lost). Hence it came to mean "the point of a weapon," "a headland" (W. rhyn), "the top of anything," "a star." 1009. *Sil* (gl. semen), W. hil. (There is another Welsh form, sil, where the *s* is unexplained.) Z. compares the names Silo, Silus, Silius Italicus. 1010. *Emnad* (gl. geminen, a doubling), O'R.'s *eamhnadh*; cf. emon, "a couple, twins," Corm. Mac na trí find*emna*, "son of the 3 fair twins," Scirglige Conc., Atlantis, ii. 386 ; mat anmann

anmann adiechta *emnatar*, and is éeen comacomol hi suidib ("if nouns adjective are doubled, there a conjunction is necessary between them," lit, *in* them), Z. 671. Cf. Skr. yama, "twins," unless we regard (e. g.) emnatar as an early corruption of geminantur. 1011. *Ara* (gl. ren), O. Ir. áru, gl. rien, Z. 20, gen. áran, W. aren, pl. ciryn, Corn. acran (Lat. rien, rénes?).

1012–1016. *Sealg no dreassan* (gl. splen, the spleen) would be in O. Ir. selg no dreassan, but I have never met either gloss elsewhere, except in O'R. (who has sealg, but not dreassan), and in O'D. Gram. 397, "mór cosmhailius risint scilg," "great resemblance to the spleen." Selg (Bret. ffelc'h) seems to stand for s(p)legû; cf. $\sigma\pi\lambda\dot{\alpha}(\gamma)\chi\nu o\text{-}\nu$, $\sigma\pi\lambda\dot{\eta}\nu$, Skr. plîhan, Lat. lien. 1014. *Int-inne iachtarach* (gl. lien), the milt or spleen, certainly a blunder, for the Irish words mean "the lower gut"—inne, "a bowel, entrail," O'R., iachtarach, an adj. from iachtar (O'R.'s iachdar), the lower part of anything, O. Ir. ichtar, Z. 147 n., 592, which seems connected with the prep. *is*, "infra." The suffix -tar (as in eehtar = W. cithyr, uachtar = W. uthr, &c., Z. 823) seems identical with the Skr. comparative suffix, -tara. 1014. *Slind* (gl. pecten) a weaver's reed or sley), so Z. 723. 1015. *Cruitire* (gl. lyricen), *v. supra*, No. 5. 1016. *Sdocaire* (gl. tubicen, a trumpeter), from *sdoc*, a trumpet, O'R., Gael. *stoc*, "trumpet," "sounding-horn."

1017–1030. *Tédaire* (gl. fidicen, lute-player), from *téd*, Gael. *teud*, string of a musical instrument, in O. Ir. tét, gl. fidis, Z. 79 = W. tant, pl. tannau, Skr. tantu, pl. tantavas, Skr. r. tan, Lat. ten-d-o, $\tau\acute{\alpha}\nu\upsilon\mu\alpha\iota$, $\tau\epsilon\acute{\iota}\nu\omega$. The *n* of this root seems preserved in scim-*tana*, gl. exilem, Z. 23, cf. Eng. thin, $\tau\alpha\nu\nu$, tenuis, &c. 1018. *Gilla adhairce* (gl. cornicen, horn-blower), lit. "lad of [the] horn;" adhairce, gen. sing. of adhare, "horn, trumpet," O'R., whence the dimin. adercéne, Z. 282, and the adj. adaredae, gl. corneta, Z. 780; cf. also adircliu (gl. cornix), Z. 727. 1019. *Séideadh* (cf. *seidedh gáithe, supra*), "blowing, blast," O'R. 1020. *Muirduchu* (gl. siren), lit. sea-music? The nom. pl. occurs in a passage from Keating, cited in O'D. Gr. 177: trialluid for muir agus teagmhaidh *murdhuchainn* dóibh, "they put to sea, and sirens met them;" cf. duchann, "i. e. ceol, music," O'R., with which our -duchu seems connected: cf. also W. dyganu, "to chant." Siren is glossed by muirmóru in Z. 28 = W. morforwyn, "sea-girl" (morynyon puellæ), Z. 202. 1029. *Mucc mara* (gl. delphin), lit. "pig of [the] sea" (cf. W. morhwch, Corn. morhoch, Bret. morhouc'h, lit. sus maris), mucc mora, gl. dolphinus, Z. 1114; cf. muccfoil, gl. hara, Z. 198 : mucc = W. moch, and cf. meichat, meichiat, "swineherd," Z. 106, 806, and the Gallo-Latin inscriptions, DEO. MERCVR. *MOCCO* (Muratori, i. 51, Orelli, 1407) MAR. ET *SVI*, MER. ET *SVI* (de Betouw, *De aris et lapidibus ad Neomagum et Santenum effossis*, &c.

A Mediæval Tract on Latin Declension. 119

&c., Neomagi, 1783). 1030. *Colach* (gl. cayn) is explained "incestuous, impious, wicked." It occurs in the gen. sing. masc. in a citation from Leab. Breacc. (Petrie, R. T. 369): ba mór tra diumus ⁊ adelos, ⁊ bocasach in ríg *cholaig* (leg. colaig?) sin, and its root occurs in Patrick's Hymn, where Patrick speaks of cech fiss a ra*chuiliu* anmain duini, "every knowledge that hath depraved man's soul." Cf. cuil (gl. piaculi), Muratori, *Antiq. Ital.* iii. 891, cuilech (gl. prostibulum, Z. 431, gl. profanus, Z. 834), cuiligim (gl. prosto), Z. 431; ærchuilecha (gl. tam nefarii ausus), Z. 838; W. cwliawg. 1030. *Deallrad* (gl. jubar, radiance, splendour, brightness), Gael. *dealradh*, masc.

1032–1036. *Aé* (gl. hepar, liver), leg. *ae*, gen. sing. *supra*, No. 975, gen. pl. in Gael. *dinean*, O. Ir. óa (gl. jecur), Z. 28 = W. afu, Corn. aui, Bret. avu, may all, notwithstanding their great dissimilarity, be connected with ἧπαρ, jecur, and Skr. yakr̥t. 1033. *Bróce* (gl. sutolar), a shoe, "brogue," in Hiberno-English, is the W. brycan, where I do not understand the *c*; Gaulish bracca seems Bret. bragez. 1034. *Ichtar na comladh* (gl. lar), "the lower part of the door." 1036. *Rí* (gl. Cæsar), a king = O. Ir. ríg, a masc. g-stem, and thus declined:—

	Sing.	Dual.	Plur.
N.	ríg	dá ríg[1]	ríg
G.	ríg	dá ríg	ríg (ṅ)
D.	ríg, rú	dib rígaib	rígaib
Acc.	ríg (ṅ)	dá ríg	ríga
Voc.	a ríg	a dá ríg	a ríga

The word occurs frequently in Gaulish proper names: nom. sing. reix, ríx (= ríg-s, n. pl. ríges, cf. Lat. rêg (rex), Goth. reik-s, Skr. râj, in samrâj, svarâj (Kuhn, Ind. Stud. i. 332)).

1037–1041. *Sruth*, a river, v. *supra*, No. 999. 1038. *Ith in arba* (gl. far, spelt, meal, grits). Ith, gen. etho, etha, Z. 15, differs from íth (gl. puls), Z. 26 = O. W. iot (gl. puls), Z. 60, now uwd, Z. 1122, Corn. iot. *Ith* (O. W. *it*-laur, gl. area, now *yd*, Corn. hit, Z. 1109) has been compared by Kuhn (I. S. 358) with O. N. aeti. *Arba*, O'R.'s *arbha*, corn, perhaps connected with W. erw, "acre," Lat. arvum. 1039. *Srón* (gl. naris), a fem. â-stem, acc. s. sróin, *supra*, srónbennach, gl. rhinoceros, Z. 28. Srón glosses nasus, Z. 28, and, like W. ffroen, seems to have lost a guttural before

---
[1] Cf. O. W. dou *rig*, Habren, "duo reges Sabrinæ," Z. 157.

before *n* : cf. Corn. fruc, Z. 89, where Norris would read *friic*, Gr. ῥύγχος. The *s* in the Irish form is put for *f*, as in srian, W. ffrwyn, Lat. fraenum, &c., and the resemblance of srón to srenim (gl. sterto, Z. 14 = sternuo, πτάρνυμαι) is therefore accidental. 1040. *Lenmunach* (gl. sequester), from lenamain, O'R.'s *leanamhain*, "following, pursuing." The root len in Z. 1022, gl. 14: *lenaid* din gutai thoisig, gl. ex superiore pendens vocali, Z. 1051, gl. 25, ar mad peethad inti for a taibre grad, *lenit* a peetbe dindí dobeir an grád, "for if he be a sinner on whom thou conferrest a holy-order [lit. a degree], his sins depend from him who confers the order" (1020). 1041. *Sbor an eich* (gl. calcar), lit. spur of the horse ; *sbor*, perhaps not from the Eng. spur. Cf. W. yspar, yspardun (óperon), Bret. spern, "thorn." *Eich*, gen. sing. of ech.

1042–1046. *Sruth* (gl. pluvinar), *v. supra*. 1043. *Clár casta* (gl. torcular, a winepress or oil-press), lit. a board of twisting (a mangle?), *clár, v. supra ; casta*, gen. of *casad*, O'R.'s *casadh*, "a bending, twisting," &c. 1044. *Buaile dam* (gl. bostar, a cow-house), *buaile*, gl. vaccaria, *supra ; dam*, "ox," *v. supra*. 1045. *C. grindi foilci* (gl. nectar), I cannot explain, unless the Irish be put for *c*[*eannach*] *grinde no foilce*, "reward of baptism, or washing." I am indebted to C. for the following curious glosses: *Biathad grinde no crinde* .i. biadh cretme .i. bathais .i. log in baistithi (H. 2, 15, MS. in the Library of T. C. D., p. 61, *b*), "food of belief, i. e. baptism, i. e. the reward of the baptized one." *Crinne* .i. ainm do baisti, ut est biathad crinne .i. logh na baisti intan imlinn ┐ imbiadh doberar .i. ó ní is credintibus bautisium [.i.] in baithis creidmedhe (O'Davoren's Glossary), "a name for baptism, *ut est* 'biathad crinne," i. e. reward of the baptism when much ale and food are given, i. e. since there is *credentibus baptisma*, i. e. the baptism of believers." With *foilce* cf. folcaim, gl. humecto, gl. lavo, Z. 78, Gaulish Volcatius, Volcae, Z. 66, W. golchi, lavare, Z. 151. 1046. *Athair* (gl. pater), O. Ir. athir, is declined *supra*, No. 3, and has, as before observed, lost the initial *p* (the root is pâ, "to protect, to support, to nourish"): hence aitherrechtaigthe (gl. patronymicum), Z. 972. Welsh has lost the word corresponding with *athair* (W. tad = Skr. tâta, carissime). The Breton compizrien (compatres) is, perhaps, a loan-word, but cf. W. athraeb, "relationship," cyfathrach, "affinity" (ach, "pedigree").

1047–1051. *Bráthair* (gl. frater) = brother, O. W. brawt, pl. brodyr, Corn. braud, broder, declined like athir, and found in all the Indo-European languages; Skr. bhrâtr (acc. bhrâtar-am), Zend. brâtar, *et v. supra*, No. 570. The root, according to Bopp (Gloss. 253), is uncertain. Prof. Max Müller, however, says that "the original meaning of bhrâtar seems to have been ‚he who carries or assists" (*Oxford Essays*, 1856, p. 16). In accordance with this view we may suppose bráthair to stand for an original

original bhrâtar, root bhrû, from bhar (bhṛ, Ir. ʙᴀʀ, rob*ar*-t, tulit, Z.). In Old Irish this noun in the nom. sing. and gen. and dat. pl. (bráithre, bráithrib) seems to have gone over to the *i*-declension. Cf. the decl. of the Lith. stems dug-ter, mo-ter, gen-ter, seser, Schleicher, *Handbuch der Lit. Sprache*, i. 193. 1048. *Braen aimsire* (gl. imber, rain-shower). *Braen* (leg. bráen) seems bróen, "pluvia," in Z. 41; so in Colmán's Hymn, l. 53:—

> In spirut nóeb ron*broena*, crist ronsóera, ronsóna.
> The Holy Spirit rain upon us! Christ deliver us (and) bless us!

Braen is explained "a drop" by O'R.; so, Gael. *braon*, and this certainly seems its meaning in Ir. Nennius, ed. Todd, 206: fofrith fer móruleach ind ⁊ *braena* fola derge tairis, "a great-bearded man was found therein, with drops of red blood over him." It is perhaps radically connected with W. bwrw, to cast, to throw : bwrw gwlaw, to rain. *Aimsire*, gen. of aimser, "time," "season," W. amser. 1049. *Cularan* (gl. cucumer, cucumber) is cularain in O'R.; cf. W. cylor, "earth-nuts," Bret. kélor. 1050, 1051. *Mí* (gl. September, gl. October), W. mis, a month. The gen. sing is mís, = mâ(n)s-as, one of the few stems in *s* remaining in Irish, if, indeed, there be another. Cf. mís-tac, gl. mensurnus, gl. menstruus, Z. 256; and Skr. mûs, "moon," "month," Zend. mâonh-, μήν, μείς, Lat. me (n)s-is (from ᴍᴀ̄ɴs, as can-is from ᴋᴠᴀ̄ɴ).

1052–1056. *Máthair* and *Bean* have been noticed *supra*, but with respect to *máthair* = mâtar-i, I may here quote Prof. Max Müller (*Oxford Essays*, 1856, p. 15): "Among the early Arians mâtar had the meaning of maker, from ᴍᴀ̄, to fashion; and in this sense, and with the same accent as the Greek μήτηρ, mâtar, not yet determined by a feminine affix, is used in the Veda as a masculine. Thus we read, for instance, *Rv.* viii. 41, 4:—Sá*h* mátâ pûrvyám padám. He, Varu*n*a (Uranos), is the maker of the old place." 1053. *Bean* (gl. mulier), O. Ir. ben, must have had some curious irregularities in its declension. I have not yet found all the O. Ir. forms, but the following list will probably prove correct so far as it goes:—

	Sing.	Dual.	Plur.
N.	ben		mnáa
G.	mnáa		ban (ṅ)
D.	mnái		mnáib
Acc.	mnái (ṅ)	(dí mnái ?)[1]	mnáa
V.	a ben		a mná

Here

[1] Dothéet cúchulainn iarsin co tard a druim frisinliic ⁊ babolo amenma leis ⁊ dofuit cotlud fair conaccai

R

Here there seem to be three bases: 1°, bani (ben) = gvani, Skr. jani; 2°, bana (ban) = gvanû = γυνή, Bœot. βάνα, Vedic gnâ, for ganâ; and 3°, a lengthened form mnâvû, for bnâvâ, for banâvâ (W. benyw, Corn. mennyw) = gvanâvû. What is the form *bándů̃*, "goddesses," Z. 280? Perhaps a double plural (nom. sing. bandea, *ibid.*, gen. sing. bandeao, Z. 1029). 1054. *Slinn criadh* (gl. linter, i. e. later), "a brick, tile;" cf. W. pridd-faen, pridd-loch, lit. "clay-stone," where pridd = *criadh*. 1055. *Cætharach* (gl. puber) = W. cedorawg, cf. W. caitoir, gl. pubes, Z. 48, hod. codor, "hair of pubescence," Bret. kezour, pubertas. 1056. *Uth* (gl. uber), leg. úth, gen. úthu, see *supra*, No. 102. I think now that úth may have lost an initial *p*; cf. W. piw, "dug," "udder."

1057-1061. *Docinelach* (gl. degener), leg. *dochinélach*, from do, the particle of quality before mentioned, and cinélach, an adj. formed from cenél, as to which *v. supra*. 1058. *Bocht* (gl. pauper), gen. sing. masc. ind aisso *boicht*, Z. 250; dat. pl. donaib *bochtaib*, Z. 823: cf. boctán, gl. pauperculus, Z. 111, and perhaps W. bychodawg (= boxâtâeo?), Corn. bochodoc, gl. inops, Z. 295. Cf. Skr. bhiksh, "to *beg*," bhikshu, "beggar." 1059. *Sine ochta* (gl. uber), if this be what the scribe meant, *sine*, nipple, has occurred *supra*, No. 151, No. 1039: *ochta*, gen. sing. of ucht, breast: *v. supra*, No. 812. 1060. *Machaire* (leg. machairech?), gl. campester, *v. supra*, No. 866. 1061. *Caillteamhail* (gl. silvester), from caill and amail (= samail, samali), apparently with the insertion of *t* before aspirated *s* (caill-t-šeamail), as in mín-t-šúilech, No. 430: however, *coill* makes its nom. pl. *coillte* in modern Irish.

1062-1065. *Uachtlanaidhe* (gl. celeber), *Uachlan* (gl. saluber), have each the peculiar mark which the scribe seems to have placed where he was not sure of the correctness of his Irish gloss. Certainly he was right in putting this mark here. Celeber is glossed by erdairc in Z.; saluber in O. Ir. would be slán, sloinech, or sláintech. 1065. *Gruamda* (gl. acer), from *gruaim*, surliness, Corm. v. Groma. Cf. W. grwm, Eng. *grum*.

1066-1074. *Etechail* (gl. volucer), in O'R. *eiteaccail*, "volatile;" cf. *eite*, quill, feather (= pettia?). 1067. *Góithamhail* (gl. paluster), cf. góithlachde (gl. paluster), Z. 41; isin *goithluch* (gl. in paludo), Z. 822. 1068. *Eithidemail* (gl. acris, leg. alacris?), *eithideamail* (gl. alacris), apparently formed from a personal subst. cithid,
"goor,"

indamndí [O. Ir. indimnái?] cucai indalanai brat úaine impe alaili brat corcra cóicdíabail imsude ("then Cuchulainn went and put his back against the rock, and his heart was low, and sleep came upon him. He saw the two women [coming] towards him—one of them [with] a green cloak around her, the other [with] a red, five-folded cloak round her").—*Seirglige Conculainn*.

"goer," which I have not met, though *eathaim*, "I go," *eathadh*, "going," occur in O'R. With *eathaim* Bopp compares the Skr. r. at, ire. 1069. *Uaidh* (gl. polyandrium), πολυάνδριον, a common burial-place) should probably be read *uaigh*, "graves." 1070. *Earrach* (gl. ver), O. Ir. errach, gen. erraig (it luathider gáith ńerraig, "they are swifter than the wind of spring;" Scirg. Conc. *Atlantis*, No. iii. p. 110). This interesting word (stem (v)erraka, for vesraka? root vas, to clothe) seems to have lost the initial *v*, like úrde, viridis, W. guyrdd, Z. 66, uisce = vad-scia? water. *Errach* is derived by Cormac from the Lat. vêr, but vêr, though it may come from the same root, is formed differently. Vêr is = verer = ves-era, the vowel-flanked *s* becoming *r* as usual, and the thematic *a* being lost, as in ἔαρ = Feσαρ, and as is usual when *r* precedes it. See Benfey, G. W. i. 309. 1071. *Corp leghas* (gl. cadaver), "a corpse that dissolves" (decomposes, decays); *corp*, gen. cuirp, now a masc. a-stem, like W. corff, pl. cyrff: both corp and corff, no doubt, were originally *s*-stems, but have gone over to the vocalic declension: *v. supra*, No. 812, and seem taken from the Lat. corpus. *Leghas*, 3rd sing. pres. relative of *leghaim*, the verbal subst. of which occurs in Z. 580, 614, illobad et *legad* (in corruption and dissolution); cf. also lechdacha, liquids (in grammar), Z. 968. *Leghaim* (cf. W. lliaw, lliad) is etymologically obscure to me, unless indeed Bopp be right in comparing it with a Skr. layâmi, r. ll (liquefacere, solvere). As to the forms legh-as (pl. legh-ate), fut. leghfas, pl. leghfate, Schleicher, Beitr. i. 503, would regard them as the participles present and future active, only preserved in the nom. form of the sing. and plur. The form in *s*, he thinks, expresses the Lat. *ns* (the loss of *n* before *s* being common in Irish), while that in *te*, in the nom. pl. m. and f., would correspond with the Lat. *ntês*. It must, however, be observed that both these forms aspirate: thus, ar cech duine *midus th*rastar dam ("against every one that meditates evil to me," Patrick's Hymn): cid druailnide *m*bes *ch*echtar in da rann, Z. 472, "quamvis sit corrupta utraque duarum partium:" *bes* chuibsech, Book of Armagh, 17 a, 1. Plur. *foilsigdde ph*ersin "quæ significant personam," Z. 198; beta *th*uicsi "qui sunt electi," Z. 197. Hence, when thepractice of aspiration was introduced, these forms must have ended in a vowel, not in *s;* and I follow Professor Siegfried in regarding them as having arisen from the agglutination of pronouns, the relative construction being originally an inverted one. 1072. *Pipur* (gl. piper), from the Lat. 1073. *Sét slighedh* (gl. iter): int-*seuit* bite hí cach crích (paths that are into every country, lit. boundary), Z. 237. Hence, sét appears to have been a masc. a-stem = senta. Glück has compared the O. Brit. name Gabro-sentum, which in Mod. Ir. would be *Gabhairséd*, "goat-path;" Cf. also W. hynt, f. Bret. hennt, m. Corn. cunhinsic, just, Z. 145; O. W. duguohintiliat (incedens), Z. 149; tidoihinto (?) per avia,

Z. 866. The Irish séitche (= sintâciâ), "wife," originally an abstract noun, like aipche, has been referred by Dr. Siegfried to sét. So much for Celtic cognates. In Gothic we have "*sinths* m. (Schulze) Mal, z. B. in *ainamma sintha, tvaim sintham* einmal, zweimal, vrm. eigentlich Gang, Reise (= Mal in mehreren deutschen Sprachen) *gasintha, gasinthja* m. Gefährte, συνέκδημος; pl. genossenschaft, συνοδία." Dicf. Goth. Wörterbuch, ii. 210, 211, where *hynt* and *seud* (= O. Ir. sét) are also compared, as well as O. H. G. sind (iter, trames), M. H. G. gesende (comes), A. S. gesið, sendan, Eng. send, &c. *Sligedh*, gen. sing. of sligi, gl. via, *supra*. 1074. *Dealg* (gl. spinter), O. Ir. delg, gen. deilg, thorn, pin, A. S. dalc, has been compared *supra* with Corn. delc(h). It occurs in the St. Gall incantations, Z. 926, imm an *delg* (around the thorn), manibé an *delg* and (unless the thorn be there). Hence, it appears to have been a neut. a-stem.

1075–1079. *Cac gabhar* (gl. ruter), "goats' dung" (excrement), leg. *cacc g.* = W. cach; cf. Lat. caco, Gr. κακκάω, κάκκη, Skr. çakṛt, in the weak cases çakan, Lith. szeku: the German kacken infringes Grimm's law. *Gabhar*, W. gafar. As to *gabhar*, v. *supra*, No. 372. 1076. *La oirrthi* (gl. juger, an acre) I cannot explain, unless the Irish be for lá-airthe, "a day's ploughing" (airthe, from aratio?), i. e. as much land as can be ploughed in a day; cf. W. aradu, to plough. There is probably some blunder in the gloss. 1077. *Nóin* (gl. vesper, evening), from the Lat. nôna (the third hour before sunset), with change of declension; W. nawn, A. S. nón, Eng. noon, Dan. noen. 1078. *Oide* (gl. nutritor), O. Ir. aite, which occurs in a gloss in Z. 1066, airdanimmart greim á *aite*, "his rearer's influence constrained him." (Note the genitivo's identity with the nom., aite, not aiti. Perhaps, however, aite is the gen. plur.) The word also occurs in the Leabhar Breacc Sermon on Brigit, cited by Dr. Todd, Lib. Hymn. 65: Isé a hathair na noemoigise intathair nemda, isé a mac Isu Crist, isé a *haite* in Spirit nóeb, "this holy virgin's father is the heavenly Father: her son is Jesus Christ, her nurturer is the Holy Ghost." The non-aspiration of the *t* in aite can hardly be explained, except by assuming its original duplication (as in cruitire = crottaria); aite would then represent a primitive attia, which may be compared with Skr. attâ, mother; Lat. atta, Fest. Gr. ἄττα, Goth. atta, father; aithei, mother; O. Bohem. ot. 1079. *Onoir* = honor, whence it is taken, but with change to the i- declension, as in preceptóir, &c.

1080–1084. *Leghtoir* is from the Latin lector [lĕgo], which would regularly become lechtóir: the Irish root LĔO, read; in ro*lég* fanacc, did he read or not? Z. 1434, exhibits a strange lengthening of the vowel: cf. W. mag*wyr* = macĕria. Lêg enters into composition: act arroilgither (ar-ro-lég-fither) ind epistilse dúibsi berthir uaib Laudocensibus et doberthar ind æpistil scríbther do suidib con arlægthar (= ar-lég-atar) duibsi,

duibsi, "when this epistle shall have been read to you, let it be brought from you to the Laodiceans; and let the epistle that is written to them be brought so that it may be read to you." Z. 1044, con arlégidsi, gl. vos legatis, Z. 1044. In legai·s, the 3rd sing. pret., the verb in question seems to have passed over to the ai (ê) conjugation:

> Inn insib mara torrian ainis, innib adrími,
> *Legais* canoin la german, ised adfiadat lini.—*Fiacc.* 6.

> In the isles of the Tyrrhene sea he remained, in them he meditated:
> He read the canon with Germanus; this histories make known.

Soleghta, soleghta, gl. legibilior, *infra*. The root scríu has also been borrowed, and we find it in what is supposed to be the oldest MS. containing specimens of the Irish language, viz., the Book of Dimma (Library of T. C. D.). Thus, at the end of St. Matthew's Gospel: oróit[1] dodimmu rod*scrib* ["pray ye for Dimma who wrote it"] pro deo ⁊ benedictione; at the end of S. Luke's: oroit dodianchridiu diaro*scribad* ["pray ye for Dianchride, for whom was written"] hic liber et dodimmu ["for Dimma"] scribenti, amen . . . (Dimma is supposed to have written this A. D. 620). 1081. *Gradh* (gl. amor). Bopp (Gloss. 107) refers this to the Skr. r. gṛdh desiderare appetere, with which gorte (famine, Goth. gredus, hunger) has been connected *supra*: cf. also O. N. grâd, Eng. greed. 1082. *Doetuir*, from the Lat. Anamchara, lit. "soul-friend," is the beautiful O. Ir. word for doctor, teacher. 1083. *Maisi* (gl. decor)—1084. *Mimaisi* (gl. dedecor), leg. maise, mímaise, et *v. supra*.

1085-1089. *Saethar* (gl. labor), in Z. sáithar (n.?), gen. sáithir: is uisse lóg a *sáithir* do chách (just is the reward of his labour to every one), Z. 1051; astorad *saithir* do (Book of Armagh, 184 *b*, top margin), acc. sing. con sáithar, Z. 251. 1086. *Tés* (gl. calor), gen. tesa, Z. 12 = W. tes, "sun-heat;" perhaps = topsu, Skr. r. tap. 1087. *Dath* (gl. color), dat. pl. secht múir gloinidi con *dathaib* examlaib in a timcholl, "seven chrystal walls, with various colours around it," Vis. Ad. 1088. *Boltanadh* (gl. odor), cf. ni *boltigetar* side *bolad*, "non odorem faciunt hi," Z. 447. 1089. *Bréntus* (gl. fetor), *v. supra*.

1090-1094. *Dénmusach* (gl. factor) from dénmus, O'R. *deanmas*, an effect, and this from dénum, "to do." 1091. *Doilbtheoir* (gl. factor) has been noticed *supra*. 1092.

Cennaidhe

---

[1] The Lat. *oráte*, hibernicised. *Oratio* was also imported: I have not met the nom. sing., which must have been orathe, oirthe (cf. coibse, from confessio), but the acc. sing. *orthain* occurs in the Lib. Hymn., p. 32: Nínine écas dorine inn*orthainse* no fiac sleibte, "N. the sage made this prayer, or Fiac of Sletty."

Cennaidhe (gl. emptor), O'R.'s ccannaidhe, "a merchant, any dealer:" cethrar imorro ros*cennaig*sim pátraic, "now four persons purchased Patrick" (Pref. to Secundinus' Hymn). 1093. *Didnighteoir* (gl. protector), O'R.'s didcanoir, "protector, guardian," from dítu, gen. díten, as to which v. supra. 1094. *Bóc* (gl. tener), hod. bog, "soft, tender, penetrable," O'R., cf. *buigi* (gl. mollior), infra, Bret. bouk, "soft;" hence the Engl. "bog."

1095–1099. *Fígidóir* (gl. textor), fígheadóir, O'R., "a weaver," from the causal verb fígim, I weave, Corm. (W. gwau, gwëu, Bret. gwéa, to weave). Bopp (Gloss. 335) refers to the Skr. r. vê, texere, suere, and compares Lat. vieo, Gr. ἤ-τριον, Lith. udis, textura; see also Diefenbach, G. W. i. 148, 431; Benfey, Gr. W. i. 287. To the Engl. "weave," web, O. H. G. web-an, &c. (see Curtius, G. E. i. 261), we cannot yet quote the corresponding forms in Old Irish and Welsh. 1096. *Triallatóir* (gl. nitor, attempter). The stem from which this noun is formed occurs in the Lib. Hymn. (pref. to Fíacc's Hymn): "dentar *trial* [mo] berthasa, ol Dubthach, con accadar Fíac, "Let an attempt be made to tonsure me," said Dubthach, "so that Fíac may perceive it." 1097. *Fliuchidect* (gl. liquor), from fliuchaide humidus, Z. 272, r. supra. 1098. *Cumdaightóir* (gl. conditor), cf. cumtach, ædificatio, Z. 229, 777, 1046. 1099. *Maigister* (gl. rctor, leg. rector), from Lat. magister.

1100–1104. *Senóir*, from the Lat. senior (which would, I think, more regularly have become sinóir); W. henwr = hen-gwr, a Gaulish senoviro-s. 1101. *Eistidóir* (gl. auditor), cf. O'R.'s *eistim*, "I hear;" by metathesis for O. Ir. étsimm, cf. héitsidi (auditores), éitset (audiunt), Z. 23, 87; foéitsider (subintelligitur), Z. 34; foétsecht, subintellectio, Z. 771: the preservation of the *t* suggests the loss of an *n*. 1102. *Croidhe* = cradia, cridio, in O. Ir. an ia-stem, neuter like Skr. hṛdaya, Zend zeredha-ya, Goth. hairtô, and Slav. srŭdĭce, while Gr. καρδία, and Lith. szirdis, are fem. The gen. and dat. of cride occur in the following gloss from Cormac: *Torc*, .i. nomen do *chridiu* ut etan dixit. Ni fó¹ in dam dom mo thuircc .i. mo *chridi* im chliab cofil forcrith. "*Torc*, i. e. a name for the heart; as Etan said, 'not good is the throbbing of my *torcc*, i. e. of my heart in my bosom which is trembling.'" Cf. also luath*chride*, gl. cardiacus in the Leyden codex of Priscian; Dian*chride*, supra, No. 1080. What is the *crid* in fom*chrid*ichfidersa (gl. accingar), Z. 475; foch*ridi*gedar (gl. accingit), Z. 476? Perhaps we may connect with this *cris*, gen. cresa, a girdle: Bret. dar-*greis*, "the girdle or the middle of the body." *Croidhe* is always spelt cride in Z. (the *o* in *croidhe* being introduced to mark the broad pronunciation of the *r*). I know not if W. craidd

---

[1] Fó (*s* being lost between vowels, and *au* becoming *ó*) = Skr. vasu, Zend vôhu.

craidd were ever a stem in ia. 1103. *Fairge* (gl. equor), v. *supra*. 1104. *Marmur*, marble, from Lat. marmor.

1105-1109. *Ainmidhe* (gl. castor), an animal. 1106. *Ad*, hoc ador *ad* should, perhaps, be read (as O'D. suggests) hoc ador *torad:* torad is "fruit" in O. Ir., dat. sing. torud, Z. 231. 1107. *Ughdur* (gl. autor), from auctor: cf. O. Ir. augtortás = auctoritas, W. awdur. 1108, 1109. *Maisi, Mímaisi, v. supra.*

1110-1112. *Cuimneach* (gl. memor), co-m'n-ech. 1111. *Micuimneach* (gl. immemor), root MAN, as to which *v. supra:* cf. ní *cuman* lim, gl. nescio; cuimnigedar (gl. reminiscentis), Z. 843. 1112. *Tecoisce* (gl. doctior), cf. *tegaisge, supra*, would have been in O. Ir. tecaisciu. The *-iu*, *-u* in the O. Ir. comparatives from iús, and this from iâs = Skr. iyâns (strong theme), O. Lat. -iōs, Goth. iza, Gr. ἰων. The *nis* (spelt *nías, niis, niis, infra*) preceding the adj., is = ní is, ní as, "a thing which is," *is*, *as*, being, as I conjecture, respectively the third sing. indic. of the roots AS, ÁS, the principal fragments of which remaining in O. Ir. are as follows:—

	Sing.	Plur.
Pres. indic. 1.	am, amm[1]	ammi (ṅ)[2]
2.	at	adib[3], ada
3.	is, it[4]	hit, it
	as, at	(at)
Pres. subj. 3.	asu, aso	atu.
Impersonal Flexion.		
1.	ismé, asmmé[5]	issnisni
2.	istú	ississi, itsib.

I cannot explain these forms solely by the root AS and the active voice. The âtmane-forms of AS given by the grammarians are fictions. One is therefore thrown upon the root ÁS and the middle voice, of which last there are, I think, clear traces in the Celtic dialects.

[1] Arnamtomnad *ndmm* (= na + amm) in duine, Z. 702.

[2] Ammi néullg, Z. 252.

[3] Adib óis muintire, Z. 478; adib atrab do dia, *ibid*. Adib iressich, Z. 252. Before *m* the *b* is assimilated: *adim*malcc, Z. 251. What is the form *abi* in Z. 1043, gl. 18: quasi dixisset *abí* mogasi dam ath far cóimdiu in nim, "as if he had said that ye are servants: your lord also is in heaven?" A misreading for adi, i. e. adim[?]

[4] Itsib ata chomarpi, Z. 894; ithé ciatu ruchreltset, Z. 570: rofess *it* fás infenechus icondelg ferb ndó, "It is known that the Fenechus is void in comparison with the words of God," Corm. v. *Ferb*.

[5] Z. 434, -mmó, from mó + mó? Cf. Lat. meme.

dialects. In the first person sing. *am, amm* is the Skr. asmi, Gr. ἐμμί, εἰμί, Lat. sum, Lith. es-mi, Goth. im, Eng. am. Here Irish has retained the old form better than her Celtic sisters, the W. being *wyf*, Corn. *of*, Bret. *off*. The plur. *ammi* (ṅ) is startlingly like the Gr. ἐσμέν, both, perhaps, standing for an original as-masmi. That the *n* is part and parcel of the Celtic form seems proved by the uninfected *m* (= *m* + *n*) in the corresponding W. *ym*, Corn. *on*, Bret. *om-p*, as well as by the fact that *ammi* does not aspirate, and must, therefore, have ended in a consonant. In the 2nd person sing. *a-t*[1], like the W. *wy-t*, Corn. *o-s*, is formed by suffixing the pronoun of this person. But the *a* in *a-t* points to the Skr. âsê, Gr. ἦσαι, the 2nd pers. of the root ĀS, to sit, to be, "from which," says Bopp, Gloss. 35, "the root of the verb subst. AS is, perhaps, shortened." Whereas the *wy* in *wy-t* rests on ê, *ai*, Skr. asi, Gr. εἶ. For the agglutination of the pronoun cf. O. N. er-t, Eng. ar-t, Goth. vas-t = Eng. was-t, O. N. var-t. The plural *ada*[2] seems from *adib*, which may = *adai* + *sib* the pers. pron. of the 2nd pers. pl.: cf. the Skr. âdhvê for âs-dhvai, Gr. ἦσθε. In the 3rd person *is* of course is = Skr. asti, Gr. ἐσ-τί(ν), Lith. es-ti, Eng. *is*. But, like the Lat. es-t, Goth. ist, it must have lost its terminal vowel at an early period, for it never aspirates. Indeed, in one instance (is nuisse, Z. 370) it seems to take a transported *n*, which would point to an old Celtic form ASTIN. But here, perhaps, Z. misread *n* for *h*. The forms *it*, *at*[3], in the sing. are obscure to me. Can they have passed over from the plur.? There *hit* (note the *metathesis aspirationis*, h-i-t = i-h-i(n)t), or *it* is = Skr. santi (for asanti), Zend. hĕnti, Gr. (σ)εντί, εἰσί, Lat. s-unt, Goth. sind: other Celtic forms are W. and Bret. ynt, Corn. yns, *ens*. *As* aspirates, and must therefore have ended with a vowel at a comparatively recent period. It is generally used in dependent or relative sentences; and was, I believe, originally identical with the Skr. âstê: *at* seems to point to ἦνται, Skr. âsatê, for âsantai, the nasal of plurality being omitted, as in dadatê = δίδο-νται. The subjunctive forms *asu*[4] (*aso*), and *atu*, only occur in connexion with the conjunctions ma,

---

[1] Z. 1129.   [2] Ada baill, Z. 251.

[3] Is and *at* gnim tengad isind huiliu labramarni, "est officium linguæ in omni quod loquimur," Z. 446. This is an example of the use of *at* as a *singular* form. But there can be no doubt that it will be found in the plural. I can, however, as yet only quote Middle-Irish examples, such as "*at* buide do láma *at* brecca do beoil *at* liatha do súile," Leab. Breacc, cited O'Don. Gr. 350. *As* is often found in an absolute position. Thus *As* du Christ as immaircide in salm-so, "*it is* to Christ this psalm is inscribed," Z. 473: Sancti et justi it hé as chorp dosom. Christus *as* chenn ind noib *as* chorp, "Sancti et justi, it is they who are his body. *Christus* is head, the saints are body," Z. 197, where note the use of *as* in the plur.

[4] M-*assu* thol, Z. 671.

ma, "if," and *cia*, *cé*, "although," Z. 671, 673. *Asu* (*aso*), the *s* of which is sometimes doubled, appears to me identical with the Skr. imperative âstâm; and *atu* (the *t* of which is unaspirable, and must, therefore, have lost a preceding *n*) seems the Indo-European âsantâm. 1113. *Laidiri* (gl. fortior), positive laidir: *laidiri*, gl. fortitudo, *supra*. 1114. *Mó* (gl. major). This form occurs in Z. 285, as well as móo, múa, má, máo, máa, W. is mwy, Corn. moy, Bret. muy (where note the preservation of the primitive *i*). One thing is tolerably clear about these forms, that they have lost a vowel-flanked *g*: cf. Skr. mahiyâṅs, Zend. maçyéhim zām = $\mu\epsilon\acute{\iota}\zeta o\nu a$ $\gamma\tilde{\eta}\nu$, Bopp; Osc. mais, Lat. major, for mag-ios, Goth. maiza, $\mu\epsilon\acute{\iota}\zeta\omega\nu$, from $\mu\epsilon\gamma\jmath\omega\nu$. So in the superl. O. Ir. maam.

1115-1119. *Lugha* (gl. minor), in Z. 283, 284, lugu, laigiu, W. llei = $\dot{\epsilon}$-$\lambda\acute{a}\sigma\sigma\omega\nu$ ($\dot{\epsilon}$-$\lambda a\chi\jmath\omega\nu$), Lat. levior, Skr. laghîyâṅs, Eng. less. 1116. *Ferr* (gl. melior) = W. Corn. and Bret. guell, Z. 286: cf. Skr. varîyâṅs, $\dot{a}\rho\epsilon\acute{\iota}\omega\nu$. The second *r* in ferr, *l* in guell, represent the assimilated *y*: W. superl. gorcu stands for varama. 1117. *Mésa* (gl. pejor), messa, Z. 285. The positive is the prefix mí- (Ebel) = Goth. missa (Dief. G. W. ii. 76) = Eng. mis: cf. Skr. mithyâ, "falsely." There are two other O. Ir. comparatives in -*sa*, viz., nesa, nessa, or nesso, "nearer," and tresa, or tressa, "firmer," "stronger." Nessa, W. nes, if connected with the Zend nazdista (proximus) = Skr. nédishṭha, may stand for nasdiâs: cf. Skr. nédîyas. (With the superl. Ir. nessam, W. nesaf, Ebel has compared Umbr. Osc. nesimo.) Tressa, W. trech, Bret. tréc'h, seems to point to a Gaul. trexiâs, but this leaves its connexion with the positive trén unexplained, unless, indeed, this be = trexna.

1120-1124. *Sanntaigi* (gl. avarior), *sanntach*, *supra*, No. 667, 1121. *Dilé* (gl. carior), posit. *dil*; is *dil* lace maid [leg. maith] do dónum dúibsi, "she likes (lit. est gratum ei) to do good to you," Z. 283: nimdil, Z. 942; compar. diliu, Z. 283; superl. dilem: is hed as *dilem* lium rath precepte, "It is this that is dearest to me, the grace of teaching," Z. 604. 1122. *Soillsi* (gl. clarior), pos. sollus, solus. 1123. *Meata* (gl. debilior) = O. Ir. mettu, from O'R.'s meata, "cowardly, fearful, timid," reminds one of the Goth. *gamaids*, Eng. mad, but perhaps the resemblance is accidental. Cf. W. meth, "a miss," methiant, failure, decay, Corn. meth, pudor, Z. 223, méza, "timide," "honteux." 1124. *Gile* (gl. albior), pos. gel (= gila), *geal* (gl. albus), *supra*, No. 659. Cf. Lat. gilvus = O. H. G. gelo, Eng. yellow. "The stem," says Lottner (7 Zeits. 184), "is widely spread, but with other suffixes: Gr. $\chi\lambda\omega\rho\acute{o}s$, Skr. hari, Sl. žlūtū, Lith. geltas."

1125-1129. *Soearthanaighi* (gl. amabilior). 1126. *Soleghta* (gl. legibilior). 1127. *Somolta* (gl. laudabilior), all formed by prefixing the particle so (= $\epsilon\mathring{v}$) to adjectives formed respectively from the roots CAR, LEG, and MOL, as to which *v. supra*, and compare with *soearthanaighi* cairddine, for cairtine, "of friendship," Z. 740, cairddinigther (amari),

(amari), Z. 1129, which, however, are formations from the participial stem, carant. 1128. *Conaichi* (gl. felicior), cf. O'R.'s conách, "prosperity, affluence." 1129. *Glica* (gl. sapientior), O. Ir. gliccu: ar ni pa *gliccu* felsub olambicidsi si in Christo estis, Z. 1040, "for no philosopher is wiser than ye will be," &c.; the abstract derived from it occurs in a gloss on "sapientes in astutia," Z. 257, viz., isin tuaichli isin *glicci*, i foili, 1130: cf. Goth. glaggvus, O. N. glöggr, A. S. gleav, N. H. G. klug, Dieffenbach, G. W. ii. 411.

1130–1133. *Cainśuaraighi* (gl. benignior), read *cainḟuarraighi?* compar. of *cdinḟuarach*, voc. sing., cain[ḟ]uarraig, occurs in Gildas' Lorica. 1131. *Dana* (gl. audacior), leg. dána: the positive of this is dána, cited *supra* from Colman's Hymn, 12, and glossing davus in Z. 20. With *dána*, Glück, 92, connects the river-name Dânuvius (N. H. G. Dônau, Eng. Danube), often wrongly written Danubius. Cf. also dánatu (audacia), Z. 769. The dat. sing of dána occurs in the Félire, Jan. 23:—

Césad cebriani	The suffering of Cebrianus
clementi consádu:	And of Clement I celebrate:
ronsnadut dondrígu	May they convoy us to the Kingdom,
conandúnad *ddnu*.	With their daring host.

1132. *Seirbe* (gl. amarior), pos. serb, O'R.'s scarbh = W. chwerw, O. H. G. sueran (dolere) cf. the Eng. *service* tree; cf. the adverb int*serbu* (gl. amarius), Z. 563. Z. has also the subst. serbe, a fem. iâ-stem: gen. sing. o cech cenélu *serbe*, Z. 257, "ab omni genere amaritudinis," acc. sing. cen *serbi* pectho (gl. azymi), "without the bitterness of sin." 1133. *Labartaighe* (gl. loquacior), pos. labartach, an adj. formed from the base labar, frequent in Celtic: cf. Corn. guir-leucriat, veridicus, gou-leucriat, falsidicus, Z. 98, W. llafarn, llefaru, to speak; aflafar, dumb (= Ir. amlabar, Z. 743), and in Irish, labrad loqui, sermo: combad an dede sin im' *labrad*-sa, Z. 460, ro*labrastar*, *supra*, "he spoke," which comes from a deponent labra-r, Z. 444. Bopp, in his Glossary, p. 297, has referred the Mod. Ir. labhraim, I speak, labhradh, speech, to the Skr. r. lap loqui, *sed qu.*; cf. the Gaulish name Labarus. A form, apparently taken from the Lat. labrum, occurs in O. Ir., but unfortunately I am as yet only able to quote its acc. pl.:—

Sén, a christ, mo *labra*	Bless, O Christ, my lips (?)
a choimde secht nime!	O Lord of seven heavens![1]

Before

---

[1] Verses prefixed to the Leabhar Breacc copy of the Félire of Oingus céle Dé ("God's companion"). In a MS. preserved in the Bodleian, however (Rawlinson, F, 95, fo. 59), this passage runs: Sén a christ mo *labrad*, a choimdiu secht nime,—and this I believe to be the true reading.

Before leaving the subject of the Celtic comparatives, I take the opportunity of referring to a paper on the subject by Dr. Ebel in the Beitr., vol. ii., pp. 78-80, and of printing a note with which I have been favoured by Prof. Siegfried: "I was long doubtful whether the Old Irish comparative in *iu, u,* was from -iân (like Greek) or -iâs (like Latin). I am now convinced it is from -iâs, whence by weakening, iûs, iu. We have the analogy of the acc. pl. of masc. a-stems, which ended in -ûs, not -ûn (ex -âns); this we know, because that case never appears with the transported *n*, as in the sing. fer (ṅ). The Welsh termination of the comparative *-ach*, the Breton *-och*, one would wish to explain likewise from -iâs. But I believe that this syllable (the Indo-European *iāns*) is totally lost in Welsh, as it is almost in Irish. No one will find this unnatural who knows that the original accent of the comparative was on the radical syllable. The termination *-ach* must then be some agglutinated word or particle, though such seems at first not offered by the Welsh lexicons. I would point to a possible connexion with ἐξ, ἔξω, ἔξοχα, W. *eh-*, Ir. *as-*, and especially with the unexplained *assa*, which occurs with the Old Ir. comparative in Z. 286. Cf. also the Welsh '*ech-doe*, day before yesterday, *ech-nos*, night before last.'"

1134-1139. *Saithech na tuise* (gl. turibulus, thurible, censer), "vessel of the incense:" *saithech*, occurs, spelt *soitheach* in the *Lebar na Cert*, p. 236. Dare we compare the W. *saig* ? *Tuise*, gen. of *tus* (which occurs in composition in *tuslestar*, gl. turibulum, Z. 1120); *tus* is from the Lat. tus, and from the inflection of the adjective dimór in the following lines, it appears to have been feminine (Lib. Hymn. 7 a) :—

Melchar tidnachtaid indóir	Melchar, giver of the gold:
Caspar tucc in*tus* dimóir	Caspar brought the excellent frankincense:
Patifarsat tacc inmirmaith	Patifarsat brought the good myrrh;
Conastarat[1] dondrig[f]laith.	He gave them to the kingly Lord.

The acc. is more correctly spelt túis in Harl. 1802, 5 b (*tuis* dodia dodégtidnaic). 1135. *Urralaisti* (gl. horologium, ὡρολόγιον) I have never met elsewhere. It is identical with the W. *orlais*, horloge. Cf. *próiste, cóiste*, from broche, coche. 1136. *Piloir* (gl. colostrigium, i. e. collistrigium, collum, stringo), French pilori, "Engl. pillory, aus dem deutschen pfilare?" (J. Grimm, Rechtsalterthümer, 725). 1137. *Compas no raing antsair*, " a compass, or the carpenter's (or mason's) divider," O'D.; *sair*, gen. sing. of sáer = W. saer, a masc. a-stem. Cf. *sáirdénmidecht*, gl. artificium, Z. 771 ; *sáer* oc suidigud sillab, Z. 1018, "an artist in placing syllables;" n. pl. nitat *sóir* huili oc snigid for sunu, Z. 460, "all are not artists in disputing respecting sounds,"

[1] Cf. contarat, Z. 360 (4).

sounds," Corn. sair artifex, faber, Z. 142. How is it that the initial *s* is retained in Welsh? Ciaran macc int*sáir* ("Céranus filius *artificis*," Book of Armagh) is a well-known person in Irish hagiology, as is also the Gobhan *Sáer* in Irish tradition. The Highland name Macintyre = mac intšáir. 1139. *Maide sgine* (gl. manubrium), handle of a knife; *maide*, lit. "wood," "stick," occurs in Corm., and Bopp compares it with Skr. manthâna (rudis); *sgine*, gen. of *sgian*, as to which *v. supra*, No. 440.

In conclusion, I have to repeat the expression of my great obligations to my friend and teacher, Professor Siegfried. To his genius or guidance are due all the novel truths brought forward in this Commentary, and he is in nowise responsible for the mistakes which it contains. I have also to request that my readers will, before forming an opinion on the contents of any of the preceding paragraphs, see whether the statements made therein have been corrected, completed, or modified in the Corrigenda and Addenda at the end of the volume.

APPENDIX.

APPENDIX.

It has been thought that the following Hymn, with the glosses thereon, would form an appropriate supplement to the foregoing Tract and Commentary. The poem in question is taken from the copy preserved in the so-called "Leabhar Breacc," or "Speckled Book" of the Mac Egans (fol. 111, *a, b*), a manuscript in the Library of the Royal Irish Academy. In the opinion of Dr. Todd, this manuscript was produced in the latter part of the fourteenth century. It is a large and well-written codex, and contains many Irish tracts and poems, of which some (such as the "Vision of Mac Conglinni," and the "Calendar of Oingus") are of considerable antiquity.

I know nothing certain about the Gillas (or Gillus—the MS. allows of either reading) to whom the scribe attributes our poem. As, however, Laidcenn, son of Baeth the Victorious (who would seem from the preface to have brought Gillas' production to Ireland), died in the year 661[1], we may perhaps presume that our Gillas was the celebrated Welshman, S. Gildas Badonicus, whose death is recorded in the Annals of Ulster, at the year 569.

[1] "This ecclesiastic was a pupil of S. Lactan, at Clonfert-Molua, now Clonfert-Mulloe, or Kyle, in the Queen's County, and died on the 12th of January (at which day he is commemorated in the Irish calendars), in the year 661."—Reeves, *Proceedings R. I. A.*, Nov. 8, 1858, where also may be found the obituary notices of Laidcenn, contained in Tigernach and the Annals of Ulster. In the latter he is called Laidggenn *sapiens*. In the Bodleian Annals of Innisfallen we find at the year 651, Quies Laidcenn mc. Baith bunnaig. For this quotation, as well as for the following extracts from the calendars, I am indebted to Dr. Reeves:—

    Crist asrúnaid rindaig   Christ's acute mystery-explainer is
    Laidcend macc Baith bandaig.   Laidcend son of Baeth the Victorious.

Félire Oingusso, Jan. 12.

(*rindaig* is glossed by *glic* in the *Leabhar Breacc*, and the first line by "is rinnaith irrúnib crist, i. e. he is sharp-pointed in the mysteries of Christ." *Bandaig*, gen. sing. m. of *bandach*, is translated "victorious" on the authority of Colgan). Laidhgenn macc Baoith o Cluain ferta molna *et* as ann ata a adhnacul, Aois Cr. 660. "L. son of B. of C. F. M. and there is his tomb, A. D. 660."—*Calendar of Donegal*, Jan. 12. So the scholiast on Marian Gorman at Jan. 12: Laidcenn ó cluain ferta molua ┐ is ann robadnacht som .i. Laidcenn mac bóith, "from C. F. M. and it is there he was buried, i. e. L. son of B." Deuis mentions a Ladkenus Hiberniensis who made an abstract from the "Moralia" of Gregory the Great. But I am doubtful if this were the same as L., son of Baeth.

569. This Gildas was the son of Caw, a disciple of Iltut, and, in the opinion of his countrymen, an "egregius scolasticus et scriptor optimus" (Rees' *Cambro-British Saints*; Llandovery, 1853, pp. 120, 343 n). The Welsh origin of the hymn is indicated by its Latinity. Thus gibra (homo), cona (oculus), sena (dens), gigra (leg. gagra? caput), are, so far as I know, only found in the Folium Luxemburgense (see Zeuss, G. C. 1096, 1097, where the forms gibras, conis, sennarum, gugras, are quoted from Mone's edition in his *Die gallische Sprache*; Karlsruhe, 1851). If Gildas Badonicus were the author, and if, as is possible, the *mortalitas hujus anni* mentioned in the fifth and sixth lines were the Yellow Plague, we might attribute the composition of our hymn to the year 547, when that visitation was first inflicted on Britain, and when Gildas was 31 years of age. Dr. Reeves, indeed, has thought (*Proceedings of the Royal Irish Academy*, November 8, 1858) that the composer of our hymn was a later writer. But I understand that this eminent scholar has recently found reason to alter this opinion, which rested, no doubt, on the statement that Gillas was a contemporary of Laidcenn, involved in the assertion that the latter " venit ab eo [scil. Gilla] in insolam Hiberniam." However this may be, I do not think it desirable to go further into the question, agreeing, as I do, with Denis (Catal. Codd. Theol. Vindob., i. 3, p. 2932), who prints from a Viennese MS. of the fifteenth century some verses of the hymn in question, and observes thereon:—"Hymnus sat mendose scriptus, rudis et superstitiosus, quo quis omnes vel minimas partes corporis sui partes Deo protegendas prorsus ἀνατομικῶς adnumerat, ubi ad membrorum censum delabitur, Plautinum te cocum aut Morlinum Coccajum audire credas."

Herr Mone, the learned Director of Archives at Carlsruhe, has published the text of the following hymn from a Darmstadt MS. of the end of the eighth century, which attributes the composition to "Lathacan Scotigena." Mone's edition ("Hymni Latini Medii Aevi," Friburg, 1853, vol. i. p. 367), is followed by a commentary in German, from which I translate the following passages:—"As an example of Irish hymn-poetry of the seventh century, the above song is not without interest, for one perceives in it a national style of treatment which differs greatly from that of the other peoples. In minuteness of detail it agrees with the drawing of the ancient Irish figures (Bildwerk), particularly with that of the illuminations in the MSS., and this particularity (Specialisiren) is accordingly a national trait. See the 'Contributions of the Antiquarian Society in Zürich,' vol. vii., p. 73-75, 92"[1].

"The song rests on Rom. xiii. 12, 2 Cor. x. 4, especially Ephes. vi. 11, 1 Thessal. v. 8.

[1] Hence it will be seen that Mone considers the author to have been an Irishman. And certainly the authority of a MS. of the eighth century is not to be despised. But I repeat that the peculiar Latinity of

v. 8. Hence also χιτὼν τῆς πίστεως in the Menœa, July 29. Quibus pro lorica Christus est, vim non metuunt. Ennod. pro syn. præf. Since the Fall, inasmuch as man's body became mortal, it has been capable of injury, and will remain so until he shall again receive an immortal body through the resurrection. And inasmuch as he has lost the garment of the original innocence, the *stola prima*, he needs against the perils of the earthly life, a defensive garment, as it were, an armour. The song moves in these ideas, to which allusion is made in other places. For example: νεκρώσεως τοὺς χιτῶνας δεξάμενος προπετείᾳ τῆς ἀκρασίας, ἀλλὰ σύ με ἔνδυσον υἱὲ τοῦ Θεοῦ, στολὴν φωτεινὴν τῆς ἀναγεννήσεως. Triodion, E. 1. Gregor. Naz. Orat. xlii. p. 681, says:—'Ἀδὰμ τοὺς δερματίνους ἀμφιέννυται χιτῶνας, ἴσως τὴν παχυτέραν σάρκα καὶ θνητὴν καὶ ἀντίτυπον."

With regard to the Irish glosses which are found between the lines or in the margin of the Leabhar Breacc copy of our hymn, and for the sake of which alone such hymn is here printed, I am of opinion that they are middle-Irish, some of them early middle-Irish, but I can see no evidence that any of them were produced before the eleventh century. Thus we find *m* for Old Irish *b* (noemaib = O. Ir. nóibaib); *d* for *t* (augdar = O. Ir. augtor); *nd* for O. Ir. *nn* (adbronda, coitchind, colaind, brond, cend). *A* is written for *e* in *sean*, O. Ir. *sen*, for *i* in *an* "in," *at* "in thy," and for *o* in *mara*, O. Ir. mora. *Iu* has become *i* in cind (capiti, W. and Corn. pyn), anciently ciunn. In declension the feminine article has in the nom. pl. masc. usurped the place of the forms proper to the masc., and we find *na* sloig, *na* hoscarait, *na* baill, which in Old Irish would be respectively *in*tslóig, *in*doscarait, *in*baill. In the dat. pl. the article and adjectives have dropt their labial ending, and we have dona hainglib, cusna hairnib, cumachtaib nemtruailnide, for the Old Ir. donaib ainglib, cusnaib áirnib, cumachtaib nobthrúailnidib. The noun, too, has suffered serious changes: thus all distinction seems lost between the nom., gen., and voc. sing. of ia-stems, and we find cride for the O. Ir. cridi (cordis) and a thigerna for a thigerni (domine). In the dat. pl. of macc, a masc. a-stem, the old accusative termination seems to have taken the place of the dative-ending, and we find maccu for the O. Ir. maccaib. In a consonantal stem, míl (= mílit), we observe in the acc. pl. a passing over to the vocalic declension, and thus ocmiled-u appears for the ancient ócmíled-a. Other such instances will be mentioned in the notes. In the verb the only remarkable form presented by the glosses is *ingerrtha* (gl. lacerandum) for the Old Irish gorrthí. The practice of thus forming the fut.

the hymn leads me to believe in its Cambrian origin. The metre, too, is un-Irish. It seems to be what Welsh writers call *y gyhydedd laes*.

fut. part. pass. by prefixing *in* to the pret. part. pass. has lasted down to the present day. It is noticed in O'Molloy's *Grammatica Latino-Hibernica*, Romæ, 1677, pp. 99, 100, where we find the following:—" Particula autem *in* addita voculæ facit voculam importare participium finiens in *dus* apud latinos, ut *faciendus*, ut *hoc non est faciendum*, hibernicè *ni bhfuil so indeunta*." This, in Old Irish, would be *ní dénti inso*¹.

The text of the hymn is printed as it stands in the MS., save that I have expanded the contractions, severed the prepositions from the words they govern, punctuated, and invariably commenced the lines and the proper names with capitals. The glosses have been placed under the text, their numerous contractions expanded, and such expansions represented by italics.

Gillas hanc loricam fecit ad demones expellendos eos qui adversaverunt illi. Peru[enit] angelus ad illum: et dixit illi angelus. Si quis homo frequentauerit illam addetur ei secul[um] septimm annis: et tertia pars peccatorum delebitur. In quacunque die cantauerit hanc orationem, oratores, homines uel demones et inimici non possunt nocere: et mors in illo die non tangit. Laidcend mac Búith Bannaig uenit ab eo in insolam Hiberniam: transtulit et portauit superaltare sancti Patricii episcopi sauos nos facere, amen. Metrum undecaisillabum quod et bracicatelecticon dicitur quod undecem sillabis constat. sic scanditur,

[S]uffragare¹ trinitatis unitas, unitatis miserere trinitas,

et sic disponitur:

Suffragare², quaeso³, mihi possito⁴

Ut

GLOSS.—¹ Forgaire ata hic onbrethir choitchiud asberar sufragor .i. fortachtaigim. sufragare .i. fortachtaigim, "this is an imperative from the common verb, which is called *suffragor* .i. I assist, *suffragare*, i. e. I assist." ² INni tra atbert intaugdar [*in marg.*] hic .i. sufragare dobeth forgaire onbrethir choitchind asberar sufragor .i. dotoet uad ifus conidinfinit gnima on brethir gneithig asberar [sufrago] .i. sufragor. fuit sufrago secundum veteres. "Now what the author has said here, i. e. that *suffragare* is an imperative from the common verb which is called suffragor, i. e. it came from it here, [or] it may be an iufinitive active, from the active verb which is called *suffrago*, i. e. *sufragor*. Fuit, &c. ³ .i. deus. ⁴ .i. iarsuidiugnd, "having been placed," lit. "after placing."

---

¹ Ebel (Beitr. 1, 162) has equated the -ti of the O. Ir. part. fut. pass. with Skr. -tavya, Gr. -τέο-ς, Lat. -tivu-s. Z. has compared the Old Breton -*toe*, the Mod. Welsh -*dwy*. Cf. also the Cornish -*dow* in cara-dow, casa-dow, (amandus, abominandus).

4. Magni[4(a)] maris[5] uelut in periculo[6].
　Ut non secum trahat[7] me mortalitas[8]
　Hujus anni[9] neque mundi uanitas[10],
　Et hoc[11] idem peto a sublimibus[12]
8. Celestis[13] milit[i]e[14] uirtutibus[15];
　Ne me linquant[16] lacerandum[17] hostibus[18],
　Sed defendant[19] me iam[20] armis[21] fortibus[22],
　Ut me illi praecedant in acie[23]
12. Celestis[24] exercitus[25] m[i]litie[26]
　Cerubin[27] et corupihin[28] cum millibus[29],
　Gabrihel[30] et Michœl[31] cum similibus[32];
　Opto tronos[33], uirtutes[34], archangelos[35],
16. Principatus[36], potestates[37], angelos[38].
　Ut m[e] denso[39] defendentes[40] agmine[41]
　Inimicos[42] uale[a]nt[43] prosternere[44].
　Dum deinde ceteros agonetetas[45],
20. Patriarchas[46] quatuor quater profetas[47];
　　　　　　　　　　　　　　　　　　　　　　　Apostolos

Gloss.—[4(a)] .i. mor, "great." [5] .i. inmara "of the sea." [6] .i. angussacht, "in danger." [7] .i. naromsraine inbas, "that the mortality may not defeat me." [8] .i. diabul iarforba mobethad, "the devil after the completion of my life." [9] .i. nahamsiresea, "of this time." [10] nadimaines intsoegail, "nor the world's vanity." [11] .i. allatum .i. impide, "a supplication." [12] onahardaih, "from the heights." [13] .i. nemdai, "of heavenly." [14] .i. calmdacht, "soldiery." [15] .i. nasualaig, "the virtues." [16] naromfacbat, "that they should not leave me." [17] .i. ingerrtha, "about to be mangled." [18] escarait, "enemies." [19] .i. corumditnet, "that they defend me." [20] .i. cobairithe, "particularly." [21] .i. arm. [22] .i. calma, "brave." [23] .i. coróremtusaigit remumm isnacathsaib, "that they may precede me in the battles." [24] nemda, "heavenly." [25] .i. nasloig, "the hosts." [26] .i. nacrodachta .i. comthinol nansingel, "of the soldiery, i. e. a congregation of the angels." [27] .i. sciencia multitudo. [28] .i. adntes, "burning host." [29] cusnahilmillib, "with the many thousands." [30] .i. fortitudo dei. [31] .i. qui sicut deus. [32] .l. cusnacosmailsib, "with the like persons." [33] .i. sedes dei interpretatur. [34] .i. innauirtute. [35] .i. summos nuntios. [36] naprincipate. [37] .i. napotestate. [38] .i. nuntios l. ministros. [39] .l. ontsluag dluith, "with the dense host." [40] .l. curaditnet, "that they may defend." [41] .l. oiluag, "with a host." [42] nabescarait, "the enemies." [43] .l. curafedat, "that they may be able." [44] aclod, "to overthrow them." [45] .l. unde dicitur agonithetas? principes belli .i. nabœnachdu. Unde dicitur agon .i. œnach. agon .l. cath l. cuimleng. Unde dicitur liber de agone Christianorum? ex quo fit agonia .i. brug L. athge. "Unde dicitur agonithetas? principes belli, i. e. the presidents of the assembly. Unde dicitur agon? i. e. an assembly; agon, i. e. a contest or conflict. Unde dicitur liber de agone Christianorum? ex quo fit agonia, i. e. anguish or struggle." [46] patres excelsos. [47] .i. aeros nuntios.

T

Appendix.

>   Apostolos[48] navis Ch[risti] proretas[49]
>   Et martires[50] omnes peto athletas[51],
>   Atque adiuro[52] et uirgines[53] omnes[72].
> 24. Uiduas[53(a)] fideles[54] et profesores[55]
>   Uti me per illos[56] salus[57] sepiat[58]
>   Atque omne malum a me pereat[59].
>   Christus[60] mecum pactum[61] firmum feriat[62],
> 28. Cuius tremor[63] tetras[64] turbas terreat[65].

Finit primus prologus graduum angelorum et patriarcharum, apostolorum et martirum cum Christo. INcipit prologus secundus de cunctis membris corporis usque ad genua.

>   Deus, inpenetrabilis tutela[66],
>   Undique[67] me defende[68] potentia[69].
>   Mei[a] gibre[70] pernas[71] omnes[72] libera[73],
> 32. Tuta[74] pelta[75] protegente[76] singula[77],
>   Ut non [t]etri[78] demones in latera[79]
>   Mea uibrent[80] ut soleant iacula[81].

Gigram

GLOSS.—[48] .i. missos. [49] .i. bruinecha l. nastiurasmaind. A prora .i. onbroine, onchuirr thussig naluinge, arite nomiua ada corr: prora. pupis, "prow-men, or the steersmen: *a prora* .i. from the prow, i. e. from the foremost end of the ship; for these are the *nomina* of its two ends, *prora, puppis.*" [50] .i. credentes. [51] .i. na hocmiledu .i. principes belli. [52] .i. atchimm, "I adjure." [53] oga, "virgins." [53(a)] nafedba, "the widows." [54] .i. indracea, "faithful." [55] nafaismedaig, "the confesors." [56] gnathugud trithu, "to use through them." [57] .i. slanti, "safety." [58] .i. coro[m]imme, "that it may surround me." [59] .i. condechat uam foreulu uleu bite foriarair chuirp ┐ anma cechoein, "that back from me may go the ills that are behind the body and soul of every one." [60] unctus. [61] .i. cairdes l. dluthad, "friendship or compact." [62] .i. curabena, "that he strike" [cf. foedus ferire]. [63] .i. in anima et in bono .i. in corpure (*sic*). [64] .i. grana, "hideous." [65] curauaimnige, "that it may terrify." [66] ininillius nemthremeta l. nemthroeta, "the security impenetrable or unconquered." [67] .i. di cech leith, "from every side." [68] ditin, "defend thou." [69] .i. dotchumachtaib nemtruailnide, "with thy incorruptible powers." [70] .i. hominis. gibre. [71] .i. artus .i. compur inchleib, "trunk (?) of the chest." [72] .i. na huile, "all the." [73] .i. saer, "free thou." [74] .i. inill, "safe." [75] .i. sciath, "shield." [76] .i. ditnet, "they protect." [77] .i. membra .i. nabaill, "the members." [78] .i. granna, "hideous." [79] .i. donatoebaib, "to the sides." [80] .i. narobertnaiget, "that they may not brandish." [81] .i. ama*l* clechtait anurcharu, "as they are used, their darts."

---

[a] In the MS. Mee.

Gigram[82], cephale[83] cum iaris[84], et conas[85],
36. Patham[86], lignam[87], senas[88] atque micenas[89]
Cladum[90], carsum[91], mandianum[92], talias[93],
Patma[94], exugiam[95] atque binas idumas[96].
Meo ergo cum capillis[97] uertici[98]
40. Galea[99] salutis[100] esto[101] capiti[102],
Fronti[103], oculis[104] cerebro triformi[105],
Rostro[106], labio[107], faciei[108], timpori[109],
Mento[110], barbæ[111], superciliis[112], auribus[113],
44. Genis[114], bucis[115], internaso[116], naribus[117],
Pupillis[118], rotis[119], palpebris[120], tutonibus[121],
Gingis[122], anclo[123], maxillis[124], faucibus[125].
Dentibus[126], lingue[127], ori[128] et guturi[129],
48. Uue[130], gurgulioni[131], et sublingue[132], ceruici[133],

Capitali,

GLOSS.—[82] .i. incloicend L inceindetan, "the skull or the top of the forehead." [83] .i. inbaithes, "the crown." [84] .i. capillis. [85] .i. oculos. [86] .i. intetan, "the forehead." [87] .i. dontengaid, "to the tongue." [88] .i. dentes. [89] .i. etiucta fiaccal, "*etiueta* (?) of teeth." [90] .i. collum. [91] .i. pectus. [92] .i. latus. [93] .i. nahinneda, "the bowels." [94] .i. nasliasta .i. infnathroic, "the loins, i. e. the waist." [95] .i. intarb sliasta l. infothoin, "the ball of the loin, or the buttock." [96] .i. manus. [97] .i. cusnafoiltnib, "with the hairs." [98] .i. mullach, "crown" (of the head). [99] .i. cathbarr, "helmet." [100] .i. slanti, "of safety." [101] .i. Christe. [102] .i. donchind, "to the head." [103] .i. donetan, "to the forehead." [104] .i. donasuilib, "to the eyes." [105] .i. doninchind tredelbdai, "to the triform brain." [106] .i. dongulbain, "to the bill." [107] .i. donbél, "to the lip." [108] .i. donagaid, "to the face." [109] .i. donaraid, "to the temple." [110] .i. donsmeich, "to the chin." [111] .i. donulchain, "to the beard." [112] .i. donamailgib, "to the eyebrows." [113] .i. donacluassaib, "to the ears." [114] i. donagruadib, "to the cheeks." [115] .i. donabóilib, "to the lower cheeks." [116] .i. donetarároin, "to the *internasus*" (the gristle between the nostrils). [117] .i. dosligtib .i. na srona, "to (the) passages, i. e. of the nose." [118] .i. dona maccu immlesaib, "to the pupils." [119] .i. donarothib, "to the irides (?)." [120] .i. donahabraehtaib, "to the eyelashes." [121] .i. donaluimmchosnib, "to the eyelids." [122] .i. donamennanib[a] l. donsmech, "to the double-chin (aux deux mentons), or to the chin." [123] .i. donanúil, "to the breath." [124] .i. donagruadib, "to the cheeks." [125] .i. dongiall, "to the jaw." [126] .i. dona fiaclaib, "to the teeth." [127] .i. dontengaid, "to the tongue." [128] .i. donbeol, "to the mouth." [129] .i. donbragait, "to the throat." [130] .i. dontengaid, "to the tongue." [131] .i. don uball bragat, "to the apple of the throat." [132] .i. doféith bic bis fontengaid this, "to the little sinew that is under the tongue below" (the frenum). [133] .i. donchulrr bragat, "to the nape of the neck."

---

[a] MS. donamennanibus.

Capitali[134], coutro[135], cartilagini[136]
Collo[137] clemens[138] adesto[139] tutamini[140].

Obsecro[141] to[142], domine[143] Jesu Christe, propter novem ordines[144] sanctorum[145] angelorum*[146].

Domine esto lorica tutisima[147]
Erga membra, erga mea uiscera[148],
Ut retundas[149] a me[150] invisibiles[151]
54. Sudum[152] clauos[153], quos fingunt[154] odibiles[155].
Tego[156], ergo, deus[157], forti[158] loricca[159]
Cum scapulis[160] humeros[161] et bracia,
Tege[162] ulnas[163] cum cubis et manibus[164],
58. Pugnas[165], palmas[166], digitos[167] cum unguibus[b].
Tego[168] spinas[169] et costas[170] cum artibus,

Terga,

Gloss.—[134] .i. donchendfiacail, "to the foretooth" (?) [135] .i. dondibechan, "to the throat." [136] .i. donloing brond, "to the cartilage (?) of the belly" (the ensiform cartilage?). [137] .i. donmuineol, "to the neck." [138] .i. achainnarraig, "O gentle one." [139] .i. aratorta, "do thou give." [140] .i. doninillius, "for the security." [141] .i. aitchimm, "I adjure." [142] .i. tu, "thee." [143] .i. athigerna, "O Lord." [144] .i. tresna .ix. nordaib, "by the nine orders." [145] .i. donanoemaib, "of the saints." [146] .i. donahaingliib, "of the angels." [147] .i. athigerna bi atluir[i]g roinill oenmimdegail aramainslb inchentair ┐ arphein inalltair, "O Lord, be thou a very secure corselet, protecting me from the wiles of this world, and from the punishment of the other." [148] .i. illeith remball*aib* ┐ illeth remindib, "overagainst my limbs and overagainst my entrails." [149] .i. curathnairge, "that thou mayest hammer." [150] .i. uaimm, "from me." [151] .i. dofaicsena, "invisible." [152] .i. inna[m]bir, "of the stakes." [153] .i. naclu, "the nails." [154] .i. delbait, "they form." [155] .i. diabuli. [156] .i. ditin, "protect." [157] .i. dia, "O God." [158] .i. calma, "brave." [159] .i. luirech, "corslet." [160] .i. cusnaclassaib dromma, "with the shoulder-blades," lit. "with the trenches of the back." [161] .i. naformnai, "the shoulders." [162] .i. ditin, "protect." [163] .i. na rigthe l. nahuille, "the radii, or the elbows." [164] .i. cusnarigthib l. cusnasliastaib l. [leg. ┐] cusnadoitib, "with the radii, or with the thighs, or [leg. and] with the hands." [165] .i. nadurnu, "the fists." [166] .i. nabassa, "the palms." [167] .i. namera l. naresi, "the fingers, or the spans." [168] .i. ditin, "protect." [169] .i. nalorgdromma, "the backbones" (the spinous processes?). [170] .i. donasnach, "to the ribs."

---

* In the Leabhar Breac this unmetrical ejaculation is written as if it comprised two lines. It does not occur in the Darmstadt MS.
b MS. unginibus.

Terga[171], dorsum[172] neruos[que] cum ossibus.
Tege[173] cutem[174], sanginem, cum renibus[175],
62. Catas[176] crinas, nates[177], cum femoribus[178].
Tege[179] gambas[180], suras[181], femoralia[182]
Cum genuclis[183] poplites[184] et genua[185].
Tege[186] talos[187] cum tibiis[188] et calcibus*,
66. Crura[189], pedes[190] plantarum[191] cum bassibus[192].
Tege[193] ramos concrescentes[194] decies[195],
Cum mentagris[196], unges[197] binos quinquies[198].
Tege[199] pectus[200], jugulum[201], pectusculum[202],
70. Mamillas[203], stomacum[204] et umbilicum[205].
Tege[206] uentrem[207], lumbos[208], genitalia[209],
Et aluum[210] et cordis et uitalia[211].
Tege[212] trifidum iacor[213] et ilia[214],
74. Marcem[215], reniculos[216], fitrem[217] cum obligia[218].
Tege[219] doliam[220], toracem[220(a)] cum pulmone[221],

Uenas,

GLOSS.— [171] .i. nadromand, "the backs." [172] .i. indruimseilg, "the back-spleen." [173] .i. ditin "protect." [174] .i. doncholaind, "to the body." [175] .i. cusnahairnib, "with the kidneys." [176] .i. nalessa, "the haunches." [177] .i. natona, "the buttocks." [178] .i. cusnasliastaib, "with the thighs" (from hip to knee). [179] .i. ditin, "protect." [180] .i. cusnahescata, "to the hams." [181] .i. nahorcni, "the calves of the leg." [182] .i. natarbsliasta, "the upper thighs (?)." [183] .i. cusnahairnib toli l. cusnafarclib glun, "with the reins of desire, or with the kneecaps." [184] .i. nahescata, "the hams." [185] .i. donaglunili, "to the knees." [186] .i. ditin, "protect." [187] .i. nahadbronda, "the ankles." [188] .i. cusnacolpthaib, "with the calves." [189] .i. donaluirgnih, "to the shin-bones." [190] .i. donacosaib, "to the feet." [191] .i. nabuind, "the soles." [192] .i. cusnasalaib, "with the heels." [193] .i. ditin, "protect." [194] .i. nagega chomforbrit, "the branches that grow together." [195] .i. dona .x. meraib, "to the ten fingers." [196] .i. cusnaladraib, "with the toes." [197] .i. donahingnib, "to the nails." [198] .i. dona .x. ningnib, "to the ten nails." [199] .i. ditin, "protect." [200] .i. donbruinde, "to the chest." [201] .i. donalt, "to the joint." [202] .i. doucht nadernainde, "to the breast of the palm." [203] .i. donacichib, "to the paps." [204] .i. dongaile, "to the stomach." [205] .i. animmlind, "the navel." [206] .i. ditin, "protect." [207] .i. donmedon, "to the middle." [208] .i. donahairnib, "to the reins." [209] .i. nahui[r]ge, "the genitals." [210] .i. donbroind, "to the stomach." [211] .i. donspirait beothaig inchride, "to the living spirit of the heart." [212] .i. ditin, "protect." [213] .i. inmacc hoe tredluigthe l. inmacc hoe treuillech, "the 3-cleft liver, or the 3-cornered liver." [214] .i. nabloingi, "of the lard (?)." [215] .i. selg, "spleen." [216] nalocha ochsal, "the armpits." [217] .i. indriscain, "the ... (?)." [218] .i. inglais, "the ... (?)." [219] .i. ditin, "protect," .i. ingaile, "the stomach." [220(a)] .i. indraip (indrapp?), "the chest (?). [221] .i. cusinscaman, "with the lungs."

---

* MS. calicibus.

142   *Appendix.*

Uenas[222], fibras[223], fel cum bucliamine[224].
Tege[225] carnem, inginem[226] cum medullis[227],
78. Spplenem[228] cum tortuosis intestinis[229].
Tege[230] ucsicam[231] adipem et pantes[232]
Compaginum[233] innumeros[234] ordines[235].
Tege[236] pilos[237] atque membra[238] reliqua[239]
82. Quorum forte præterii[240] nomina[241].
Tege[242] totum[243] me cum quinque sensibus[244],
Et cum decem fabrefactis* foribus[245].
Uti[b][246] a plantis[247] usque ad uerticem[248]
86. Nullo[249] membro[250] foris[250(a)] intus[251] egrotem[252].
Ne de meo posit[253] uitam[254] trudere[255]
Pestis[256], febris[257], langor[258], dolor corpore[259].
Donec iam deo dante seniam[260]
90. Et peccata mea bonis factis deleam[261].
Et de carne lens[262] labis[263] carcam

Et

GLOSS.—[222] .i. nahéte ochta, l. na cuislenna, "the *ete* (?) of the breast or the veins." [223] .i. nafethi, "the sinews." [224] .i. cusintóin .i. coelan nageralne l. muine. [225] .i. *ditin,* "protect." [226] .i. inbleoin, "the groin." [227] .i. cusna hindib, "with the entrails." [228] .i. inlu leith, "the spleen." [229] .i. cusna-findchoelanaib cammaib, "with the tortuous intestines" (lit. "white guts"). [230] .i. *ditin,* "protect." [231] .i. lamannan, "bladder." [232] .i. omnes. [233] .i. nacomdluta, "of the joints." [234] .i. dirim, "innumerable." [235] .i. innahuird, "the orders." [236] .i. *ditin,* "protect." [237] .i. nafoilt, "the hairs." [238] .i. nabúill, "the limbs." [239] .i. cobulide, "entirely," "altogether." [240] .i. asarsechmaillius, "of which I have passed by." [241] .i. ananmand ("their names") .i. prætarii per concisionem causa metri. [242] .i. ditin, "protect." [243] .i. imlan, "the whole." [244] .i. cusna .u. sians[aib], "with the 5 senses." [245] .i. cusna .x. ndoirsib dentaib .i. quinque sensibus anma, "with the 10 doors of . . . i. e. quinque sensibus of the soul." [246] .i. gnath[ogud], "to use." [247] .i. nabuind, "the soles." [248] .i. inbaithis, "the top of the head." [249] .i. cenni, "without anything." [250] .i. sic. [250(a)] .i. allamuig, "abroad, without." [251] .i. allaastig, "at home," "within." [252] .i. nasroin, "that I may not be sick" (?). [253] .i. nafeda, "that it may not be able." [254] .i. botha, "life." [255] .i. curasroena, "that it may defeat." [256] .i. plag, "plague." [257] .i. fiabrus "fever." [258] .i. indiangalur, "the lethargy." [259] .i. incorp, "the body." [260] .i. curaoentaige dia dam curbainsean friforba mobetbad ind etlai ⁊ indendgal, "that God may grant to me that I may be old at the end of my life in purity and in innocence." [261] .i. curadichuirer mopecda domdeggnimarthaib, "so that I may displace my sins by my righteous doings." [262] .i. inategim, "in which I go." [263] uel himis .i. onabasaib, "from the deaths (?)."

---

* MS. fabrifactis: *in marg.* vel fabricatis f. .i. cusna .x. ndoirsib cumda*ch*taib.
b MS. utii.

Et ad alta euolare[264] ualeam,
Et miserto deo[265] ad etheria[266]
94. Letus[267] uchar[268] regni refrigeria[269].
Fin. it. amen.,

GLOSS.—[264] .i. *curaetelaiger cusnahardaib* .i. *cusnanemdaib*, "that I may fly to the heights, i. e. to the heavenly (places)." [265] .i. *curaerchisse dia dim*, "that God may have mercy on me." [266] .i. *cusnanemdaib*, "to the heavenly (places)." [267] .i. *cofailid*, "blithely." [268] .i. *corumimarchoirther*, "that I may be borne." [269] .i. *etarfuarad*, "coolness"?

NOTES.

PREFACE.—*Superaltare* (sr. altare, MS.) "bifariam sumi videtur, nempe pro Ciborio, quod altari imminet, et Altari portatili."—Du Cange. *Savos*, i. e. salvos. *Undecaisillabum*, i. e. ἑνδεκασύλλαβον. *Bracicatelecticon*, i. e. βραχυκατάληκτον.

TEXT.—V. 4. I take the following quotations from Mone *(Hymni Lat.* i. 370) :—An non est mare hoc sæculum, ubi se invicem homines quasi pisces devorant? an parvæ procellæ et fluctus tentationis perturbant hoc mare? an parva pericula sunt navigantium, id est in ligno crucis patriam cœlestem quærentium? S. *Augustini*, sermo 252, 2. *Chrysost.* contra anom. 7, 1. ὁ τῆς δικαιοσύνης ἥλιος τοῦτον ἡμῖν κατευθύνει τὸν πλοῦν. Minæ undæque mundialium nimborum *Sidon. Apoll.* Ep. 9, 4. Salum jactantis sæculi, S. *Cyprian.* Ep. 1. Tibi hoc sæculum mare est; habet diversos fluctus, undas graves, sævas tempestates et tu esto piscis, ut sæculi te unda non mergat.—*Ambros.* de sacram. 3, 1.

V. 19. *Agonetetas*, i. e. ἀγωνοθέτας.

V. 21. Says Mone : A similar putting together of the saints is often found in the Greek songs, e. g. θεηγόροι προφῆται, θεοειδεῖς μάρτυρες, θεῖοι μαθηταὶ τοῦ σωτῆρος, τοῦτον αἰτήσασθε.—*Triodion*, E. 3.

V. 24. *Atque adjuro*. This and the next line are not given by Mone.

V. 25. For *uti* (which, as in v. 85, the scholiast mistakes for ūti) Mone gives *ut*.

V. 28. For *cujus tremor*, Mone has *timor, tremor*. Note the alliteration in this line.

V. 29. *Inpenetrabilis tutela*, Mone.

V. 31. *Gibræ*, i. e. hominis (*gybrœ* in the Darmstadt MS.), gen. sing. of gibra, apparently a corruption of the Chaldee gabrā (Syriac gabrŏ, Hebrew gĕber, Arabic gabrun).

V. 31. *Tetri dæmones*. Again I quote Mone : "The devil has destroyed the divine order in the creation, and this is expressed in his form, which is an image of the wildest distortion (*verzerrung*), neither human being nor beast, but a self-contradictory mixture of both. To this essentially belongs his black colour, for he is an enemy of the divine light; be shines only as a destroying fire, and has fallen
like

144   *Appendix.*

like a lightning-flash from heaven, Luke, x. 18, Matt. xxv. 41. All these representations rest on the Revelation of John, xii. 3, 9, xiii. 2, and other places. Strictly speaking, the devil should only be named serpent, so far as regards the aforetime and the present, for only at the end of the world does he appear as a dragon. *Augustin.* sermon. ined. ed. Denis, p. 39, calls him leo et draco; quando ut draco serpit non ut leo rugit. *Tertullian.* adv. Marcion, 4, 24, diabolus in serpentis et draconis et eminentissimæ cujusque bestiæ nomine deputatur penes creatorem. *Sever. Sulpit.* epist. 3, calls him cruenta bestia."

V. 34. Mone's MS. reads "mea librent, ut solent, iacula." Here, of course, iacula is a quadrisyllable (i-acula). "The darts of the devil," says Mone, " are called in the Menæa ἰοὶ ψυχόλεθροι. Oct. 11. Thereby is the heart poisoned : ἡ καρδία μου φαρμαχθεῖσα ἰῷ τοῦ ὄφεως, Jul. 27. They are a poisonous snake-bite: δρακόντιον δῆγμα, ibid. ἐτραυμάτισεν ὁ ὄφις ὁ παμπόνηρος ὅλην μου τὴν ψυχὴν πονηρῶς. *Triodion,* II. 3."

Vv. 35-38. These difficult lines stand thus in the Darmstadt MS. :—

> Gigram cepphale cum iaris et conas
> patam liganam sennas atque michi: nas
> chaladum charassum madianum talias
> batma exugiam atque binas idumas.

Gigram, better *gugram* (gugras, i. e. capita, Z. 1097), is possibly taken from Hebr. gulgōleth, or Syriac gōgūltō. *Cephale (cepphale)* is of course κεφαλή. For *Iaris* (gl. capillis), leg. *saris,* abl. pl. of sara (-us, -um ?), formed from Heb. sē'ār, Arab. sha'run ? This ingenious conjecture is due to Professor Wright. *Cona,* "eye," and *patha (pata)* "forehead," have not yet been referred to their sources, whence Eng. pate ? *Ligna (ligana),* "tongue," perhaps for lizna, lizana, a corruption of Syr. leshōnō (Heb. lāshōn, Arab. lisānun). *Sena (senna),* "tooth," obviously, as Dr. Todd remarks, from Syr. shennō, fem. (Hebr. shēn, Arab. sinnun). *Micenas* (i. e. etiucta fiaccal). *Micena* must be some part of a tooth, the enamel, the fangs ? but unfortunately the meaning of *etiueta* is unknown, and *micena* is equally obscure. *Cladum (chaladum),* i. e. collum. If this be not from Gr. κλείς, gen. κλειδός, the collar-bone, we must regard it as for cadlum (cadalum), and compare the Arab. qadbālun (Syr. q'dhōlō), which, as Prof. Wright informs me, is "the back of the head and upper part of the neck." *Carnum (charassum),* gl. pectus. I suspect the scholiast has blundered here, for carsum is probably the Chaldee ḥarsā, "the loins." *Mandianum (madianum),* i. e. latus. Perhaps from Hebr. *mothnayim,* which, however, means lumbi. *Talias* (gl. na hinneda, "the entrails, bowels") is obscure to me. *Patma (batma),* i. e. na aliasta .i. iu fuathroic, "the thighs, i. e. the waist," is also obscure. *Exugiam* (i. e. in tarb aliasta no in fotboin, "the ball of the thigh or the buttock"). Exugia is glossed by *gihsunga* l. *gesceinco* (shank ?). Dief. Ælfric has exugium *mecgern.* No one of these A. S. words do I understand. *Idunas (edumas)* seems formed from Hebr. yādhayim. The abl. sing. occurs in the Book of Hymns, *Altus,* line 70, "Suffulta dei *iduma* omnipotentis valida," where the scholiast says, ".i. manu, iduma ebraice, cirus [χείρ] græce, manus latine"*.

V. 39.

---

* I am ignorant of the Shemitic languages, and am indebted for the above Shemitic words to Professor Wright and Dr. Todd.

V. 39. Mone's MS. has meo ergo cum capillis et vertici, which is bad metre and bad grammar. The construction is obviously " Be therefore a helmet of safety to my crown (meo . . . vertici), head (capiti) forehead, eyes, and triple brain (right and left lobes, cerebellum), nose, lip, face, temple."

V. 44. *Internaso.* Ælfric has "internasus, nose-*grýstle*."

V 45. For *Tutonibus*, Mone's MS. has tautonibus, and *tautones* is glossed by A. S. *bruwa*, "eye-brows," in Diefenbach's Med. Lat. Glossary. *Rota* (whence *rotis*) I take to be the circulus pupillæ, ðæs eeo bringe of Ælfric.

V. 45. *Gingis.* I have been unable to find this word elsewhere. *Anele*, i. e. anhelæ.

V. 46. Mone's MS. has:—

> Dentibus linguæ ori uvæ gutturi
> gurgulioni et sublingua cervici.

Uva, "tongue," hence uvula (κίων, columella). *Gurgulio*, "Adam's apple," is glossed by Ælfric *throtbolla* (throat-ball). As to *sublinguæ*, Ælfric has *sublingium huf*, which Bosworth explains as "a round spongy substance covering the glottis."

V. 49. *Capitali, ceutro,* with the meanings given in the gloss, are, so far as I know, ἅπαξ λεγόμενα. With *ceutro*, we may, perhaps, compare chautrum, which Ælfric glosses by *eal throtbolla*. But what is *eal* here? The ejaculation *obsecro te*, &c., is not in Mone's MS.

V. 51. For *domine*, Mone gives *deinde*.

V. 53. For *retundas*, Mone gives *retrudas*, and in illustration of the verse he cites *Triodion*, L. 4, ὁρατῶν καὶ ἀοράτων ἐχθρῶν ῥῦσαι ἡμᾶς, κύριε.

V. 57. *Cubis* (i. e. rigthib). Ælfric glosses the nom. sing. *cuba* by *elboga*.

V. 62. Read *catacrinas* for *catas crinas*; first, because Mono's MS. has the former reading; secondly, because Ælfric has "catacrina *hýpeban*," hip-bone, which comes tolerably near the meaning of the Irish gloss.

V. 64. *Genuclis.* The gloss attributes two meanings to this word. The first is "reins of desire;" and here the word probably stands for *genialibus* (though genialia properly means "marriage bed," "marriage"). The second is "knee-caps;" and here it stands for *geniculis* (Ælfric glosses *geniculi* by *cneoicwyrste*).

V. 68. *Mentagris* (i. e. ladraib, "toes"). This meaning suits in the following passage from Cummian's Epistle (*Usher's Works*, iv. 436): "An Britonum Scotorumque particulæ qui sunt *pene extremi*, et, ut ita dicam, *mentagræ* orbis terrarum." Dr. Reeves has kindly referred me to a story in the Acts of S. Baitheno (*Acta Sanctorum*, Junii, tom. ii. p. 237, *b*), where the devil says of a possessed man, "per *mentogram* irrepsi in eum."

V. 69. *Pectusculum.* Ælfric glosses this word by *breost-ban*, breast-bone.

V. 74. *Mareem* and *Fitrem* are to me ἅπαξ λεγόμενα. *Obligia* occurs in Ælfric's glossary, explained by *nýtte*, and Somner thinks it means ἀκρομφαλον, i. e. the centre of the navel.

V. 75. *Doliæm*, apparently for dolium, which properly means a large jar, but may well have got the secondary signification of "stomach" (*gaile*).

V. 76. *Buctiamine: bucleamen* is glossed by *heorthama* ("midriff, covering of the heart") in an Anglo-Saxon MS. quoted by Diefenbach.

V. 81. *Pantes*, of course πάντες. This conceit of using Greek words when Latin would have done as well, or better, may be further exemplified by the hymn to Abbot Comgill (Z. 1138):—

> Audite *pantes ta erga* (πάντες τὰ ἔργα)
> allati ad angelica, &c.

V. 91. *Labis* (MS. *iabis*) is for labibus.

GLOSSES.—No. 1. *Forgaire*, "an imperative" (= ver-garia): cf. *forgair* imperat., Z. 440. In co *forṅgairiu apstil*, "with an apostle's authority," Z. 1060; *forṅgarthaid*, an imperative, Z. 767, 853, 979; *forṅgarti juasi*, Z. 473, the preposition seems *forn* (*farnóeadcilb*, *forn-óin ûdeilb* "secundum idem exemplar," Z. 583) = Bret. and Corn. *warn*, unless, indeed, this be the Ir. *íarn* = ivarn. The root is GAR. See Commentary, No. 469, and compare γῆρυς, Eng. crow.

Fortachtaigim, I assist, a denominative from *fortacht*, or, as spelt in the Tract, No. 727 (Comm. p. 90), *furtacht*. It may be interesting to put together here the verbal forms found in these glosses:—

Active, Pres. indic. 1st. sing. (ĭ-stems), *fortachtaigi-m*, 1; *atchi-mm*, 52; *aitchi-mm*, 141; *tegim*, 261.
    3rd pl. *ditnet*, 76; *it*, 49.
Pret. act., 1st sing. *sechmaillius*, 240. 3rd sing. *atber-t*, 2 (an ă-stem); *dotóet*, 2.
Imper. 2nd sing. act., *ditin* passim; *bi*, 147.
Conjunctive 1st sing., *sroin*, 252 (leg. *sróinam* ?); *dichuirer*, 261; *etelaiger*, 264.
    2nd sing., *torta*, 139; *tûairge*, 149.
    3rd sing., *bena*, 62; *féda*, 253; *srocna*, 255.
         „   *erchisse*, 265; *imme*, 58; *óentaige*, 260; *sraine*, 7; *úaimnige*, 65.
    3rd plur., *bertnaiget*, 80; *remtúsaigit*, 23; *chomforbrit*, 194; *ditnet*, 19; *didnet*, 40; *fédat*, 43; *dechat*, 59.
Relative present: *bis*, 133.
Passive, 3rd sing. pres.: *asberar*, 1, 2 (an ă-stem), for asberthar; *imarchoirther*, 268 (conjunctive).
Pret. participle: *nemtroeta* (troeth-ta), 66; fut. participle: *ingerrtha*, 19.
Verbal noun: *clód*, 44; *iindegail*, 147; *gnáthugud*, 56; *suidiugud*, 4.

No. 4. *Iar suidiugud* (gl. posito). This mode of making the pret. part. pass. is common in Middle Irish; see, for example, Leab. Breacc, 79 *b* (cited Petrie, R. T. 437), where coilech in cboimded *iarna* chumtach translates the "calix Domini scriniolo reconditus," of what is said to be the Ven. Bede's abstract of Adamnán's work, *De Situ Terræ Sanctæ*, &c.

No. 6. *Guassacht*, danger; *gûassacht*, in Z. 28, 61. Cf. the man's name, Gósact (*Gosactum filium Milcon Maccubooin*, Book of Armagh, 11 *a*, 1).

No. 7. With *sroene* we may perhaps connect W. rhynod, "agitation;" rhynu, "to shiver, to shake;" *sroin*, 252; *sroena*, 255; Mod. Ir. *sraoinim*, "I defeat;" Gael. *sraon*, "make a false step," "fall sideways," "stumble," "rush forward with violence;" *sróin*, "deviate."

No. 8. *Forba*, cf. *forbe*, Z. 15, dat. sing. iar *forbu* in gnímo, "after the completion of the work," Z. 1068.

No. 10. *Dimainee* would now be *diomhanas*. *Soegail*, gen. sing. of soegal, O. Ir. saigul, Z. 731. I know
not

not if this be connnected with W. hoedel (vita), Z. 125, Bret. hoal. The resemblance to së-culum is, perhaps, deceptive.

No. 11. *Impide* is, perhaps, = *imb-bide*. Cf. Goth. bidjan, bidan, A. S. gebede, Eng. *bid*, *bead*sman, &c.

No. 20. *Co-hairithe* for co-hairighthe, an adverb formed from the adjective airighthe (O. Ir. airegde, Z. 233), by prefixing *co*, now *go;* connected are *airechas* (principatus), Z. 233 ; *airech* ("primus, anterior," Z. 67, note) = W. arg in arg-lwydd?

No. 28. *Adntes*, apparently adan-tes; *adhanaim*, "I kindle" (W. en-*ynu*, root AN?). As to tes, v. Commentary, No. 5.

No. 39. *Dluith, v. supra*, Commentary, No. 636. Cf. dluthad, *infra*, No. 61, and W. dyludo, "to adhere," from the W. word it would seem as if dluith stood for du-luith : cf. dliged = W. dyled.

No. 43. *Fedat* (gl. valeant), *feda*, gl. possit, 89, read *fédat, féda*, and compare nir *fétsat* a hescaine do forchúlu, "they could not avert his malediction." Fled dúin nan ged, 28 ; ni *fédann* fer fingaile a toglunsacht, "a parricide cannot move it," ibid. 82.

No. 44. *Clód* = W. cludd, "an overwhelming." Clód for co-lód. Cf. O. Ir. imchlóud (imm-co-lóud), Z. 768, 847; *imchloud* cenelúil na dill, "change of gender or declension," Z. 664: timluad (du-immlód) agitatio, Z. 847 : im*luad*ad (gl. saltabat), ib. ; imm*luadi* (gl. exagitat), ib.

No. 45. *Cuimleng*, cf. bid *cuimlengaithi* .i. bid conflechtaigthi (gl. congrediendus), Z. 474 : coimpleanga, O'R., "a race," Skr. root, *langh ?* With *brug* cf. the Mod. Ir. bruighedn, "strife."

No. 49. *Ænach, œnachdu*, in Old Ir. óinach, óinachdu : in oinach l. i taibderce (gl. in theathrum), Book of Armagh, 183 *b.* Óinach is derived from óin, W. un, Old Lat. oinos, Goth. ain-s, Eng. one. M. Pictet (the morning-star of Celtic philology) has compared the Mod. Ir. *aon* with the Skr. demonstrative *êna. Bruinecha* (gl. proretas), *bruine, broine,* "prora," are O'R.'s *braine*, "prow," *braineach .*l. taoiscach, a leader. (Cf. W. blain, *blaenor*, a leader; *blaenu*, to precede, and Corn. brenulat, gl. proreta?). *Stiurasmaind* is a Teutonic word, probably Old Norse, in which language there may have been *styrismenn*, n. pl. of *styriamaðr*, though I cannot quote either of these forms. Cf. A. S. steóres man, L. Æðelb., *foresteórda* proreta Somn. The Danish styrmand means "a mate." In Breton we have *stûr* and *sturia*. *Corr* fem. agrees in gender with Bret. *ker*, a sharp edge. W. *cwr* (for *cwrr*) is masc.

No. 52. With *atchimm* cf. *itge*, a prayer. Book of Armagh, 18 *b*, 1.

No. 53. *Fedba*, nom. sing. *fedb*, i. e. *fedv* = W. gweddw, Corn. guedeu, Lat. vidua.

No. 54. *Indracca* (gl. fideles) cf. O'R.'s *ionnracan*, and perhaps the O. Ir. *inricc.*

No. 55. *Faismedaig :* the gen. plur. of this word occurs in Patrick's hymn : in cruaigthib huasalathrach, i taircetlaib fátha, hi praiceptaib apstal, in hiresaib *fuismedach,* for which we should read fóismedach : cf. fóisite (confessio), Z. 41 ; fóisitnib (professionibus), Z. 589.

No. 58. *Imme*, apparently from a verb, immim, imbim, formed from the prep. imm, imb = ambi.

No. 59. *Dechat* has here, perhaps, a transitive meaning ; but in Z. 1129, arna *decha* means ne veniat. *Uleu ;* this is the O. Ir. acc. pl. masc. of *ole* (= Ulko-s, which is found on a Gaulish coin ?). *Iarair*, a derivation from the prep. *iar :* cf. rofersam ar*ni*arair, Oingus ; ar ar*ni*arair, Corm. Ecc. 60.

No. 62. *Bena*, from *benim*, Z. 933, I strike, now beanaim. Cf. Goth. *banja* (πληγή, ἕλκος), Engl. bane, Gr. φόνος. The root is concealed in W. cyminedd, "conflict," cyn-binedd.

No. 64. *Grdnna*, cf. perhaps W. graen, "rough."

No. 65. *Uaimnige*, a denominative from *ómun*, fear ; cf. W. ofni, to frighten ; Gaul. Exobnus.
No. 66. *Inillius* (gl. tutela, gl. tutamini, *infra*, No. 140), derived from *inill* (gl. tuta, *infra*, No. 74); *ro-inill* tutissima, No. 147. Z. 731, has *inill* (gl. tutor), but he says the reading is doubtful. *Tremeta* (leg. tremetha?) in nemthremeta (cf. neimhthreabhthe, O'R.), seems a deriv. from the prep. *tremi*, which occurs in composition (tremi-berar " transfertur," tremi-tiagat " transgrediuntur," Z. 850). *Troeta* in nemtroeta appears to be the part. pret. pass. of the verb *troethaim* (O'R.'s *traothaim*), I subdue.
No. 69. With *truailnide* in *nemthruailnide*, cf. ro-*truailled*, "was corrupted," Corm. v. *Bráthair*, Eng. *trull*, Bret. trulen, "femme malpropre," are perhaps connected.
No. 71. *Compur*, O'R.'s *compuir*, "body, chest, trunk," is etymologically obscure to me.
No. 75. *Sciath*, Z. 21 = W. ysgṅyd, Old Bret. scoit, Z. 114 (= scêtâ), the relations of which with scûtum, σκῦτος, if existing, I am unable to settle.
No. 80. *Bertnaiget* (gl. vibrent), Z. 436, has *ro-bertaigset*, gl. vibraverunt. Has he left out *n* ?
No. 81. With *urchar*, "a dart," cf. W. ergyr-waew, " a flying spear."
No. 82. *Cloi-cend* seems the W. *pen-glog*.
No. 83. *Clechtait* (gl. soleant), from *clechtaim*, now *cleachdaim*. The same form occurs in the Leab. Breacc : ⁊ *clechtait* doine a thadnll ⁊ a póccad, "and men are used to touch it and kiss it" (Petrie, R. T., 437). This seems the W. preithiaw, " to *practise*."
No. 93. *Inneda*, acc. pl. of inne, O. W. engued, Z. 149 ; the Corn. eneder-en (gl. extum) is from ἔντερον.
No. 94. *Sliasta*, nom. pl. of *sliasait* (now *sliassaid*), *sliassit*, gl. poples, Z. 22 ; *sliastaib*, gl. femoribus, gl. cubis, *infra*. *Fuathroic*, *fuathrog*, "girdle," O'R., cf. W. gwregys, Corn. grugus.
No. 95. *Fothoin*, I have not met elsewhere, and cannot say whether it is a nom. sing. *fem*. or a nom. pl. *masc*. ; probably the former, as *na* is used in these glosses for the nom. pl. masc. of the article. May we compare the W. *gwadn*, "foundation"? Z. 261, has fotha (gl. crepido), dat. sing. fothu, Z. 999 (rob-fothiged, "ye were founded," ibid ; no-fothaiged, "it was founded," Lib. Hymn., ed. Todd, p. 73), which seems cognate.
No. 99. *Cath-barr*, "battle-hat ;" barr (gl. cassis, Z. 51) = O. W. barr (gl. colomaticus). With these, I suspect, are connected Fr. *barrette*, Ital. *berretta*. Diez, however, refers them to the late Latin *berrus*.
No. 106. *Gulbain* (gl. rostro), cf. nom. *gulba* : cf. O. W. golbinoc (gl. rostratam), Z. 111 ; W. *gylf*, a bill, or beak, Corn. gelvin.
No. 107. *Bél*, "lip," cf. W. gwefl = vo-bel.
No. 109. *Araid* (gl. tempori) for *araig*, dat. sing. of *are*, gen. *arach*. The acc. dual of this word occurs in the charm against *cenngalar* (headache), Z. 926 : im du da *are* ⁊ fort chulatha, "round thy two temples and on the back parts of thy head" (*clais culad*, "hollow of the poll," C.); Corn. *erieu*, gl. timpus, W. ar-lais.
No. 112. *Malg*, "eyebrow ;" Bret. *malven*.
No. 113. *Cluassaib* (gl. auribus), from cluas = W. clust.
No. 114. *Gruadib* (gl. genis), from gruaid, W. grudd.
No. 115. *Oilib* (gl. bucis), from *oil*, now written *aoil*, with which the W. *ael* may be connected, though this means " a brow."

No. 121.

No. 121. *Imchoenib* (gl. tutonibus) is to me an ἅπαξ λεγομένον: the root seems that of *cosanaim*, I defend. Though *tantones*, according to an A. S. glosser, signifies eyebrows, I think that the Irish scribe understood it as meaning eyelids, especially as eyebrows (*mailgib*) occurs before, No. 112.

No. 123. *Anail* (gl. anele), W. *anadl*, Skr. r. ᴀɴ; an-imus, ἄν-εμος, Skr. anila, wind.

No. 125. *Giall* (gl. faucibus): cf. A. S. ceole, Eng. *jowl?*

No. 135. *Dibechan*, throat: *neascóid dibeachain* (gl. apostema gutturis), C.

No. 137. *Muineol* (gl. collo), W. *mwnwgl*.

No. 138. For *edinuarraig* read *edinfuarraig*, and cf. fuarrech (gl. clemens), Z. 778; fuairrech, Z. 986.

No. 147. *Bi at lúirig*, " be thou a corselet," literally " be thou *in thy* corselet," an idiom inexplicable by me. See O'Don. Gram., 165: bhí sé 'n a rígh, " he was a king," lit. " he was in his king." The same idiom is found in the case of the verb subst. *tá*: tá sé 'n a sagart, " he is *in his* priest," i. e. " he is a priest," ibid.; *imdegail*, protection, so in Patrick's hymn: lám dó domm imdegail; and see Colmán's hymn, cited *supra*, p. 57, *oentair*, *altair*, genitives sing. of formations from *cen*, " cis," and *all* = ἄλλο, by means of the suffix *-tar* = Skr. tara; with *amainsib* cf. *dimaines*, *supra*, No. 10.

No. 149. *Túairge* (gl. retundas), v. *supra*, No. 722.

No. 151. *Dofaicesna* (gl. invisibiles), apparently an adjectival n- stem, nom. sing. dofaicse, O'R., from the particle *do* and *faicse*, which I have not met, though *faicsinach*, " visible," occurs. Retla mongach ... do *faicsin*, " a bristly star was seen," Tighernach, cited O'Don. Gr. 443; *faiçfi*, 3rd sing. fut. act. of *faicim*, I see, occurs *ibid.*, 179. With this verb M. Pictet (Beitr. ii. 87) compares Skr. paç, W. paith, " glance (from pakti),; Skr. spaça, " spier;" Lat. specio, specto, &c. I have not found this form (with unaspirated *c*) in Old Irish. Z. 933 has a word, *fegad*, which seems connected:—

Mucholmoc ramcharastar ar *fégad*, ar fis
Is airai ramcharastar nair is tend mo chris.

" Mucholmoc (" my little Colum") loved me, for (my) insight, for (my) knowledge.
It is for this he loved me, since my girdle is strong."

Oc *fegad* (fégad), " seeing;" *fégaid*, " see ye;" *Seirgl. Conc.* Aingil, apstail, ard *fegad*, " angels, apostles, a high vision!" Colm. 44; cf., too, the Mod. Ir. *feuchaim*.

No. 152. *Bir*, gen. *bera* = Lat. veru; birdae, berach (gl. verutus), Z. 46; W., Corn., and Bret. ber. Benfey connects veru with the Skr. r. hvṛ; and this would go far to explain the strange phenomenon of initial Celtic *b* = Lat. *v*.

No. 153. *Clu*, clói (gl. clavi), Z. 67.

No. 160. *Classaib*, cf. W. *clais*, trench.

No. 163. *Uille* (gl. ulnas), W. and Corn. elin. Cf. ul-na, ὠλ-ένη, ellen bogen, Eng. el-bow.

No. 166. *Bassa*, from *bas*, " palm of the hand," probably identical with W. *bas*, shallow, flat.

No. 170. *Asnach* (gl. costas): cf. W. and Corn. asen (there is a W. plur. asen-au). Radically connected with Skr. asthi (by-theme asthan), ὀστέον, os, oss-is.

No. 177. *Tóna*, buttocks: cf. W. *tin*, " a tail, a bottom."

No. 185. *Glúnib* (gl. genua), from glún, W. glin, Corn. (irregularly) clin.

No. 187. *Adbronda* (gl. talos): O. Ir. odbrann, gl. talus, Z. 1102: Leyden Priscian, 37 *b*, Gael. aobrunn (where note the non-aspiration of the *b*), W. uffarn. Probably a compound, the first element of which has,

150   *Appendix.*

has, as Dr. Siegfried suggests, perhaps lost an initial *p :* cf. ποδ-ός, pĕd-is, Skr. pad (Eng. *foot,* Goth. *fótu* is Skr. pâda).

No. 189. With *luirgnib,* nom. *lorga,* cf., perhaps, W. llorp, shank.

No. 192. *Salaib* (gl. bassibus), from *sal* = W. ff'al (or sawdl?).

No. 194. *Géga,* " branches," from gág = W. caog, as dég (10) = W. deng. Perhaps we may compare the Ir. (and British) tribe-name, Gangani (Γάγγανοι).

No. 196. *Ladhar* now means a fork, a prong, the space between two fingers or two toes. O'Reilly, however, has *ladhar,* "a toe," and in Gaelic the word means hoof as well as prong, fork.

No. 198. *Dona .x. ningnib, read* dona deich n-ingnib, and note the occurrence of the transported *n* after *deich* (10), that number (Skr. daçan, Lat. decem) having originally ended in a nasal. So we have secht(n) 7, and ocht (n) 8, *ingnib,* dat. of *inga* = W. ewin, Skr. nakha, ὄνυξ, Germ. nag-el, Eng. *nai*-l.

No. 200. *Bruinde,* " breast, bosom." St. John is called Sean na bruinne ; W. and Corn. bron.

No. 203. *Cich* = W. cyg, flesh.

No. 205. *Immlind,* navel. Radically connected with ὀμφαλός, umbilicus, navel, Skr. nâbhi.

No. 216. *Ochsal* (which in form is almost identical with Lat. axilla, O. H. G. ahsala) is, I suspect, by metathesis for oschal, aschal: cf. W. asgall, "wing."

No. 220. *Raip* (?) I have never met elsewhere. Can it be connected with A. S. hrife, Eng. mid-*riff*? But the word may, perhaps, be *indraip,* or *draip.*

No. 221. *Scaman* (gl. pulmone), cf. O. W. *scamn*hegint (gl. levant), W. ysgyfaint, "the lights ;" Bret. scŏvent, Corn. skefans.

No. 224. *Cusin tóin,* "with the anus, i. e. *coelan na geraine no muine,* the gut of fat or lard ;" i. e. the large intestine which is covered by the omentum : *coelan,* a deriv. from cóil, "slender :" *geraine,* gen. sing. of some word having the same root as *geir,* tallow : *muine,* " the lard which lines the intestines of a pig," C. The Highland Society's Dict. has *muin,* " fat adhering to the entrails of an animal."

No. 228. *Lu leith* "the spleen." Perhaps the mysterious *lewilloit* (gl. splen) of the Cornish vocabulary, may be connected with this.

No. 229. *Find,* "white," W. gwyn, Gaulish, Vindos; root vid, for cvid, Skr. çvid album esse, Goth. hveita, Eng. white. *Cammaib,* nom. sing. *camm,* W. cam = cambo in Cambo-dunum, &c., see Z. 75.

No. 231. *Lamannan,* "bladder," perhaps connected with W. *lla*fanog, "liverwort."

No. 238. *Baill,* nom. pl. of báll, "a member" = φαλλός (Prof. Siegfried).

No. 240. *Asarsèchmaillius,* i. e. asa-r'-sèchmaillius, *asa,* "whose," (sing. and plur.), I cannot explain. It occurs at least twice in the Félire, and also, spelt *isa,* in the *Battle of Magh Rath.* See O'Don. Gr. 131, 132. *Sechmaillius* is the 1st. sing. pret. act. of a verb which in Z. appears to belong to the â-conjugation (the Latin first): nad *sechmalla* (gl. non omittit), Z. 849; *sechmalfam*-ni (praeteribimus), Z. 437; sechmalfaider, Z. 1067. In Mod. Ir. the verb in question has passed over to the î-conjugation (the Latin fourth), as we see from the form *scachmaill-i-m* ; and this change seems to have taken place when our gloss was written, *sechmaill-i-us* being identical in form with rocinn-i-us (gl. definivi), Z. 434; baits-i-us, ibid.; tocuir-i-us (Patrick's Hymn), &c.

No. 245. I do not understand this gloss. Can *dentœib* be for d'óen-tóib, " of one side"?

Nos. 250, 251. *Allamuig,* "outside;" *allaastig,* " on the inside." I cannot explain these adverbs. They occur in O'Don. Gr. 263, 269.

No. 258.

No. 258. *Diangalur* (gl. languor). This gloss enables me to correct my reading and version of part of one of the S. Gall incantations, Commentary, No. 222. *Diangalar fúail* (languor urinae) is the ailment against which the charm is directed.

No. 260. *Endgai*, innocence, O. Ir *eneae*, fem., Z. 262; innan ennac (gl. innocentum), Z. 1003. S. Brigit is said to have been *endac*, "innocent," Leb. Breacc, cited Todd, Lib. Hymn, 65. The true spelling is *enneae*, *ennae*, and the words are probably cognate with in-nocens (noceo = Skr. nâçayâmi, "I slay"). *Etlai*, dat. of *etlae*, *etla* ? an abstract from the adj. *etal*, the gen. sing. neut. of which occurs in H. 2, 15, fo. 64, *a* (T. C. D.): co fortacht cach *etail* .i. co forithin cach glain.

No. 261. *Deg-gnimarthaib*. I have not met the nom. sing. of the *simplex* of this word, which must be *gnimarad*, whence O'R.'s *gniomharthach*, "actual, active."

No. 265. *Erchisse*, better *airchisse*. Cf. airchissi (gl. parcit), Z. 199; airchissa, arcessea, "parcat," Z. 839; hond erchissecht (gl. propitiatione), Z. 839. The root is probably identical with that of *cessacht*, "sparingness," *supra*, p. 64, No. 280.

No. 267. *Cofáilid* (gl. laetus). Cf. fáilte, "gaudium," Z. 94, which Z. connects with Goth. bleiths, O. H. G. blîdi, A. S. blîde, Eng. *blithe*. He also compares Lat. *laetus*, which he supposes to stand for *flaetus*.

No. 268. *Co-ru-m-imarchoirther* exemplifies the system of impersonal flexion which has attained such a development in the Celtic verb, in consequence of the early loss of the first and second persons in the tenses of the passive. Cf. *do-chuirur*, gl. ascisco, Z. 844; *imm-e-churetar* "qui tractant," Z. 447 (where the *e* is the infixed relative, changed from *a* by progressive *umlaut*); *erchuiretar*, Z. 1016, 467; "ponuntur," *adchuireddar*, "adhibentur," Z. 467; *cuirctar*, "ponunt," Z. 314; *cuire* uait, "pone a te," Z. 457. The third sing. pret. act. of the verb in our gloss occurs in the *Irish Nennius*, p. 110: ro-*imarcor* Artur delb [deilb ?] Muire for a gualaind ⁊ ro-teilgistar na Pagain, "Arthur carried the image of Mary on his shoulder, and cast out the Pagans."

No. 269. *Etarfuarad* (gl. refrigeria), cf. *fuar*, cold. I do not understand the force of *etar-* here.

CORRECTIONS

CORRECTIONS AND ADDITIONS.

Page 2, *for* caraic *read* carric (Old Ir. *carric*, Book of Armagh, 10 *b*, 1; Med. W. *carrec*, Z. 814).

Page 4, note 15, *for* amann *read* lamann.

Page 5, No. 55, iolla is for hilla: see Commentary, No. 1005, p. 116.

Page 5, No. 57, *for* placaipe *read* placaipe.

Page 7, No. 132, scama is for squama, and lanb is the O. Ir. *lann*. "Cenni am. blosce am. *lanna*" is the gloss in the Book of Armagh, 176 *b*, 2, on "ceciderunt ab oculis ejus tamquam scamae."

Page 7, No. 147, *for* caip *read* capp.

Page 8, No. 211, *for* fistula *read* festuca.

Page 9, No. 237, *for* manipicina *read* monificina.

Page 9, No. 254, scupa is certainly for stupa, not scopac.

Page 10, No. 169, *for* cnaimpiað *read* cnaimpiað.

Page 10, Nos. 272, 273, *for* chiromantia *read* chiromachia. For pcupna *read* sturna.

Page 11, No. 305, *for* eipinnað *read* éipinnað.

Page 12, No. 328, *for* pepga *read* pepgaðc.

Page 14, note 4, read merlaime, mer coisi.

Page 17, No. 503, read cnaimpiað. No. 520, read Locanus, Loðan.

Page 18, No. 575, *for* paipge *read* paipge.

Page 19, No. 621, *for* piappuileð *read* piappuilech.

Page 20, No. 643, delete [ventossus].

Page 24, No. 811, the MS. has "creocledus inleman."

Page 25, No. 826, I should now read this as follows: "hic sibilus est hominis (i. e. is of the masc. gender) sibela [est feminae "is of the fem. gender"]: sermo pri[m]us in péð popu.

Page 25, No. 831, delete [pileus].

Page 27, No. 863, *for* uipci *read* uipci. No. 872, read pemcheðcap.

Page 28, No. 890, read péibe.

Page 31, No. 1019, read péibeað.

Page 32, No. 1057, read bochinélach.

Page 37,

Page 37, No. 4, *sái, súi*, seems the W. *syw* (Davies). The acc. sing. of the derivative *súithe* occurs (spelt súidi(ṅ)) in the *Cris Finnáin* (Z. 933):—

<pre>
cris coin mnchris   "May my girdle be the girdle of John,
ralég súidi nglan   Who read pure science."
</pre>

Page 37, No. 5, *for* crottârias *read* crottâria-s. As to *cruit*, I am indebted for the following note to Mr. S. H. O'Grady, who has read and annotated the foregoing Commentary with the kindness generally found among men of his wide and accurate attainments:—" Figuratively *cruit* at the present day means 'a hump on the back' (from the shape of the Irish harp), and the word has been introduced into the Anglo-Irish dialect. *He put a critt on himself* (do léig sé cruit air féin) is applied to any one assuming a humpy attitude, as a jockey does when he works himself along in a race," &c.

Page 37, No. 6, the *timpan* (gen. *timpain*), whence *timpanach* was a stringed instrument. See C.'s *Battle of Magh Léna*, p. 50, where occurs the expression an *tiompan* téad-bhinn, "the sweet-stringed *timpan*." Cf. also Girald. Topogr. Hib., "Hibernia quidem tantum duobus utitur et delectatur instrumentis cythara scilicet et *tympano*: Scotia tribus, cythara, *tympano* et choro: Gwallia vero cythara, tibiis et choro."

Page 37, No. 9, cf. the Cornish *renniat*, divisor, which is synonymous with partista.

Page 38, line 10, read 10, *Luchtaire*. I think this word is radically connected with the Latin lucta, "wrestling," luctor, luctator.

Page 38, No. 13, I have now no doubt that *cathir*, &c., are stems in c. The stem of cathir (*i* a weakening of *a*) is *catharac*. With *uasal-athair* compare Corn. *huheltat*, A. S. heahfæðer = "high-father." In the second line from the bottom of p. 38 read áth *for* ath, and in the last line of the note *for* philosophy *read* poetry.

Page 39, No. 14, read *crosán*. Hence the Mod. Ir. *crosántachd*, which Mr. O'Grady explains as "a kind of composition, part prose, part verse, generally consisting of very far-fetched jokes, and couched in the most difficult and out-of-the-way language at the command of the composer."

Page 39, No. 15, *cestunach*, now *ceisteamhnach*, O'G.

Page 39, No. 16, in O. Ir. the *a* of *ard* is long.

Page 39, No. 17, *cinn* I now regard as the gen. (cf. *gilla nan each, gilla adairce*). The locative sing. of masc. a-stems is in O. Ir., as in Latin, identical with the gen. sing. Thus *puirt, supra*, No. 676, is the loc. of *port*, gen. *puirt*. For examples of locatives sing. of other declensions, see Beitr. i. 335, 336.

X   Page 40,

Page 40, No. 18, perhaps *birria* stands for *birrus*, "a cloak for rainy weather;" unsméðe hrægel, "unsmooth raiment," Ælfric.

Page 40, No. 19, W. *gwydd*, Corn. *gúdh*. See Diefenbach's *Celtica*, i. 134, 135.

Page 40, No. 20, *Ríghan* should be *Ríghain* (W. *rhiain*), as it is in the modern language. In Old Ir. it seems declined like a fem. i-stem. Thus the gen. pl. *rignae* occurs in an O. Ir. poem to one Áed, for a copy of which I am indebted to Herr Mone, of Carlsruhe:—

"Is bun cruinn máir miad soerda, fri baig is bunad findae,
is gasne arggait arddbrigg, di oblaind chéit rig céit rignae,"

where, though Mone's copy has *phinda* and *ignae*, the corrections are certain.[1]

Page 40, No. 24, the *t* in sagart may be also explained by reference to the ordinary rise of *rt* from *rd*. See Z. 70.

Page 40, No. 26, cf. the W. *clopen*, *clopa*, pen-*glog*.

Page 40, No. 27, read *táiplis*. Cf. A. S. tœfel (gl. alea) Ælf., W. *taflu*, to fling. Perhaps *táiplis* is a Celtic word.

Page 40, No. 30, the Lat. *manus*, O. N. *mund*, should have been compared with *muin*-cille. Cf. also W. *mun*, man.

Page 40, Nos. 33, 35, the genitives sing. of *ciabh* and *dias* are respectively *céibh*, *déise*.

Page 41, No. 36, cf. the Mod. Ir. *pras*, "hasty, quick, rash;" W. *pres* seems = praestus, *presto*, *prêt*.

Page 41, line 11, *for* fit *read* faithful.

Page 41, No. 37, I strongly suspect that *fallaing* is cognate with pallium, though Zeuss seems not to believe that a Celtic *f* can ever represent a Latin *p*. Cf., however, con*f*oirem "comparamus," Z. 841, and M. Pictet's paper, Beitr. ii., 84.

Page 41, No. 39, now *gruadh*, pl. gruadhna. Cf. also W. *grudd*.

Page 42, No. 42, hence the Anglo-Irish *losset*, "the long wooden box, with a lid and lock, often standing on trestles in a farmer's bed-room, and in which he keeps his linen and valuables," O'G.

Page 42, No. 44, W. *canwyl*, where *wy* as usual = *é*.

Page 42, No. 46, I have blundered here. The hard *d* in *fedán* = an O. Ir. *t* (= O. Celtic *tt*), and *fedán* is the W. *chwythu*.

Page 42, No. 47, the root may be VAKS, to grow: cf. the line in Morte d'Arthur, "mixed with the manly GROWTH that fringed his lip."

Page 42, No. 48, cf. *les*mac, which glosses privignus, in a ninth-century MS. of Priscian,

[1] The MS. from which this poem is taken is preserved in the monastery of S. Paul, Carinthia.

Priscian, fo. 30, *a*, written by one Dubthach, and preserved in the University Library of Leyden, No. 67. For this and the other glosses in the same MS. I am indebted to Professor Siegfried.

Page 42, No. 49, *sesrach* now means "a yoke of horses," O'G.

Page 42, No. 50. Can this *rón* (gen. *róin*) be = the A. S. *hrón*, "whale"?

Page 42, No. 51, cf. the Gael. *ceann-bhdrr*-easpuig, "a bishop's mitre."

Page 42, No. 55, iolla is hilla, see No. 1005, p. 117. *Maróc* = W. *monochen*.

Page 43, No. 59, also *adirc-liu* (gl. cornix), Z. 726 (is *liu* = Gaul. λουγος?).

Page 43, No. 61, *riaghail* (*ia* from *ê*) is the W. *rheol*.

Page 43, No. 64, perhaps mitreta is for metreta.

Page 43, No. 65, the Mod. Ir. *meadar* means "a vessel," generally a churn. Hence the Anglo-Ir. *mether*.

Page 43, No. 70, *sess* is now "the board thrown out from the gunwale of a boat to the strand, to enable one to walk in dryshod," O'G.

Page 44, No. 71, Gael. *taobhan*, "rafter, beam." "*Taoíbhín* means a small patch in the side (*taobh*) of a brogue," O'G.

Page 44, No. 73, *lainnéir* is a living word along the Shannon, and means "lanyard," C. Perhaps both the English and Irish words are taken from the French *lanière*.

Page 44, No. 75, now *coróinn*, gen. *coróinneach*, O'G.

Page 44, No. 77, the reading of the quatrain here given is justified by the fac-simile given by Dr. Ferdinand Keller in his *Bilder und Schriftzüge u. s. w.*, plate xi.: *reimm* should be *réimm*, and *oa*, *óa*.

Page 45, in the paradigm of the article the hypothetical stem is inaccurate. In the masc. it should be SANDA (ex SANNA, SA-SMA (?)); in the fem. SANDÂ (ex SA-SMÂ (?)): in the neut. nom. and acc. sing. SA. In lines 3 and 6, *for* sanad? *read* sa-n?

In the dat. pl. of *dia* read déib = dévâbo (?), and compare ματρεβο ναμαυσικαβο, p. 100, the discovery of which forms overturns Ebel's theory (here followed) as to the origin of the Ir. dat. pl. from an instrumental. O. Ir. *aib* (-*ib*), Gaul. *abo* = *âbus* (fem.), Skr. *âbhyas*.

Page 46, No. 86, *oigheann* now means "a large cauldron," O'G., who quotes from an old song, "do thuit mo bhean a n-*oigheann* na feola."

Page 46, No. 88, *for* panthera *read* pantera. Perhaps this is the French *pantière*, "a draw-net for partridges, &c.," Old Eng. *paunter*:—

> "Pride hath in his *paunter* kaoht the heie and the lowe,
> So that unnethe can eny man God Almihti knowe."
>
> *Political Songs of England*, ed. Wright, p. 344.

Page 46, No. 90, *leth*, W. *lled* = Lat. lătus, Gr. πλάτος (Ebel). Other examples of *leth*, meaning half-, are *leathlobhtha*, "half rotten," *leathmheisge*, "half drunk."

Note 1. If *doiros* in the following Gaulish inscription on the handle of a patera (found in 1853 near Dijon) be = the O. Ir. *dóir*, the opposite of *sóir*, the truth of the conjecture here made is established: DOIROS SEGOMARI IEVRV ALISANV, "a slave of Segomaros made (this) for Alisanos."

Page 47, No. 92, "*craos na haoine*," lit. "gluttony of the Friday," is a phrase now used of eating meat on that day, O'G.

Page 47, No. 93, *mataxa* vel corductum vel stramentum, *stræl* vel *bedding*, Ælfric.

Page 47, Nos. 94, 95, the gen. of *bas* is *baise*. *Read* baság.

Page 47, No. 98, dare we connect *cáin* with poena, ποινή?

Page 47, No. 99, with *féith* cf. Corn. *guiden*, gl. cutulus, i. e. catulus, a kind of fetter; also Skr. vétasa, arundo.

Page 48, No. 104. In the quotation from the Tripartite Life for *atcondaire* we should probably read *atcondare*, cf. *adcondarc*, "*I* perceived," Z. 930.

Page 48, No. 106, *read* scála, now "a cup;" *caitheamh na scála*, "cup-tossing on Hallow-e'en," O'G.

Page 48, No. 108, "*talamh*, gen. *talmhan*, is now used by correct speakers for the earth = the world, as in *druim na talmhan* = dorsum terræ, the face of the earth. But *talamh*, gen. *talaimh*, is earth in the sense of land, e. g. *dá aera talaimh*, two acres of land," O'G. (O'D. and C. do not recognise this distinction.)

Page 48, No. 110, an earlier instance is in the Book of Armagh, 11, *a*, 2 (top margin), "*is báile inso sis as incertus*," "there is a place here below that is *incertus*."

Page 49, No. 118, as to *grunna*, also gronna, gromna, see Z. 735, note ¹.

Page 50, No. 122, "An old saying is *eró roimh oirc*, 'stye before pigling' = 'counting your chickens before they are hatched,'" O'G. (*cró roimh na horcaibh*, C.).

Page 50, No. 128, *lasair* (= laxarac) is the W. llachar.

Page 50, No. 129, *camradh* is, perhaps, cognate with W. cafn.

Page 50, No. 130, *read* sen (old) = sena-s, W. hen: cf. Zend hana.

Page 50, No. 131, *sech-rán* is obviously a deriv. from the prep. *sech*, W. hep. Lat. sécus; Zend, haca.

Page 51, No. 133, delete the statement that in O. Ir. *liacc* is a cc-stem, into which I was led by a misreading of Zeuss's (corrected *supra* p. 80, No. 573); *liacc* was and is a fem. â-stem. As to *lógmar*, *v*. No. 792, p. 96.

Page 51, No. 137, *ossadh* is cognate with *sossadh* and *fossadh*, the common root being STHÂ.

Page 51,

Corrections and Additions.

Page 51, No. 138, cf. A. S. melc (patera), Ælfr.

Page 51, No. 139. I suspect *cogad* (O. Ir. cocad) is con-cata, the *eata* being cognate with Gaul. *eatu*, Ir. cath.

Page 52, No. 141, the dat. sing. *bairgin* is in Z. 738.

Page 52, No. 142, *read* O. W. petguerid in the masculine. And in the third line *read* nómad (Z. 1076) *for* nóim-ed.

Page 52, No. 145, *cogar* is probably con-gar. See p. 76, No. 469.

Page 52, No. 148, at the end *read* san(d)islindeni.

Page 52, note 2, *bliadne*, Book of Armagh (cited *supra*, No. 676), nom. bliadain, is another example of the gen. plur. of a fem. i-stem. So ilar *fochraice*, Patrick's Hymn; nom. fochric: *fochide*, Z. 992, 481; nom. fochaid: *infinite*, Z. 979; nom. infinit.

Page 53, No. 152, cf. the Eng. *butteris*, Fr. boutoir.

Page 53, No. 154, compare with *lúirech*, in its secondary sense, the Vedic charman, lit. a hide.

Page 53, No. 156, cf. W. mèr, a particle, Gr. μέρος, which Benfey connects with Skr. mṛsh. Cf. *tir* with tarsh.

Page 55, No. 170, so biocon, from Viscount.

Page 55, No. 173, *abbdaine* (abbacy) is solely applicable to the office.

Page 55, No. 177, W. *eglwys*, *e* becoming *wy* as usual.

Page 55, No. 179, W. *blisgyn*. *Blaesc* is now *plaosg*, "pod," and, jocosely, the "head," O'G.

Page 55, No. 180, *for* sabribarra *read* sarabara: "sarabara sunt fluxa ac sinuosa vestimenta de quibus legitur in Daniele." Isidor.

Page 55, No. 183, see, however, Ebel, Beitr. ii. 82, on the *Vertauschung der spiranten, f, s, h (ch)*, in Celtic.

Page 55, No. 191, *bile* also means lip (of a jug, &c.), O'G.

Page 56, No. 194, *faechog* is cognate with W. gwichiad, Corn. guihan.

Page 57, No. 207, read *dreolán*, now *dreoilin*, from *deroil*, Corm., now *deireoil*, diminutive.

Page 57, No. 209, *conn* = Lat. canna: W. cawn, conyn.

Page 57, No. 211, *read* festuca *for* fistula.

Page 57, No. 216, *ga* also means "beam:" *ga gréine*, sunbeam; *ga gealaighe*, moonbeam, O'G.

Page 58, No. 217. I think now that the right reading may be *seideth gáithbulga*, the second word being the gen. of a *gáithbuilg*.

Page 58, No. 220, for gen. *bláthaig* read gen. *bláthaighe*.

Page 58, No. 222, *diangalar* is wrongly rendered here: a gloss in Gildas' Lorica shows that its meaning is *languor*. As to the note, I now see that the *t* in perfects like asruhur-t, &c., is nothing but the *d* (of the root.dhâ), which, when following *r* or *c*, becomes *t*. This is proved by the occurrence of the form rodam*datar*, "they suffered," in the poem following the Félire (Leab. Breacc):—

| iarna techt don rígiu | after their coming to the kingdom |
| rodamdatar sóethu | they suffered pains. |

(The second line is glossed by ".i. rodamsat soethu .i. piana.") And I now believe that the unaspirated *t* in *domeltis*, &c., was preceded by *n*. Cf. dognítis, adsaitis, dofuaircitis.

Page 59, No. 227, cf. in "hello *Roth*," where Adamnán (Vit. Col.) alludes to the battle of Mag-Rath (= Rotomagus).

Page 60, No. 233, the spelling *sirogra* seems to show that chiragra was pronounced *sheeragra*.

Page 60, No. 240, "*cliath fuirsidhe* is a rude kind of harrow, made with a hurdle and stones to weight it, for light work like bush-harrowing. A regular harrow is *bráca*, or *práca*," O'G.

Page 60, No. 245, Schleicher thinks *popina* a loan-word from one of the other Italic dialects (Zeits. vii. 320).

Page 61, No. 246, and lapillula, of course, for lapillulus.

Page 61, No. 248, read *Luch francach*. "A rat is now called simply *franncach*," O'G.

Page 61, No. 251, C. says there is a phrase tug sé *amaisc* air, "he made a grab at him."

Page 61, No. 254, *read*, possibly from *es*.

Page 61, No. 256, for *onesta* read *ouesta*, *oresta*, and cf. *obesta* boost, Ælfr.

Page 62, No. 257, "*baineachlach* occurs in the sense of a female retainer (unconnected with horses) in the tale of Diarmid and Grainne," O'G. (*Toruigheacht D. 7 G.*, p. 98).

Page 62, No. 262, in the fourth line of the quatrain *read* has stuck.

Page 62, No. 264, in the paradigm *read* dib mbethaih.

Page 62, No. 265, is *tiar* = du-iar?

Page 63, No. 266, *ól cormae* would be better rendered "a drinking of ale."

Page 63, No. 272, from dorn comes duirnín, a small handle: *read* nom*durni*.

Page 63, No. 274, *spline*, "a sharp look;" splincín, "a long splinter of bog-pine, used as a candle," O'G.

Page 64,

Page 64, No. 279, *for* cumail *read* comal, and delete the words *Gaulish ver.*

Page 64, No. 287, I think Ebel (Beitr. i. 163) errs in denying a vowel-changing power to *o, u,* for *lenomnaib* (gl. lituris), Z. 739, is surely from *linomnaib,* Lat. līno, cercol = *ci*rculus, Z. 594; felsub = ph*i*losophus; and I believe that *betho, etho* (from bith, ith), may also be quoted as examples of the power possessed by *o*. Ebel says that in the latter instances the *o* stands for a prior *a;* and we certainly have *betha, etha.* But these are surely mere instances of *a* for *o.* Cf. the Ogamic genitive *Atilogdo,* which Dr. Graves reads *Apilogdo,* in Mr. Wilde's *Catalogue of the Antiquities in the Museum of the Royal Irish Academy.* Dublin, 1857, p. 136.

Page 65, No. 290. "*Nighean* is heard in Ireland, in names like Nóra *nighean* Aodha, Nora Hays," O'G. (O'D. and C. say this should be written N. *ni n-Aodha*).

Page 66, No. 296. These words seem not Indo-European. "Orientis partibus Adventavit *asinus*" is probably true in more senses than one.

Page 66, No. 300, cf. A. S. feohstrang (pecuniosus), feohhus (ærarium), Ælfr.

Page 66, No. 303, cf. the Corn. diures (gl. exul).

Page 66, No. 305. The theory here set forth is so extremely ingenious that I could not help inserting it. For my part, however, I believe that *Hérinn* is nothing but *Ivernya* ('Ιουερνια), the *v* having passed into spiritus asper, which has then shifted, the *é* standing for *i* (Z. 25), the *nn* for *ny,* as in the Prakrit aṇṇa from Skr. anya, the O. Ir. *moirtchenn,* from morticinium. Thus, Ivernia, hierna ('Ιερνη), whence by metathesis hirenn, hérenn. As to the irregularity in the acc., *enn* for *inn,* I have found the correct vowel in the Tripartite Life: dorat dia *heirind* duitsiu ("God has given Ireland to thee"), Egerton, 93 (Mus. Brit.), fo. 16 *a,* 2.

Page 68, line 4 from top. The *b* in marb (W. marw) is really a *v,* as in O. Ir. *tarb* = Gaulish tarvos, W. tarw, *fedb* = Lat. vidua, W. gweddw, *garb* = Skr. garva, W. garw, *nonbar* = a Skr. navanvara-m.

Page 69, note 2, add: ind réta ad*gúsi* optait, Z. 978, "the things which the optative desires:" assa*guss*im én cechtar mo dá gúaland, "I wish a bird on each of my two shoulders." Scirgl. Conculainn.

Page 70, No. 370, now *macámh.*

Page 70, No. 372. The statement of the regular *lautvertretung* in Old Irish, and the other Indo-European languages, is here given with a brevity which, perhaps, may mislead. The following Table will be useful, and may be relied on so far as it goes, being, with the exception of the Old Irish column, taken from Curtius' *Grundzüge der Griechischen Etymologie* (Leipzig, 1858):—

Appendix.

Indo-European	Old Irish	Sanskrit	Greek	Latin	Gothic	Old High German	Slavonic	Lithuanian
K	c, ch (g)[a]	k, kh, ch, ç	κ	c, q	h (g)	h (g)	k, č, c, s	k, sz
G	g	g, j	γ	g	k	k (ch)	g, ž, z	g, ž
GH	g	gh, h	χ	h[b], g[c]	g	g (k)	g, ž, z	g, ž
T	t, th (d)[d]	t, th	τ	t	th (d)	d	t	t
D	d	d	δ	d	t	z, sz	d	d
DH	d	dh	θ	f[b], d, b[e]	d	t	d	d
P	lost[b], c, f[e]	p, ph	π	p	f	f, v (b)	p	p
B	b	b	β	b				
BH	b	bh	φ	f[b], b[c]	b	b (p)	b	b
Ṅ	ṅ, lost ?[f]	ṅ	γ before gutturals	n	n	n	n	n
N	n, or lost[g]	n, ṇ	ν	n	n	n	n	n
M	m, n[h]	m	μ, ν[i]	m	m	m	m	m
R	r	r	ρ	r	r	r	r	r
L	l	l	λ	l	l	l	l	l
Y	lost, h ?[k]	y	ζ, ʽ	j	j	j	j	j
S	s or lost[l]	s, sh	σ, ʽ	s (r)	s (z)	s (r)	s, ch, š	s
V	f, v[m]	v	F	v	v	w	v	v

[a] When c is, or has been, flanked by vowels, it becomes ch, for which g (i. e. gh) is found.
[b] At the beginning of a word (in anlaut).
[c] In a word (in inlaut).
[d] When t is, or has been, flanked by vowels, it becomes th, for which d (i. e. dh) is found.
[e] O. Ir. f ex p is very rare. See p. 154, addendum to No. 37. I have little doubt that p occurs in inlaut (probably in combination with some other letter), but cannot yet quote a sure example.
[f] In the combination ṅc, so far as I know, the nasal is always lost in O. Ir.
[g] In the combinations nt, ns.
[h] In auslaut, e. g. in the acc. sing., and gen. plur. of a-stems, what I call the transported n represents a primitive m.
[i] In auslaut.
[k] I suspect that initial y is sometimes represented by h, it having (as often in Greek) passed into the spiritus asper.
[l] Lost between vowels, as I believe, invariably : sometimes also in anlaut, e. g. in the nom. and gen. of the article.
[m] Initial v always becomes f. In anlaut and auslaut v (written b, sometimes f in Old Irish, bh in Modern Irish) is preserved in combination with d, l, n, r. It also occurs in varu, "your" (cf. Goth. izvara), written barn or farn in O. Ir., uorh in the Tripartite Life, bhar n- in the modern language.

Page 72,

Page 72, No. 397, a left-handed man is *ciotach*: ciotóg, "the left-hand," O'G. Lhuyd has compared W. *chwith*, "left;" *chwithig*, "left-handed."

Page 72, No. 411, *for* guitter *read* guilter.

Page 72, No. 412, "*breall* is the *glans penis*: also the round knob at the end of the *buailteán*, or striking part, of a flail, by which the thong is kept from flying off," O'G.

Page 73, No. 423, line 8 from top, *read*, 423, Tuata (gl. laicus); cf. Τουτιυς; and in the translation of the Gaulish inscription *read* made this temple for Belesama. Dr. Siegfried now explains ειὁrυ, ιετευ by the Old Ir. root ιυr, found in fritammi*u*rat "me adficiunt," fritammi*o*rsa (gl. me adficiet), Z. 336; fúrad (gl. factum est), Book of Armagh, 189 *b*, 1. In the note delete the first sentence. M. Pictet is undoubtedly right in identifying Ουιλλονεος with Villonius (Gruter, 488-5). See his learned and ingenious *Essai sur quelques Inscriptions en langue gauloise*. Genève, 1859.

Page 74, No. 428. I have no doubt now that the MS. is right in its *ruaimnech dubain*. Cf. the Skr. rôman horschair (from rôhman), and the O. Ir. ruamnae (gl. lodix), Z. 27; W. rhawn, Bret. reûn, Ir. *ruainne* (No. 463) seem connected.

Page 74, No. 429. I think *dilechta* is the pret. part. pass. of a verb *dileicim*: cf. leicim = linquo.

Page 74, No. 430, cf. aon-t-suim, "grand total," O'G.

Page 74, No. 431, delete, gl. tener, *infra*.

Page 74, No. 434, O'G. thinks cúisi (for cúise) the gen. sing.

Page 75, No. 446, read *tige*, gen. of *tig*.

Page 75, No. 462, the acc. plurals here quoted seem (with the exceptions of cairtea, náimtea) to be rather examples of metathesis rather than extension.

Page 75, line 3 from bottom, *for* 469 *read* 463.

Page 76, No. 465, cf. Fr. doigt de pied.

Page 76, No. 479, W. cwpan.

Page 76, No. 482, perhaps W. *od*-n in *eb-odn*, "horse-dung," may be connected.

Page 77, No. 484, *sgagaim*, "I strain, sift, winnow," O'G.; cf. Eng. *shake?*

Page 76, No. 498, delete, compare Eng. *whelp*.

Page 77, No. 508, *preachán* and *préachan* are now "a crow;" préachán na cccare, "a kite," O'G.

Page 78, No. 545, *c* is *not* aspirated by the influence of *n*. In *sancht* the *cht* has regularly arisen from *ct*. Cf. O. Persian Bakhtris, durukhta: A. S. tœh-te, vœh-te, sôh-te, from tœc-an, wœc-an, sêc-an. *Conch*oimnucuir, conchechrat, are probably written in the MS. ochoim, ochech, and should have been read cochoim, cochech.

Page 79, No. 561, cf. the N. H. G. *eber*-esche.

Page 79, No. 565, hence *fraochan*, whortleberry, and cf. ἐρείκη, erica.

Page 80, No. 570, *bráthair* now means cousin; *dearbhbhráthair*, "brother," pronounced *driтháir*, derbráthir (gl. germane), Z. 834.

Page 81, line 7, *for* the earth *read* earth.

Page 81, No. 577, *sroll* now always means *satin*; *sioda* is silk, O'G.

Page 81, No. 587, "a bramble-brake is now *drisearnach*, with the termination of which cf. *sgealparnach*, "continued pinching" (*sgealp*, a pinch); *siosarnach*, "continued whispering," O'G.

Page 82, No. 595, the W. *pyrchwyn*, "crest of a helmet;" *pyrgwyn*, "crest of a plume," may be connected.

Page 83, No. 606, *ór* is a neut. a-stem in O. Ir., and occurs in the nom. sing. with the transported *n* in the following verses, for which I am indebted to Herr Mone:—

"Is én immo ṅiada sás,   He is a bird round which the trap is closing,
is nau tholl diant eslinn gúas,   He is a leaky ship in perilous danger,
is lestar fás, is crann crín   He is an empty vessel, he is a withered tree,
[nach digni toil ind ríg túas.]   Whoso doth not the will of the King above.

Is ór ṅglan, is nem im gréin,   He is pure gold, he is heaven round the sun,
is lestar ṅarggit ca fín,   He is a vessel of silver with wine [in it],
is son, is alaind, is nóeb   He is prosperous, is beautiful, is holy,
cach óen digni toil ind ríg."[1]   Every one that doth the will of the King.

Page 85, No. 641, read *luathgdirech*.

Page 85, No. 650, *coisinech* would properly be "small-footed."

Page 85, No. 652, add, from *gearb*, a scab.

Page 86, No. 660, *for* sochoise *read* sochoise. I cannot but think the *coscitir* here quoted is cognate with the Lat. consequor. Cf. madu coscedar (gl. ipsa consequatur), Leyden Priscian, 17 *b*.

Page 86, No. 666, *taithneamh na gréine*, "the shining of the sun," is a common phrase.

Page 87, No. 674, delete line 5 as far as *cruaidh*.

Page 88, No. 700, cf. O. W. cruitr (gl. pala, a winnowing-shovel).

Page 89,

---

[1] This is from the before-mentioned MS. in the monastery of S. Paul. I have ventured to correct Mone's *sar* into sás, his *nan* into nan, his *sin* into fín. Mr. Curry has found a poem in the Book of Ballymote, in which the above verses are incorporated.

Page 89, No. 709. I have now no doubt that sgeota and sgéotha are different words. *Sgeota* (gl. cartesium, i. e. chartaceum) seems a loan-word from scheda. As to *scéotha*, see Reeves' Vit. Col., 106. Du Cange, sub v. scota.

Page 89, No. 716, with *bile*, "leaflet, blossom," cf. the Gaulish *Beliocanda*, "Achillæa millefolium." Is not this = folium, φύλλον ?

Page 89, No. 717, *cassock*, Fr. casaque, Ital. casaccia, Lat. casa (Diez, E. W., 91), has nothing to do with ceis.

Page 89, No. 720, in Sanskrit svapna sometimes means a dream : cf. Old Eng. *sweren*, somnium, ὕπνος.

Page 90, No. 725. If O'R. be correct in explaining *long* as enclosure, *long-phort* = castrum becomes intelligible.

Page 91, No. 735, *for* ûivs-i-s *read* âius-ti-s?

Page 91, No. 740, *for* iii. *read* 111. No. 741, read *Sealladh*.

Page 92, No. 744, Z.'s *muinæ* is right. Cf. *myne*, monile, Ælfr., *mene*, Beowulf, 2403.

Page 92, No. 745, druim (notwithstanding the irregularity of *d* = *t*) is the W. trwm; so días = W. twys.

Page 93, No. 752, *arbe* (not arpe) is the right form. Cf. Goth. arbja, heir, and Skr. arbha, prolos.

Page 94, line 5, *for* yûvas *read* yavas.

Page 94, No. 769, read *Bidhgadh*.

Page 96, No. 782, now *leamhnacht*. Cf. W. *llefrith*.

Page 96, No. 792, *Leasughadh* means, 1, to improve ; 2, to manure, O'G.

Page 97, No. 795. Two other forms are *foileastrom*, *oileastrom*, O'G.

Page 97, No. 796, cf. Do *sgairt* sí fú gháiridhe, "she burst out into a roar of laughter," O'G.

Page 97, No. 797, I feel sure that the true reading of Z.'s *uudimm* is rudimin.

Page 98, No. 812, Dia (= divas), "day;" in the acc. sing. *dei* (fri *dei*) is still declined like an s-stem. But in the dat. diu (in*diu*) it has gone over to the vocalic declension.

Page 99, note, *for* Celtic *v* read Gaulish *v* ; see, however, p. 154.

Page 100, line 12 from top, *for* 847 *read* 843.

Page 100, No. 845, for *Coindealbthadh* we should certainly read *Coindealbháthadh*: coindeal, from candela ; *báthadh*, "destruction, extinguishment." Cf. bathach, leg. báthach (gl. moribundus), Z. 777.

Page 100, No. 846, *Taidbsiu* may be du-ad-*vad*-s-tiân. Cf. W. *gwedd*, "shape," Z. 860; a-gwedd = adgwedd.

Page 100, note, line 11, *read* ad-coth-*ded*-ac; coth = Gaulish cata, W. cyd.
Page 101, No. 851, cf. W. *cor*-lan, "sheep-fold."
Page 101, No. 853, *for* now aifrin *read* now aifrionn: with *aiffrend* cf. W. offeren.
Page 101, No. 854, gradale for graduale; W. *gris*-lyfr, from gressus; W. grisiau, "steps."
Page 102, No. 859, corporale is the napkin which covers the sacred elements.
Page 102, No. 864, now scóraid.
Page 105, No. 884, *read* sólás, happiness, the opposite of dólás.
Page 106, No. 892, read *compántus*.
Page 107, line 11, *for* di[a]áis *read* dia és (dom-h*éis*-se, "after me," Z. 1053). No. 899, *read* denid (facito), Z. 458.
Page 108, No. 903, *read comthromugud*. Comhthrom now means "just, fair."
Page 108, No. 908, now *leoirghntomh*.
Page 109, No. 913, now *comháircamh* (áram = ad-ram ?).
Page 109, No. 916, now *lámhágan* (applied to a child's first attempt at creeping on all-fours), from *lámh*, just as *lapadóireacht*, "groping;" from *lap* and *lapa*, "the hand," O'G.
Page 109, No. 918. *Comma* is, perhaps, a loan-word; κόμμα taleatio (talea, a cutting).
Page 111, No. 937, *for* finlorg *read* fri lorg, "on (the) track."
Page 111, No. 940, cf. in*gerr*tha, gl. lacerandum, Gildas' Lorica.
Page 112, No. 945, now sméaróid: cf. sméar, "a blackberry," O'G.
Page 112, note, frecuirthe céill (gl. recole, i. e. repone sensum), Z. 1130.
Page 113, No. 952, Ir. *gres*, W. *gres*, seem likewise connected with ghrans.
Page 113, No. 955. In the last line of the quotation from Ultán's hymn I should now render *biam* by "may I be!"
Page 114, No. 967. In his A. S. lexicon, p. 690, Ettmüller gives "secóta -an m. tructus, trocta piscis."
Page 114, line 11 from bottom, *for* 995 *read* 975.
Page 114, No. 976, there is no such word as *ainmidheach*, according to O'D. and C.
Page 116, No. 999, delete (from sbhrav ?).
Page 117, No. 1006. In the dialect of Vannes, *blonec* means graisse, abdomen. De Courson, *Hist. des origines*, &c. Paris, 1843, p. 409.
Page 118, No. 1017, add W. tenou.
Page 118, No. 1029, *miuco mara* is a porpoise.
Page 119, line 8, read 1031.

Page 120,

Page 120, No. 1040, cf. W. er*lyn*, "pursuit; dy-*lynu*, "to adhere;" can-*lyn*, "to follow;" g*lyn*, "adhesion."

Page 120, No. 1045. The *c* stands, I now believe, for céd, first; and I suspect that *céd grindi foilci* is some kind of warm lotion. The expression occurs in a passage from a medical tract with which C. has furnished me. *Log in baistithi* (nom. *baistedh*) should have been rendered "price of baptism." In the passage from O'Davoren's Glossary *read* intan is i linn ⁊ im biud doberar, "when it is in ale and in food it is given."

Page 121, No. 1052, read *máthair* = mâtar. The *ai* (*i*) is a weakened *a*. So is the *ai* (*i*) of *bráthair*, *athair*.

Page 125, note. I have erred in regarding and translating *oróit* as from orate. It is explained as a subst. in Cormac, and occurs unmistakeably as such in a piece following Sanctáin's hymn in Lib. Hymn., Rombith *oróit* let a mairc, "sit mihi oratio apud te, O Maria!" See also the inscription on the case of the Book of Durrow, *supra*, p. 56.

Page 126, No. 1102. In the quotation from Cormac, *dam* should have been rendered "suffering." See the quotation and gloss from the *Leabhar Breacc*, *suprà*, p. 158.

Page 128, line 12 from top. I have erred in quoting cr-t, var-t, &c., as instances of pronominal agglutination. The *t* here is the regular termination of the 2nd pers. sing. of the Teutonic preterite. The pronoun, however, is agglutinated in the O. H. G., A. S., and Eng. termination of the 2nd pers. sing., *s-t*.

Page 129, line 8 from bottom, *before* méza *insert* Bret.

Page 130, note, *for* Rawlinson *read* Laud.

Page 134, line 20 from top, *read* minimas corporis sui partes.

Page 135, line 19 from top, the Welsh *pyn* occurs in cr-*byn*, "against" (Norris).

Page 145, line 8 from top, *for* v. 45 *read* v. 46. *Gingis* (gl. oslaicib, "openings") occurs in Cormac's Glossary, v. *Gin* (this word is not in the Academy copy).

Page 146, to the verbal forms under the conjunctive 1st sing., add *cu-r-bam*, No. 260. This, indeed, seems the only true form here given of the conjunctive in the 1st pers. sing.

Page 150, No. 220, the gen. plur. *rap* occurs twice in a medical MS. in the library of the Royal Irish Academy (⁴⋅¹), is ann bis an caor ar muine duib n[a] *rap* (p. 2): Leges gaire in gaile ⁊ na *rap* (p. 12). No. 245, *dentaib* is for *déntaib*, "fabrefactis."

Page 151, No. 260, *oentaige*, better *óentuige*, from *óen-tuigim* = O. Ir. óintuccu, "I am of one mind with," "I assent," "I grant." Tuccu (an ia-stem?) seems cognate with the O. Latin tongêre, Goth. thagkjan, Eng. think, O. Norse thekkja, O. H. G. denchan.

denchan. Can the Eng. slang-word *twig* (= understand) have been taken from the Mod. Ir. *tuigim?*

Page 151, No. 261, gnimarthaib is for gnímradaib. For *gnímarad* read *gnímrad*. The dat. pl. of *daggnímrad* occurs in the opening of the sermon in the Codex of Cambray (Z. 1003): aire sechethar sclictu ar fédot [nom. féda, fiadu] in *dagnimrathib*, "ut sequatur vestigia dei nostri in bonis operibus," C. *Gníomh* now makes its nom. pl. *gníomha* and *gníomhartha*.

GLOSSES FROM THE BOOK OF ARMAGH.

[The following selection from the Old Irish glosses scattered through the Book of Armagh, may fitly fill a space which would otherwise remain vacant. Of these glosses, as well as of the other contents of that invaluable MS., we may soon expect a complete edition from the Rev. Dr. Reeves.]

Ochen (gl. benignus), 9, *b.* 1; *totmáel* (gl. aurigam totum), 13, *b.* 2; *enga* (gl. aqua supra petram, i. e. fons), ibid.; *duferti martur* (gl. ad sargifagum martyrum), 21, *b.* 2; *gabdl oblann* (gl. acceptis autem v. panibus et ii. piscibus), *gabis ailli* (gl. benedixit illis), *combach* (gl. fregit), *fodil* (gl. distribuit), 77, *a.* 1; *diledu* (gl. stercora), 81, *a.* 1; *indloingtis* (gl. disecabantur), *dúnsit l. congabsat* (gl. continuerunt, aures suas), 175, *b.* 1; *cuimte* (gl. ionuchus), 176, *a.* 2; *tarsende* (gl. Tarsensem), 176, *b.* 2; *etalaeda* (gl. Italica, nom. sing.), 177, *a.* 2; *coibdelig* (gl. necessariis amicis), 177, *b.* 2; *tecelsid* (gl. acceptor, personarum), 178, *a.* 1; *nudebthi*[*tis*], (gl. disceptabant), 178, *a.* 2; *rechtire forru* (gl. regerent[ur], 179, *a.* 1; *fornuichthib .i. moirtchenn* (gl. subfucatis, i. e. suffocatis), 181, *a.* 1; *huasalsichire* (gl. ariopagita), *huasalterchomrictid* (gl. archisinagogus), 182, *b.* 2; *immact* (.i. jecit), 183, *a.* 1; *sachilli* (gl. saudaria), *debai* (gl. simicintia), 183, *a.* 2; *et l. indeb l. tarsichid* (gl. ndquæsitio), 183, *b.* 2; *berensdæ* (gl. Beroensis), *derbensde* (gl. Derbius), *arunn*[*f*]*ethitis* (gl. sustinebant nos), 184, *a.* 1; [*ad*]*sluindim* (gl. appello), 187, *b.* 1; *arbir* (gl. co[h]ortis), 188, *b.* 1; *muiride* (gl. civitas Thalasa), *dugaimigud* (gl. ad h[i]emandum), 188, *b.* 2; *dinmuirdgu* (gl. cum sustulissent), *erus* (gl. pupi), *innaluæ* (gl. juncturas gubernaculorum), 189, *a.* 2; *fernn siúil l. seól* (gl. artimone), *cimbidi* (gl. custodias), *dlúthsit .i.* infigerunt, navim, 189, *b.* 1; *dindirect .i. rith folo* (gl. disintiria), 189, *b.* 2.

General Index.

GENERAL INDEX.

[*The numbers refer to the paragraphs of the Commentary, except when the letter "*p.*" is prefixed; then they refer to the pages of this book.*]

Â weakened to *ai*, p. 155; *a* weakened to *ai* (*i*), p. 153, p. 165.
Acta Sanctorum cited, p. 145.
Adamnán's Vision (in the Leabhar Breacc and the Lebar na huidre), cited or referred to, 90, 103; p. 95, note [1]; 1008, 1087.
Adverbs formed by the prefix ∞ (*go*), p. 147.
Agglutination, pronominal, 1071; p. 165.
Ælfric's Glossary cited, p. 144, p. 145, &c.
Amra Choluim Chille, cited, p. 37, note.
Archives des Missions Scientifiques et Littéraires, vol. v,. referred to, p. 97, note.
Armagh, *Book of*. See *Manuscripts*.
Article, Old Irish, declined, 78; and see Addenda, p. 155; nom. pl. masc. of article in Mid. Irish, p. 135; article in Old Welsh, Cornish, and Breton, p. 45, note [1].
Assimilation, retrogressive, 458; progressive, 705.
Aspiration, 5, p. 45, note [1]; p. 46, note [1]; 139, 287, 1071.
Aufrecht, Dr. Theodor, referred to, 423, 776.
Autun, Gaulish inscription of, p. 104, note.

B in Old Irish corresponds with Skr. *b*, Gr. β, Lat. *b*; and also with Skr. *bh*, Gr. φ, Lat. *f* (at the beginning of a word), *b* (in a word), 372; p. 160; Indo-European *b*, see p. 160; *b* sometimes for *g*, 784; apparent instance of Ir. *b* = Lat. *v*, p. 149 (No. 152).
Benary's law, 372.
Benfey, Theodor, referred to, 426.
—— his *Griechisches Wurzellexicon* referred to, 700, 1070, 1095.
Beowulf. See *Thorpe*.
Bh, Indo-European, p. 160.
Böhtlingk and Roth, their Skr. Dictionary referred to, 870, 952.

Bopp, Franz, cited or referred to, 158; p. 58, note; 224, 250, 290, 420, 546, 621, 776, 860, 904, 1000, 1068, 1071.
—— his *Vergleichende Grammatik*, quoted, 387, 703.
—— his *Glossarium Sanscritieum* referred to, 1047, 1081, 1133, 1095.
Brogán's hymn (*Liber Hymnorum*), cited 218, 280, 424, 966, 977.
Burn's *Ecclesiastical Law*, cited, 854, 855.

C. Stems in *c*. See *Declension*, and p. 153. Old Irish *c* corresponds with Gr. κ, Lat. *c*, *q*, Skr. *k*, *kh*, *ch*, ç, 372, p. 160; *cc* in Welsh becomes *ch*, 439; *ct* in Irish becomes *cht* (sanct = sancta, 545, see Addenda, pp. 161-162), but *th* in Welsh, 915.
—— *c* (in *inlaut*) lost in combination *cr*, 621, 724; in combination *cn*, 118, and Addenda.
Cianan of Daimliac (Duleek), 35.
Ciaran, St., 1137.
Civilization, material, of Irish ecclesiastics, 740.
Colmán's hymn (Liber Hymnorum), cited, 214, 338, 588, 640, 738, 890, 955.
Columcille, p. 37, note.
Comgell, hymn to Abbot, p. 146.
Comparatives, formation of some Old Irish, 1112, 1115, 1133.
Conjugation. See *Verb*.
Cormac's *Glossary* cited or referred to, 38, 42, 70, 90, 112, 115, 120, 136, 146, 155, 159, 184, 216, 218, 255, 256, 266, 555, 578, 588, 651, 814, 843, 873, 889, 897, 933, 966, 1065, 1102; p. 127, note [4]; p. 148, p. 165.
Cormacan ócces, cited 39, 56, 226, 866; p. 147.
Ct becomes *cht* in O. Irish, pp. 161-162.
Cummian's Epistle, cited, p. 145.
Curry, Professor Eugene, cited or referred to, pas-

sim ; his *Cath Maighe Léna* cited, 580 ; and see
    Seirglige Conculainn.
Curtius, G., referred to, p. 58, note; 245, 860, 871;
    his *Grundzüge der Griechischen Etymologie* cited
    or referred to, 792, 948, 999, 1095 ; p. 159.

D becomes *t* before aspirated *s*, 148, 734; stems in
    d, see *Declension* ; Old Irish *d* corresponds with
    Skr. and Lat. *d*, Gr. δ, and also with Skr. *dh*,
    Gr. θ, Lat. *f* (at the beginning of a word), *d*, *b*
    (in a word), 372, p. 160; *d* assimilated to *n*,
    914; to *l*, 915; *gh* written for *dh*, 604 (*boghar*
    for *bodhar*) ; Indo-European *d*, see p. 160.
Dative plural in Irish, origin of, p. 155.
De Belloguet, Baron, his *Ethnogénie Gauloise* referred to, 423, and note.
De Betouw, his *De aris*, &c., referred to, 1029.
Declension, Old Irish :—
    I. Vocalic : . . . 1. masc. a-stems, 17, 81 ; neut.
            a-stems, 139 ; masc. iā-
            stems, 9 (there are neut. ia-
            stems).
        2. fem. ā-stems, 9 ; fem. iā-
            stems, 158.
        3. masc. and fem. i-stems, 2,
            42 ; p. 52, note [2], p. 157 ;
            neut. i-stems, 1008.
        4. masc. u-stems, 264 (there
            are also neut. u-stems, but
            no fem. u-stems).
    II. Consonantal : 1. Guttural stems : c-stems,
            13 ; g-stem, 1036.
        2. Dental stems : t-stems, 4 ;
            ant-stems, 292, 444 ; ent-
            stems (*lóche*, gen. *lóchet*) ;
            d-stems, 1 ; n-stems, 108 ;
            mann-stem, 991.
        3. Liquid stems : r-stems, 13.
        4. S-stems, 812 ; p. 163 ; ns-
            stems, 1315.
    III. Monosyllabic stems in *i*, 987.
    IV. Adjectival : a-stems, 803 ; iā-stems, 803 ;
            i-stems, 661 (*ili*, nom. pl.
            of *il*, 565 ; and see *Beitr*. i.,
            464).
    V. Pronominal. See *Pronouns, Article*.
    Flexion in adjectives preceding the nouns with
    which they agree, 565 ; passage over from one
    declension to another, 87, 726, 1047 ; p. 135,
    p. 163 ; extension of stems, 462, but see p.
    161; loss of labial ending in dat. pl., p. 135.
    See *Article, Pronoun*.
Declension in Welsh and Cornish, trace of, p. 135
    (*pyn*, dat. of *pen*).
De Courson, his *Hist. des Origines*, &c., cited, p. 164.
Denis, cited or referred to, p. 133, note; 134.

Dh, Indo-European, see p. 160.
Diefenbach, Dr. Lorenz, referred to, 387 ; his *Celtica* referred to, 121, 266 ; p. 154; his *Glossarium Med. Lat. Germ.*, cited or referred to, 152, 574, 793, 866 ; p. 145; his *Gothisches Wörterbuch* quoted, 1073 ; referred to, 1095.
Diez, his *Etymologisches Wörterbuch* cited or referred to, 107, 708, 852 ; p. 148.
Dimma mace Nathi, 133, 1080.
Diminutival suffixes, 934; p. 111, note.
Dioscorides, cited, 765.
Dual in Irish, 773.
Dubthach, his MS. of Priscian, p. 155.
Du Cange, his *Glossarium* cited or referred to, 59, 98, 797 ; p. 143.

Ebel, Dr. Hermann, cited or referred to, 74 ; p. 61, note[2]; 287, 288, 289, 315, 328, 735; p. 99, note; 1117; p. 136, note; p. 156, p. 157, p. 158.
Eclipsis, phenomena of, 905.
Ettmüller, his *Lexicon Anglosaxonicum* cited, p. 164.

F = *sv*, 777 ; initial *f* from *v*, 157, 468 ; from *p*,
    p. 154.
Felire Oingusso, cited or referred to, 35, 36, 168, 234 ; p. 65, note [1] ; 391, 812 ; p. 100, note ; 1131, 1133.
Ferguson, Mr. Samuel, quoted, 708.
Festus, referred to, 18.
Fermoy, Book of. See *Manuscripts*.
Fiacc's Hymn (*Liber Hymnorum*), cited, 154, 588, 605, 729, 870, 897, 943, 1080 ; Preface to, cited, p. 112, note.
Förstemann, referred to, 55.

G, loss of, between vowels, 378, 1114 ; in combination *gn*, 459, 683. Stems in *g*, see *Declension*. Old Irish *g* corresponds with Skr. *g*, *j*, Gr. γ, Lat. *g* ; and also with Skr. *gh*, *h*, Gr. χ, Lat. *h* (at the beginning of a word), *g* (in a word), 372, and p. 160; *gg* for *ng*, 879 ; Indo-European *g*, see p. 160.
Gaulish Inscriptions. See *Inscriptions*.
—— derivatives in *anco*, &c., 1006.
Gh, Indo-European, see p. 160.
Gildas, 17.
—— Badonicus, p. 133.
—— *Lorica*, p. 136, *et seq*.
Giraldus Cambrensis, his *Topogr. Hib.* cited, 37; p. 153.
Glück, C. W., his *Keltische Namen* cited or referred to, 46, 133, 139, 258, 328, 430, 533, 558, 656, 666, 667, 957, 999, 1073, 1131.
Gothic *h* (*g*) = O. Ir. *c*; Goth. *k* = O. Ir. *g* ; Goth. *g* = O. Ir. *g* ; Goth. *th* (*d*) = O. Ir. *d* ; Goth. *t* = O. Ir. *d* ; Goth. *d* = O. Ir. *d*. See Addenda, p. 160.

Greek κ = O. Ir. c; γ, χ = O. Ir. g; δ, θ = O. Ir. d; β, ϕ = O. Ir. b, 372; and see Addenda, p. 160.
Graves, Rev. Dr., mentioned, p. 159.
Grimm, Jacob, referred to, 387, 423; his *Geschichte der deutschen Sprache* referred to, 250, 784.
—— his *Deutsche Rechtsalterthümer* cited, 1136.
Gunation in Old Irish, 380, 392, 959.

H in Old Irish, p. 68, note.
Haug, his *Die Gâthâ's* referred to, 682.
Highland Society's *Dictionarium Scoto-Celticum* cited or referred to, 66, *et passim*.

Imperative active, Old Irish rare form of 2nd pers. sing., p. 112, note, and Addenda, p. 164.
Indo-European consonants, how represented in Old Irish and other sister languages, p. 160.
Inscriptions, Old Irish, on the case of the *Book of Durrow*, 203; copied by Dr. Petrie, 398; Gaulish, Vaison, 423, p. 161; Nismes, p. 100, note; Dijon, p. 156. See *Ogham*.
Irish Nennius. See *Todd*.

J (= *y*) lost at beginning of Old Irish words, 758; assimilated to preceding *l*, 765, 884; to *n*, p. 159; to *r*, 1116; passing into spiritus asper, p. 160.

K, Indo-European, how represented in the O. Ir. and sister languages, p. 160.
Keller, Dr. F., his *Bilder und Schriftzüge*, u. s. w., referred to, p. 155.
Kelly, Rev. Dr., his Calendar of Irish Saints cited, 223.
Kirchhoff referred to, 423.
Kuhn, Dr. A., cited or referred to, 108; p. 68, note, 423, 1036, 1038.

L, Indo-European, p. 160; O. Ir. *l*, ibid.
—— assimilating a following *d*, 915.
-lach, 933.
Laideenn mac Báith Bannaig, p. 133, and note.
Lassen, referred to, 758.
Latin *c*, *q* = O. Ir. *c*; Lat. *g* = O. Ir. *g*; Lat. *h* (at the beginning of a word) = O. Ir. *g*; Lat. *t* = O. Ir. *t*; Lat. *d* = O. Ir. *d*; Lat. *f* (at the beginning of a word) = O. Ir. *d*, *b*; Lat. *d*, *b* (in a word) = O. Ir. *d´* (and *b*?), p. 160.
Leabhar Breacc, mentioned, p. 132. See *Manuscripts*.
Lebar na huidre cited, see *Manuscripts*.
Lithuanian consonants, correspondence of, with those of the O. Ir., and other sister-languages, p. 160; declension of Lith. stems in -*ter*, 1047.
Locative sing. in O. Irish, p. 153 (and cf. the Mod. Ir. *cois na habhann*, *láimh re fairge*).
Lottner, Dr. Carl, cited or referred to, 831; p. 100, note; 977, 1124; and see *Verb*.

M, Indo-European, p. 160; *m* in *auslaut* weakened into *n* in O. Ir., p. 160, note; *m* in Welsh represents *mm*, *mn*, *mb*, 108.
Macintyre (*Mac int śáir*), 1137.
Manuscripts cited :—
  Book of Armagh (T. C. D.), cited, 75, 114, 203, 264, 342, 366, 383, 387, 390, 398, 424, 425, 427, 439, 580, 583, 588, 607, 616, 676, 693, 729, 745, 746; p. 95, note[2]; 781; p. 100, note; p. 103, note[3]; 871, 879, 909, 948; p. 112, note; 994, 1071, 1085; p. 146, p. 147, p. 152 (bis), p. 156, p. 166.
  Book of Dimma (T. C. D.) cited, 133, 1080.
  Book of Fermoy (Dr. Todd) quoted, 710.
  Book of Leinster (T. C. D.) cited, 555.
  Egerton, 88 (Mus. Brit.), referred to, 301.
  Harl., 1802 (Mus. Brit.), cited, 232; p. 68, note; 1134.
  H. 2, 16 (T. C. D.), p. 37, note. H. 2, 15, (T. C. D.), 1045. H. 3, 18 (T. C. D.), 371, 862.
  Laud, 610 (Bibl. Bodl.) cited, 428; Laud, F. 95 (Bibl. Bodl.), p. 130, note.
  Leabhar Breacc (R. I. A.), p. 103, note. See *Félire*.
  Lebar na huidre (R. I. A.), cited, p. 37, note.
  Liber Hymnorum (T. C. D.) cited or referred to, 128, 130, 560, 639, 770, 775; p. 95, note[2]; 867, 894; p. 125, note; 1096, 1134. See *Fiacc's hymn*, *Brogán's hymn*, *Colmán's hymn*, *Patrick's hymn*, *Sanctáin's hymn*, *Ultán's hymn*.
  Medical MS. ($\frac{52}{1}$), (R. I. A.) p. 165.
  O'Davoren's Glossary (Egerton, 88, Mus. Brit.), p. 44, note.
  Tripartite Life of St. Patrick (Egerton, 93, Mus. Brit.) cited, 104, 110, 189, 320, 518, 784, p. 159; and see *Cormac's Glossary*, *Félire Óingusso*, *Mone*, *Priscian*.
Medials, Irish, 372, and Addenda, p. 160; and see in this Index, *B*, *D*, *G*.
Metathesis aspirationis. See *Spiritus asper:* Metathesis vocalium, p. 161.
Middle-Irish, some characteristics of, p. 135.
Middle voice, traces of, in Celtic, 1112.
Mommsen, Theodor, his *Römische Inschriften der Schweiz* cited, 957.
Mone, Franz, his edition of the Lorica of Gildas, p. 134; his commentary thereon cited, ibid., and pp. 143, 144, 145; his copies of poems from a Carinthian MS. cited, p. 154, p. 161.
Müller, Professor Max, quoted or referred to, 584, 1047, 1052.
Muratori, *Thesaurus Veterum Inscriptionum* cited, 1029; his *Antiq. Ital.* cited, 1030.

Z

Myvyrian Archaiology referred to, 21.

N, stems in, see *Declension*. The so-called prosthetic *n*, 85; the combination *nth*, 287; *n* lost before *s*, 285, 807, 880; before *t*, 192 and note ², 490, 1017; before *f*, 519; *n* from *m*, 305, p. 160, note ʰ; the combination *nt* preserved in Welsh and Breton, 772; the transported *n*, 776 and note; p. 103, note ⁸; p. 108, notes; 946; p. 150; this *n* becomes *m* before *b*, p. 95, note ¹; *n* assimilates a following *d*, 914, and *y*, p. 159; Indo-European *n*, p. 160.
N Indo-European, p. 160.
Nasalization of initial medials, 776.
Nennius, the Irish translation of his *Historia Britonum*. See *Todd*.
Nismes, Gaulish inscription of, p. 100, note.
Norris, Mr. Edwin, his *Cornish Drama* referred to, p. 109, note, 937, 1039, p. 165.
Numerals, Cardinals, 772–777; Ordinals, 588–593; and see 930, 931.

O possesses umlauting power, p. 159.
O'Davoren's *Glossary*. See *Manuscripts*.
O'Donovan, Dr. John, cited or referred to, *passim*; his *Irish Grammar* quoted or referred to, 90, 139, 155, 161, 168, 208, p. 58, note; p. 70, note; 868; p. 103, note ³; p. 128, note ⁸; pp. 149; his *Fled dúin nan Géd* quoted, 193, 781, p. 100, note; p. 147; his *Battle of Magh Rath*, 303; his *Lebar na Cert*, 747, 837; and see *Cormacán éices*.
Oghams, 534.
—— inscriptions referred to, 80; p. 159.
O'Grady, Mr. S. H., his assistance acknowledged, p. 153.
Oingus *Cele Dé*. See *Félire*.
Old High German, correspondence of its consonants with those of the O. Ir., and other Indo-European languages, p. 160.
O'Molloy, his *Grammatica Latino-Hibernica* quoted, p. 136.
O'Reilly, his Irish Dictionary cited or referred to, *passim*.
Oreilli, 957, 1029.
Oxford Essays. See *Müller*.

P, loss of initial, 13, 493, 746; p. 150; change of initial *p* to *f*, p. 154; change of *p* to *c*, 224; loss of *inlautend p* in the combination *pn*, 720; Indo-European *p*, see p. 160.
Participles in ωυ, -οντος, represented by Irish ant-stems, 292; future participle passive, how formed in Old Irish, p. 135, p. 136, note; how in Middle and Modern Irish, p. 136; pret. part. passive, how formed in Middle Irish, p. 146.

Patrick's hymn (*Liber Hymnorum*) cited, 369, 580, 867, 872, 1071; p. 147, p. 149; Patrick's altar, p. 136; Lassar takes veil from Patrick, 676.
Petrie, Dr. George, referred to, 398; his *Round Towers* referred to, 55, 125; p. 58, note; 847, 933; p. 146; p. 148; his Essay on Tara cited or referred to, 173, 602, 784.
Pictet, M. Adolphe, cited or referred to, 97, 290, 302, 305, 578, 940, 999; p. 147, p. 149, p. 161; his *Essai sur quelques Inscriptions*, &c., p. 161.
Political Songs of England, ed. Wright, cited, p. 155.
Pott, cited or referred to, 746, 819; his *Etymologische Forschungen* referred to, 426.
Prefixes, *do*, *so*, 85; *mo*, p. 107, note ¹.
Priscian, Leyden Codex of, cited, 1102; p. 162.
Pronoun, possessive, of 2nd pers. sing., 570; of 3rd pers. sing., 420; relative, Mid.-Ir. gen., p. 150.
Pronunciation of *e*, *t* before *i*, 884, and note.

R, Indo-European. See p. 160.
Reduplication in Old Irish verb, p. 65, note ¹; p. 100, note; in the Welsh verb, 655.
Reeves, Dr., referred to, p. 133, p. 134, p. 145; his edition of Adamnan's *Vita Columbæ* cited or referred to, 121, 159, 191, 203, 303, 390, 724; p. 163; his list of names in *-gus*, p. 69, note ⁸; p. 133, p. 134.
Relative verbal forms in Irish, 1071.
Resolution of *é* into *ia*, 61; of *ó* into *ua*, 955.
Revue Archéologique, referred to, p. 100, note.
Rumann cited, 428.

S between vowels lost, 296; *sn* becomes *nn*, 305; *sv* becomes *v*, p. 160, note ᵐ; *s* from *x*, Skr. *ksh*, 386, 466; 426; *s* for *f*, 1039; *s* assimilated to following *t*, 556; stems in *s*, p. 163; Indo-European *s*, p. 160.
Sanctáin's hymn (*Liber Hymnorum*), cited, 937.
Sanskrit consonants corresponding with those of the O. Ir., and other Indo-European languages, p. 160.
Schleicher, Professor A., referred to, 1071; p. 158.
—— his *Handbuch der Litauischen Sprache* referred to, 1047.
Scirglige Conculainn, ed. by Mr. Curry (*Atlantis*, Nos. 2, 3), cited, p. 44, note ⁸⁰; p. 69, note ⁸; 486, 1010; p. 121, note; 1070; p. 159.
Semitic words latinized, p. 144.
Siegfried, Professor R. T., cited or referred to, 89, 99; p. 68, note; 342, 682, 746, 758, 784; p. 100, note; 884, 952, 1071, 1073, 1133; the editor's great obligations to him, p. 132.
Singulative forms, 765.
Slavonic consonants, correspondence of, with those of

the O. Ir., and other Indo-European languages, p. 160.
Spiegel cited or referred to, 55, 96, 130.
Spiritus asper, shifting of in Old Irish, 305; p. 68, note; in Welsh and Cornish, 608.
Suffixes, superlative, 43; -tar, 1014; p. 149; Skr. suffix, -ta, Lat. tu-s, Gr. ro-ç, found in Irish, p. 61, note[2]; O. Ir. -the, -te = -taya, ibid.
Syntax, curious construction with bhi and td, p. 149.

T, use of, in Mod. Ir. declension, p. 58, note; in verbal forms, ibid. (but see *Addenda*, p. 158); stems in *t*, see *Declension*; *t* between vowels, 227; *tt* becomes *th* in Welsh, 230, 957; Old Irish *t* corresponds with Skr. *t*, *th*, Gr. τ, Lat. *t*, Goth. *th* (*d*), 372, see Addenda, p. 160; *t* in composition, 430, 1061; loss of *t* before *r*, 466; *t* worn down to *d* in the possess. pron. of 2nd pers. sing., 570; final *t* becomes *s* in Cornish, 772; medialization of *t* by *n*, and subsequent assimilation, 991; Indo-European *t*, p. 160.
Táin Bó Cuailgne cited, 481, 747.
Tenues, Old Irish, 372; and see in this Index, *C, P, T*.
Thorpe, Mr. Benjamin, his edition of *Beowulf* referred to, 752, p. 163.
Todd, Rev. Dr. J. H., his *Irish Nennius* cited or referred to, 14, 229, 557, 817, 975, 1048; p. 151.
—— his edition of the *Liber Hymnorum* cited or referred to, p. 51, note; 218, 267, 320, 481, 691, 695, 727, 745, 770; p. 95, note[2]; 784, 894, 923, 977, 1078, 1092; p. 148, p. 151.
—— his *Cogad Gaedil re Gallaib* cited, 866.
—— his help acknowledged, p. 2, p. 144.
Tooke, Horne, cited, 595.

U possesses umlauting power, p. 159.
Ultán's hymn (*Liber Hymnorum*) referred to, 943; cited, 955.

Umlaut, 5, 287; p. 159; progressive umlaut, p. 151.
Usury, Old Irish word for, 740.

V between vowels lost, 174, 477; passing into spiritus asper, 305; found in Irish (written *b*) in the combinations *dv*, *lv*, *nv*, and *rv*, p. 159, p. 160; also as representing *dv* (aibherseoir, abhcoide, 432); Indo-European *v*, p. 160.
Vaison, Gaulish inscription of, 423; p. 161.
Verb. Old-Irish conjugations: â-stems, p. 150, No. 240; aI-stems, 1080; å-stems and î-stems, p. 146 (these were first pointed out by Dr. Lottner); ia-stems, p. 165; the *t* in the perf. act. of a-stems, p. 158; pret. part. pass., formation of, p. 146; and see *Imperative, Middle Voice, Participles, Reduplication, Relative Verbal Forms*.
Verbal forms in the Lorica-glosses, p. 146; impersonal flexion in passive, p. 151.
Villemarqué, Vicomte H. de la, referred to, 797.
Vocalism, 5, 287 (but see Addenda, pp. 151, 159).
Vriddhation, 34, 948.

Weakening of *â* and *a* into *ai*, p. 164; p. 153.
Weber, A., cited or referred to, 205, 758.
Welsh, see *C, M, N, Reduplication, Spiritus asper, T*; Welsh Latinity, p. 134; trace of declension in Welsh (*pyn* in *crbyn* is the dat. of pen), p. 135.
Wilde, Mr., his *Catalogue* referred to, p. 159.
Words and forms, historical value of evidence given by, p. 2.
Wright, Professor William, his help acknowledged, p. 144.

Y, Indo-European, p. 160; sometimes passes into *spiritus asper*, ibid., note [h]. See *N, T*.

Zeitschrift für vergl. sprachforschung, cited or referred to, *passim*.
Zeuss, his *Grammatica Celtica* cited or referred to, *passim*.

INDICES VERBORUM.

[The numerals refer to the paragraphs of the foregoing Commentary, except when the letter "p." is prefixed; then they refer to the pages of this book.]

I. OLD-CELTIC INDEX.

AD-namatius, 666.
Aedui, 948.
Alisanos, p. 156.
ambi, 670.
Ambitui, 921.
ande, 734.
Andebrocirix, 947.
are, 704.
Argento-ratum, 607.
Argentomagus, 607.
Ar-morica, 704.
asno-s, 296, p. 159.
Atilogdo (gen. sing.), p. 159.
Atrebat-es, 315.

Becco, 664.
Belesama, 423.
belinus, 545.
bello-canda, p. 163.
Bovinda, 21.
brâtu-de, p. 100, note.
Brâtu-spantium, 366.
bretos, 328.
Brettania, 957.
Brettanos, 957.
Brigantes, 292.
Britovius, 957.
Britta, 957.
Britte-burgum, 957.
broci-rix, 947.
Brittus, 957.
Droco-magus, 947.
Ilrogi-mârus, 663.
bulga, 217.

Cambodunum, p. 150.
casses, 46.
cata-, p. 164.
catu, p. 157.
Catu-slôgi, 1003.
cinco (stem), p. 86, note.
Cintu-genus, 588.
Cluniâcum, 723.
Cocidius, 139.
Cogidumnus, 139.
Com-bretonium, 957.
Cono-maglus, 545.
Con-snanetes, 667.
Con-textos, p. 104, note.
Coslum, 556.
crotta, 5.
Cuno-belinus, 545.
curmen, curmi, 266.

Dânuvius, p. 130.
Darvernon, 554.
dede, p. 100, note.
Dexsiva, Dexivia, 386.
Doiros, p. 156.
Dubis, 381.
Dubra, Dubri-s, dubron, 375.
dula, 765.
dumnos, 994.
dûnon, 21, p. 150.
duron, 608.

eiðru, 423.
Epasnactus, 296.
Epo-mûlus, 295.

ex, 393.
Ex-cinco-mârus, p. 86, note.

Gabro-magus, 372.
Gabro-sentum, 372, 1073.
Galaatl, 216.
Gangani, p. 150.
genos, 588.
Glana, 671.
glastum, p. 91, note.
Gobannitius, 369.
Grannos, 952.

Iantu-mârus, 663.
Iartai : : p. 100, note.
Ierne, p. 159.
ieuru, p. 73, note ; pp. 156, 161.
Isaruo-durum, 608.
Ivernio-s, Iverni-s, Ivernia, p. 67, note 1 ; p. 159.

Labarus, 1133.
Laurentius, 908.
Lauriâcum, 908.
Lauro, 908.
Lîcca, 133.
Lucterios, 10.
lugos, p. 155.

Magalius, 902.
Magalus, 902.
maglos, 545.
magus (mago-s), 21.
mâros, 423, 621, 663, 902.

matos, 661.
mâtrebo, p. 100, note.
Mello-dunum, 258.
Mellosectum, 258.
Moccon (stem), 664.
Moccus, 1029.
Mogit-mârus, 902.
Mogounus, 952.
mori, 860.
mûlos, 295.

namatios, 666.
namausatis, 423.
namausicâbo, p. 100, note.
nemeton, 423.
Nerto-mârus, 663.
novios, 21.

pempe-dula (?), 765.
pompai-dula (?), 765.

raton, 607.
rîx, 423.
Rotomagus, p. 158.

sages, 450; sagi, 872.
Salusa, 977.
Santones, 667.
secton, 258.
Sego-mâros, 423; p. 156.
senton, 372.
Silius, 1009.
Silo, 1009.
Silus, 1009.
Sirona, 952.
slôgos, 1003.
sole, 558.
sosin, 423.
spantion, 366.
Suanetes, 667.

tarbelodathion (tarvo-tabatio-n), 40; tarvos, p. 159.
Tecto-sages, 450.
Tecto-sagi, 872.
Teuto-matus, 661.
textos, p. 104, note.
Togiacus, 994.
Togidia, 994.
Togius, 994.

Togitius, 994.
Togi-rîx, 994.
Togo-dumnus, 994.
Toutio-rîx, 423.
toutius, 423; p. 161.
tragos, 74.

Ulkos, p. 147.

Velleda, 1.
ver, 74; p. 99, note.
Vergivios, 328.
Vergo-bretus, 328, 366.
Verno-dubrum, 375.
Verno-sole, 558.
ver-tragi, 74.
vidu, 46.
Vidua, 46.
Vidu-casses, 46.
Villoncos, 423.
Villonius, p. 161.
Vindos, p. 150.
Virdomârus, 663.
Volcæ, 1045.
Volcatius, 1045.

II. OLD-IRISH INDEX.

á (prep.), 200, (pron.) 420.
a (interject.), p. 165.
aball, 555.
abbaith, 948.
ached, 159, 580, 909.
acher, 77.
act, 614, 745.
acus, 203.
adaltras, 882.
adarcdae (-de), 59, 1018.
adbail, 954.
adbar, 161.
adchodadoessa, p. 100, note.
adcondare, p. 156.
adcotedæ, p. 100, nota.
adebuiriur, p. 151.
ade, 676.
adercóne, 1018.
adfiadat, 1080.
adgaur, 869.
adglúdastar, 128.
adgúsimm, p. 159.
adib, adim, abi (?), p. 127.
adiecht, 1010.
adircliu, 1018; p. 155.

adnacul, 693.
adopart, 948.
ad-ra-nact, p. 61, note; 693.
adrimiter, 738; adrimi, 1080.
adroigegrannatar, p. 100, note.
adslaindimm, p. 166.
Λ'ed (Aid), 948.
águr, 77.
aidacht, 948.
aidche, 546.
aig, 758.
ail, 91.
aile, 158.
ailedu, p. 166.
ailigud, 462.
aill, 924.
aille, p. 166.
ainis, 1080.
ainm, 56, 991.
Ainmire, 13.
áir, 873.
airchissim, p. 151.
Airdllacc, 573.
aireeb, p. 147.
airechas, p. 147.

airgech, 586.
airegda, p. 147.
airi, p. 100, note; 639.
airlam, 884.
airle, 884.
airm, 729.
airthir, 150.
áis, 735, 812.
aith, 155.
aithech, p. 100, note.
aithle, 155.
ala, 150.
alaile, 872.
álaind, p. 162.
álgenaigim, 917.
altóir, 745.
am-, 392.
am, 1112.
amail, 262.
amiressach, 943.
amlabar, 1133.
amml(ñ), 85, 1112.
amréid, 890.
an (neut. art.), 78.
án, 682.

anacul, 570.
anairtúaid, 353.
anais, 897.
analchi, 752.
anamchara, 1082.
and, 676.
anfolmithe, 676.
aníar, 305.
aníartúaid, 353.
antúaid, 353.
apgitir, 21.
ar (prep.), 98, 608, 614.
ara (ń), p. 100, note.
araile, 112.
áram, p. 164.
arbar, p. 166.
arbe, p. 163.
arbiathim, 477.
archiunn, 35.
Ard-machæ, 948.
ardbrig, p. 154.
ard-fégad, p. 149.
are, p. 148.
aren, 752.
ar-unn-fethitis, p. 166.
argat, 607; argget, p. 162.
ar-id-rálastar, 128.
arin, 729.
arbe, p. 163.
ar (ń), 884.
arsidi, 722.
artu, 812.
áru, 246, 1011.
as(ń), 565, 1112.
asbiur, 639.
asbert, 879.
asbertar, 639.
asigthe, p. 112, note.
asin, 128.
asindisset, p. 100, note.
aslach, 933.
as-m-berar, 578 (asbiur).
ass, 555.
assa, 812.
assagússim, p. 159.
m-aso, m-asu, 1112.
astoidet, 1008.
at, 1112.
atá(ú), 565.
athair, athir, 13, 1046.
atlaigthe, 943.
atomsnassar, 817.
atrab, p. 127, note [a].
atrópert, p. 100, note.
m-atu, 1112.
háue, p. 67, note [a].

augtortás, 1107.

bú, 115.
bachal, 262.
bachall, p. 103, note [a].
bad, 729.
bál, 128, 676.
baig, p. 154.
baile, p. 156.
bainne, 966.
bairgen, 141, 722; p. 157.
baithes, p. 100, note.
baitsium, p. 150.
ball, 638.
bán, 738.
bandach, p. 133, note.
bandea, 289, 1053.
banna, 966.
banteriamid, 287.
bar(ń), p. 160, note [m].
barr, 28.
bas, 881.
bás, 200, 614, 745.
báthach, p. 163.
batar, 36.
bebais, p. 100, note.
bebe, p. 100, note.
becc, 439, 664.
bed, 290, 880.
beith, p. 154.
bél, 425, 636.
bélre, 176.
ben, 369, 884, 1053.
bendacht, benedacht, 203, 914.
berenade, p. 166.
bertaigimm, p. 148.
béa, 722 (= bias); 745, 1071.
bésgnae, 890.
bethu, 605, 870.
bi, 56.
biad, 477.
biam, 954; p. 164.
bid, 154.
biis, 35.
bind, 115.
bir, 184.
bís, 740.
bithbethu, 640.
bite, 1071.
biu, 154.
bliadain, 676, 745; p. 157.
bláth, 954.
blosce, p. 152.
bó, 424.
bóchaill, 583.
bocc, 498.

bocht, boctán, 1058.
ból, 948.
Boind, 21, 462.
bolad, 1087.
bolc (bolg), 217.
boltigur, 1087.
bommar, 815.
borg, 555.
bou, 159.
brúge, 292.
brasse, 36.
brúth, 154, 366, 948.
bráthair, 1047; p. 165.
brée, 958.
brécairecht, 958.
brénaim, 683.
bréntu, 683.
Bretan, 909.
bretha nemid, 578.
briatbar, 812, 897.
brichta (acc. pl.), 369.
Brigit, 954.
brithem, 366.
rou-broena, 1048.
bró, 784.
brónach, 427.
bronnait, 647.
búachaill, 583.
bnbe, p. 100, note.
bnide, adj. 803; subst. 943.
buideeh, 884.
buith, 930.
bun, p. 154.
bunad, p. 154.

cúch, 154, 729, 815.
cadessin, 948.
cae, 218.
cáer, 267.
cáera, cúira, 13, 851.
Caichán, 676.
caill, 115.
caille, 676.
cáindías, 35.
caindlóir, 44.
caingel, 745.
cúintaidlech, 287.
cáirchuide, 851.
cairtine, 1127.
cairtinigther, 1127.
Callrige, 745.
calad, 280.
canoin, 1080.
car, 280.
cara, 292.
caraim, 280, 815.

carcar, 262.
carpat, 112, 424.
carric, p. 152.
cathim, 280.
cathir, 13.
cach, 214.
cechaing, p. 100, note.
cechladar, p. 100, note.
cechtar, 1071 ; p. 159.
cél (celaim), 371.
céle, 882.
celebirsimme, 746.
cell, 203, 948.
cen, 120, 640.
cenél, 676, 745.
cenéla͠e, 822.
cenn, 17, 120.
cenngalar, p. 148.
Cennsalach, p. 67, note ²; 616.
cep, 480.
cercdae, 196.
cercol, p. 159.
cerd, 218.
cerd-chae, 218.
césad, 892, 1131.
céss, 892.
cessacht, p. 151.
cessachtach, 280.
cét, 772; p. 154.
cétamus, 578.
cétlaid, 3.
cétach, 909.
cethir, 775.
cethrar, 398.
ciad-choloml, 203.
Ciaran, 200.
ciatu, p. 127, note ⁴.
cid, 1071.
cil, 90.
cimbidi (acc. pl.), p. 166.
cinnim, p. 150.
cis, 954.
cith (cid), 637.
claar, 67.
clam, 424.
cland, 745, 991 ; p. 154.
cli, 387.
cliab, 1102.
clocc, p. 103, note ³.
clóen, 870.
clú, 812.
clúain, 200, 723.
cluas, 867.
cluichech, 518.
ro-cluinetar, 902.
clum, 262.

cnám, 269.
co, 128.
coccilsine, 882.
cocert, 888.
cofil, 1102.
colbdelach, p. 166.
coibse, 745.
cóic, 776.
cóicur, 398.
coill (caill), 115.
cóimdiu, 812; p. 127, note ³; 1133.
coimet, p. 103, note ³.
cóimsa (gen. sing.), 757.
coire, 724.
coirnea (acc. pl.), 75.
cóis (acc. sing.), 434.
coisecrad, 880.
coitchenn, 872.
col, 1030.
colann (colinn), 120.
colcaid, 262.
collde, 556.
colinn, 919.
Colmán, 909.
Colomb, 203.
colpa, 146.
comacomol, 1010.
comadnacul, 889.
comain, 897.
comairle, comairlle, 884.
comalnad, 760.
comarpe, p. 127, note ⁴.
combach, p. 166.
comdlúthad, 636.
comeisséirge, 889.
coméitged, 817.
comirsire, p. 105, note.
comman, 897.
comnactar, 897.
coimthúarcon, 722.
con (conj.), 120; (prep.) 580.
conaicertus, 888.
con-a-til, 729.
Conchad, 948.
conchechrat, p. 100, note; p. 161.
conchoimnuculr, p. 161.
Conchubor, 545.
condaig, 450.
condelg, p. 127, note ⁴.
confil, 614, 745.
conflechtaigimm, p. 147.
confoirem, p. 154.
congabaimm, 676; p. 166.
contarat, p. 131, note.
contubart, 948.

conicim, 570.
conmir, 156.
consádu, 1131.
consan, 930.
contuil, 729.
contesbad, 966.
coór, 938.
corcur, 224.
core, 938.
corp, 98, 812; p. 128, note ³.
cos (= coxa), 637.
cosc, 660.
coscedar, p. 162.
coscitir, 660.
coth (?), p. 164.
crag, 203.
cráibdech, 745.
crann, 719; p. 154, p. 162.
creitem, p. 100, note.
Cromthann, 693.
Cremthinne, 909.
cretim, p. 127, note ⁴.
cretmech, 817.
criathar, 700.
crich, 781, 1073.
cride, 67, 1102.
crin, p. 162.
cris, 1102.
crith, 1102.
croch, 738, 812.
cro-chaingel, 745.
crocann, 56.
crocenn, 56.
croeb, 955.
crottichther, 5.
cruithnecht, 778.
cruithnechtide, 778.
cruth, 380.
cu (co), 168.
cuanene, 986.
cucan, 245, 572.
cucann, 245.
cuibsech, 745, 1071.
cuil (acc. sing.), 262.
cuilech, 1030.
cuilennbocc, 498.
cuiligim, 1030.
ra-chuiliu, 1030.
cuimlengaimm, p. 147.
cuimnigur, 1111.
cuimte, p. 166.
cuintgim, 871.
cuirimm, p. 151.
cuiriur, p. 151.
cuirm, 266.
culatha (acc. pl.), p. 148.

Indices Verborum.

cumal, 909.
cuman, 1111.
cumbre, 678.
Cummen, 909.
cumtach (cumddach), 203, 569, 871, 881, 1098.
curchas, 933.
cúrsagad, 924.
curu (acc. pl.), p. 74, note.
cusecraimm, 879.
cutrumme, 903.
cutrummus, 903.

dú, 112, 773.
dagairle, 884.
dagcomairle, 884.
dagforcitlid, 902.
daggnimrad, p. 166.
daingen, daingnigim, 674.
dairde, 554.
Dallbrónach, 427.
dúltech, 569.
daltæ, 676.
dam (mihi), 1071 ; (etiam), 752.
dam (bos), 722, 858.
dam (dolor), 1102.
ro-damdatar, p. 158.
damde, 858.
con-dan, 878.
dán, 565 ; p. 109, note.
dána, dúnatu, 1131.
daneu, 738.
darmchennsa, 635.
daro (gen. sing., nom. *dair?*), 676.
dartinn, 870.
daú (ei), 745 ; dáu (2), 773.
daur, daurde, 554.
daurauch, 554.
dé-, 773.
dea, 289.
debai, p. 166.
debthimm, p. 166.
décrud, 745.
déed, 815.
deichenbar, 398.
déirec, 626.
delb, 642 ; p. 146.
demnai (acc. plur.), 214.
dénmid, 899.
dénim, 899.
dénmusach, 899.
dénom, 141, 722, 899.
deóg lái, 120.
derbbráthair, p. 162.
derbensde, p. 166.
derc (oculus), 675.

derc (ruber), 565, 738, 939.
dercaide, 939.
dernad, 203.
derucc, 554.
des, 386.
deserce, 626.
dessam, 937.
di (prep.), 676.
di (2), 745, 773.
dia (suo), 450.
dia (deus), 21, 81.
dia (dies), p. 163.
diabul (diabolus), 863.
diabul (duplex), 930.
diade, p. 109, note.
diall, p. 95, note [1].
Dianchride, 1080.
diangalar, 222 ; p. 151.
dianid, 555.
diant, p. 162.
diar(n), 284, 890.
días, 35.
dib(n), 773.
dichéin, 878.
dídiu, 41.
digóni, 909.
digni, p. 162.
diib, 745.
díl, 1120.
Dimma, 1080.
din, 112.
dind (L dinn ?), p. 37, note.
diudirect, p. 166.
dínu, 292.
dirrógel, 580.
ditbrubach, 214.
diliu, 153, 762.
dliged, 87.
dláith, 636.
dláth, 636.
dláthe, 636.
dláthait, p. 166.
do- (pref.), 85 ; (prep.), 112.
do (prep.), 605.
do (pron.), 570.
dó, deo, 817.
doadbadar, 565.
doadbat, 846.
donirbiur, 660.
doaurchanim, 704, 837.
dobiur, 133, 745.
dochuiriur, p. 151.
docbum, 943.
dodcaid, 262.
dofaith, 128.
dofarci, 873.

dofoirnde, 1008.
doformgut, 756.
dofuairce, 722.
dogegat, p. 100, note.
dogniu, 908.
dogrés, 222.
doilbthid, 642.
Doilgus, 342.
dóir, 85 ; p. 156.
dolbud, 642.
do-m-farcai, 371.
domnu, 812.
doman, 280.
domunde, p. 109, note.
donn, 909.
drochgnim, 752.
dorút, p. 159.
dorchæ, 331.
doroega, 555.
dorencanas, 837.
dorodba, 954.
doroigu, p. 100, note.
doroiier, 890.
dorónta, 112.
do-s-fiuscad, 605.
dosiathach, 578.
draigen, 559.
driss, 587.
dristenach, 587.
druailnide, 1071.
druid, 369.
druimm, 676, 745.
du (pron.), 570.
du (prep.), 738.
dúaib, p. 100, note.
dub, 381.
dubber, 745.
dubchorcur, 224.
Dubloch, 781.
duécastar, 745.
dúibsi, 1080.
dúil, p. 52, note.
duine, 89, 738.
duit, 943.
dulluid, 879.
du-m-esurcsa, 222 (*tesurc*).
dún, 674.
dunad (dúnad ?), 1131.
dúan, 98.
dúnsit, p. 166.
durind, 880.
durni, 272.
dús in, 745.

e, 637.
hé, 128.

Old-Irish Index.

ech, 17, 909.
Echaid, 13.
écen, 1010.
eclais, 177; eclis, 948.
écosc, 660.
ecsamlus, 904.
edocht, 745; edoct, 948.
heirp, 205.
éitach, 757.
éitset, 1101.
héitsid, 1101.
Éladach, 909.
ellach, 933.
emnatar, 1010.
emon, 1010.
én, 371, 746; p. 162.
encae, p. 151.
enga, p. 166.
ennac, p. 151.
eólas, 85.
epistil, 1080.
epscop, 948, 982.
ercbissecht, p. 151.
ercboltech, 935.
erchuiriur, p. 151.
hErinn, 154, 305, 870; p. 159.
erlabrai, 867.
erlam, 906.
érlam, 955.
ermaisse, 927.
ernaigthe, p. 147.
ernais, 280.
ercbuilech, 1030.
erochairchétlaid, 3.
erochuir (-air), 3.
eros, 70, 580; p. 166.
érpimm (airbimm), 752.
errach, 1070.
erreud, 1006.
erthnaiscertach, 305.
és, día és, dom héis-se, p. 164.
ésca, 234.
óscac, 234.
escaicbaill, 115.
éscide (-caide), 234.
easgre, 738.
eslinn, p. 162.
éstecht, 867.
ót, 635; p. 166.
étach, 501, 757; étacht, 757.
etalacda, p. 166.
ethar, 70.
Etan, 1102.
etar, 745.
etarscarad, 254.
étmar, 635.

étrad, 166.
étruimm, 639.
étsecht, 176, 1101.
étrumme, 903.
étsid, 902, 1101.

faca, 120.
fácab, 676; fáccab, 948.
fa-des, 128.
fáilte, 161; p. 151.
fairgge, 77.
fúith, 2; p. 147.
fáithsine, 882.
fanacc, 1080.
fannall, 934.
far(h), p. 127, note [3]; p. 160.
fás, p. 127, note [4]; p. 162.
feblæ, 948.
fóda, p. 166.
fóisne, p. 100, note.
féith, 99.
fel, 371.
felsub, 1129; p. 159.
fenechua, p. 127, note [4].
fer, 841.
ferh, p. 127, note [3].
ferenn, 390.
ferg, 328.
Fergus, 342.
fergach (fercach), 328.
fernn, p. 166.
ferr, 41, 1116.
ferte, p. 166.
fescor, 224.
fésóc, 47; p. 155.
fess, p. 127, note [4].
fésur, 392.
féuil, 150.
Féth, 745.
fiach, 269.
Fiachu, 13, 115.
fiacail, 150.
Fiacc, 880.
fiaclach, 150.
Fiachra, 13.
fiad, 36.
fiadnisse, 959.
fiadu (fóda), 292; p. 166.
fiasur, 392.
fichtea (acc. pl.), 676.
fid, 580.
fidbaide, 371.
figim, 1095.
fili, 1.
filus, 738.
fin, p. 162.

Find, 120.
findae, p. 154.
findfolt, 77.
finechas, 745.
Fio, 745.
firián, 681.
firiánigedar, 682.
firinnugud, 682.
firinne, 927.
fir-óg, 954.
fis, 846.
fiss, 1008.
flaith, 338; p. 100, note.
Flaud, 203, 948.
fliuchaidlatu, 675.
fliuchaide, 675.
fliuchaigim, 675.
fliuchderc, 431, 675.
fó, 1102.
foncanim, 837.
fochaid, p. 100, note; p. 157.
focheirt, 35, 888.
focertar, 222.
fochétóir, 588.
fochlaid, 229.
fochric, p. 157.
fochridigur, 1102.
fochun, 371.
fodil, p. 166.
foedes, 890.
foétsecht, foéitsimm, 1101.
fogbaidetn, 740.
foglaim, 890.
fognam, 815.
fogrigur, 611.
fugur, 469.
foigde, 815.
foile, 1129.
foilsigud, 895.
Foirtchernn, 871.
folcaimm, 1044.
follus, 895.
fo-m-chain, 371.
for, 387; p. 99, note; 729, 745.
forchanim, 837.
furcetal, 139.
fochell, 98.
forcital, 837.
forcitlaidecht, 837.
forcitlid, 837.
focul, 873.
fóisite, p. 147.
forbe, p. 146.
forculu, 873.
forchun, 837.
fordingair, 578.

2 A

178 Indices Verborum.

forcir, 660.
forgair, p. 146.
forlóg, 909.
formuichthe, p. 166.
for(ṅ), pron. 635.
forn, prep., p. 146.
forūgaire, p. 146.
forṅgarthaid, p. 146.
for-ōenu, 36.
forosna, 168.
forru, p. 166.
fortacht, 727, 890.
fortachtid, 727.
fortiag, 727.
fortrumme, 903.
fot, 677.
fota, 677.
fotha, p. 148.
fothaigim, p. 148.
fotharcud, 740, 822.
fri, 112, 369, 635, 815.
frisdúnaim, 287.
friss, 346.
frithiúraim, p. 161.
fróich, 565.
fuacht, p. 103, note ³.
fúal, 222.
fúan, 29.
fuar-both, 120.
fuarrech, fuairrech, p. 149.
fuasnad, 927.
fufuasna, 77.
fuilib (dat. pl.), 608.
fuireitis, 729.
fuismedach, p. 147.
fulsam, p. 100, note.
furruimtis, 729.

gabais, 676; gabis, p. 166.
gabál, p. 166.
gabor, 372.
gabsi, 948.
gabul, 135.
gádatar, 870.
gaib, 262.
gáid, 870.
gaide, 216.
gainnigud, p. 166.
gair, 115.
gáith (subst.), 77.
gáith (adj.), 884.
galar, 222.
galla (acc. pl.), , p. 112, note.
gasne, p. 154.
geinti (acc. pl), p. 100, note.
gelgrian, 168.

geumnai (dat. sing.), 214.
German, 1080.
giall, 216.
gigestesi, p. 100, note.
gilcach, 933.
gilither, 168.
giuil, 262.
glais, 781.
glan, p. 162.
glanaim, 671.
glas, 738.
glasán, 226.
glicc, gliccu, 1129.
glicce, 1129.
glúne (acc. pl.), 740.
gní (acc. sing.), 902.
gním, 682, 908; p. 128, note ³;
    p. 146.
gó, 897.
gobann, 369.
góithlach, 933, 1067.
gonas, 940.
gorith, 637.
gorte, 620.
grád, 1040.
grán, 722.
grant, 651.
gres, p. 164.
gréssich, 815.
grian, 952; p. 162.
gruad, 90.
gúala, p. 159.
gúas, p. 162.
guide, 870, 943.
guidimm, 870.
gutae, 1040.

hi, 91.
iach, 216.
iada, p. 162.
iar, 305; p. 100, note.
hiarn, 216, 608, 812.
iaruaid, 676.
iarsichid, p. 166.
iar-suidiu, 879.
iarum, 120.
iasc, 13.
iathmaige, 390.
iarthuaisceerddach, 305.
Ibar, 561.
icc, 758.
iccaid, 605.
icfed, 897.
ichtar, 1014.
idón, 1; page 103, note ³.
ídul, 569.

iffern, 519.
il, 13, 565.
ilar, p. 157.
ilmrechtrad, 957.
im, 128.
imb, 578, 784.
imbed, 670, 921.
imber, 465.
imchomarc, 112.
imchlóud, p. 147.
imda, 200.
imdegail, 214, 867; p. 149.
imdergud, 873.
imdu, 299.
imm, 670.
immact, p. 166.
immaircide, p. 128, note ³.
immchuiriur, p. 151.
immib, 757.
immluadi, p. 147.
immo(ṅ), p. 162.
imm-r̄ordad, 878.
immunn, 305.
immut, 154.
imorro, 555.
impe, 954.
imthised, 870.
in (prep.), 637.
in (art.), 78.
inad, 516.
inbaid, 954.
ind (art.), 78.
ind (prep.), 734.
indarbe, 752.
indeb, p. 109, note; p. 166.
indlaid, 424.
indlinech, 371.
indiung, p. 166.
indocbáil, 450.
indoilbthid, 642.
infinit, p. 157.
ingen, 676.
ingenas, 290.
ingor, 68.
ingraimmim (dat. s.), p. 100, note.
ingrented, p. 100, note.
inill, p. 148.
inis, 462, 1080.
iuniain, 955.
inna, inna(ṅ), 78.
innocht, 77.
innunn, 954.
insin, 262.
insnastis, 817.
inso, 222, 745; p. 156.
int, 78.

intan, 897.
inte, 745.
intech, 872.
intṡerbu, 1132.
intáliucht, 734.
iráil (eráil, hod. *furail*), 91.
ire, 13.
hires, 91, 752; p. 147.
iressach, p. 127, note 3.
irladigur, 884.
irlam, 906.
irlithe, 884.
is, 1112.
Isin, 262.
I'su, 758, 954.
it', 154.
it, 1112.
ith, 1038.
ith, 758, 1038.
itge, p. 147.
ithim, 40.
i-timchuairt, 338.
ithland, 132.
iudeiu (acc. pl.), p. 100, note.
iúrad, p. 161.

la, p. 100, note; 605.
labrad, 1133.
labrar, 812; p. 128, note 3.
ro-labrastar, 812.
laechraid (dat. sing.), 77.
Laigen, 954.
Laigiu, 923.
laith, 266.
laithe, 154.
laithoirt, 266.
lám, 34, 387, 637, 867.
lámbrat, 740.
lán, 13.
land, 132.
lann (adj.), 77.
lann (subst.), p. 152.
lasan, 203.
lase, 746.
lassais, 128.
Lassar, 676.
lat, 41.
laur, 908.
lebar, 371.
lecbdach, 1071.
ledmarb (*recte* lethmarv), 90.
legad, 1071.
légend, 853.
rolég, 1080.
léine, 38.
leis, 879.

lenaimin, 1040.
lendan, 38.
lenomun, p. 159.
lenu, 580.
leosom, 722, 858.
les, 424, 580.
lesc, 382, 815.
lesmac, p. 155.
lestar, p. 162.
let, p. 165.
leth, p. 156.
lethan, 13, 925.
lethchil, 90.
lethgute, 90.
lethit (acc. sing.), 925.
lethmaethail, 90.
lcthóm, 90.
lethn (dat. sing.), 640.
lethu (adv.?), 870.
lia, 13.
lia, 424.
liacc, 133, 573; p. 156.
Liás, 676, 745.
libur, 371.
lige, 812.
lim, 614.
lín, 863.
line, 1080.
linn, p. 100, note.
lobad, 1071.
loc, 879.
loch, 637, 781.
lóche, 292; p. 168.
Lochland, 77.
lóeg (lóig), 424.
lóg, 133, 792, 1085.
lóid, 371.
Lóig-les, 424.
Loiguire, 424.
lon, 371.
lonach, 115.
long, 574.
lór, 860, 908.
lorg (lorc), 937.
losait, 42.
loscud (dat. sing.), 737.
lóthor (-ur), 740.
loure, 908.
luxe (acc. pl.), p. 166.
lúath, 371.
lúathchride, 1102.
lub, 114.
lubgartoir, 114.
lubgort, 114.
Lugaid, 13.
Ingimem, 923.

luid, 36, 948.
lúrech, 154.
luscu (acc. pl.), 605.

ma, 637, 745.
mac, 115, 200, 757.
maccán, 337.
maccu, 200.
maccu-Nois, 723.
Machae, 943, 948.
mad, 41, 1040.
madu, p. 162.
maethail, 90.
mag, 580.
maglster, 365.
maigen, 222.
Máilduin, 200.
Mál Odræ, 909.
Máilsechnaill, 203.
Maire, p. 165.
maisse, 927.
maith, 450, 661, 745.
malducht, 915.
manach, 745.
manestrech (gen. s.), 726.
mani, 745.
mann, 299.
múr, 663; p. 154.
marb, 90, 605; p. 159.
martir, 214.
martre (gen. s.), 738.
martur, p. 166.
máthair, 954.
mátharlach, 933.
mathim, 280.
mélt, 168, 922.
menme, 927.
menn, 77.
menstir, p. 103, note 3.
mór, 465.
mesraigthe, 807.
mess, 154.
messa, 1117.
mi-, 1117.
miad, p. 154.
midus, 1071.
mil, 133.
milte, 133.
mimasclach, 933.
mír, 156.
mirtchaill, 115.
mistae, 1050.
mo (pron.), 371; (pref.), 897.
Mochoe, 745.
moirtchenn, p. 159, p. 166.
moithiu (compar.), 394.

molad, 873.
molor, 902.
Monach, 115.
mór, 663.
mórféser, 777.
móru, 1020.
mrecht, 957.
mrechtrad, 927, 957.
mu, p. 107, note.
mucc mora, 1029.
muccfoil, 1029.
mug, 403, 882; p. 127, note 3.
muinæ, 744. p. 163.
muiode, 744.
muine, 128, 583.
muinntore, 744.
muinter, 745; p. 127, note 3.
muir, 77, 812, 860.
muirágu (dat. sing.), p. 166.
Muirchad, 200.
muiride, p. 166.
muirmóru, 1020.
Muirscc, 69.
mulcnn, 701.
múl, múldae, 295.

na, na(n), 78.
nach, "not," 817.
nád, 371, 639, 745.
náma, 292.
nand, 879.
nascad, 817.
natbir, 13; nathair, 88.
nau (naui?), p. 162.
naneirchinnech, 449.
neb-, 987.
neblesc, 382.
nech, 745.
necht, 224.
neim, 280.
nem, p. 52, note 2; 812, 943;
  p. 127, note 3.
nenaid, 208.
neph-, 987.
nephéscide (-caide), 234.
nascóit, 347.
nessa, nessam, 1117.
ní, 77, 614.
ní (res), 987.
nim, 812.
Ninine, p. 125, note.
nit (gen. sing.), 781.
nóeb, 214, 954; p. 162.
nól, 21.
nóib (nom. pl.), p. 128, note 3.
nóibe, 168.

nóib-briathar, 812.
nóin, 262.
Nóindruimm, 745.
nónbar, 400.
Nos, 200.
nu, 637.
núæ, 578.
Nuada, 292.
núe, 21, 803.
nus (nús?), 256.

ó, 555.
óa, 77.
óa (minor), 758.
óa (jecur), 1032.
oblann, p. 166.
oc, 299, 815.
óc, 758.
ochen, p. 166.
óclach, 933.
óclachde, 758.
ócmíl, 758.
ochter, 580, 909.
odbrann, p. 149.
óg, 954.
óiuach, p. 147.
óindæ, 565.
Oiugus, 342.
oipred, 889.
óis, 812; p. 127, note 3.
oitherroch, 948.
ól, 266, p. 158.
olambieidsi, 1129.
olc, 578, 662, p. 147.
olachaill, 115.
óm, 90.
omne, 262.
ood, 752.
optait, p. 159.
or, 184.
ór, p. 162.
órd, 943.
órddan, 943.
hóre, p. 100, note.
oróit, 203, 1080; p. 165.
ort, 266.
oslaícib (dat. pl.), p. 165.

Pátricc, 676, 745.
pé, 745.
pellec, 136.
peccad, 1040.
pecthad, 1040.
persan, 87.
pólire, p. 103, note 3.
port, 676, 725.

praintech, 729.
precept, 91.
pronn, 815.

ra-, 13.
ráith, 115.
rann, 9, 1071.
ro-ratha, p. 109, note.
rechtaire, 450; p. 166.
réga, 943.
régat, 154.
réid, 890.
rélmm, 77; p. 155.
rem, 745.
remtbechtas, 872.
remunn, 890.
rét, p. 159.
riagol (-gul), 61.
riat, p. 109, note.
riched, 168.
rici, 254.
rig, 36, 203, 1036; p. 154,
  p. 162.
rigad, 879.
rigain, p. 154.
rige, 1131; p. 158.
rind, p. 67; 1008.
rindaig, p. 133, note.
rith folo, p. 166.
rithæ, 909.
ro-, 13.
ro-bai, 214.
robbem, 640.
ro-bet, 338.
ro-cét, p. 61, note.
róis, 262.
ro-m-bith, p. 165.
ro-p, 214, 614, 890.
roth, p. 158.
ro-t-checuladar, 656.
ro-t-bia, 161.
ruamnae, p. 161.
ruire, 13.
rúnaid, p. 133, note.
ru-n-dlúth, 636.
sab, p. 37, note.
sachilli, p. 166.
súebchore, 938.
sáer, 1137.
shethar, 133.
sáibapstal, 635.
saiget, 214.
saigid (dat. sing.), 1137.
saigul, p. 146.
saile, 651.
sáirdénmidecht, 1137.

Old-Irish Index.

sáithar, 1085.
salann, 977.
Salchan, 724.
salm, p. 128, note 3.
-san, -sa, 78.
sancht, p. 161.
santach, 280, 667.
sás, p. 162.
scatán, 967.
scél, 223.
sciath, 214.
scíth, 614.
sclictn, p. 166.
scol, 338.
scribend, 853.
scuchad, 112.
sé, 777.
sech, 112.
sechethar, p. 166.
sechmall, p. 150.
secht(n), 224.
Segéne, 948.
seib, 109.
séim, 636.
séimtana, 1017.
seirge, 924.
selb, 580.
sem, 420.
sen, 735.
sén, 1132.
ron-séna, 1048.
soól, p. 166.
serbe, 1132.
ses, 580.
sesaimm, p. 100, note.
sess, 70.
sét, 280.
sét (iter), 490, 729, 1073.
setharoircnid, 320.
sétfethchaib, 826.
siasair, p. 100, note.
síb, 1112.
side, 1088.
síl, 555.
-sind, -sin, 78.
siniu, 130.
-sin(n), 78.
sís, p. 156.
sissi, 1112.
siur, 216.
sinrnat, 320.
slabreid, 890.
slóte, 586.
Sléibte, 693, 948.
slemon, 639.
sliassit, p. 148.

slige, 112.
sliss, 32.
slúag, 36, 1003.
slucht, 734.
ron-snádut, 1131.
snáthe, 817.
sned, 649.
sni, 305; snisni, 1112.
so-, 85.
sochoisc, 660.
sóer, 954; ro-n-sóera, 1048.
socrda, p. 154.
sóeth, p. 158.
sóir (sóer), p. 156.
sóirmug, 404.
solam, 740.
som, 420.
son (sonus), 1137.
son, p. 162.
sprut, 565, 1048.
srathar, 262.
suldigud, 1137.
srcibnaide, 794.
sruim, 1039.
srian, 109, 1039.
srón, 1039.
srnth, 999.
suide, 366, 812.
suide (pron.), 1010.
súil, 425.
sunt, 565.
súithe, p. 37, note

t', 570.
tabuirt, p. 100, note.
tacúir, 98.
tadbat, 846.
taibderec, p. 147.
taibre, 1040.
taidbsiu, 844.
taidlech, 287.
tairchechuin, 837.
tairchet, p. 61, note; 837.
tairchetal, p. 147.
tairmthechtas, 872.
taispenad, 894.
talam, 108, 578.
tamlacht, 781.
tana, 1017.
tanise, p. 58, note.
tar, 740.
tarési(n), 676.
tarfarcennsi, 738.
tarsende, p. 166.
tarslacc, 890.
taschide, 760.

Tassach, 897, p. 104, note.
tech, 569.
tecelsid, p. 166.
tecmallad, 299.
tecnate, 569.
techt, 450, 872; p. 158.
techtaire, 450.
techtat, 639.
teglach, 933.
ten (dat. sing.), 128.
tenge, p. 128, note 3.
teoir, 774.
teora, 774.
terismid, 287.
tét, 1017.
tes, 942.
tiach, 41, 371.
tiarmoracht, 872.
tic, 120.
tigerne, 450, 909.
timlnad, p. 147.
tinne, 760.
timtherecht, 898.   }
timthirecht, 368.   }
timthirthid, 368.
tintarrad, 870.
tintathach, 927.
tír, 703.
Tirechán, p. 95, note 2.
tirim, 703.
tirme, 703.
tised, 879.
tissad, 870.
tochuirimm, p. 150.
togu, 878.
Toiguire, 994.
toirthech, 289.
tóisech, 21, 1040.
tol, p. 100, note; p. 162.
toll, p. 162.
torad, 289, 1085, 1106.
tórand, 880.
torc (eor), 1102.
torc, 744.
torcc, 373, 729.
torcde, 373.
tórmach, 756.
tórmachtae, 756.
tórmachtaid, 756.
tórúther, 1006.
Torrian, 1080.
tosach, p. 100, note.
totmáel, p. 166.
traig, 74.
trastar, 1071.
trefocla, 873.

tróide, 578.
tremiblur, p. 148.
tremitiagat, p. 148.
trón, 299, 1117.
tress, 873.
tressa, 1117.
trí, 676.
trí (prep.), 636, 752.
trían, 897.
trimi-ro-thorndiussa, 1008.
triroch, 371.
tróg (truag), 383.
trógán, 383.
tromchride, 903.
tromm, 903.
truag, 262.
truscu (acc. pl.), 605.
tú, 1112.

tuaichle, 1129.
túarcun, 722, 858.
túath, 423, 870.
túathum, 937.
tucad, 555.
tuccu, p. 165.
tuirind (dat. sing.), 35.
tuisled, 927.
tús (tuus), 21.
túslestar, 1134.
tuus, 21, 937.

húad, 879.
úadib, 729.
úair, p. 95; note [1].
uan (uainn), 214.
húare, 639.
úas, 371.

húasalathair, 13; p. 147.
húasalsichire, p. 166.
húasalterchomrictid, p. 166.
ucht, 262, 812.
huile, p. 100, note.
huinnius, 557.
uisce, 69.
uisceán, 69.
uisce, 36, 758, 881, 1085.
Ultán, p. 95, note [2].
humae, 611.
úr, 578.
húrde, 578.
urfaisiu, 777.
utmall, 815.

ymmon, 154.

III. MIDDLE-IRISH INDEX.

[Where there is no commentary on a word, the numerals in this Index refer to the articles in the text, pp. 4-35. Numerals with "gl." prefixed to them refer to the Glosses on the Lorica, supra, pp. 136-143.]

a (pron.), 420, 421.
a (interj.), p. 112, note.
abb, see banab.
abhall, 555.
abdaine, 173; p. 157.
abhcoide, 432.
abhracht, gl. 120.
accai, 104.
accadhar, 1096.
aclaidhi, 456.
acra, 869.
adh (agh) allaidh, 387.
adhalg, 866.
adhailtrach, 619.
adhalltras, 883.
adharc, 59, 1018; p. 155.
adhastar, 820.
adhbhar, 161, 849.
adhbhardacht, 835, 848.
adbrond, gl. 187; p. 149.
ad[b]clos, 1030.
adblacadh, 759, p. 23.
adblucadh, 693.
adntes, gl. 28; p. 147.
áe, 975, 1032.
ænach, ænachde, gl. 45; p. 147.

Aengus, 342.
agaidh, gl. 108.
agarb, 385.
aghat, p. 44, note.
aibhirseoir (oibhirseoir), 517.
aiceeht, 868.
aidbhendh (gen. pl.), 709.
aidhchidhe, 546.
aier, 105.
aiffrend, 853; p. 164.
áil, 91.
Ailech, 39.
Ailell, 481.
ailghinecht, 917.
aimfesach, 392.
aimsir, 1048, gl. 9; 847.
ainder, 223.
ainfírénach, 682.
aingil, 460; -gel, gl. 26, gl. 146.
ainim, 288.
ainm, 991; gl. 241.
ainmech, 428.
ainmidhi, 976.
ainmneachadh, 885.
air, 226.
airai, p. 149.

airchindech, 449.
airdi (-de), 926.
airdeasbog, 447.
aire, gl. 109; p. 148.
airecht, p. 37, note; p. 95, note [1].
airgi (-ge), 586, 754.
airgeach, 586.
airged, 787.
airgedach, 607.
ait, 191.
aitchimm, gl. 141.
aiteand, 933.
aitbléini, 155.
alaind, 226, 234.
Alba, 191.
albanach, 306.
allaastigh, gl. 251; p. 150.
allaidh, 297, 417.
allamuigh, gl. 250([2]); p. 150.
Alldghus, p. 69, note.
alltar, gl. 147; p. 149.
almanach, 312.
alt (= artus), gl. 201.
amadán, 302.
amalnsibh (dat. pl.), gl. 147.
amaisc, 251; p. 158.

ainbal, gl. 81.
amhnas, 226.
an (prep.), p. 135; gl. 6.
ro-an, 193.
anál, gl. 123; p. 149.
ancoire, 68.
anmach, 654.
anmain (dat. sing.), 232.
anoir (onoir), 1079.
anum, 406; gl. 59.
Aodh, 948.
aoir, 104.
ar (pron.), 847.
ar (conj.), 847.
ara (d-ara), 589.
úra, 1011; gl. 175, gl. 208.
úirnibh toll (dat. pl.), gl. 183.
arachend, p. 95, note 1.
arain, 163.
arán geal, 236.
arbha, 213, 1038.
archaingel, 462.
ard, 16; gl. 12, gl. 264.
ardeaspoc, 16.
ardríg, 161.
arg, 198.
arm, gl. 21.
arrecaim, 481.
arson anma, 996.
artán (?), 111.
Artgbus, p. 69, note.
asa, gl. 240; p. 150.
as-a-altbli, 193.
asnach, gl. 170; p. 149.
asóer, 937.
assal, 296, 416; p. 159.
assan, 72.
atanach, 596.
at cluic, 26; p. 154.
at pill, 831.
at ("in thy"), p. 149; gl. 147.
athair, 3, 1046.
athair-talmhan, 178.
atharmarbhthach, 317.
atbél-sa, 104.
atcondaire, 104; p. 156.
atchumiledh, 909.
athfiana, 330.
atchimm, gl. 52, gl. 141; p. 147.
atbgbabhtúil, p. 44, note.
athgo, gl. 45.
atuaith, 937.
augdar, gl. 2.

ba, p. 37, note.
baccach, 605.

bachlach, 410.
bachlach brcallán, 412.
bachlóg, 696.
bagar, 339.
baile, 110; p. 156.
bainde, 966.
baindea in toraidh, 289.
baindi cich, 326.
baineachlach, 257; p. 158.
baintigherna, 287.
bairín, 28.
bairghen, 141; p. 157.
baistedh, p. 165.
baithes, gl. 83, gl. 248.
ball, gl. 77, gl. 148, gl. 238; p. 150.
ballach, 638.
bam, gl. 260; p. 165.
banab, 22.
bancoig, 247.
bauchara, 293.
bannach, p. 133.
bunphricir, 23.
bansagart, 24.
bansaer (-sóir), 292.
bantaisech (-tóisech), 21.
bantracht, 39.
Baothghas, p. 69, note.
bara, 320.
baramhail, 877.
bás, gl. 7, gl. 263.
hasóg, 95.
bass, 94; gl. 166; p. 149, p. 156.
báthadh, p. 163.
bathais, 1045.
batar, 36.
bealach, 793.
bean, 1053.
bean do bhráthar, 570.
bean do mheic, 571.
beanmharbhthach, 321.
bec, gl. 132.
beithi, 560.
beg, 194, 664, 673, 806.
bél, gl. 107; p. 148.
benim, gl. 62; p. 147.
bennacht, 914.
beol, gl. 128; p. 128, note 3.
beóthach, gl. 211.
bérla, p. 37, note.
berradh, 1096.
bertnaigbim, gl. 80; p. 148.
betha, 113; gl. 8, gl. 254, gl. 260.
bí, gl. 147.
bladh, 1045; p. 165.
biathadh, 1045.

bicairecht, 171; p. 157.
bidbgadh, 769.
bile (orlus), 191; p. 157.
bile (ventilogium), 716; p. 163.
biun, 223.
bir, gl. 152; p. 149.
biror, 184.
birrach, 18; p. 154.
birur, 823.
bis, gl. 132; bite, gl. 59.
blaesc, 179; p. 157.
bláthach, 220; p. 157.
bláthmhar, 491.
bleoin, gl. 226.
bliadain, 173.
bloingi (acc. pl.? *die weichen ?*), gl. 214.
blonac, 236, 1006; p. 164.
bó, 159, 583.
boc, 1094.
bocasach, 1030.
bocht, 1058.
bocoidech, 653.
bodhar, 604.
bolltanadh, 1088.
bond, 96; gl. 191, gl. 247.
bonn, 190.
bó-álnaighedh, 300; p. 159.
bothán, 120.
braen aimsire, 1048.
brúghe, gl. 129, gl. 131.
braiccin, 714.
bráighdech, 444.
braise, 36.
brat, 29.
bráthair, 1047; p. 162.
brátharmarbhthach, 319.
breallach, 657; p. 161.
brece, p. 128, note 3.
brégach, 958.
breitheamh, 366.
brén, 683.
bréntus, 1089.
bretnach, 957.
bríathar, 628; gl. 1.
briathrach, 628.
bróce, 1033.
bróg, 445.
broine, gl. 49; p. 147.
brondmar, 647.
brothrachan, 180.
bruach, 947.
brú, gl. 210; b. na hóighe, 576.
brugh, gl. 45; p. 147.
bruinech, gl. 49; p. 147.
bruinde, gl. 200; p. 150.

buachaill bó, 583.
buachaill mucc, 584.
buaile, 174.
buaile dam, 1044.
buain, 502.
buathbhallán liath, 182.
buidhen, p. 95, note [1].
buidhe, buidhi, 803; p. 128, note [3].
buigi, 1119 (see boc).
butun, 152; p. 157.

ca, 218.
cabillanacht, 172.
cac gabhar, 1075.
cách, p. 37, note.
caech, 426.
caemh-Dhaire, 191.
caenuaraigh, 1130.
cáer fíuemach, 267.
caera, 851; p. 164.
cætharach, 1055.
cai, 770.
Caid, 949.
caílc, 58.
caile dabhca, 158.
caillech, 847; a. ligheoc, 282.
caillné, 336.
cailtteamhail, 1061.
cáin, 98, p. 156.
cain (adj.), 234.
cainuarrach, 1130, gl. 138; p. 149.
cairdes, gl. 61.
caire, 36.
caisc, 298.
calma, gl. 22; gl. 158.
calmdacht, gl. 14.
calpach, 164.
calptach, 162.
camm, gl. 229, p. 150.
camra, 123.
camradh, 129; p. 156.
canauach, 437.
cantair, 239.
cantairecht, 63.
caog, 101.
caor, p. 165.
cara, 293, 413.
caraim, 191.
ra-m-charastar, p. 149.
carr, 70, 263.
casadh, 1043.
casnoidhi, 253.
casta, 632.
cat, 499.
cath, gl. 23.
cathair airdeasbuig, 176.

cathbharr, gl. 99, p. 148.
catholica, 521.
cealg, 325, 500.
cech, p. 37, note; gl. 59.
céd (primus), 588; (100), 772.
céd grindi foilci, 1045; p. 165.
cedir, 560.
ceilebhradh eoin, 746.
ceindetan, gl. 82.
céir, 225.
cúirin, 836.
ceis, 717; p. 163.
ceithri, 775.
cenbaran, 181.
cend, gl. 102.
cendaidhi (cennaidhe), 1092.
cend-fíacail, gl. 134.
cengal, 149, 911.
i-cenn, 894.
cennaighim, 1092.
cennais, 232.
cennbharr, 51; p. 155.
centar, gl. 147, p. 149.
cep, 480.
cerc, 196.
cércaill, 979.
cercall, 475.
cerd, 218, 508.
cerdcha, 218.
cernach, 486.
certachadh, 888.
cessacht, 280.
cestugadh, 891.
cestunach, 15; p. 153.
cethardubhladh, 931.
cét-bliadhain, 588.
cét-chathach, 772.
cethramhadh, 142.
cethrar, 400, 1092.
cethri, 775.
cothruma, 591.
ciabh, 33; p. 154.
ciarsech, 200.
cich, 100, gl. 203, p. 150.
cichin, 101.
cindchércaill, 481.
cis, 784.
cisti (ciste), 199.
clais dromma, gl. 160, p. 149.
clár, 67, 560.
clár casta, 1043.
clas guail, 273.
claustra, 818.
cleath, 485.
clechtaim, gl. 81, p. 148.
cléirech, 422, 710.

Clement, 539.
clesamnach, p. 44, note.
co-clethi, p. 37, note.
cliabh, gl. 71.
cliambuin, 377, 322.
cliamhuinmharbhthach, 322.
cliath, 126.
cliathach, 712.
cliath fuirsidh, 240, p. 158.
clibhún, 697.
cluc, 26.
cloch, 552; p. 112, note.
clódh, gl. 44, p. 147.
cloicend, gl. 82, p. 148.
cloidheamh, 461.
clu (acc. pl.), gl. 153; p. 149.
cluain gabhála, 723.
cluas, gl. 113; p. 148.
cluithi (-the), 518.
clúmhar, 655.
cnúimh, 193, 296.
cnaimfiach, 269, 503.
cohairithe, gl. 20, p. 147.
cochall, 121, 56.
cocan, 245.
cochtair, 283.
codaltoch, 729.
coelán, gl. 224, p. 150.
cofúilidh, gl. 267, p. 151.
cogadh, 139, p. 157.
cogar, 145, p. 157.
coi, 770.
coibhlighe, 847.
coileach, 506.
coiloch gáithi (-the), 510.
coill, 115.
coimpert, 847.
coindealbhúthadh, 345, p. 163.
coin-mir, 276.
coinnill, 44, p. 154.
coinnlin, 210.
cóir, p. 44, note.
coire (-ri), 724.
coisinech, 650; p. 162.
coisreagadh, 285.
coissegradh, 880.
coitchend, gl. 1.
colach, 1030.
colaud (dat. sing.), gl. 174.
coll, 556.
colpa, 146, gl. 188.
colum, 203, 504.
Columcille, p. 37, note.
colund, 919.
combadas, 36.
comhaightech, 314.

comhaineachadh, 897.
comhainm, 993.
comhairle, 884.
comhairemh, 913.
comhaistiu, 518.
combalta, 486.
comhaltudh, 518.
comhdhlúta (gen. pl.), gl. 233.
combfoccul, 873.
chomhforbrit, gl. 194.
combla, 71, 125.
comma, 918.
companach, 378.
compantus, 892.
comparaid, 875, 896.
compas, 1137, 1138.
compur, gl. 71, p. 148.
combradh, 481.
combruc, 847.
combsólás, 884.
combthinól, gl. 26.
comhthrom, 960.
comhthromugudh, 903.
conaichi, 1128.
Conall Cernach, 486.
concró, 261.
Conchubhar, 545.
conidh, gl. 2.
conn, 209; p. 157.
Conn, 772.
connlach, 209.
connargaibh, 320.
copán, 479.
coraidh, 457.
co-r-bo, 4.
corcach mara, 206, 505.
Corcaigh (dat. sing.), 4.
corcair, 224.
Cormac, 173.
coróin, 75, 76.
corónta, 601.
corp, 812; gl. 259; c. leghas, 1071.
corporas, 859; p. 164.
corr, gl. 49; corr brághat, gl. 133.
corróg, 167.
cos, 466, 560; gl. 190.
coslatra, 36.
cosmhailius, 904.
cosmhailsibh (dat. pl.), gl. 32.
cosolamh, 36.
cotun, 270.
cobulidhe, gl. 239.
cráes, 92; p. 156.
cráessach, 644.
crand gíus, 563.

crand glésta, 719.
crand lauir, 564.
crand mucor, 566.
crand tochartaigh, 746.
crebhar, 204.
criadh, 1054.
criathar, 700; p. 162.
cridhe, gl. 211.
cris, 720, 1102; p. 149; p. 153.
cris tribhuis, 706.
crisdal, 552.
crismal, 840.
cristaighi (-e), 323.
cristin, 313.
cró, 122, 261; p. 156.
cró caerach, 851.
crocan, 56.
crodhacht, gl. 26.
croicinn madra alta, 275.
croidhi (-e), 1102.
croindtille, 651, 844.
croindtillech, 651.
crombéol, 708.
crosán, 14.
Cruachan Ráith Chonrach, 481.
cruaidh, 674.
crusaidhi, 1118.
crubh dich, 442.
cruit, p. 153.
cruitire, 5, 1015.
cruithnecht, 778, 189.
crupán na lámh, 233.
cú allaidh, 417.
cuailli (-e), 495.
Cuangus, p. 69, note.
cugan, 572.
cúig, 776.
cúigedh, 592.
cuigel, 567.
cúigur, 401.
cuilen, 498.
cuimhleng, gl. 45; p. 147.
cuimhneach, 1110.
cainchidh, 783.
cuindeóg, 165.
cuisle, 99; gl. 222.
cularan, 1049.
cumhacht, gl. 69.
cumair, 678.
comea, 737.
cumdach, 881.
cumdachta, p. 141, note. } cumh-?
cumdaightóir, 1098. }
cumtach, 871.
cupris, 560.
curach, 488.

curchuslach, 933.
curracach, 595.
curu (acc. pl.), 428.
cusle, 99.

dú, 773.
dabhach, 158, 277.
daingen, p. 37, note.
daingin, 674, 679.
dair, 554.
Daire, 191.
dail, 249, 427, 623.
dallsúilech, 622.
damb, 758, 858, 1044.
dúna, 1131.
darabósi, p. 112, note; darmési, 937.
dath, 1087.
des, 289.
dealbh, 642, 936.
dealbhdha, 642.
dealg, 1074.
dealradh, 1031.
deas, 386.
dóc, 173.
decháin, 454.
dechinhadh, 43.
Dechtere, 320.
decredech, 12.
deganach, 451.
degh-ghnímbradh, gl. 261; p. 151, p. 166.
deirgech, 78.
delbhait, gl. 154.
dénamh, 899.
déninhusach, 1090.
dónta, gl. 245; p. 165.
dóntar, 1096.
deóir, 550.
deoradh, 303; p. 159.
dér, 39, 724.
dércach, 627.
derg, 1048.
dergi (-ge), 939.
dergudh, 481.
dermhár, p. 95, note¹; 1008.
des, p. 69, note.
di, gl. 67.
dia, 405, 232; gl. 157, gl. 265.
diabhul, 527.
diadhacht, 81, 334.
dianghalur, gl. 258; p. 151.
Diarmaid, 540.
dias, 398.
dias, 35.
dibechan, gl. 135; p. 149.

dibblínaibb, 104.
dibh(ṅ), p. 95, note [1].
dichuirer, gl. 261.
didean, 153.
dídin, 762, 995
dídnighteóir, 1093.
díghlach, p. 69, note.
dílé, 1121.
dílechta, 429; p. 161.
dílechtach, 83.
dim, gl. 265.
dimaines, gl. 10; p. 146.
dín, 193.
dindsenchas, p. 37, note.
diner, 699.
dinghhala, 668.
dirimb, gl. 234.
d'then, 718.
ditoin, 472.
discibul, 438.
dlaliugudh, 910.
disle, 496.
ditín (acc. sing.), 602.
ditin, gl. 68; dítnet, gl. 19, gl. 76.
dithrebhach, 315.
diumus, 1030.
dlighedh, 87, 879; p. 147.
dlighi, 87.
dlightinech, 433.
dlistinach, 433, 439.
dlúith, 636; gl. 39; p. 147.
dlúthadh, gl. 61.
dó, 193.
doheth, gl. 2.
dobhrán, 375.
dochinélach, 676, 1057.
dochotar, 894.
doctuir, 1082.
Doedbghus, p. 69, note.
dóenna (= O. Ir. dóinde), 85.
dofalcsena, gl. 151; p. 149.
dogni, 847; dogniat, 1008.
doib, 481.
doilbhtheóir, 1091.
doilbhiblugudh, 900.
dóit, gl. 164.
dolléci, 747.
domblas áe, 975.
Donnchadh, 525.
Donnghus, p. 69, note.
dorátadh, 560, 867.
dorchadhus, 331, 332.
dorine, p. 125, note.
dornadóracht, 272.
dornán buana, 502.

dorus, 124; gl. 245.
dorus lis, 580.
dot, gl. 69.
dótbengtach, 626.
dothóet, gl. 2.
do-da-trascair, 847.
dreassan, 1012.
dreolán, 207.
dris, 587, 933.
driscain, gl. 217.
droigbin, 559.
dromand, gl. 171.
druim, 745; druimseilg, gl. 172.
co-druimne, 4.
dubh, 381, 802.
dubhán, 428.
dubbrudau, 721.
Dubhthach, 1096.
duchu, 1020.
dúil (dúl), 267.
duillen, 765.
duine, 89, 953.
duine beg, 436.
dúl, 1008.
dunmharbhthach, 316.
durnu (acc. pl.), gl. 165.

each, 17, 414, 442.
Eachtghus, 69, note.
eaglas (eaglais), 177.
ealadan, 85.
eallach (?), 71.
earrach, 1070.
eás, 259.
easbog, 448.
easpog, 982.
écas (éccas), p. 125, note.
écna, p. 38, note.
édach, 501, 757.
édail, 694.
édaingen, 680.
édmhur, 635.
edrath, 166.
egeomhthrom, 961, 962.
egeusmhai'ius, 905.
eideand, 933.
Eighipt, 581.
eineeb, p. 58, note.
éirindach (éirinnach), 305.
eistidhóir, 1101.
eitelladh, 912.
eithidheannhail, 1068.
ela, 509.
embnadh, 1010.
endae, p. 151.
endgae, gl. 260.

Eoghan, 543.
éolus, 85, 901.
eorna, 779.
erlabhra, 867.
erchissiu, gl. 265; p. 151.
escaine, p. 147.
escara, gl. 18.
escart, 254; p. 158.
escata, gl. 180, gl. 184.
escuinge urchoideeb, 935.
esga, 234.
eslán, 393, 634.
esláni (-e), 928.
etal, p. 151.
etan, gl. 86, gl. 103.
etarfuaradh, gl. 269.
etarsróin, gl. 116.
éte ochta, gl. 222.
etechail, 1066.
etelaigher, gl. 264.
etixeta, gl. 89.
etlae (?), gl. 260; p. 151.
eturru, 481.
examail, 1087.

fabhra (O. Ir. *abra*, gen. -*at*), 79.
fácbat, gl. 16.
fada, 677.
faecbóg, 188, 194.
Faelghus, p. 69, note.
falcim, p. 149.
faidi (-e), 929.
faidiugudh, 907.
faighin, 157.
failgheach, 631.
fáinleóc, 934.
fairei (fairge), 1103.
fairge, 575, 1103.
fairsing, 640.
faismedhach, gl. 55; p. 147.
faisncis, 751.
fáistine, p. 38, note.
fáith, 2, 350, 351, 352, 958.
falling, 37; p. 154.
fallaingech, 599.
farcún, 238.
fareli glún, gl. 183.
farsinge, 640.
feam, 97.
feclug, 185.
fecht, 481.
féd fose[laidh], 826.
fódaim, l. 43, gl. 253; p. 147.
fédán, 46; p. 154.
fedhbh, gl. 53²; p. 159.
fégadh, p. 149.

fóith, gl. 132, gl. 223; p. 156.
feóil, 193.
feóil na fiacal, 150.
feorus, 582.
fer, 395, 1048.
fer clí, 397.
fer cuisi do condmail, 434.
fér, p. 70, note.
ferand, 390.
ferbóg, 205.
fergacht, 328.
Ferghal, 533.
Ferghus, 486.
fernóg, 558.
ferr, 1116.
fersaid (-said), 568.
fersán, 468.
fesach, 392.
fesóg, 47; p. 154.
fesógach, 645.
fétaim, p. 147.
fiabhrus, gl. 257.
Fiac, p. 125, note.
fiacail, 150, gl. 89, gl. 126.
fiadh, 183.
fiadhnaisi (-e), 959.
Fianghus, p. 69, note.
fiar, 621.
fiarsúilech, 621.
fichabhall, 562.
fidh, 46, 267.
fidhbha, 797.
fidhbhuidhe, p. 70, note.
fidhchat, 260.
fidhchillí (gen. sing.), 747.
fighidóir, 1095.
fil, 104.
filidh, 1.
filidhecht, 833; p. 38, note; 1002.
find-choelán, gl. 229.
find-emhon, 1010.
finemach, 267.
finemain, 267.
finghalle, p. 147.
firénach, 681.
firmamint, 749, 1008.
fis, p. 149.
Flathghus, p. 69, note.
fliuch, 675.
fliuchaidhe, p. 111, note.
fliuchidhecht, 1097.
fobith, 486.
fochétóir, 320.
fochluidh (-aidh), 229.
fód, 119.
fofrith, 1048.

foghnr, 469.
foighl, 815.
foilci, 1045.
foillsiugudh, 895.
foiltfind, 39.
foiltnilih (dat. pl.), gl. 97.
foiltnin, 464.
foircedal, 837.
foirmtech, 602.
folt, 77, 78; p. 70, note; gl. 237.
fon, gl. 132.
fonamhaideach, 630.
forba, gl. 8, gl. 260; p. 146.
forculu, gl. 59.
forgaire, gl. 1; p. 146.
foriarair, gl. 59; p. 147.
forithin (dat. sing.), p. 151.
format, 602.
formnai (acc. pl.), gl. 161.
forsgath, 839.
fortachtaigbim, gl. 1; p. 146; 727.
fortaigbim, 727.
fothoin (acc. sing.), gl. 95; p. 148.
fotbragadh, 822.
fraech, 565, 933; p. 162.
francach, 248.
frangcach, 309.
fria, 847; frim, 937.
friss, 125, 847.
fual, 222.
fuathrole, gl. 94; p. 148.
fuil, 1048.
fulltin, 463.
fuindeóg, 134.
fuindseóg, 557.
fuiseóg, 140.
fundamintech, 612.
furachair, 984.
furtacht (fort-), 727.

ga, 216, p. 157.
gabhúiltech, 594.
gabhal, 135.
gabhann, 369.
gabhar, 372.
gaethanmhail (góith-), 1067.
gaeth, 428; g. atúaidh, 353.
gaethmhar, 646.
gaibhthi, p. 112, note.
gaile, gl. 219, gl. 220, p. 165.
gaill-mhias, 478.
gaire, p. 165.
gairleóg, 31.
gáith, 1070; gáithbhuilg? p. 157.
galar, 281.

gall, 478.
galldach, 307.
gamain arain, 163.
ganmhech, 428.
garbog, 186.
garrga, 702.
geal, 168, 286, 801, 659, 1124.
gealan na súl, 168.
no-t-gebhtha, p. 112, note.
góg, gl. 194; p. 150.
gúidh, 19; p. 154.
geimhel, 226.
gein, 104.
geind, 560.
geinemhain, 887.
gemhan, 834.
geocach, 513.
gerraine (gen. sing.). gl. 224; p. 150.
gerbach, 652.
geredh (gen. sing.), 125.
gerreach, 494.
gerrchend, 125.
gerrghuin, 940.
in-gerrtha, gl. 17; p. 135.
glaii, gl. 125; p. 149.
gileach, 933.
gile, 1124.
gilla adhairce, 1018.
gilla cinn eich, 17; p. 153.
gilla Crist, 523.
gilla Martain, 526.
gilla na naomh, 345.
gilla nan-each, 946.
gilla l'átrice, 537.
Gilliam, 532.
Gilliberd, 534.
glas, 563, 560.
glac, 1008; glac-arbha, 213.
glac saighed, 214.
gluine, 191.
glais, gl. 218.
glan, 671, p. 153; glan-mhét, 29.
glas, 29; p. 91, note.
glass(serra), 226.
glecaire, 986.
glic, 1129.
gloinidhe, 1087.
glún, gl. 183, gl. 185; p. 149.
gnáthughudh, gl. 56; gl. 246.
gnéthigh (dat. sing. fem.), gl. 2.
gnimh, 908, gl. 2.
gnimhradh, p. 151, p. 166.
gocan, 66.
god, 603.
goirt, 637.

gortach, 620.
grádh, 1081.
grainsech, 195.
gramatach, 82.
granna, grana, gl. 78, gl. 64.
gredháil, 854.
greidell, 107.
greim, 144.
grian, 952, 973, 989, 990.
Grighoir, 544; -ghuir, 894.
grinn, 39.
grindi (-e), 1045.
groigh, 742.
gruaidh, 39; gl. 114, gl. 124; p. 148.
gruamdha, 384, 1065.
gruth, 784.
gual, 273.
guala, p. 151.
guasacht, 727; gl. 6.
guidhi (-e), 870, 893.
guirin, 255.
gulban, gl. 106; p. 148.
gus, p. 69, note.

iachtarach, 1013.
iarnaighi (-e), 608.
iarund, 790.
iar-sein, 4.
ibhar, 561; p. 162.
ibrach (?), 832.
ichtar na comhladh, 1034.
idh urchumail, 279.
ifearnadha, 827.
ifern, 519, 520, 825.
ifus, gl. 2.
igha, 244.
ilmhíle, gl. 29; ilrátha, p. 70, note.
ilar, 197.
imad (-adh?), 921.
imarchuirim, imarchor, gl. 268; p. 151.
imdha, 670, 805.
imdheghail, 154; gl. 147; p. 149.
imell, 69.
imlán, gl. 243.
imun, 784.
immchosuibh (dat. pl.), gl. 121; p. 149.
imme, gl. 58; p. 147.
immles, gl. 118.
immlind, gl. 205; p. 150.
immun, 894.
impidhe, gl. 11; p. 147.
in (prep.), p. 37, note.
inadh, 516.

inada, 329.
inar, 29.
inarach, 597.
inbher, 428.
inchinn, 747; inchind, gl. 105.
ind (prep.), gl. 260.
ind (subst.), 154.
indibh (dat. pl.), gl. 148.
indracc, gl. 54; p. 147.
indte, p. 103, note 1.
infinit, gl. 2.
ingar, 839.
ingbin, 290; inghen, p. 150; 291.
ingnadh, 229.
inga, gl. 197, gl. 198; p. 150.
inill, gl. 74.
inillius, gl. 66, gl. 140; p. 148.
iumhus, 333.
innarbadh, 752.
innarbthach, 983.
inne, gl. 93, gl. 227.
inne iachtarach, 1013.
inniit, 25.
innraice (nom. pl.), 36.
inntindeach, 876.
instrumint, 761.
int, 78, 1013.
interiacht, 874.
inti, 867.
inntlecht, 734.
irriabhra, p. 103, note.
isat, 1008.
ith in arbha, 1038.
iummus, p. 37, note.

la (prep.), 722.
ro-la, 428.
labhar, 376.
labhartaighe, 1133.
lacht, 250.
ladhar, gl. 196; p. 150.
laegh, 424.
láidire, 920.
láidiri, 1113.
láimtech, p. 69, note.
laindér, 73; p. 155.
láir, 294.
laithirt, 266.
lámh, 34, 233, 465; p. 128, note 3.
lámhaccan, 916; p. 164.
lámhann, 34.
lamhannan, gl. 231; p. 150.
lámh-thuagh, 857.
lán, 1008.
land (laun), 132; p. 152.

lá-oirrthi, 1076.
lár, 747.
lasair, 128; p. 156.
lauir (gen. sing.), 564.
Laurint, 538.
leabaidh in daimh allta, 858.
leabhar, 371.
lear, 13.
lebaidh, 481.
lebhar aiffrind, 853.
leca, 89.
léc in árain, 246.
lég, 133, 573.
ra-légh, p. 153.
leghaim, 1071.
leghes, p. 165.
léghtóir, 1080.
léine, 38.
leitheld (acc. sing.), 104.
leithni (-e), 925.
lemhnacht, 782.
lenmbunach, 1040.
lepaidh, 481.
Lerghus, p. 69, note.
lesc, 382.
lesmháthair, 48.
less, 580.
lessa (acc. pl.), gl. 176.
leth, 90; gl. 67; p. 156.
leth-ail, 90.
lethchaech, 426, 624.
lethenach, 232.
lethfer, 396.
lethómh, 90.
lethsáthach, 403.
lethtoin, 471.
lexaire, 11.
liath, 182; p. 128, note 3.
ligheóc, 282.
lin uisci, 863.
lind, 221.
line, 232.
linn (lind), p. 165.
liriu, p. 70, note.
liter, 230.
litó, 767.
liubhar, 371.
lubbra, 268.
locha ochsal, gl. 216.
loch, 781.
Locban, 522.
Lochlann, 541.
Lóegh, p. 112, note.
lóghmhar, 133.
loighed, 923.
long, gl. 49; long luath, 574.

Middle-Irish Index.

long brond, gl. 136.
longphort, 725, 813; p. 163.
lór, 908.
lorg, 52.
lorgarecht, 937.
lór-ghnímh, 908.
lorgdromma, gl. 169.
losa feadha, 933.
losad, 42.
loscadh, 737.
lu leith, gl. 228; p. 150.
luach faisnéisi, 751.
luach lesa, 792.
luaidhe, 60, 788, 609.
luaidheamhail, 609.
luath, 574; luathidher, 1070.
luathghúirech, 641.
luch dhall, 249.
luch francach, 248.
luchtaire, 10; p. 153.
lugha, 1115.
luibh (lubh), 114.
luidh, 894.
lúirech, 154; gl. 147, gl. 159.
luirgnibh (dat. pl.), gl. 189; p. 150.
lus, 810, 104, 933.
lus na fiadh, 183.

mac, 407, 408.
mac dilechta, 429; p. 161.
mac immlesen, 80; gl. 118.
mac imresan, 80.
maccu Immlesaib (dat. pl.), gl. 118.
mac na hoidhchi (-e), 546.
mac-bóe, gl. 213.
macámh, 370.
macámh gennti, 473.
machaire, 866, 1060.
madair, 275.
Máel-issu, 232.
maeth, 394.
maethsúilech, 431.
maghisder, 365, 392.
maide sgine, 1139.
maighister, 1099.
mailgibh (dat. pl), gl. 112; p. 148.
maindsér, 861.
mainister, 726.
mainn, 299.
maise, 1083, 1108.
maissi, 927.
maith, 661, 798, 1134.
mallacht, 915.
mallci, 866.
manach, 435.

mani, 104.
Maolsechlainn, 346.
marbhadh, 14.
marbhnudh, p. 70, note.
marcach na comhladh, 127.
marclach, 189.
maróc, 55, 1005; p. 155.
maróg, 1005.
martra, 738.
marmur, 1104.
Matha, 549.
máthair, 130, 1052.
matal, 490.
mátharmarbhthach, 318.
mathghamhain, 418.
meall, 258.
meata, 1123.
medal, 235.
Medhbh, 481.
medhg, 783.
medhón, gl. 207.
medughudh, 763.
móld, 922.
méirsi (-e), 780.
mér, 465; gl. 167, gl. 195.
mér-coise, 466.
mér-láimhe, 465.
merdrech, 187.
merlach na comhladh, 944.
mésa, 1117.
mesgán, 219.
mesurdha, 807.
mí, 1050, 1051.
mias, 478, 193.
michlúmhar, 656.
michuimhneach, 1111.
midhingbhala, 669.
míl, 974.
mil édaigh, 501.
mil mór, 428, 865.
milan, 138.
milchú, 411.
milech, 648.
mimhaise (-i), 1084, 1109.
min, 430.
mintsúilech, 430.
Miodhghus, p. 69, note.
mír, 156; p. 157; m. pluc, 750.
mirr, 1134.
mirbhail, 695.
mitall, 791.
mithormach, 756.
mó, 1114.
móin, 118.
moladh, 902; -ludh, 894.
Molua, p. 133, note.

monadh, 237, 841.
monadan, 212.
mong in-t-álindéin, 148.
mór, 428, 663, 809; gl. ".
mórmhargad, 327.
mór-ulchach, 1048.
mucc, 584.
mucc mara, 1029; p. 164.
Mucholmóc, p. 149.
mucor, 566.
mughsaine, 882.
muilleand, 711.
mullind, 701.
muime, 784.
muin, 709.
muinchille, 30; p. 154.
muinchilloch, 598.
muine, gl. 224; p. 150, p. 165.
muine, 585.
muine draighin, 110.
muinél, 744; muineol, gl. 137.
muir, 144, 860; gl. 5.
múl, 295, 415.
mulcán, 243.
mullach, 1007; gl. 98.
mullach tighi (-e), 838.
múr, 476.
Murchadh, 542.
murdhuchu, 1020.

náit, 935.
námha, 1008.
naomh, 345.
nathari (nathair?), 88.
neach (O. Ir. nech), 379.
neimhni, 987, 988.
neimh, 602.
néll, 337.
nélladóracht, 271.
nemh, 812.
nemhdha, gl. 13, gl. 24, gl. 264.
nemhdhuine, 954.
nemhfurechair, 985.
nemhmharbhdha, 1008.
nemhthindismech, 617.
nemhthremeta, gl. 66; p. 148.
nemhthroeta, gl. 66; p. 148.
nenntóg, 208.
nertmhar, p. 37, note.
nescóid, 843.
ní, 987, 1112; gl. 249.
Nialghus, p. 69, note.
noemh, gl. 145.
nóin, 1077.
nóine, 335.
nómhadh, 173.

normanach, 308.
nús, 256.

ó, gl. 41.
ochtmhadh, 229.
óen, gl. 59.
oibriugudh, 889.
oidhche, 546.
oidi (-e), 1078.
oighen, 86.
oilemhain, 753.
oilithrech, 311.
oinmhid, 512.
oirenin, 493.
ohair, 614.
ómhil, gl. 51.
ocum, gl. 147.
óentaighim, gl. 260; p. 165.
ógh, 955; gl. 53.
ógdhamh, 758.
oite, 232.
ol, 847, 1096.
olc, 662, 799; gl. 59.
ómh, 90.
ón, 613.
ór, 606, 786, 1134.
orcnl (acc. pl.), gl. 181.
ord, 943; gl. 144; gl. 235.
árdbaighe, 606.
organaidh, 7.
orlár, 704.
ortha, p. 125, note.
osaadh, 137; p. 156.
otrach, 482.

pagún, p. 151.
paiper, 579.
paisti bróg, 445.
parrtus, 553.
partan, 374 (*see* torpan).
pecadh, gl. 261.
pell, 831.
pellec, 136.
penn, 53.
persunacht, 170.
pethair (?), 320.
Petar, 528.
pian, 54; gl. 147.
piloir, 1136.
pipur, 1072.
plag, gl. 256.
Plait, 950.
Ploit, 951.
pluc, 750.
póccadh, p. 148.
pólaire (tólaire?), 371.

port, 110.
prebach, 658.
prechún, 507.
prelait, 452.
presen (persen), 524.
primaidecht, 354.
prioir, *see* banphrioir.
priv, 97.
proindtech, 728.
proisté, 852.
próvinse, 175.
punc, 474.
punnann, 45.
pupul, 458.

raing ant-šair, 1137.
rain (rapp?), gl. 220([a]); p. 165.
raith, 933.
rannaire, 9.
rastail, 814.
rechtaire, 784.
redla, 1008.
réidhi (-e), 890, 191.
reilic, 691.
rem, gl. 148.
remhainm, 992.
remhthechtas, 872.
remhthúsaighit, gl. 23.
rembum, 937; remhamm, gl. 23.
rési (acc. pl.), gl. 167.
retla, 103.
rí, 1035, 1036.
riablhach, 804.
co-riacht, p. 37; note.
riaghail, 61; p. 155.
riccedh, p. 37; note.
righan, 20; p. 154.
rigflaith, 1134; rig-lepaid, 481.
righthe (acc. pl.), gl. 163; gl. 164.
rind, 1008; rinn, 267.
robbeg, 808.
Roiberd, 529.
roinill, gl. 147.
rómhánach, 310.
rón, 50.
roth, 227; gl. 119.
rotaidhe, p. 111, note.
Ruaidhri, 535.
rnaimnech dubbáin, 428; p. 161.
ruaindi, 463.

sah, p. 37; note.
Sabbull, p. 107, note [1].
sacc, 489.
shebhchoire, 938.
saer, 292, 379, 409.

saer (libera), gl. 73.
saer (artifex), 1138.
Saerghus, p. 69, note.
saethar, 1085.
sagart, 24, 367; p. 154.
sai, 4.
saighed, 215.
sailmchétlaidh, 3.
saithech na tuise, 1134.
súl, gl. 192; p. 150.
salach, 616, 684.
salann, 977.
salm, 467, 3.
saltair, 766.
sanntach, 667.
sanntaighi, 1120.
sáthach, 402.
sbegach, 629.
sblinach, 274.
sbor, 1041.
sborún, 514.
sbruileach, 1004.
ru-scaith, 894.
scúls, 106; p. 156.
scamban, gl. 221; p. 150.
scáraidh, 864.
sciath, gl. 75; p. 148.
scithech, 613, 614.
scola, 338.
scolb tighe, 446.
sdair, 84.
sdau, 789.
sdocaire, 1016.
sé, 777.
scalladh, 741.
Seán, 151.
sechmaillim, gl. 240; p. 150.
Sechnall, 894.
secbrúu, 131; p. 156.
seghdha, 847.
seichi (-e), 732.
séideadh, 1019.
séideth gáithbhulga, 217; p. 157.
seimin, 211.
seirbe, 1132.
séisedh, 593.
séitche, 1073.
seig, gl. 215; sealg, 1012.
sen, 130; seau, gl. 260.
senadh naomh, 551.
senúis, 735.
seuathnir, 419.
senmbáthair, 130.
senóir, 29, 1100.
seomra, 123.
serrach, 494.

Middle-Irish Index.

ses, 70; p. 155.
searach, 49.
sét slighedh, 1073.
sgadan, 967.
sguignen, 484.
sgartach, 796.
sgél, 223.
sgeota, 709; p. 163.
sgeotha, 710; p. 163.
sgian, 440, 441, 1139.
sgingidóir, 515.
sgiursi (-e), 109.
sgornachán, 707.
si, 847.
siadaire, 57.
sians, gl. 244.
sidhan gaeithe, 997.
sil, 1009.
sillad, 231.
sillaidhi, 231.
sin, 420, 421.
sine ochta, 1059.
sine Saüin, 151.
sitheal, 241.
siur-marbhthach, 320.
slaitin, 117.
slán, 393, 633.
slúnti (-e), gl. 57.
slat, 116.
slataidhi (-e), 956.
Sleibte, p. 125, note.
slemain (slemon), 639.
slestán, 32.
slissit, gl. 94, gl. 164, gl. 178.
slighe, 112, 613; gl. 117.
slind, 1014.
slindén, 148.
slinnchriadh, 376.
sliseóg, 1001.
sluagh, 1003; gl. 25, gl. 39, &c.
smech, gl. 110, gl. 122.
smeróid, 945.
smir, 193.
snáithi (-e), 817.
snúmbach, 391.
Snedbghus, p. 69, note.
snethach, 649.
so-abb, p. 37, note.
no-sóadh, p. 37, note.
socharthanaighi, 1125.
sochruidhe, 380.
sodain, 747.
socgni, gl. 10; p. 146-7.
sogh allaidh, 297.
soifist (soiphist), 842.
soller, 740.

soilestar, 795.
soillsi (-e), 998, 1122.
soléghta, 1126.
solus, 665; see follus.
somholta, 1127.
sophistighi (tidhe?), 8.
speilp, 730.
spideóg, 202.
spin, 933.
spirait, gl. 211.
spuirech, 764.
sraine. gl. 7; p. 146.
srathar, 262.
srebhand (-bhan), 794.
srian, 819.
srocuaim, gl. 255.
sroin (?), gl. 252.
sról, 577.
srón, 1039; gl. 117.
srubhan, 143.
srubán mara, 144.
sruth, 999, 1037, 1042.
stanambuil, 610.
stiurasmund, gl. 49; p. 147.
stoc-ronnadh, 705.
stól, 748.
stuidis, 856.
subhachus, 301.
subdecháin, 455.
sualach, gl. 15.
sui, 4.
sui abb, p. 37, note.
súidhe, p. 153.
suidheocan, 850.
suidhiugbudh, gl. 4.
súil, 168, 425; gl. 104; p. 128, note[s].
súilech, 430, 431.
suirgech, 618.
suisti (-te), 278.
súithe (sapientia), p. 37, note.
suithe, 941.
sust, 109.
sútbemlacht, p. 37, note.

tabhaill, 62.
tadbbhais, 846; p. 163.
Tadhg, 548.
tadhull, p. 148.
taemhan, 71.
tacs, 241.
taibherne, 169, 689.
taill (-e), 739.
tailm (acc. s.), p. 112, note.
táiplis, 27; p. 154.
tairis, 1048.

tairrnge, 443.
tairrsech, 1000.
talsbenadh, 894, 846; p. 163.
taisech, see bantaisech.
taisech cethrair, 400.
taisech cuigir, 401.
taithneamhnach, 800.
taithnemach, 666.
túl, 252.
talumh, 108.
tanic, 110.
tarbh-sliasta, gl. 95, gl. 182.
tardadh, 193, 226.
tarr, 147.
tarrach, 284.
teach, 569.
teachtaire, 450.
teallach, 511.
tech na merdreach, 713.
techat, gl. 59.
tecoisce, 1112.
techtaire, 747.
tédaire, 1017.
tegalsge, 660.
teghim, gl. 262.
teilgim, p. 151.
téine creasa, 720.
teirc, 672.
teircl (-e), 924.
tempoll, 688.
tend, p. 149.
tenga, 560; gl. 87, gl. 127, gl. 130; tengadh, 40.
tengthach, 625.
tés, 942, 1086.
tiach, 41, 371.
tiarach, 265.
tidhnachtaidh, 1134.
tigh, 446; p. 161.
tighearna, 287, 404, 453; gl. 143, gl. 147.
tigherna dóise, 398.
tigherna trir, 399.
tigherna, 886.
timchell, 691, 1087.
timna, 760.
timpanach, 6; p. 153.
timthirigh, 368.
timthirecht, 898.
tinnisnech (-nach), 615.
tiradh, 703.
tis, gl. 132.
titul, 560.
tochartaigh, 746.
toebh, gl. 79.
togha, 878.

toghluasacht, p. 147.
toin, 470.
tomhllur, 104; toimhlld, 193.
tón, gl. 177, gl. 224.
toradh, 289.
torc, 373, 483.
Tordhelbach, 161.
tormach, 755.
torpan, 269 (*see* partan).
torta, gl. 139.
tra, 1030.
tredhelbhdha, gl. 105.
tredhluigbthe, gl. 213.
tres, 590.
treuillech, gl. 213.
trethe, 560.
tri, 774.
trial, triallatóir, 1096.
tri-bhith, 229.
tribhus, 324.
tribhusach, 600.
tripulta, 930.
trithu, gl. 56.
triur, 398.
troethaim, p. 148.
troibel, 855.
truagh, 383.
túsidh, 353.
truailnidhe, gl. 69; p. 148.
tú, gl. 142.

tuairgin, 722; tuairgim, gl. 149.
tuata, 423.
tucadh, p. 103, note [1].
tucc, 1134.
tuighi (-e), 994.
tuireóg, 64; p. 155.
tunna, 731.
tus, 1134.
tús, 232.
tússigh (dat. s. fem.), gl. 49.

nachtlan, 1064.
uachtlanaidhe, 1063.
uachtar, 192.
uadh, gl. 2.
uaigh, 1069.
uaimm, gl. 150.
uaimhnighim, gl. 65.
uainin, 492.
Uaithne, 547, 768.
uallghubha, 1008.
uam, gl. 59.
uan, 459.
uas, p. 37, note.
uasalathair,' 13.
Uater, 530.
ubhall brághat, gl. 131.
ucht, 1059; u. na demainde, gl. 202.

uchtach, 264.
uchtard, 643.
uchtghel, 223.
ughdur, 1107.
uile, gl. 72.
uille, gl. 163; p. 149.
Uilliam, 531.
uinneamhain, 862.
uinnimint, 785.
uir, 578.
uirge (= ὄρχις), gl. 209.
uisci (-e), 160, 863.
uisce imill, 69.
uisgemhlacht, 932.
uisa (nom. pl. m.), 36.
ulbu, 93.
ulcha, gl. 111.
umhail, 36.
umhamhail, 611.
uraicecht, 868.
urchar, gl. 81.
urchoidech, 935.
urchumail, 279; p. 159.
urlabhradh, 867.
urlamhas, 906.
urraidh, 304.
urralaisti, 1135.
urtan (artán?), 111.
uth, 102, 1056.

IV. WELSH INDEX.

[*The Old-Welsh words in this Index are marked with an asterisk.*]

*aballon, 555.
adan, 746.
ael, p. 148.
*ætlnet, p. 59, note; 746.
aflafar, 1133.
afu, 1032.
aguedd, p. 163.
aidd, 948.
amm, 670.
alarch, 509.
amser, 1048.
anadl, p. 149.
augor, 68.

aradu, 1076.
arddangos, 660.
aren, 246, 1011.
arglwydd, p. 147.
ariant, 607.
arlais, p. 148.
ason, p. 149.
asen, asyn, 296.
atar, 746.
athrach, 1046.

bach, 439, 664.
bachawg, 605.

ball, 638.
bara, 141.
*barr, p. 148.
bas, p. 149.
bedw, 560.
bendithio, 914.
benyw, 1053.
ber, p. 149.
berw, berwr, bery, 823.
*bicoled, 339.
blas, 975.
blain, blaenor, blaenu, p. 147.
blawd, 491.

Welsh Index.

blisgyn, p. 157.
blodeuog, 491.
bloneg, 236.
bod, 120.
*bou, 158.
*bontig, 158.
braen, braenu, 683.
*brawt, 1047.
*braut, 366.
breuant, 292.
*brith, 957.
bron, p. 150.
*bronnbreithet, p. 59, note; 957.
bru, 647.
brycan, 1033.
brysiaw, 36.
Brytbon, 957.
bugail, 583.
bun, 21.
bwgwth, 339.
bwrw, 1048.
bwyt, 477.
bychodawg, 1058.
byddar, 604.
bygyliaeth, 339.
byr, 678.
*bywyt, 113.

cach, 1075.
*cae, 218.
cafael, 594.
cafn, p. 156.
cair, 267.
*caitoir, 1055.
calaned, 919.
calch, 58.
calon, 919.
cam, p. 150.
cang, p. 150.
canlyn, p. 165.
cant, 772.
canwyll, p. 154.
caraut, 292.
cath, 499.
cawn, p. 157.
cedor, cedorawg, 1055.
ceiliawg, 506.
celliog gwynt, 510.
celc, 325.
cell, 115.
cengl, 149.
*cenitol, 676.
ceryddn, 888.
cesail, p. 150 (No. 216).
eig, p. 150 (No. 203; correct *eyg*?).
ciglif, 655.

clais, p. 149.
clas, 273.
*claud, 229.
*claur, cloriou, 67.
cledd, 387.
cleddyf, 461.
cloddiaw, 229.
clodfawr, 655.
clopa, p. 154.
clopen, p. 154.
cludd, p. 147.
clust, p. 148.
clyn, 723.
clyw, 655.
*coc, 245.
cogail, 567.
coegfran, 201.
collen, 556.
colomen, 203.
colwyn, 498.
conyn, p. 157.
cor, 457.
corff, 1071.
corlan, p. 164.
craidd, 1102.
cranc, 374.
creyr, 204.
crochan, 56.
croen, 56.
croesan, 14.
croesaw, 92.
*cruitr, p. 162.
crwth, 5.
cunnawg, 165.
cwliawg, 1030.
cwpan, p. 161.
cwr, p. 147.
cwrw, 266.
cwrwgl, 488.
cwyr, 225.
cwyren, 836.
cyd, p. 164.
cyfathrach, 1046.
cyfenw, 993.
cyfrif, 913.
cylor, 1049.
cymanfa, 897.
cymharu, 896.
cyminedd, p. 147.
cymyn, 897.
cynnull yd, 210.
cysegriad, 879.
cystudd, 892.
cystwyad, 891.

chwaer, 320.

chwant, 667.
chwech, chweched, 777.
*chuechet, 588.
chwiawr, 320.
chwegr, 570.
chwerw, 1132.
chwith, chwitbig, p. 161.
chwyth, 826.
chwythiad, 217.
chwythu, 57; p. 154.

dafad, dafates, 858.
dalen, deilen, 765.
dall, 249.
dangaws, 660.
delw, 642, 936.
dehen, 386.
deng, p. 150.
derwen, 554.
didryfwr, 315.
delehedion, 87.
*diminid, 237.
dieet, 87.
*doguomisur., 807.
*dou, *dui, 773.
*duguobintiliat, 1073.
draen, 559.
drws, 124.
dtywyn, 207.
dryssien, 587.
du, 381.
duw, 404.
dwrn, 502.
dy, 570.
dyfrgi, 375.
dyled, p. 147.
dyludo, p. 147.
dylynu, p. 165.
dyn, 953; llys dyn, 718.
dysgybl, 438.

eawg, 216.
ebodn, p. 161.
eddestr, eddestl, eddestlawr, 810.
einyf, 666.
ednyw, 666.
edyn, 746.
efydd, 610.
eglwys, p. 157.
eirif, 913.
elthyr, 1014.
elin, p. 149.
*emed, 610.
emennydd, 747.
*emmeni, 784.
*engued, p. 148.

2 C

Indices Verborum

ennill, 694.
enw, 991.
enynu, p. 147.
erbyn (= O. Ir. archlunn), p. 165.
erfin, 213.
ergyrwaew, p. 148.
erlyn, p. 165.
erw, 1038.
eryr, 197.
*escip, 982.
*eterinn, 746.
*etncoilhaam, 746.
ewin, p. 150.
ewyll, 884.
ewyrdonic, p. 67, note 1.

ffa, 109.
ffal, p. 150.
ffaling, 37; p. 154.
ffroen, 1039.
ffrowyll, 109.
ffrwd, 999.
ffrwyn, 109, 819, 1039.
ffurfafen, 749.
ffust, 109.

gafl, 135.
gafr, 372; gafar, 1075.
galar, 281.
garw, p. 159.
gebel, 135.
gefell, 834.
gel, 940.
Gildas, 17.
glân, 671.
glin, p. 149.
glo, 273.
glwys, 719.
glyn, p. 165.
gof, 369.
goglawdd, 229.
*golbinoc, p. 148.
golchi, 1045.
goreu, 1116.
gorfynt, 602.
goryn, 255.
graen, p. 147.
*gratell, 107.
gro, 742.
gres, p. 164.
grisiau, p. 164.
grislyfr, p. 164.
grudd, p. 148, p. 154.
grûg, 565; p. 162.
grwm, 384, 1065.
grwn, 390.

grwysen, 582.
*gudif, *gudhyf, 797.
*guell, 1116.
gwadn, p. 148.
gwaew, 216.
gwain, 157.
gwarchad, 984.
gware, 641.
gwau, 1095.
gwedd, p. 163.
gweddi, 870.
gweddw, p. 147, p. 159.
gwefl, p. 148.
gwol, 1.
gwennol, 934.
*guerg, 328.
gworonn, 558.
gwerthyd, 568.
gwêu, 1095.
gwichell, 140.
gwichiad, p. 157.
gwirion, 681.
gwlybwr, 675.
gwlyp, 675; *rogulipias, 675.
Gwraldeg, 533.
gwregys, p. 148.
Gwrwst, 342.
gwydd, 959.
gŵydd, p. 154.
gwyddif, 797.
gwyn, p. 150.
gŵyr, 621, 724.
gwyth, 99.
gylf, p. 148.
gyth, 603.

haearn, 608.
hafal, 609, 904.
halen, 977.
hebawg, 1006.
hen, p. 156.
*henmam, 130.
henwr, 1100.
*hep, p. 156.
hidl, 241.
hil, 1009.
*binham, 130.
*hint, 490.
hoedel, p. 147.
hosan, 72.
hotan, hotyn, 596.
bun, 720.
hydd, 183.
hynt, 1073.

iâ, 758.

iau, 758.
iawn, 681.
*iechyt, 758.
ieuaf, 758.
ieuanc, 758.
*iot, 758.
*iouenc, 758.
*itlaur, 1038.
iwrch, 205.

kentaf, kyntaf, 588.

llachar, p. 156.
llaeth, 250.
llafanog, p. 150.
llafaru, 1133.
llai, 923.
llan, 132.
llath, 116.
llawen, 393.
llawer, 908.
llawn, 13.
llawr, 704.
lloch, 573.
lled, p. 156.
llefaru, 1133.
llefrith, p. 163.
lleiad, 923.
lleiaf, 923.
Iliad, Illiaw, 1071.
llin, 38.
llith, 767.
llo, 424.
*logod, 248.
llong, 574.
llongborth, 725.
llorp, p. 150.
llosg, 128, 737.
lln, 1003.
*lult, 182.
lluryg, 154.
llydanedd, 925.
llyfn, 639.
llyfrith, 268.
llyfyr, 371.
llyg, 248.
llygod ffrengig, 248.
llyn, 221.
llynghes, 574.
llyriad, 937.
llys, 580.
llysdad, 48.
llysenw, 48.
llysiau, 810.
llysieuyn, 183.
llythyron, 230.

Welsh Index.

mad, 661.
magwyr, 866.
maidd, 783.
main, 430.
maint, 922.
malu, 701.
man, p. 154.
mantell, 490.
*map, 80.
march, 189.
*marchauc, 127.
marw, p. 159.
marwydos, 945.
mawl, 902.
mawn, 118.
mawr, 663.
maws, 927.
*meichat (-iat), 1029.
meistyr, 365.
mel, 968.
melin, 701.
melldith, 915.
mer, 193.
mêr, p. 157.
*merchet, p. 59, note.
merthyr, 738.
meth, methiant, 1123.
mign, 118.
milgi, 411.
mis, 1050.
moch, 1029.
moel, 258.
moel-ron, 50.
monochen, p. 155.
mor, 860.
morforwyn, 1020.
morhwch, 1029.
*motrwy, 466.
morynyon, 1020.
mul, 295.
mum, p. 154.
mur, 476.
mwnai, 841.
mwng, 744.
mwnwgl, 744; p. 149.
mwyd, 431.
mwy, 1114.
mwyn, 430.
mwyth, 394.
mynydd, 237.
myr, 55.

nadr, 88.
nawf, 391.
nawn, 1077.
nedden, neddog, 649.

nef, 812.
nes, nesaf, 1117.
nifwl, niwl, 337.
nith, 224.
*notuid, 817.

oen, 459.
offeren, p. 164.
ofni, p. 148.
*ois, *oisouð, 735.
orlais, 1135.

pair, 724.
paith, p. 149.
paradwys, 553.
pawl, 495.
pedwardyblyg, 931.
penglog, p. 148, p. 154.
*petguerid, p. 157; *petguared, 142.
*petnar, 775.
*pimphet, 588.
piw, 1056.
plygu, 930.
porch, 493.
porphor, 224.
preithlaw, p. 148.
pren, 719.
pres, p. 154.
priddfaen, 1054.
priddlech, 1054.
pump, 776.
pwn, pynlaw, 45.
pyrchwyn, p. 162.
pyrgwyn, p. 162.
pŷsg, 13.
pystylwyn, 265.

rhagenw, 992.
*rannam, rhan, 9.
*rhascl, rhasgl, 814.
rhawn, p. 161.
rhiain, p. 154.
rhif, 913.
rhod, 227.
rheol, p. 155.
*ro-gulipias, 675.
rhol, p. 109, note.
rhyn, 1008.

sach, 489.
saer, 1137.
saeth, 214.
sawdl, p. 150.
*scamnhegint, p. 150.
senedd, 551.

serch, 618.
sil, 1009.
sill, 231.
swta, 941.
syw, p. 153.

tad, 1046.
tafiu, p. 154.
tafod, 40.
tair, 774.
taith, 450, 872.
tal, 739.
talm, 108.
tant, 1017.
tarw, p. 159.
tes, 942, 1086.
teyrnas, 886.
*tig, 159.
tin, p. 149.
to, 994.
toes, 242.
*traet, 74.
trawa, tros, 1000.
*treb, 315.
trech, 1117.
*tri, tair, 774.
triphlygiad, 930.
trothwy, 1000.
truan, 383.
trwm (adj.), 903.
trwm (subst.), p. 163.
trws, 324.
*tût (tud), 423.
twrch, 373.
twysen, 35; p. 163.
tynell, 731.
ty, 569.

uchedydd, 140.
uffarn, p. 149.
uffern, 519.
*unvet, 142.
urdd, 943.
uthr, 1014.
uwd, 1038.

*vudimin (?), 797; p. 163.

wyf, 1112.
wyt, 1112.

ym, 85, 1112.
ymenin, 784.
ynfyd, 512.
ynt, 1112.
ysborion, 764.

196 Indices Verborum.

ysbwrial, 764, 1004.
ysgadan, 967.
ysgiaw, 440.
ysgïen, 440.
ysgin, 515.

ysgŵyd, p. 148.
ysgyfaint, p. 150.
yslath, 116.
ysnoden, 817.
ystlys, 32.

ystrodyr, 262.
yspardun, 1041.
yspar, 1041.
yw, 561.

V. CORNISH INDEX.

acran, 1011.
ail, 460.
ancar, 68.
arhanz, 607.
asen, p. 149.
avallen, 555.
avi, 1032.

banne, 966.
bara, 141.
barth, 14.
beler, 823.
ber, p. 149.
blez, 491.
bloneg, 236.
bochadoc, 1058.
bothar, 604.
braud, 1047.
brenniat, p. 147.
bron, p. 150.
bugel, 583.
buit, 477.

cans, 772.
cantuil, 44.
kat, 499.
keghin, 245.
chelioc, 506.
kelli, 115.
kigel, 567.
clin, p. 149.
cog, 245.
coir, 225.
coloin, 498.
colviden, 556.
croider, 700.
cugol, 121.
cuic, 426.
curun, 75.

darat (-raz), 124.
delc, 852.
delen, 765.
den, 953.
discibel, 438.
diures, p. 159.
dreis, 587.
duv, 381.
duy, 404.
dyghow, 386.

ehog, 216.
elin, p. 149.
enederen, p. 148.
enef, 288.
ens, 1112.
er, 197.
ericu, p. 148.

fichren, 562.
fruc (fruc?), 1039.
firmament, 749.

ghel, 940.
gelvin, p. 148.
glibor, 675.
gof, 369.
grud, 39.
gùdh, p. 154.
guedeu, p. 147.
guein, 157.
guell, 1116.
guennol, 934.
guernen, 558.
guiden, p. 156.
guihan, p. 157.
gurhthit, 568.

haloin, halein, 977.
hivin, 561.

hoern, 608.
huethaf, 217.
huheltat, p. 153.
huis, 735.

idne, 746.
iffarn, 519.
impinion, 747.
ispak, 982.

lait, 250.
lergh, 937.
loski, 128.
leveriat, 1133.
lewilloit, p. 150.
liver, 371.
loch, 424.
lorch, 52.
losc, 737.
luu, 1003.
luworch guit, 114.

maister, 365.
manach, 435.
march, 189.
marhaz, 327.
mel, 968.
melin, 701.
mennyw, 1053.
meth, 1123.
mor, 860.
morhoch, 1029.
moy, 1114.

nef, 812.
noden, 817.

of, 1112.
oin, 459.
on, 1112.

onnen, 557.
oe, 1112.

peis, peus, pows, 717.
pepel, 458.
pêr, 724.

renniat, p. 153.

sair, 1137.

scala, 106.
sened, 551.
skefans, p. 150.
snoden, 817.
soler, 740.
stoc, 705.

tavot, 40.
tes, 942.
ti, 569.

tonnel, 731.
torch, 373.
truit, 74.
trulerch, 937.

warn, p. 146.

yns, 1112.
yorch, 205.

VI. BRETON INDEX.

amann, 784.
arc'hant, 607.
avu, 1032.

bannec'h, 966.
bara, 141.
beler, 823.
ber, p. 149.
blonec, p. 164.
bouzar, 604.
bragez, 1033.
buez, 113.

cant, 772.
c'houćzaf, 217.
chwant, 667.
compizrien, 1046.

da, 570.
dargreiz, 1102.
delien, 765.
du, 381.

empenn, 747.
éné, 288.
env, 812.
eor, 68.
erer, er, 197.

felc'h, 1012.

gof, 369.
gonin, 157.
guell, 1116.
guénnóli, 934.
gwéa, 1095.

gwelaouen, 940.
gwernen, 558.
gwerzid, 568.

hal, halen, holen, 977.
hennt, 1073.
hoal, p. 147.

ioul, 884.
iourc'h, 205.
ivinen, 561.

kaz, 499.
kegel (kigel), 567.
keler, 1049.
kelvézen, 556.
ker, p. 147.
kezour, 1055.
kleiz, 387.
klom, koulm, 203.
koar, 225.
kolen, 498.
kougoul, 121.
krouezer, 700.

lerc'h, 937.
lestad, 48.
lesvab, 48.
lorchen, 52.
losk, 737.
lue, 424.

malven, p. 148.
mel, 968.
melin, 701.
meulet, 902.

méza, 1123.
moan, 430.
morhouc'h, 1029.
muy, 1114.

nadoz, 817.
noud, neuden, 817.
niz, 649.

oan, 459.
off, 1112.
omp, 1112.
ounnen, 557.

reûn, p. 161.
reiz, 890.

scévent, p. 150.
scoit, p. 148.
skéja, 440.
spern, 1041.
stûr, sturis, p. 147.

tez, 942.
ti, 569.
tonel, 731.
tourc'h, 373.
tréc'h, 1117.
treûzou, 1000.
trulen, p. 148.

warn, p. 146.

yen, 758.
ynt, 1112.

VII. LATIN INDEX.

aedes, 948.
acr, 104.
aea, 812, 216.
acstas, 948.
aestus, 948.
agnomen, 991.
agnus (= avignus?), 492.
ago, p. 44, note.
alo, 486.
amb-, 670, 921.
ancora, 68.
animal, 428.
animus, p. 149.
arduus, 16.
argentum, 607.
arvum, 1038.
asinus, 296; p. 159.
atta, 1078.
aurum, 606.
axilla, p. 150.

betula, 560.
bi-, 773.
bos, 159.
brevis, 678.
brocchus, 852.
bubulcus, 583.

caco, 1075.
caecus, 426.
calx, 58.
canis, 411, 1050.
canus, p. 157.
cano, 837.
capor, 372.
carex, 933.
cavea (= O. Ir. cae?), 218.
censeo, 837.
census, 285.
centum, 772.
cera, 225.
certus, 888.
cognomen, 991.
columba, 203.
communis, 897.
comparo, p. 154.
consequor, p. 162.
coquino, 245.
coquo, 245.
corpus, 812.
corylus, 556.
coxa, 466.

crates, 126.
cribrum, 700.
crotta, 5.
cucullus, 121.

dama, 858.
dea, 289.
decem, p. 150.
deus, 81.
dexter, 386.
duo, 773.

edo, 40.
equus, 17.
erica, p. 162.
esox, 216.
est, 1112.
esucins, 216.

faba, 109.
faber, 369.
fero, 835.
fervere, 952.
fircus (Sabine), 205.
flagellum, 109.
flos, 491.
folium, 765; p. 163.
fores, 124.
forma, 642.
frater, 570, 1047.
frenum, 109, 819.
fundus, 96.
furvus, 381.
fuscus, 381.
fustis, 109.

genus, 812.
gilvus, 1124.
grex, 742.
gustus, p. 69, note 2.

hirpus, 205.
hircus, 205.

inclytus, 655.
innocens, p. 151.
inter, 490.

jecur, 1032.
justus, 758.
juvencus, 758.
juvenis, 758.

lac, 250.
lacus, 781.
laetus, p. 151.
lătus, p. 156.
lātus (πλατύς), 13.
Laverna, 792.
laxus, 382.
lena, lendis, 649.
levior, 923, 1115.
levir, 397.
lien, 1012.
lingua, 40.
lino, p. 159.
linquo, p. 161.
lippus, 675.
liquor, 675.
lorica, 154.
lucrum, 792.
lucta, p. 153.

magnus, 663.
major, 1114.
mantellum, 490.
manus, p. 154.
marceo, 860.
mare, 860.
mater, 130, 1052.
mel, 968.
meme, p. 127, note 5.
mensa, 478, 285.
mensis, 285, 1050.
molendinum, 701.
molo, 701.
mors, 315.
mulceo, 243.
mulgeo, 243.
mulus, 295.

natrix, 88.
navis, 21.
nebula, 337.
necto, 817.
neptis, 224.
nex, 693.
noceo, p. 151.
nomen, 991.
nox, 693.

opus, 889.
ordo, 943.
ornus, 557.
os, ossis, p. 149.

pallium, p. 154.
palumba, 203.
pater, 13, 1046.
pectus, 812.
pecus, 389.
penna, 746.
pes, p. 150.
piscis, 13.
plecto, 930.
plenus, 13.
plerus, 13.
plico, 930.
poena, 98; p. 156.
popina, 245; p. 158.
porcus, 493.
pro, 13.
pulsus, 99.
purpura, 224.

quatuor, 775.
quinctus, 588.
quinque, 776.

raetrum, 814.
regina, 20.
ren, 246.
rex, 1036.
rien, 1011.
rivus, 999.
rota, 227; p. 158.

rumis, 999.
ruo, 999.

sacer, 724.
saccus, 489.
sagitta, 214.
sal, 977.
salax, 616.
salicastrum, 795.
salio, 616, 977.
salum, 977.
scutum, p. 148.
seculum, p. 147.
secus, p. 156.
sedeo, 70.
semi, 392.
Seneca, 130.
senex, 130.
septem, 224.
sex, 777.
sextus, 588.
similis, 609, 904.
sisto, p. 100, note.
socrus, 570.
somnium, p. 163.
soror, 216, 320.
specio, specto. p. 149.
stannum, 610.
sum, sunt, 1112.

talea, 252.
taurus (= Gaulish *tarvos*), p. 159.
tellus, 108.
tendo, 1017.
tepere, 942.
theca, 41, 371.
tongeo, p. 165.
torreo, 703.
trana, 1000.
tres, 774.
tribus, 315.

ulna, p. 149.
umbilicus, p. 150.
unguis, p. 150; No. 198.
unio, 862.
unus (oinos), p. 147.

vagina, 157.
varus, 621.
vates, 2.
veru, p. 149.
vespera, 224.
vieo, 99, 1095.
vidua, p. 147, p. 159.
vir, 395.
vita, 477.
vitis, 99; p. 156.
vivus, 113.

VIII. MEDIÆVAL LATIN INDEX.

[*Numerals to which the letter "L." is prefixed refer to the lines of the Lorica, pp. 136–143.*]

abacia, 173.
admidulum, 824.
aglossus, 629.
agoneteta, L. 19; p. 143.
allea, 31.
alminiatrum, 793.
amusca, 251; p. 158.
anlūs, 558.
antela, 264.
anticula, 155.
aptempna, 70.
arcimantrica, 16.
asugia, 236.

babana, 284.
batma, p. 144.

baudaca, 220.
benna, 163.
berrus, p. 148.
binna, 162.
birria, 18; p. 154.
biturrea (-ia), 152.
braxatua, 600.
brecia, 184.
brucus, 565.
brunus, 559.
bucealla, 144.
bucliamen, L. 76; p. 145.

cabn, 277.
cadibulta, 274.
callidiba, 278.

camisa, 38.
candaléna, 63.
capitali (dat. s.), L. 49.
caphia, 51.
capula, 266.
carsum, L. 37; p. 144.
cartesium (= chartaceum), 709.
cartilago, L. 49.
cataerina, L. 62; p. 145.
caustoria, 59.
cavicula, 229.
celopidus, 635.
cephale, L. 35; p. 144.
cepus, 480.
centro (dat. s.), L. 49; p. 145.
chautrum, p. 145.

chorus, p. 153.
cipus, 479.
ciratheca, 34.
ciromancia (chiromachia), 272.
cirra, 33.
citola, 241.
cladum, L. 37; p. 144.
clerica, 76.
collacanius, 486.
colomaticus, p. 148.
colosdriginm, 1136.
comprisura, 238.
cona, L. 35; p. 144.
corductum, p. 156.
corporale, 859; p. 164.
corrolus, 556.
creta, 126.
crotella, 107.
cuba, L. 57; p. 145.

dactura, 153.
delipin, 1029.
digma (?), 127.
dolia, L. 75; p. 145.
ducendum, 773.

ea, 186.
edihulta, 275.
emenda, 98.
episcopum, p. 13.
ereocledus, p. 24.
eripica, 240.
crundo, 934.
ethera, 104.

falinga, 37.
fascllus, 488.
ferina, 183.
fessica, 57.
festula (festuca?), 211.
fetbma, 844.
fitrem (acc. s.), L. 74.
fixio, 900.
forcuratio, 899.

gamba, L. 63.
ganea, 187.
garga, 141.
gelima, 45.
genimen, 1010.
genuclis (abl. pl.), L. 64; p. 145.
gernoodum, 708.
gerra, 139.
geta, 19.
gibra, L. 31; p. 143.
gigra, L. 35; p. 144.

gingis (dat. pl.), L. 46; p. 165.
glabella, 78.
glassin, 243.
gletealla, 189.
grangia, 195.
gredale, 854.
grimaga, 257.
grunna, 118; p. 156.
gugra, p. 144.
gurgulio, L. 46; p. 145.
gyrgyrium, 746.

honplata, 148.
bonumculus, 436.

iaris (abl. pl.), L. 35; p. 144.
iduma, L. 38; p. 144.
igniferrium, 720.
impedica, 192.
internasus, L. 44; p. 145.
iolla (= billa), 55, 1005.
ionuchus (= eunuchus), p. 166.
irundo, 935.

jacor, L. 73.
juntura, 149.

lapifulta, 246.
lectorie, 856.
licór, 1097.
ligna, L. 36; ligana, p. 144.
limpa, 69.
lucifugia, 204.

malosus, 411.
mancellus, 490.
mandiannm, L. 37; p. 144.
manuale, 857.
marcem (acc. s.), L. 74.
mataxa, 93; p. 156.
mentagra, L. 68; p. 145.
mersiamentum, 780.
micena, L 36; p. 144.
milgus, 507.
mitreta, 64; p. 155.
monetola, 201.
monificina, 237.
morellus, 499.
múcledia, 165.
mulera, 166.

nauaula, 71.
nuchum, 794.

oba, 167.
obesta, p. 158.

obligia, L. 74.
obtolmia, 281.
odomen, 1006.
onesta, 256; p. 158.

panca, 235.
pantera, 88; p. 155.
pantes, L. 79; p. 146.
partista, 9.
patha, L. 36; pata, p. 144.
patma, L. 38; p. 144.
pavimentum, 769.
pectusculum, L. 69; p. 145.
pensa, 245.
pestucula, 147.
picuta, 258.
pilomena, 202.
piromanxia, 271.
plumba, 60.
plumpeus, 609.
postolla, 265.
presena, 247.
prespiter, 367.
prissura, 244.
profeticum, 796.
proseumeticum, 792.
prostrinum, 711.
pumnatus, 473.

quadricentum, 775.
quincentum, 776.

retor, 1099.
romineda, 311.
rostigola, 206.
rotis (dat. pl.), L. 45.
rula, 248.
ruter, 1075.

sabribarra, 180; p. 157.
sargifagum (= sarcophagum), p. 166.
saudarium (= sudarium), p. 166.
scama (= squama), 132; p. 152.
scauum, 748.
scilarotica, 168.
scircu, p. 26.
scupa (= stupa), 254.
sena, L. 36; senna, p. 144.
senester, 387.
sope, 862.
sera, 226.
sexcentum, 777.
simicintium, p. 166.
sindula, 253.
sirogra, 233.

sturna, 273.
sista, 199.
sitarista, 5.
stipifortifartium, 705.
straulium, 717.
subfucatus, p. 166.
sublingua, L. 48; p. 145.
superaltare, p. 136; p. 143.
susurra, 145.

talia, L. 37.
tempe, 866.
tethologia, 81.
tignus, 485.
tipia, 146.
tomūs, 587.
treoga, 137.
tribula, 109.
trica, 279.
tricendum, 774.

troclia, 239.
trobialo, 855.
trolla, 42.
tutones, L. 45; p. 145.
tympanum, p. 153.

ugula, 151.
uolua, 181.
urla, 191.
uva, L. 48; p. 145.

IX. GREEK INDEX.

ἄγλυ, 509.
αἰθίοψ, αἴθος, αἴθω, 948.
ἅλλομαι, 616, 977.
ἄλλος, p. 149.
ἄλς, 977.
ἀμέλγω, 243.
ἀμφί, 670.
Ἀμφίμαρος, 860.
ἀμφίπολος, 898.
ἄνεμος, p. 149.
ἀνεψιός, 224.
ἁπλόος, 930.
ἄργυρος, 607.
ἀρείων, 1116.
ἀρτοκόπος, 245.
ἀρτοπόπος, 245.
ἄττα, 1078.
αὖρον = O. Ir. ór(ń), p. 162.
ἄχεται, p. 44, note.

βάνα, 1053.
βίος, 113.
βίοτος, 477.
βολγός, 217.
βοῦς, 159.
βουκόλος, 584.
βραχύς, 678.

γάλα, 250.
γένος, 812.
γεύω, p. 69, note ².
γλακροφάγος, γλάγος, 250.
γυνή, 1053.

ϝαήρ, 397.
ϝάκρυ, 724.
ϝεξιός, 386.
ϝιπλόος, 930.

δόρυ, 554.
ϝρῦς, 554.
ϝυς·, 85.

ἐγκέφαλος, 747.
εὖος, 812.
εἰ, εἰμί, εἰσί, 1112.
ἕκτος, 777.
ἐκυρά, 570.
ἐλάσσων, 923, 1115.
ἔλος, 977.
ἐμέω, 97.
ἐμμί, 1112.
ἐξακάτιοι, ἐξήκοντα, 777.
ἐρείκη, p. 162.
ἔργον, 328, 533.
ἐσμέν, ἐστί(ν), 1112.
ἐυ-, 95.
εὐρύς, 578.

ζέα, 779.

ἧπαρ, 1032.
ἤσαι, ἤσθι, 1112.
ἤτριον, 1095.

θερμός, 952.
θύρα, 124.

Ἰάων, 758.
ἰθαίνεσθαι, 948.
ἱπποβουκόλος, 584.
ἵππος, 17; p. 68, note; 675.
ἴστημι, p. 100, note.
ἰτέα, 99.

κακκάω, κάκκη, 1075.
κανάζω, 837.

κάπρος, 372.
καρδία, 1102.
κίρκος, 507.
κλέος, κλυτός, 656, 812.
κνήμη, 269.
κόνις, κόνιδος, 649.
κόρυλος, 556.
κρησέρα, 700.
κριός, 158.
κύων (= eú, gen. con), 411.

λαμβάνω, 34.
λάτρις, 792.
λείπω, cf. O. Ir. leicim.
λευκός, cf. O. Ir. lóche, 292.
λέχος, 812.
ληΐς, 792.
λόχος, 1003.

μακρός, 621, 724.
μᾶνος, 430.
μαραίνω, 860.
μεγάλου, 663, 902.
μέγας, 663.
μέθυ, 968.
μείζων, 1114.
μέλι, 968.
μέρος, p. 157.
μῆνις, 602.
μήτηρ, 130.
μολγός, 217.
μύλη, 701.

ναῦς, 21; p. 162.
νέκις, 693.
νεφέλη, 337.
νέφος, 812.
νέω, 817.

2 D

νήθω, 817.
νυός, 570.

ὄϊς = O. Ir. ói.
ὀμαλός, 609, 904.
ὀμφαλός, p. 150.
ὄνομα, 991.
ὄνος, 296.
ὄνυξ, p. 150.
ὀργή, 328, 533.
ὀρθός, 16.
ὄρχις (= uirge), gl. 209.
ὀστέον, p. 149.
οὖθαρ, 102.

παρά, 704.
πάτος, 13.
πέμπε, πέντε, 776.
πατήρ, 13.
πιεπαῖος, 13.
πιτεηνά, πέτομαι, 746.
πλάτος, p. 156.
πλατύς, 13.
πλείων, 13.
πλέκω, 930.
πλήρης, 13.
ποίνη, 98; p. 156.

πολύ, 13.
πόρκος = orc, 492.
πούς, p. 150.
πτάρνυμαι, 1039.
πυθμήν, 96.

ῥεῦμα, 999.
ῥέω, 999.
ῥύγχος, 1039.
ῥυτός, 909.

σάκκος, 489.
Σελήνη, 952.
σκῦτος, p. 148.
σπλάγχνον, 1012.
σπλήν, 1012.
στέργω, 618.
στοργή, 618.
σχίζω, 441.

τάνυμαι, 1017.
τανυ, τανάός, 1017.
ταῦρος = Gaul. tarvos, p. 150.
ταφ, 942.
τέγος, 569.
τείνω, 1017.
τεῖχος, 871.

τέκος, 871.
τελέω, τέλος, 739.
τέρσομαι, 703
τοῖχος, 871.
τόκος, 871.
τρίχω, 74.
τύκος, 871.

ὕδωρ, 69.
ὕπνος, p. 163.
ὑψηλός, p. 68, note.

φαίθω, φάος, 846.
φαγ, 109.
φαλλός, p. 150.
φέρω, 835.
φόνος, p. 147.
φρητήρ, 570.
φύλλον, 765; p. 163.
φώγειν, p. 61, note.

χλωρός, 1124.

ὠλένη, p. 149.
ὠμός, 90.
ὥρα = úair, p. 95, note 1.

X. SANSKRIT INDEX.

aksha, akshi, 426.
anganâ, 290.
anji, 784.
at, 1068.
ati, 155.
attâ, 1078.
adlû, 752.
an, 428; p. 149.
anila, p. 149.
antar, 490.
abhi, 670.
amati, 302.
ayas, 608.
arbha, p. 163.
avara, 305.
açva, 17; p. 68, note.
as, 1112.
asthi, p. 149.
asmad, 305.

âma, 90.
âyu, p. 68, note.
âyus, 812.
âs, 1112.

indh, 948.
ishira, p. 68, note.

utsa, 69.
und, 69.
uru, 578.
urvî, 578.
ush, 606.

ûdhas, 102.
ûrdhva, 16.

edha, edhas, 948.
ena, p. 147.

ûidh, âidha, 948.

kanyâ, 158.
karsha, 703.
kûla, 200.
kṛ, 700.
kravya, 919.

gad, 870.
garva, p. 159.
go, 159, 784.
gṛdh, 620.
gṛha, 702.
gnâ, 1053.

gharma, ghṛmi, 952.
ghruṇs, ghraṇsa, 952; p. 164.

chatur, 775.

Sanskrit Index.

charman, p. 157.

chhid, 441.

jan, 290.
jani, 1053.
janiman, janman, 886.
jalukâ, 940.
jîva, 113, 784.
jîvita, 477.

takma, 871.
taksh, 871.
tanch, 872.
tan, 1017.
tantu, 1017.
tap, 942, 1986.
tava, yushmad, 570.
tishṭhâmi, p. 100, note.
tu, 423.
tṛ́, 898.
tṛksh, 74.
tṛsh, 703.

dakshiṇa, 265, 386.
daçan, p. 150.
dah (dabh), 942.
dâ, p. 100, note.
dâru, 554.
dus-, 85.
dṛç (paç), p. 149.
dêva, 21, 81.
dûvara, 397.
dvâra, 124.
dvi-, 773.

dhanvan, 108.
dhâ, p. 158.
dhṛ, 642, 819.

nakhu, p. 150.
naptrî, 224.
nabhas, 812.
navya, 21.
naç, 693.
nâçayâmi, p. 151.
nah, 817.
nâbhi, p. 150.
nêdîyas, 1117.

pach, 245.
panchan, 776.
pad, pâda, p. 150.

parichara, 898.
paç (dṛç), p. 149.
pâthas, pathin = O. Ir. *dth*, 13.
pitṛ, 13.
puru, ved. pulu, 13.
pṛch, 930.
pṛthu, 13.
pṛ́ (par), 13.
pra, 13, 428.
plîhan, 1012.

badhira, 604.
budhna, 96.
bṛhat, 292.

bhaksh, 109.
bhiksh, 1058.
bhû, p. 100, note.
bhṛ, 835, 1047.
bhrâtṛ, 570, 1047.
bhrû, 79.

maghavan, 952.
mati, 302.
madhu, 968.
man, 302, 1110.
manu, 302.
manthâna, 1139.
mah, 756.
mahat, 663.
mahîyas, 1114.
mâ, 1052.
mâtṛ, 130, 1052.
mâs, 1050.
mithyâ, 1117.
mur, p. 76, note.
mṛ, 860.
mṛiṇ, 860.

yam, 635.
yama, 1010.
yavn, 779.
yavîyas, 758.
yu, 758.
yuvan, 758.
yushmad, 570.
yos, 758.

rajata, 607.
ratha, 227.
râj, râjnî, 20.
ruch, 331.
rôman, p. 161.

laghîyas, laghu, 923.
langh, p. 147.
labh, 34.
lûta, 792.

vakra, 621.
vad, 870.
vam, 97.
vara, 397.
varama, 1116.
varîyas, 1116.
vas, 1070.
vasu, p. 126, note.
vâr, vâri, 222, 860.
vid, 392.
viṭikû, 99.
vîra, 397.
vṛ, 884.
ve, 1095.
vetasa, p. 156.

çaus, 63, 837.
çakṛt, 1075.
çakra, 724.
çatam, 772.
çravas, 655, 812.
çrî, 387.
çvaçrû, 570.
çvid, p. 150.

sad, 70.
sadas, 812.
sama, 904.
saras, 977.
sarit, 977.
salila, 977.
sahas, 663.
sâmi, 392.
sṛ, 977.
sthag, 569.
sthâ, p. 100, note.
snâ, 391.
anushû, 570.
spaça, p. 149.
sru, 999.
srotas, 999.
svapna, p. 163.
svasṛ, 320.

hari, 1124.
hṛdaya, 1102.
hvṛ, p. 149.

XI. ZEND INDEX.

kainô, 158.
khsvas, 777.
tafnu, 720.
tanch-, 872.
thrishva, 588.
dačna, 89.
nazdista, 1117.
naçu, 693.
panchan, 776.

peretu, 725.
bi-, 773.
maçyêhîm, 1114.
maoiriuãm, 55.
mûonh, 1050.
yava, 779.
yaos, 758.
yâna, 681.

rathaêstâ, 227.
verez, 533.
vôhu, p. 126, note.
çatĕm, 772.
hacha, p. 156.
hana, 735; p. 156.
hiçtâmi, p. 100, note.
zeredhaya, 1102.

XII. GOTHIC INDEX.

ailus, 17.
ains, p. 147.
aithei, 1078.
andalauul, 792.
ara, 197.
arbja, 752; p. 163.
asilus, 296.
atta, 1078.

balgs, 218.
hanja, p. 147.
bidjan, bidan, p. 147.
bleiths, p. 151.
brôthar, 570, 1047; brôthrahans, 13.

daigs, 242.
daur, 124.
dulg, 433.

eisarn, 608.

faihu, 389.
faihnthraihna, 300.
fidvór, 775.
fisu, 13.
fimf, 776.
fiska = *iasc*, 13.
fulla = *lán*, 13.
fôtu, p. 150.

gamalds, 1122.
gamains, 897.
gasintha, -thja, 1073.
glaggvus, 1129.
gredus, 1081.

hairtô, 1102.
hana, 837.
hardus, p. 64, note ¹.
hleiduma, 387.
hunda, 772.
hveita, p. 150.

im, ist, 1112.
izvara, p. 160, note ᵐ.

jór = *úair*, p. 95, note ¹.

kiusan, p. 69, note.

laufs, 114.
laun, 133, 792.

magus, 882.
maiza, 1114.
marei, 860.
mikils, 663.
miluks, 243.
missa, 1117.

qvairnus, 784.
qvius, 113.

reiks, 1036.

sakkus, 489.
salt, 977.
sama, 904.
siud, 1112.
sinths, 490, 1073.
skalja, 106.
suur, 570.
svaihro, 570.

triu, 554.
tuggo, 40.

vair, 395.
valdan, cf. *flaith*, 338.
vast, 1112; p. 165.
viljan, 884.

thagkjan, p. 165.
thaurp, 315.
thauraja, 703.
thiuda, 423.
thragja, 74.

XIII. ANGLO-SAXON INDEX.

ád, 948.
blíðe, p. 151.
braðean, 366.
ceole, p. 149.
dale, 1074.
elch, 205.
feohstrang, p. 159.
garleac (O. N. geirlaukr), 31.
gebede, p. 147.
gerim, 913.
gesið, 1073.

gleav, 1129.
heahfæðer, p. 153.
heado = *eath*.
hlæden, 126.
hrife, p. 150.
hrón, 50; p. 155.
lagu = *loch*, 781.
mele, p. 157.
mene, myne, p. 163.
naca, 21.

nón, 1077.
rót, 5.
rim, 913.
sceóta, p. 164.
sendan, 1073.
tæfel, p. 154.
treov, 554.
tvi-, 773.
vudu, 46.
yrfe, 752.

XIV. ENGLISH INDEX.

am, 1112.
apple, 555.
art, 1112, p. 165.

bake, p. 61, note 1.
bane, p. 147.
beadsman, p. 147.
bellows, 217.
bid, p. 147.
blithe, p. 151.
booth, 120.
bother, 604.
bottom, 96.
Briton, 957.
brooch, 852.
brogue, 1033.
brother, 570, 1047.
butteris, p. 157.

car, 70.
cat, 499.
choose, p. 69, note.
chough, 201.
clean, 671.
coal, 273.
coracle, 488.
corn = *grán*, 722.
corry, 724.
cow, 159.
cowl, 121.
crowder, 5.
curd, 784.

door, 124.
dough, 242.
dusk, 381.

elk, 205.
ewe = O. Ir. ói.

farrow = *ore*, 492.
father, 1046.
feather, 746.
fell, 136.
five, 776.
ford, 725.
four, 775.
fun, 630.

gallon, 106.
garlick, 31.
gavelock, 135.
grail, 854.
greed, 620.
grill, 107.
grum, 1065.

hame, 444.
hard, p. 64, note 1.
hat, 831.
hazle, 556.
hedge, 218.
hound, 261, 411.
hundred, 772.
hurdle, 126.

iron, 216, 608.
is, 1112.

jowl, p. 149.

lanyard, 73; p. 155.
lead, 609.
less, 1115.
linseed, 38.
list, 655.
load, 609.
loan, 133, 792.
loud, 655.
lurcher, 937.

man, 89.
market, 327.
midriff, p. 150.
milk, 243.
mill, 701.
mis-, 1117.
mother, 130.

nail, p. 150.
navel, p. 150.
nit, 649.
noon, 1077.

one, p. 147.
onion, 862.
ore, 608.

206   *Indices Verborum.*

paunter, p. 155.
pillory, 1136.
pismire, 55.

quern (Goth. qvaírnus), 784.
quick, 113.

rhyme, 913.

salt, 977.
same, 904.
send, 490, 1073.
service-tree, 1132.
shake, p. 161.
shell, 106.
sister, 320.
slaughter, slay, 1003.
six, 777.
smear, 193.

stream, 999.
spur, 1041.
sweven, p. 163.

tailor, 252.
thin, 1017.
think, p. 165.
thirst, 703.
thorp, 315.
three, 774.
tongs, 674.
tongue, 40.
tree, 554.
trowsers, 324.
truce, 137.
trull, p. 148.
tun, 731.
twinge, 674.
two, 773.

udder, 102.
um-, 670.

warm, 952.
wast, 1112; p. 165.
weave, 1095.
white, p. 150.
will, 884.
window, 134.
wit, 392.
withe, 99.
wood, 46.
work, 328, 533.

yellow, 1124.
yew, 561.
young, 758.

XV. OLD HIGH GERMAN INDEX.

blîdi, p. 151.
bodam, 96.
chuo, 159.
cuncla, 567.
denchan, p. 166.
diota, 423.
dwingan, 674.
ehu, 17.
eit, 948.
esil, 296.
furah = *orc*, 492.
fichtan, 930.
gelo, 1124.
Hadumâr, p. 86, note.
hafr, 372.

hag, 218.
Hincmar, p. 86, note.
Hlodomâr, 655; p. 86, note.
hlût, 655.
hrêo, 919.
hrotta, 5.
hunta, 772.
îwa, 561.
jâr = *úair*, p. 95.
kisal, 216.
korn = *grán*, 722.
meri, 860.
metu, 968.
miluh, 243.
muli, 701.

nacho, 21.
prawa, 79.
salo, 616.
scala, 106.
sind, 1073.
slahan, 1003.
stroum, 999.
sueran, 1132.
umbi = *imm*, 670.
wâr = *fir*, 954.
weban, 1095.
wîda, 99.
wiho, 269.
witu, 46.
zunga, 40.

BENDACHT DÉI FOR HUILI CARATE HÉRINN OCUS A SENDÉLRE.

CORRIGENDA.

[The following have been noticed during the passage of the Indices through the press.]

P. 49, line 4, *for* carpat *read* charpat.
P. 52, line 16, *for* 145 *read* 144.
P. 65, note a, delete the latter part of this note: *nis gignetar tola* means "desires (lusts) did not wound them," and we have here the 3rd pers. plur. pret. active of the root GON. The 3rd pers. sing. of the same tense—*geguin*—occurs in the Féilre, Oct. 23.
P. 107, line 20, *for* tṛ *read* tṝ.
P. 109, in the paradigm, nom. and voc. sing., *for* rig *read* rí.
P. 111, line 5, *for* tracing from), lorg *read* tracing), from lorg.
P. 114, line 11 from bottom, *for* 995 *read* 975.
P. 120, line 4 from bottom, *for* bhrátr *read* bhrátṛ.
P. 131, line 11 from bottom, *for* inmirmaith *read* inmir maith.
P. 144, line 16, *for* lens *read* lens.
P. 155, line 11 from bottom, *for* dévabo *read* dĕvabo.
P. 160, note =, *for* anlaut *read* inlaut.
P. 166, line 13, *for* aurigam totum *read* totum calvum.
P. 166, line 14, and p. 179, *for* martur *read* martar.
P. 167, col. 2, line 6, *for* Sanscritleum *read* Sanscritum.
P. 168, col. 2, line 3 from bottom, for O. Ir. d *read* O. Ir. *t*.
P. 170, col. 2, at *Prefixes* insert ro (ru, ra), 13, 428, 808.
P. 174, at *barr* insert a reference to p. 148.
P. 181, *insert* tarb, p. 189.

THE IRISH ARCHÆOLOGICAL AND CELTIC SOCIETY.

MDCCCLIX.

Patron:
HIS ROYAL HIGHNESS THE PRINCE CONSORT.

President:
HIS GRACE THE DUKE OF LEINSTER.

Vice-Presidents:
THE MOST NOBLE THE MARQUESS OF KILDARE, M. R. I. A.
THE RIGHT HON. THE EARL OF DUNRAVEN, M. R. I. A.
THE RIGHT HON. LORD TALBOT DE MALAHIDE, M. R. I. A.
VERY REV. CHARLES W. RUSSELL, D. D., President of Maynooth College.

Council:

EUGENE CURRY, M. R. I. A.	PATRICK V. FITZPATRICK, ESQ.
REV. THOMAS FARRELLY.	JOHN C. O'CALLAGHAN, ESQ.
REV. CHARLES GRAVES, D. D., F. T. C. D., M. R. I. A.	JOHN O'DONOVAN, LL. D., M. R. I. A.
	GEORGE PETRIE, LL. D., V. P. R. I. A.
REV. JAMES GRAVES, A. B.	REV. WM. REEVES, D. D., V. P. R. I. A.
THOMAS A. LARCOM, Major-General, R. E., M. R. I. A.	W. R. WILDE, F. R. C. S. I., M. R. I. A.

Secretaries:
J. H. TODD, D. D., Pres. R. I. A. | J. T. GILBERT, M. R. I. A.

THE materials for Irish history, although rich and abundant, have hitherto been but to a small extent available to the student. The few accessible authorities have been so frequently used, and the works compiled from them are so incomplete, that the expectation of any accurate history of Ireland has been generally deferred, under the conviction that vast additions must be made to the materials at present available before any complete work of that nature can be produced. The immediate object of this Society is to print, with accurate English translations and annotations, the unpublished documents illustrative of Irish history, especially those in the ancient and obsolete Irish language, many of which can be accurately translated and elucidated only by scholars who have been long engaged in investigating the Celtic remains of Ireland; and should the publication of these manuscripts be long delayed, many most important literary monuments may become unavailable to the students of history and comparative philology. The Society will also endeavour to protect the existing monumental and architectural remains of Ireland, by directing public attention to their preservation from the destruction with which they frequently are threatened.

The publication of twenty-one volumes, illustrative of Irish history, has been completed by the Irish Archæological Society, founded in 1840, and the Celtic Society, established in 1845. The present Society has been formed by the union of these two bodies, under the name of the "Irish Archæological and Celtic Society," for the preservation of the monuments illustrative of Irish history, and for the publication of the historic, bardic, ecclesiastical, and topographical remains of Ireland, especially such as are extant in the Irish language. Since the union of the two Societies, two important volumes have been published.

The Books of the Society are published solely for the use of its Subscribers, who are divided into two classes: Members, who pay three pounds admission, and one pound per annum; and Associates, who pay an annual subscription of one pound, without any entrance fee. The Fundamental Laws of the Society regulate the privileges of each class of Subscribers, who can also obtain the publications of the two former Societies, at the rates, and under the conditions specified in the present Prospectus.

FUNDAMENTAL LAWS.

I. The Society shall consist of Members and Associates.

II. The affairs of the Society shall be managed by a Council, consisting of a President, five Vice-Presidents, Treasurer, two Secretaries, and fourteen others, to be elected annually by the Society from the Members.

III. All Members and Associates shall be elected by the Council, on being proposed by a Member; and no person shall be elected either a Member or an Associate of the Society until he has made the requisite payments.

IV. Each Member shall pay four pounds on the first year of his election, and one pound every subsequent year. Associates shall pay one pound per annum only, without any entrance fee. All subscriptions to be paid in advance, and to become due on the first day of January, annually.

V. Such Members as desire it may become Life Members, on payment of the sum of thirteen pounds, or ten pounds (if they have already paid their entrance fee), in lieu of the annual subscription.

VI. Every Member whose subscription is not in arrear shall be entitled to receive one copy of each publication of the Society issued subsequently to his admission; and the books printed by the Society shall not be sold to the Public.

VII. Associates may become Members, on signifying their wish to the Council, and on payment of the entrance fee of three pounds.

VIII. Associates shall receive a copy of all publications issued by the Society during the year for which they have paid a subscription; but shall not be entitled to any other privileges.

IX. No Member who is three months in arrear of his subscription shall be entitled to vote, or to any other privileges of a Member, and any Member who shall be one year in arrear shall be considered as having resigned. Associates who are in arrear shall cease, *ipso facto*, to belong to the Society.

X. The Council shall have power to appoint officers, and to make By-Laws not inconsistent with the Fundamental Laws of the Society.

PUBLICATIONS OF THE IRISH ARCHÆOLOGICAL SOCIETY,

Founded MDCCCXL.

1841.

I. TRACTS RELATING TO IRELAND, vol. I., containing:
1. The Circuit of Ireland; by Muircheartach Mac Neill, Prince of Aileach; a Poem written in the year 942 by Cormacan Eigeas, Chief Poet of the North of Ireland. Edited, with a Translation and Notes, and a Map of the Circuit, by JOHN O'DONOVAN, LL. D., M. R. I. A.
2. "A Brife Description of Ireland, made in the year 1589, by Robert Payne, vnto xxv. of his partners, for whom he is vndertaker there." Reprinted from the second edition, London, 1590, with a Preface and Notes, by AQUILLA SMITH, M. D., M. R. I. A. (Out of print.)

II. THE ANNALS OF IRELAND, by James Grace, of Kilkenny. Edited from the MS. in the Library of Trinity College, Dublin, in the original Latin, with a Translation and Notes, by the Rev. RICHARD BUTLER, A. B., M. R. I. A. Price 8s.

1842.

I. Cath Muighi Rath. The Battle of Magh Rath (Moira), from an ancient MS. in the Library of Trinity College, Dublin. Edited in the original Irish, with a Translation and Notes, by JOHN O'DONOVAN, LL.D., M. R. I. A. Price 10s.

II. TRACTS RELATING TO IRELAND, vol. II. containing:
1. "A Treatise of Ireland; by John Dymmok." Edited from a MS. in the British Museum, with Notes, by the Rev. RICHARD BUTLER, A. B., M. R. I. A.
2. The Annals of Multifernan; from the original MS. in the Library of Trinity College, Dublin. Edited by AQUILLA SMITH, M. D., M. R. I. A.
3. A Statute passed at a Parliament held at Kilkenny, A. D. 1367; from a MS. in the British Museum. Edited, with a Translation and Notes, by JAMES HARDIMAN, Esq., M. R. I. A. Price 10s.

1843.

I. AN ACCOUNT OF THE TRIBES AND CUSTOMS OF THE DISTRICT OF HY-MANY commonly called O'Kelly's Country, in the Counties of Galway and Roscommon. Edited from the Book of Lecan in the Library of the Royal Irish Academy, in the original Irish; with a Translation and Notes, and a Map of Hy-Many, by JOHN O'DONOVAN, LL. D., M. R. I. A. Price 12s.

II. THE BOOK OF OBITS AND MARTYROLOGY OF THE CATHEDRAL OF THE HOLY TRINITY, commonly called Christ Church, Dublin. Edited from the original MS. in the Library of Trinity College, Dublin. By the Rev. JOHN CLARKE CROSTHWAITE, A. M., Rector of St. Mary-at-Hill, and St. Andrew Hubbart, London. With an Introduction by JAMES HENTHORN TODD, D. D., V. P. R. I. A., Fellow of Trinity College, Dublin. Price 12s.

1844.

I. REGISTRUM ECCLESIÆ OMNIUM SANCTORUM JUXTA DUBLIN; from the original MS. in the Library of Trinity College, Dublin. Edited by the Rev. RICHARD BUTLER, A. B., M.R.I.A. Price 7s.

II. AN ACCOUNT OF THE TRIBES AND CUSTOMS OF THE DISTRICT OF HY-FIACHRACH, in the Counties of Sligo and Mayo. Edited from the Book of Lecan, in the Library of the Royal Irish Academy, and from a copy of the Mac Firbis MS. in the possession of the Earl of Roden. With a Translation and Notes, and a Map of Hy-Fiachrach. By JOHN O'DONOVAN, LL.D., M. R. I. A. Price 15s.

1845.

A DESCRIPTION OF WEST OR H-IAR CONNAUGHT, by Roderic O'Flaherty, Author of the Ogygia, written A.D. 1684. Edited from a MS. in the Library of Trinity College, Dublin; with copious Notes and an Appendix. By JAMES HARDIMAN, Esq., M. R. I. A. Price 15s.

1846.

THE MISCELLANY OF THE IRISH ARCHÆOLOGICAL SOCIETY: vol. I. containing:

1. An ancient Poem attributed to St. Columbkille, with a Translation and Notes by JOHN O'DONOVAN, LL. D., M. R. I. A.
2. De Concilio Hiberniæ; the earliest extant record of a Parliament in Ireland; with Notes by the Rev. R. BUTLER, M. R. I. A.
3. Copy of the Award as concerning the Tolboll (Dublin): contributed by Dr. AQUILLA SMITH, M. R. I. A.
4. Pedigree of Dr. Dominick Lynch, Regent of the Colledge of St. Thomas of Aquin, in Seville, A.D. 1674: contributed by JAMES HARDIMAN, Esq., M. R. I. A.
5. A Latin Poem, by Dr. John Lynch, Author of *Cambrensis Eversus*, in reply to the Question *Cur in patriam non redis?* Contributed by JAMES HARDIMAN, Esq., M. R. I. A.
6. The Obits of Kilcormick, now Frankfort, King's County; contributed by the Rev. J. H. TODD, D. D., M. R. I. A.
7. Ancient Testaments; contributed by Dr. AQUILLA SMITH, M. R. I. A.
8. Autograph Letter of Thady O'Roddy: with some Notices of the Author by the Rev. J. H. TODD, D. D., M. R. I. A.
9. Autograph Letter of Oliver Cromwell to his Son, Harry Cromwell, Commander-in-Chief in Ireland: contributed by Dr. A. SMITH, M. R. I. A.

10. The Irish Charters in the Book of Kells, with a Translation and Notes, by JOHN O'DONOVAN, LL.D., M. R. I. A.
11. Original Charter granted by John Lord of Ireland, to the Abbey of Mellifont: contributed by Dr. A. SMITH, M. R. I. A.
12. A Journey to Connaught in 1709 by Dr. Thomas Molyneux: contributed by Dr. A. SMITH, M. R. I. A.
13. A Covenant in Irish between Mageoghegan and the Fox; with a Translation and historical Notices of the two Families, by JOHN O'DONOVAN, LL.D., M. R. I. A.
14. The Annals of Ireland, from A.D. 1453 to 1468, translated from a lost Irish original, by Dudley Firbise; with Notes by J. O'DONOVAN, LL.D., M. R. I. A. Price 8s.

1847.

The Irish Version of the HISTORIA BRITONUM of Nennius, or, as it is called in Irish MSS. Leabar breatnac, the British Book. Edited from the Book of Ballimote, collated with copies in the Book of Lecan and in the Library of Trinity College, Dublin, with a Translation and Notes, by JAMES HENTHORN TODD, D. D., M. R. I. A., Fellow of Trinity College, &c.; and Additional Notes and an Introduction, by the Hon. ALGERNON HERBERT. Price 15s.

1848.

THE LATIN ANNALISTS OF IRELAND; edited with Introductory Remarks and Notes by the Very Rev. RICHARD BUTLER, M. R. I. A., Dean of Clonmacnois,—viz.:

1. The Annals of Ireland, by John Clyn, of Kilkenny; from a MS. in the Library of Trinity College, Dublin, collated with another in the Bodleian Library, Oxford.
2. The Annals of Ireland, by Thady Dowling, Chancellor of Leighlin. From a MS. in the Library of Trinity College, Dublin. Price 8s.

1849-50.

MACARIÆ EXCIDIUM, the Destruction of Cyprus; being a secret History of the Civil War in Ireland, under James II., by Colonel Charles O'Kelly. Edited in the Latin from a MS. presented by the late Professor M'Cullagh to the Library of the Royal Irish Academy; with a Translation from a MS. of the seventeenth century; and Notes by JOHN C. O'CALLAGHAN, Esq. Price 1l.

1851.

ACTS OF ARCHBISHOP COLTON in his Visitation of the Diocese of Derry, A. D. 1397. Edited from the original Roll, with Introduction and Notes, by WILLIAM REEVES, D. D., M. R. I. A. (Not sold.)

[PRESENTED TO THE SOCIETY BY THE REV. DR. REEVES.]

1852.

SIR WILLIAM PETTY'S NARRATIVE OF HIS PROCEEDINGS IN THE SURVEY OF IRELAND; from a MS. in the Library of Trinity College, Dublin. Edited, with Notes, by THOMAS A. LARCOM, Esq., R. E., V. P. R. I. A. Price 15s.

1853.

CAMBRENSIS EVERSUS; or, Refutation of the Authority of Giraldus Cambrensis on the History of Ireland, by Dr. John Lynch (1662), with some Account of the Affairs of that Kingdom during his own and former times. Edited, with Translation and copious Notes, by the Rev. MATTHEW KELLY, Royal College of St. Patrick, Maynooth. Three volumes. Price, 1l. 10s.

PUBLICATIONS OF THE CELTIC SOCIETY,

FOUNDED MDCCCXLV.

1847.

Leabar na g-Ceart, or, The Book of Rights; a Treatise on the Rights and Privileges of the Ancient Kings of Ireland, now for the first time edited, with Translation and Notes, by JOHN O'DONOVAN, LL. D., M. R. I. A. Price 10s.

1848-50-51-52.

CAMBRENSIS EVERSUS, &c. as above. Three volumes.

[Given to Members of the Celtic Society for 1848, 1850-52; and to Members or Associates of the United Society for 1853.]

1849.

MISCELLANY OF THE CELTIC SOCIETY, containing:

A Treatise from the Book of Leacan on O'h-Eidirseceoil's (O'Driscol's) Country, in the County of Cork.

A Historical Poem on the Battle of Dun (Downpatrick), A.D. 1260.

Sir Richard Bingham's Account of his Proceedings in Connacht, in the reign of Elizabeth.

A Narration of Sir Henry Docwra's Services in Ulster, written A.D. 1614; together with other original Documents and Letters illustrative of Irish History. Edited by JOHN O'DONOVAN, Esq., LL. D., M. R. I. A. Price 10s.

1853.

CATH MUIGHE LENA: The Battle of Magh Lena; an ancient historic Tale, edited by EUGENE CURRY, Esq., M. R. I. A., from original MSS. Price 10s.

A few complete Sets of the foregoing Publications (with the exception of that of the Archæological Society for 1851), can still be had by Members and Associates. Application to be made to EDWARD CLIBBORN, Esq., Royal Irish Academy, Dawson-street, Dublin.

PUBLICATIONS OF THE IRISH ARCHÆOLOGICAL AND CELTIC SOCIETY.

UNITED MDCCCLIII.

1854.

LIBER HYMNORUM: The Book of Hymns of the Ancient Church of Ireland; from the original MS. in the Library of Trinity College, Dublin. Edited by the Rev. JAMES HENTHORN TODD, D. D., Pres. R. I. A., Senior Fellow of Trinity College. Part I. Containing the following Latin Hymns, with Irish Scholia and Gloss:—
1. The Alphabetical Hymn of St. Sechnall, or Secundinus, in praise of St. Patrick. 2. The Alphabetical Hymn in praise of St. Brigid, attributed to St. Ultan, Bishop of Ardbreccan. 3. The Hymn of St. Cummain Fota. 4. The Hymn or Prayer of St. Mugint.

1855 and 1856.

THE LIFE OF ST. COLUMBA, by ADAMNAN, Ninth Abbot of Hy [or Iona]. The Latin text taken from a MS. of the early part of the eighth century, preserved at Schaffhausen; accompanied by Various Readings from six other MSS., found in different parts of Europe; and illustrated by copious Notes and Dissertations. By the Rev. WILLIAM REEVES, D.D., M.B., V. P. R. I. A. With Maps, and coloured Facsimiles of the MSS.

The two Parts are bound in one Volume, for the convenience of Members.

1857.

A Mediæval Tract on Latin Declension, with examples explained in Irish. From a Manuscript in the Library of Trinity College, Dublin. Together with the *Lorica* of Gildas, and the Middle Irish Gloss thereon, from the *Leabhar Breac*. Edited, with a Commentary, Notes, and Indices Verborum, by WHITLEY STOKES, A. B.

1858.

Three Fragments of Ancient Irish Annals, hitherto unpublished. Edited, from a MS. in the Burgundian Library, Brussels, with a Translation and Notes, by JOHN O'DONOVAN, LL. D., M. R. I. A., Professor of Irish Literature in the Queen's College, Belfast. (*Nearly ready.*)

1859.

LIBER HYMNORUM: The Book of Hymns of the Ancient Church of Ireland; from the original MS. in the Library of Trinity College, Dublin. Edited by the Rev. JAMES HENTHORN TODD, D. D., Pres. R. I. A., Senior Fellow of Trinity College. Part II. (*In the Press.*)

1860.

The Topographical Poems of Seaan O'Dubhagain and Gilla na-naomh O'Huidhrin, enumerating the principal Families and Territories of Ireland, and their Chiefs, at the period of the Anglo-Norman Invasion. The Irish Text edited, with Translation and copious illustrative Notes, by JOHN O'DONOVAN, LL. D. (*In preparation.*)

PUBLICATIONS SUGGESTED OR IN PROGRESS.

I. A TREATISE ON THE OGHAM OR OCCULT FORMS OF WRITING OF THE ANCIENT IRISH; from a MS. in the Library of Trinity College, Dublin; with a Translation and Notes, and Preliminary Dissertation, by the Rev. CHARLES GRAVES, D. D., M. R. I. A., Fellow of Trinity College, and Professor of Mathematics in the University of Dublin. (*In the Press.*)

II. The Annals of Tigbernach, and Chronicon Scotorum, from MSS. in the Bodleian Library, and that of Trinity College, Dublin. Edited by the Rev. W. REEVES, D. D.

III. The Martyrology of Donegal.

IV. Cormac's Glossary. Edited by J. H. TODD, D. D., with a Translation and Notes, by J. O'DONOVAN, LL. D., M. R. I. A., and EUGENE CURRY, ESQ., M. R. I. A.

V. The Annals of Ulster. With a Translation and Notes. Edited from a MS. in the Library of Trinity College, Dublin, collated with the Translation made for Sir James Ware by Dudley or Duald Mac Firbis, a MS. in the British Museum.

VI. The Annals of Innisfallen; from a MS. in the Bodleian Library, Oxford.

VII. The Genealogy and History of the Saints of Ireland: from the Book of Lecan.

VIII. An Account of the Firbolgs and Danes of Ireland, by Duald Mac Firbis, from a MS. in the Library of Trinity College, Dublin.

IX. boɲama. The Origin and History of the Boromean Tribute. Edited from a MS. in the Library of Trinity College, Dublin, with a Translation and Notes, by EUGENE CURRY, Esq., M. R. I. A.

X. Leabaɲ Ɉabala, or, The History of the Invasions of Ireland, by the Four Masters.

XI. Foɲuʃ Feaɲa aɲ Eiɲinn, or, The History of Ireland, by Dr. Geoffrey Keating.

XII. Leabaɲ Oinn Seanċuɲ, or, History of the Noted Places in Ireland.

XIII. The Works of Giraldus Cambrensis relating to Ireland.

XIV. Miscellany of the Irish Archæological and Celtic Society.

The Council will receive Donations or Subscriptions to be applied especially to any of the above Publications.

Subscriptions are received by EDWARD CLIBBORN, Esq., Royal Irish Academy, Dawson-street, Dublin. Persons desirous of becoming Subscribers to the Society are requested to communicate, by letter, with the Hon. Secretaries, at No. 19, Dawson-street, Dublin.

La Ouilech cain Clochaıp.—Feilire of Ængus, Ninth Century.

ST. DOULAGH'S CHURCH,
COUNTY OF DUBLIN.

Preservation Committee:

THE LORD VISCT. DUNGANNON, Brynkinalt, North Wales.
LORD VISCT. MONCK, Charleville, Enniskerry.
THE LORD TALBOT DE MALAHIDE, Malahide.
H. DARLEY, ESQ., Newgrove, Raheny, } *Church*
W. F. KNIPE, M. D., St. Doulagh's, } *Wardens.*
THE VERY REV. R. M. KENNEDY, Dean of Clonfert, and Precentor of St. Patrick's.
REV. J. H. TODD, D.D., S. F. T. C. D., Pres. R. I. A.
REV. WILLIAM REEVES, D.D., M. B., V.P.R.I.A.
GEORGE PETRIE, LL.D., M. R. I. A.
MR. JOHN HENRY PARKER, Oxford.
REV. RICHARD BARTON, Precentor of Christ's Church, and Patron of St. Doulagh's Benefice.
REV. WILLIAM DE BURGH, D.D., Sandymount.
REV. J. W. STUBBS, F.T.C.D.
D. H. KELLY, ESQ., D. L, J. P., M. R. I. A., Castle Kelly, Mount Talbot.

REV. W. SLOANE EVANS, Totness, Devon.
E. H. CASEY, D. L., J. P., Raheny.
REV. WILLIAM BLACK, Rectory, Raheny.
REV. WILLIAM MACONCHY, Rectory, Coolock.
REV. WILLIAM B. ADAMS, Rectory, Cloghran.
REV. D. H. ELRINGTON, Vicarage, Swords.
REV. J. H. MONAHAN, Preb. St. Michan's, Dublin.
REV. E. S. ABBOTT, Rector of St. Mary's, Dublin.
HENRY RUTHERFOORD, ESQ., St. Doulagh's.
JON. ALLEY, ESQ., Spring Hill, St. Doulagh's.
EDMUND CUPPAGE, ESQ., Clare Grove, Raheny.
L. STUDDERT, ESQ., EX.-S.T.C.D., Bar.-at-Law.
REV. C. B. KNOX, Rathfriland, county of Down.
REV. J. C. FLOOD, Hollywood, county of Down.
REV. J. SMYTHE, A. M., Rector of Ballyclug, Ballymena.
REV. H. L. KENNEDY, Strabane.
L. S. KENNEDY, ESQ., Mountrath.

Treasurer:
THE LORD TALBOT DE MALAHIDE.

Secretaries:
REV. WILLIAM STUDDERT KENNEDY, A. M., Curate of St. Doulagh's.
REV. WILLIAM REEVES, D. D., M. B., V. P. R. I. A., Vicar of Lusk.

Architect.
J. S. SLOANE, A.M., C.E., 5, Richmond-st., North.

Banker.
THE ROYAL BANK, Foster-place, Dublin.

This Committee, with power to add to their number, was appointed at a Meeting held in the Board-room of the Royal Irish Academy on the 19th of August, 1859.

The work they have undertaken is, to *collect*, and *apply* money for the preservation of the ancient buildings at St. Doulagh's, so far as those venerable remains are in the possession of the Incumbent.

It would be vain to attempt, by written description, to convey an adequate idea of this curious structure. The view given above of the exterior is, necessarily, partial; whilst the interior, to be appreciated, must be the subject of actual examination.

The Chapel commemorative of St. Duilech of Clogher, who flourished, it is said, about the year 600, has been visited by Antiquaries and Ecclesiologists, the most learned and careful, from various countries; and all these, though agreeing as to its great antiquity, differ, and are in some measure at fault, when they attempt to explain its original design and subsequent use and history.

It exhibits the strangest incongruities of style; and every period of Church Architecture—from the primitive square-headed doorway and window to the ornate Perpendicular—has some representative in the building. The outer walls are in excellent preservation, and the *stone roof* is, perhaps, without an equal in these kingdoms; although, according to some of our antiquaries, it must now be at least *seven centuries* old.

The building contains seven apartments, to which different names have been given by writers anxious to advance different theories. Archdall, for instance, describes it as an abbey; others, as an anchorite's cell. But setting aside theories, one fact remains, and that is, that this building, in danger of being lost to the world, is unique, and, as an architectural enigma, unmatched in Europe.

The simple task which the Committee propose to themselves is to preserve and hand down for future study the conditions left of this unsolved problem. To accomplish this, they appeal to the general Public; they seek the sympathy and assistance of those who love to study the History and Monuments of Ireland; and they remind all, in the concluding words of Dr. Reeves's "Memoir," that "just as England has inherited her noble cathedrals from a religion which she now disowns, so we may blamelessly, nay, laudably, cherish so precious an architectural gem as St. Doulagh's Chapel, though it be diverted from its original use; and, without sacrifice of principle, or misapplication of money, admire and preserve it."

The Committee will present to each Subscriber of £1, or Collector of £2, a Copy of the beautiful Photograph of the building, lately taken by Mr. Allen, together with Dr. Reeves's "Memoir of the Church of St. Duilech," containing a Paper read before the Royal Irish Academy, on the 11th April, 1859.

Subscriptions will be thankfully received by the Treasurer, LORD TALBOT DE MALAHIDE, Castle, Malahide; or at the ROYAL BANK, Foster-place, Dublin; or by any Member of the Committee.

ARCHITECT'S REPORT.

The following is the Report of the Architect, Mr. SLOANE, as read before the meeting held in August at the Royal Irish Academy :—

"AT the request of the Rev. W. S. Kennedy, I visited the ancient building of St. Doulagh's, in this county, on the 2nd of June last, and made a survey of same, with the view of laying before you a statement of what is required to place the building in a state of repair sufficient to insure its preservation for many years hence; and I have prepared drawings to exhibit the appearance of the building externally, when those repairs shall have been made. Commencing with the cell in which is the supposed tomb, I find that there are eight openings, now wholly or in part blocked up with masonry: those I propose to have filled with metal sashes, glazed in quarries with moderately strong glass. I propose to repair the tomb by restoring the cavetto moulding, a portion of which remains, and flagging over the top; I would hack off the plastering, which appears modern, and wedge up the vaults with slates in Portland cement, giving the whole a thorough cleansing. I propose to adopt the same course with the next apartment, which I call the *Oratory*, thoroughly repairing the vault and cementing it with Portland cement; and, to impart extra strength, I would tile the floor of the apartment over it with a layer of fire-clay tiles, laid in cement. I would also repair the stairs in this part of the building, and rebuild the parapet wall to a height of about two feet nine inches, which would not interfere with the light from the principal south window; the *hagioscope* to be glazed with ribbed glass. The different recesses I would have repaired, and the *Piscina* restored to its original niche in the south wall. In the long apartment over the Oratory, I propose plastering the vault with Portland cement, and forming the curve, as far as possible, to its original shape; the pieces of concrete with which it is composed affording an excellent key for the plaster. I would repair the seat of the south window, and restore the west window to correspond with the east; repairing its seat also, and restoring the steps that lead up to the floor of the west end, over the small *mezzanine* cell which is over the tomb cell. As for the exterior, I propose raking out all the old joints carefully, and re-pointing with cement. The only portion that is at all ruinous is the western corner, and that I would have shored up, each stone carefully removed, and reset exactly in its proper position. The battlements of the tower should be all repaired, the stone roofs re-pointed in cement, and all vegetation carefully removed."

The amount of Mr. Sloane's estimate for these necessary repairs is under £150.

He concluded his Report thus:—

"It may be perceived that I have avoided any attempt at *restoration*, excepting, as in the parapet of the tower, I could do so without any doubt of its propriety. I have thus, in a general way, endeavoured to show what I would propose to effect in the way of repairs. These repairs completed, and the whole finished, I could not consistently recommend the building to be locked up and left to its fate; but, for the preserving of it, I would suggest that it be used as a school, for which I believe it is amply extensive; and very little beyond what I have recommended as necessary repairs for its preservation would make it available for that purpose. I further beg leave to state, that I have examined this subject in various ways, and thought of it for years, and the pleasure I would otherwise have enjoyed in contemplating the interesting object in question, both in an architectural and antiquarian point of view, has always been marred by the existence of the modern structure adjoining, which is calculated to offend the experienced and practical eye; and while I think of the comparatively easy task of removing this deformity, and erecting a chapel more in keeping with the building which we all wish to preserve, I feel the matter has only to be brought under the notice of such a meeting as this to have the desired ends accomplished. Of the former existence of some building that was removed to make way for the present church, I have no doubt; and it is on the supposed site of that building I would erect the chapel or nave, using the cell in which the tomb stands as a vestry. The expense of such a chapel would be under £500."

Mr. Sloane produced the ground plan and a full design of such a nave, to give one hundred sittings in twenty-five open pews, extending north the tower, having the reading-desk and pulpit at the end next the *hagioscope*, the side slant of which would then again transmit to the congregation the light of the old east window.

ABSTRACT OF Mr. SLOANE'S ESTIMATE, SUBMITTED TO MEETING.

	£	s.	d.
Exterior,	61	17	6
Cell,	16	11	6
Oratory,	25	17	0
Chamber over Cell,	7	2	6
Chamber over Oratory,	15	16	6
Staircases,	3	10	0
	130	15	0
Contingencies, at 10 per Cent.,	13	1	0
Total,	£143	16	0

St. Doulagh's Well.

www.ingramcontent.com/pod-product-compliance
Lightning Source LLC
Chambersburg PA
CBHW021843230426
43669CB00008B/1056